Aural Skills
In Context

Aural Skills
In Context

A Comprehensive Approach to Sight Singing,
Ear Training, Keyboard Harmony,
and Improvisation

Evan Jones and Matthew Shaftel
with Juan Chattah

New York   Oxford
OXFORD UNIVERSITY PRESS

Oxford University Press is a department of the University of Oxford.
It furthers the University's objective of excellence in research, scholarship,
and education by publishing worldwide.

Oxford   New York
Auckland   Cape Town   Dar es Salaam   Hong Kong   Karachi
Kuala Lumpur   Madrid   Melbourne   Mexico City   Nairobi
New Delhi   Shanghai   Taipei   Toronto

With offices in
Argentina   Austria   Brazil   Chile   Czech Republic   France   Greece
Guatemala   Hungary   Italy   Japan   Poland   Portugal   Singapore
South Korea   Switzerland   Thailand   Turkey   Ukraine   Vietnam

For titles covered by Section 112 of the US Higher Education Opportunity
Act, please visit www.oup.com/us/he for the latest information about
pricing and alternate formats.

Published by Oxford University Press.
198 Madison Avenue, New York, NY 10016
www.oup.com

Oxford is a registered trademark of Oxford University Press

Library of Congress Cataloging-in-Publication Data
Jones, Evan.
  Aural skills in context : a comprehensive approach to sight-singing,
ear training, keyboard harmony, and improvisation / Dr. Evan Jones,
Dr. Matthew Shaftel, and Dr. Juan Chattah.
     pages cm
  Includes bibliographical references.
  ISBN 978-0-19-994382-1 — ISBN 978-0-19-933731-6 1. Ear training.
2. Sight-singing. 3. Harmony. I. Shaftel, Matthew R. II. Chattah,
Juan. III. Title.
  MT35.J76 2014
  781.4'24—dc23
                                    2013011576

Contents

Wherein consists the art of playing at first sight? In this: in playing the piece in the time in which it ought to be played, and in playing all the notes, appoggiaturas and so forth, exactly as they are written and with the appropriate expression and taste, so that you might suppose that the performer had composed it himself.

—Wolfgang Amadeus Mozart

Preface

This textbook presents multiple solutions to several persistent pedagogical problems, foremost among which is the unavailability of singable selections drawn from "real music" in their harmonic context. Some textbooks rely on author-composed materials; others provide melodic extracts for sight singing but omit harmonic context. In either case, the student is unnecessarily handicapped in many ways. The authors of this book are convinced that the use of real music—art music, folk music, and music from other sources, both vocal and instrumental—has tremendous advantages in the aural skills classroom. First, it reinforces the relevance of the aural skills curriculum to the students' other classes, as well as to their performance and listening interests. Students gain exposure to many examples of music that they will surely revisit as performers, scholars, or educators, and it extends their knowledge of the musical repertoire. Although the exclusion of examples from the repertoire may level the playing field, inasmuch as every melody will be equally unfamiliar to every student, the use of musical materials that may already be familiar enables a student to reach a deeper understanding of musical abstractions such as scale-degree function, chord progression, and phrase structure. When an excerpt is familiar, or even quite familiar, to a student, he or she may reach a deeper understanding of musical abstractions such as melodic function, chord progression, and phrase structure. Indeed, a great number of cognitive studies have shown that regular and repeated exposure to the many melodic, harmonic, and rhythmic patterns of "real music" can be extremely beneficial to music practitioners (see below). Finally, the pervasive use of real music allows a student to glean characteristics of musical structure beyond what he or she may "know" in any formal way—thus affording inestimable musical benefits to the student's future growth.

Another crucial characteristic of our approach is that every melodic extract is consistently retained in its harmonic and/or contrapuntal context. This allows an overall organization along harmonic lines, paralleling a written theory curriculum and resulting in a more comprehensive engagement than the typical sight-singing manual. Melodies presented without harmonic context are often of limited use in class because the harmonic support, the cadential articulation, and even the phrase structure may be unknowable or ambiguous from the melody alone. Knowledge of the harmonic underpinnings of a melody is essential for the performance of melodic leaps and provides insight into the function of particular melodic tones. To deny students what might be essential information about a melody is to impose artificial limitations and to diminish their chances for successfully acquiring the necessary aural skills.

Further, the availability of the complete harmonic texture enriches the students' musical experience in class, and it permits a great variety of possible uses for a given extract. Students can perform at sight directly out of the book or prepare certain selections as assigned. The memorization of assigned melodies on scale-degree numbers or solfège syllables is particularly beneficial. Examples may be rendered as a vocal solo, in ensemble combination with students on other parts, or with the student accompanying himself or herself on the piano or another instrument. Students might also enjoy improvising an alternate melody above the given bass line, or an additional "obbligato" voice above the given melody or between the outer voices. Further, many of the suggested dictations at the end of each chapter include contrapuntal or accompanimental parts; they provide an opportunity to practice multipart listening skills. We find it to be of pedagogical benefit to alternate between staff-based dictation (given the clef, key, meter, and number of measures) and scale-degree or solfège dictation (given only the meter and number of measures); purely rhythmic dictation would also be worthwhile.

This book also offers a large number of drills, keyboard harmony explorations, and improvisatory exercises. The consistent goal is to help students become fluent in musical patterning while providing them the freedom and opportunity to manipulate those patterns in a creative and real-time manner. In particular, the strong emphasis on improvisation allows students to focus on musical "communication," teaching students to attend to the sound being produced and to trust their own ears. Furthermore, improvisation is a powerful vehicle for musical expression, which demonstrates a synthesis of theoretical understanding and musicianship. The choices students make while improvising reflect their musical thinking processes and musical understanding. Naturally, this opens up windows for assessment, as students are able to express musical ideas spontaneously only after thoroughly internalizing the underpinning musical structures. We have provided the student with a number of online backup tracks over which they may record and submit improvisations for evaluation. The wealth of drill and improvisation activities in this textbook distinguishes it from all other options.

Finally, this book provides an additional, unique resource in its compilation of binary, ternary, rondo, and sonata forms, selected and arranged for "singability." Because music students must already specialize to such a great extent in order to progress in their studies, not every student gets the chance to perform music in these various forms, and when they do, their attention (and that of their conductor or coach) may be directed toward other aspects than the form of the music. Several fugues are also included in certain activities. With the materials presented in this volume, students have an invaluable opportunity to get to know a range of standard and nonstandard examples of each of these forms, both as a performer and as an active listener to Contextual Listening examples. The musical examples in every chapter are complemented by a selection of rhythmic, harmonic, and melodic drills and exercises, designed to solidify a student's understanding of the position of every pitch within the tonal context and to further support the development of fluency with a large number of typical rhythmic, harmonic, and melodic paradigms. Improvisational activities allow students to develop their musical spontaneity and confidence.

Ultimately, the programmed arrangement of musical extracts and exercises is designed to foster a heightened awareness of melodic function, rhythmic patterning, and the harmonic-contrapuntal structure of tonal music. Though no particular pedagogical approach is advocated, every chapter ends with a set of possible weekly assignments, designed to further the learning that is started in class. Listening and dictation-type exercises that approach twentieth-century works in both popular and classical styles can be found in the Expanding the Repertoire sections of every chapter. Although they are supplementary, these exercises allow students to engage in listening beyond the traditional paradigms. Links to commercial recordings, and free, studio-released videos of these works are available on our website, although many of the works will already be in the students' collections.

An online resource, www.auralskillsincontext.com, provides streaming audio at various tempos to be used for Contextual Listening assignments, several of which can be found in every chapter. Many of the excerpts also include an online mixer that can be used to rebalance the parts in a multivoiced excerpt, or to add a metronome click. The website is available only to students and instructors.

Another major innovation of this text is that it has been designed to be used with Finale SmartMusic,[1] an inexpensive software program that will evaluate, track, and report the student's progress in accurate singing, while providing the harmonic context of real music examples that is at the root of our philosophy. Most excerpts have been turned into assessable exercises, which students complete weekly by singing into a microphone on their computer. The computer calculates a score and provides the student with immediate feedback, but it also creates a recording that is automatically uploaded to SmartMusic's online gradebook. The instructor can see the computer's assessment, listen to the recording, enter other assignment grades, and provide additional feedback. The students

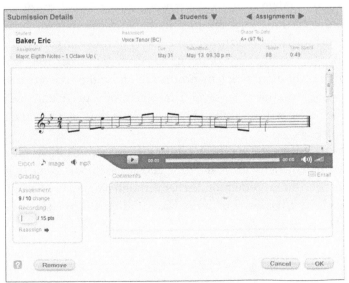

[1] SmartMusic logo and screenshots used with permission of Make Music, Inc.

can also see their own grades and comments every time they log on. In addition, we have provided improvisation assignments, where the students improvise a melody over a repeating harmonic progression (typically in a jazz or popular style). The recording can be submitted for the instructor to evaluate through the online gradebook.

At a minimal cost to students, this software provides invaluable feedback and offers an exciting practice tool that includes accompaniments for virtually any piece of standard repertoire. Indeed, virtually every major method book has standard accompaniments that are available for free to SmartMusic subscribers. Although the book can be used successfully without employing SmartMusic, it is an invaluable tool to allow students to practice at their own pace with immediate feedback. The end of every chapter includes a set of suggested SmartMusic assignments, any of which may be easily assigned by the instructor with just a few mouse clicks from a shared online SmartMusic library.

Aural skills instructors have always been faced with a choice between texts that engage and enhance their students' harmonic-contrapuntal hearing and texts that acknowledge and capture their students' love of music (which prompted them to commence its study in the first place). This textbook obviates the need for such a choice—thus optimizing a student's learning experience in every way.

Support from Leading Scholars in Music Cognition

The paradigmatic approach found in this text employs real stylistically based harmonic progressions, melodic patterns, and specific rhythmic shapes to give students an aural vocabulary, which they can then use in all of their musical activities. Several studies have shown that students who learn to label musical paradigms consistently are more successful in meaningfully parsing the musical surface. According to these studies on statistical learning, repetitions of musical patterns of all types (even atypical ones) lead to the creation of new knowledge structures, which ultimately can lead to significantly more efficient processing and more accurate predictions. Ultimately, as the student is exposed to several instances of a particular melodic or rhythmic paradigm, he or she will be able to perform music that contains the paradigm more fluently and accurately.[2]

The paradigmatic approach has significant ramifications for musical memory as well. As students engage with real music and its harmonic context in a way that focuses on accurate musical reproduction (either through singing or through the Contextual Listening exercises), they learn to apply the paradigms in the segmentation of the music into

---

[2] Roland Eberlein and Jobst Peter Fricke, *Kadenzwahrnehmung und Kadenzgeschichte: Ein Beitrag zu einer Grammatik der Musik* (Frankfurt am Main: Peter Lang, 1992); David Huron, *Sweet Anticipation: Music and the Psychology of Expectation* (Cambridge: MIT Press, 2006); Crystal Peebles, *The Role of Segmentation and Expectation in the Perception of Closure* (Ph.D. diss., Florida State University, 2011).

logical, nameable events. As Zacks et al. have shown,[3] this sort of segmentation into meaningful groups results in significantly improved memory of the larger whole.

As explained previously, the current pedagogical text progresses rapidly toward larger excerpts, always expressed with their harmonic context. One clear advantage is that it allows students to engage in accurate prediction within a stylistic context, a critical component of fluent sight reading and engaged hearing. A study by Joichi, for instance,[4] demonstrated that longer excerpts of music within a harmonic context led participants to more clearly anticipate points of cadential arrival, consequently allowing them to intuit certain details about phrase and structure.

Finally, this book's coordination with SmartMusic permits consistent *targeted* or *deliberate* practice, following the principles set out by Ericsson.[5] The graded approach to varied melodies, rhythms, and bass lines from real music combined with SmartMusic's instant feedback and adaptability to the individual student supports an ideal practice scenario. Thus, greater fluency and efficiency with the basic materials of tonal music can be easily achieved.

Curricular Planning

As with any textbook, there are many possible pathways through the materials herein. What follow are some possible ways to divide the chapters across the curriculum. To promote a great deal of flexibility, an introductory chapter, "The Foundations of Aural Skills," has been provided. It is substantially different from the remaining chapters, offering little by way of real musical excerpts, but instead presenting an introduction to all the materials of aural skills through drill, improvisation, and practice. The underlying materials and philosophy of the book are presented in the introductory chapter in short sections that include prose descriptions and a large number of musical exercises. It would be perfectly possible for students to spend the first three or four weeks of instruction carefully perfecting the exercises in that chapter and attempting one of the Contextual Listening assignments each week. This would be an ideal basis for a student with some musical experience but little exposure to the kind of aural skills required for Chapter 1. Many college-level curricula, by contrast, have a music-theory fundamentals course that students take before they begin serious musicianship training. If this is the case, one week

---

[3] Jeffrey M. Zacks and Khena M. Swallow, "Event Segmentation," *Current Directions in Psychological Science* 2007, 16: 80–84; Jeffrey M. Zacks, Nicole K. Speer, and Jeremy R. Reynolds, "Segmentation in Reading and Film Comprehension," *Journal of Experimental Psychology* 2009, 138 (2): 307–327.

[4] Janet M. Joichi, *Closure, Context, and Hierarchical Grouping in Music: A Theoretical and Empirical Investigation* (Ph.D. diss., Northwestern University, 2006).

[5] K. A. Ericsson, R. Th. Krampe, and C. Tesch-Römer, "The Role of Deliberate Practice in the Acquisition of Expert Performance," *Psychological Review*, 1993, 100: 363–406; K. A. Ericsson and A. C. Lehmann, "Expert and Exceptional Performance: Evidence on Maximal Adaptations on Task Constraints," *Annual Review of Psychology*, 1996, 47: 273–305.

on the basic materials of the introductory chapter will be ample to prepare students to move into Chapter 1. Finally, the pacing required for student success depends greatly on the number of class meetings per week, the percentage of music majors in a particular curriculum, the student commitment and preparation level, and the pacing of the written theory curriculum. Instructors are encouraged to take a very flexible view of the materials in the present text.

Depending on the path taken through this book, it is possible that some harmonic topics may be encountered earlier than in a companion class in music theory. If this is the case, instructors may find success in introducing harmony as an aural and physical experience (at the piano and on an instrument). Part writing, melody harmonization, and thoughtful analysis are complex cognitive tasks, but hearing a simple phrase model is something that many young musicians are already prepared to do. Alternatively, instructors may always choose to introduce the Chorale Workshop progressions more slowly than presented in this text. Virtually all excerpts and most exercises will work just fine at a different pace from that of the Chorale Workshop assignments.

Two-Year Aural-Skills Curriculum Begun *After* a Fundamentals Course:

SEMESTER 1:   The Foundations of Aural Skills (first week), then Chapters 1 through 7
Introduction of materials through simple excerpts using the entire octave

SEMESTER 2:   Chapters 8 through 14
Sequences through simple, nonmodulatory chromaticism

SEMESTER 3:   Chapters 15–21
Basic modulation through binary and ternary forms

SEMESTER 4:   Chapters 22–27
Advanced chromaticism and larger forms

Two-Year Aural-Skills Curriculum with *No* Fundamentals Course:

This division of the material may also work well for institutions where the students are primarily nonmusic majors or come in with little exposure to musicianship skills.

SEMESTER 1:   The Foundations of Aural Skills (weeks 1 through 3 or 4), then Chapters 1 through 4
Introduction of materials through melodies with limited pitches of the scale

SEMESTER 2:   Chapters 5 through 10 (no chromaticism until semester 3)
Simple excerpts using the entire octave through multiple phrase types

SEMESTER 3:   Chapters 11–16
                Simple chromaticism through modulation

SEMESTER 4:   Chapters 17–23
                Binary forms through nineteenth-century harmony and rondo
                form

Practicalities

www.auralskillsincontext.com

Contextual listening exercises must be completed by listening to the excerpts found on the website. Complete access will be provided to adopters and students through the higher-education division of Oxford University Press. Limited guest access may be acquired with the guest login.

Login: guest
Password: guest

SmartMusic

A desk copy of SmartMusic may be acquired through Make Music's manager for the higher-education division.

Make Music has a number of useful tutorials that the instructor may watch, but setting up a class is easy and intuitive. Once a class is created, a student must register in order for the instructor to assign exercises. It is recommended that the instructor *also* set up a student account so that the student's perspective may also be evaluated.

Depending on the location of the instructor's school, the SmartMusic assignments may be shared directly through the "shared assignments" folder in the instructor's "assignment library." SmartMusic exercise files will also be available for instructors to download, at www.auralskillsincontext.com.

For SmartMusic tips directed to the student, see the introductory chapter.

Acknowledgments

Many instructors, students, friends, and colleagues have been involved in the evolution of this text. We would particularly like to thank Richard Carlin and Sheena Kowalski at Oxford University Press, as well as all of the many reviewers whose comments were invaluable to the refinement of this text, including the following:

David Easley
Oklahoma City University

Robert L. Glarner
Radford University

Melissa Hoag
Oakland University

Laila Kteily-O'Sullivan
University of Memphis

Cindy Moyer
Humboldt State University

Susan Piagentini
Northwestern University
Bienen School of Music

Robert A. M. Ross
Community College of Philadelphia

Louise A. Weiss
Greenville College

We would also like to thank the following people for their editorial and testing work:

Rafael Almario
Matthew Bell
Michael Broder
Joshua Burel
Christopher Burton
Evan Bushman
Szu-Yu Chen
Ya-Hui Cheng
Fabrice Curtis
Gregory Decker
David Easley
Margaret Erdman
Roger Foreman
Andrew Gades
Sarah Gaskins
Emily Gertsch

Chelsey Hamm
Sarah Horick
Bryn Hughes
Brian Jarvis
Lewis Jeter
Joshua Keeling
Doron Kima
Jeremy Klumpp
Benjamin Krock
Megan Lavengood
Kimberly Loeffert
Micah Lomax
Marc Magellan
Greg McCandless
Joshua Mills
Judith Ofcarcik

Jon Overholt
Crystal Peebles
John Peterson
Stephanie Pieczynski
Nastassja Riley
Gillian Robertson
Tyler Roe
Sarah Sarver
Jay Smith
Jennie Smith
Jayme Wagner
Jamie Whitmarsh
Evan Williams
Tara Young
Richard Zarou

In addition, we would like to extend our eternal thanks to our wonderful colleagues at Florida State University and the University of Miami, and of course to our families, who are the foundation upon which all of our professional efforts stand!

Aural Skills
In Context

The Foundations of Aural Skills

Introduction for the Student

Everyone who enjoys music, from beginners to professionals, can benefit from improved aural skills. The ability to use one's ear to engage critically with music of all styles and origins translates not only into dramatically improved musicianship but also into increased enjoyment, as the intricacies of the music become clear. This book presents exercises and excerpts chosen to help you improve these skills in an appropriately gradual and musically engaging manner. Although certain excerpts and exercises may seem quite challenging at first, it is important to remember that aural skills cannot develop without thoughtful daily practice (even just a few minutes per day) and tenacity. These basic underlying skills must be practiced with the same intensity that a musician brings to a challenging new piece of music, or that an athlete uses to prepare for an event.

"Real Music" from Multiple Styles and in Multiple Parts

This book seeks to help you acquire the skills of critical listening and sight singing through excerpts of actual music from a wide variety of styles and composers presented in an appropriate harmonic context. Your practice will closely replicate the kind of holistic musical engagement undertaken by musicians in their other musical endeavors. All of the excerpts in this book are arranged to be sung, either by yourself with a piano (or other instrument) or in a group with people singing each part. It is critical that you always be prepared to sing every part of an excerpt—melody, bass, and inner voices—since it is from simultaneous familiarity with all the parts that you will best be able to negotiate the relationship between harmony and melody.

Feel free to listen to recordings of professional musicians playing these excerpts so that you may experience some of the interpretive decisions they have made. Do try, however, to avoid using recordings or a piano keyboard as a crutch for your own learning. Remember that a little struggle is part of the learning process. When you are learning an excerpt, try to work directly from the score, never playing the "part" that you are learning on an external instrument. Instead, use your knowledge of the scale, harmony, and function of each pitch within the scale and the harmonic context to "sound" out an excerpt with your voice. Be sure to try singing nearly every voice in the multipart excerpts. The goal is for you to be able to audiate (to sing in your head) the other parts while you sing your own part. In order to build your facility in this regard, try simultaneously singing your part while playing the other parts on an instrument so that you can have the harmonic context of the other voices as a reference.

Familiar Excerpts and Audiation

Some of the excerpts may be familiar to you, in which case you should use them as reference points, singing them with solmization syllables (such as scale-degree numbers or solfège) so that the relationships between notes on a page and actual music making are reinforced. When you come across an excerpt that you do not already know, you will be able to quickly transfer the good habits that you create in singing familiar tunes to the unfamiliar ones. It is also essential that you audiate, as it is this skill that allows musicians to prepare by thinking "ahead" of the actual music and be able to critique their own playing. Dictation exercises are invaluable in developing audiation skills, but do not forget to practice singing silently!

Contextual Listening and Expanding the Repertoire

Throughout the book, listening exercises that are designed to expand your listening skills will reinforce concepts that you will have explored in your singing and internal ear. These excerpts (and, in some cases, entire works) are drawn from a wide variety of repertoires, including popular musics. Although single-line melodic dictation, multipart dictation, and harmonic dictation help to focus your hearing, the exercises ask you to listen for other musical elements, such as formal design, phrasing, harmonic planning, and motivic construction. Audio for all the excerpts are available through the website that accompanies this text, www.auralskillsincontext.com.

Keyboard Orientation and Chorale Workshops

Playing, singing, listening, and thinking from the keyboard are critical skills for all musicians, even for those who have little experience with a piano. The strong historical connections between the keyboard and the development of Western music can hardly be overstated. Indeed, the familiar keyboard layout has been associated with Western musical practice for more than six centuries, and some of the most basic elements of our musical heritage (such as the twelve-note chromatic scale) find their roots in the keyboard. This book does *not* furnish instruction for piano technique, which should be sought in a studio or class setting, but the exercises here are designed to reinforce the connections among melody, harmony, hearing, and singing through a *total physical response* to music. Because the piano offers the advantages of fixed pitch, clearly defined duration, a wide range (encompassing that of all Western instruments), the ability to sound multiple voices simultaneously, and an organization that shares characteristics with musical notation, it is the ideal instrument through which to experience and to transfer many of the skills that are taught in this book. Although all students are encouraged to develop some level of piano proficiency, it is not required or even expected for this book. Instead, students and instructors should focus on the experience of the simultaneous playing of harmonic and melodic patterns, or of playing one line while singing another. That is, technical limitations should not get in the way of slow, but fluid and rhythmic, practice at the keyboard.

Drills

Musical patterns and fluent aural skills go hand in hand, and thus this book provides more than one hundred drills. These may seem to be secondary to the part singing and contextual listening that is found throughout the book, but we believe that successful aural skills center on the fluid and flexible experience and implementation of musical patterning. Learning to immediately recognize, audiate, and manipulate these patterns in actual music will reinforce overall musicianship while building better connections between musical execution and the musical ear.

Improvisation

Improvisation is the real-time composition that occurs when the fluent use of musical patterns, such as those explored in the excerpts and drills, meets creativity and musical communication! It has been a vital part of music making throughout history (from early plainchant to improvised cadenzas of the Classical period, to contemporary jazz), and it represents the ultimate synthesis of musicianship skills. In addition to the improvisation suggestions at the end of every chapter, many of the contextual listening assignments include improvisational exercises that will allow you to reconceive the musical materials explored in the contextual listening. You will be able to practice improvisation with on-line backup tracks and then submit recordings of your improvisations to your instructor. All improvisation exercises you will encounter in this book feature a balance between structure (the use of formulas and models) and creativity (taking risks) that offers a great diversity of choices and results. Explore with confidence, find your personal boundaries, and push your musical limits!

Thinking, Singing, and Hearing Holistically

Since the language of this text is music, prose will be kept to a minimum. Some selections, however, will be accompanied by small points that may be worth considering. Remember that hearing and performing music isn't just about pitches and/or rhythms; it also requires an ability to understand phrase, motive, gesture, form, and so forth. All of these additional parameters play an important role in this text.

The Materials of Aural Skills

The drills and exercises in this chapter are designed to introduce the basic materials of music: scales, triads, chord tones, nonchord tones, intervals within the diatonic system, rhythm, meter, and rhythmic subdivisions. In addition, we will be outlining the fundamental skills that underlie successful aural skills: singing, hearing, solmization syllables, harmonic hearing, singing in parts, improvisation, and familiarity with the keyboard. You may have encountered all of these materials and concepts in your previous musical study, in which case we would encourage you to move quickly through the exercises below. Do not ignore the improvisation or keyboard orientation parts of this chapter, however, as these are absolutely integral to the development of reliable and flexible aural skills. Finally, although many of these materials are initially presented in isolation, remember that the goal of musicianship (and thus, the goal of this textbook) is for you to be able to successfully integrate all of your musical skills. As such, you will note that many of the later exercises build on skills that are introduced on the earlier ones.

Major and Minor Scales with Solmization Syllables

The major and minor scales are the underlying organizational scheme of all Western musical melodies and harmonies. Becoming familiar with the scale and its constituent intervals is critical for successful aural skills. Using a solmization system, a set of syllables linked to individual members of the scale, will eventually help you understand the unique position and tendencies of each pitch of the scale (scale degree). As you have surely learned in your music theory classes, the minor scale may include alterations to the sixth and seventh scale degrees. Some instructors and students find it useful to employ the syllable "raised" whenever there is an accidental as part of a stepwise ascent (and "low" whenever there is an accidental as part of a descent). The minor scale is typically employed with one of these sets of alterations:

a. With scale degrees $\hat{6}$ and $\hat{7}$ raised on the way up and lowered on the way down as shown below, commonly called "melodic minor"
b. With scale degree $\hat{7}$ raised in both directions, commonly called "harmonic minor" (watch out for the unusual space between scale degrees $\hat{6}$ and $\hat{7}$)
c. With scale degrees $\hat{6}$ and $\hat{7}$ lowered both on the way up and on the way down, commonly called natural minor, or Aeolian mode

Major scale:

Minor scale(s):

Scale Practice/Singing in Parts

Exercise F.1.   Sing the scales with solmization syllables in unison. Be sure to practice all possible iterations of the minor scale.

Exercise F.2. Sing scales with note names. Try this in several major and minor keys. If you have a partner, ask your partner to identify the name of the scale after you sing.

Exercise F.3. Sing major and minor scales in a simple round in which the second voice enters with the third note of the scale. Make the adjustments as found below to accommodate the second voice and the adjustments to the minor scale. Sing using solmization syllables and note names.

Improvising with the Scale, and Locating the Scale Degrees Within the Scale

Exercise F.4. Write the scale on a piece of paper or on the board. Have a friend or instructor make up a melody by pointing to pitches. Respond to the visual cues by singing the pitches accurately as they are pointed out.

Exercise F.5. Sing phone numbers as though they were scale degrees. You may simply ignore the 0 and 9 digits, or substitute them for scale degree $\hat{1}$.

Exercise F.6. Make up a melody from small scalar subsets. Whenever possible, work with a partner, so that you can trade off. Have your partner pick up whenever you finish a scale segment and vice versa (e.g.: $\hat{1}$–$\hat{2}$–$\hat{3}$–$\hat{4}$–$\hat{5}$–$\hat{5}$–$\hat{5}$–$\hat{4}$–$\hat{3}$–$\hat{2}$–$\hat{1}$/ do–re–mi–fa–sol–sol–sol–fa–mi–re–do).

Rhythm and Subdivision

Rhythm is, of course, another essential component of music. Becoming fluent in the common rhythmic patterns of music is essential for successful aural skills. As you have no doubt learned in your previous music studies, the rhythmic values of Western notation relate to one another through specific ratios. That is, any note of a longer duration may be subdivided into a group of evenly spaced notes in shorter durations. The chart shown here summarizes many of the ratios, while providing some common solmization approaches to various durations.[1] Although rhythmic solmization is not nearly as standardized as scale solmization, employing some system of syllables will help you to accurately "sound out" rhythmic patterns. It is important to keep in mind, however, that durations often combine to make very common rhythmic gestures or patterns. Becoming familiar and fluent with the larger patterns is as important as being able to sound out a new pattern for the first time by subdividing. Just as it would be difficult to read and comprehend this paragraph by having to sound out each individual word, "sounding out" a piece of music by subdividing each and every duration would be a challenging task indeed.

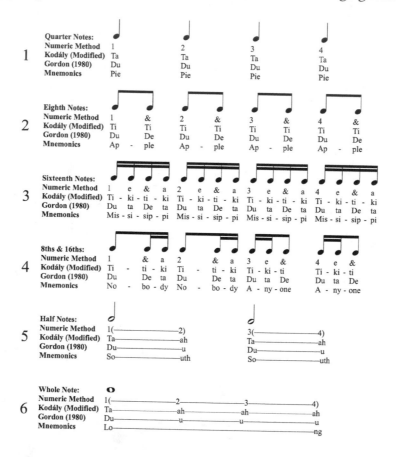

Exercise F.7.   Practice each pattern above. Start with the quarter notes (no. 1), and, as you work down to the whole note (no. 6), continue tapping the quarter notes with one hand while speaking the other rhythms.

Exercise F.8.   Make up your own mnemonic devices for each rhythmic pattern, keeping the emphases found in the mnemonics we have supplied.

[1] Another popular system, *Takadimi*, uses syllables that change according to the exact point of attack (or point of onset) within each beat. A complete explanation may be found at http://www.takadimi.net.

Exercise F.9.   *Audiation*: in order to practice *internalizing* the rhythmic patterns, start singing or playing a rhythmic pattern above. Then, take a quarter note's worth of duration and perform it differently (try tapping, whistling, or humming). Now leave out that quarter note's worth of duration altogether, just imagining the durations that you left out while maintaining the same speed. See the example that follows:

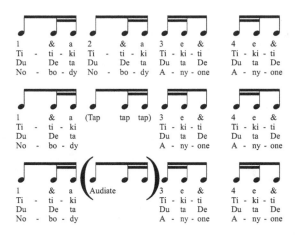

Exercise F.10.   *Simon says*: have a friend or your instructor play or sing one of the rhythmic patterns above. Sing or play the rhythmic pattern in imitation, and then identify which pattern it was. Now expand to two different rhythmic patterns and try imitating, and then identifying, them both. How many rhythms can you identify in a row?

Rhythmic Improvisation

Exercise F.11.   Have a friend or your instructor point to the rhythms numbered 1–6 in the rhythmic syllable chart above. Try a random order at first, and then attempt to build a longer rhythmic phrase (a complete musical idea, with a beginning, middle, and end) by stringing together several rhythmic patterns. Which patterns tend to sound more like beginnings and endings? Which are more climactic?

Exercise F.12.   Now, build a rhythmic phrase as in Exercise F.11, and then add text, using the example of the mnemonic devices you created in Exercise F.8. Try to create a short story in rhythm. Pay particular attention to retaining the rhythmic emphases in the mnemonic devices provided. Be prepared to perform this in class.

Dotted Rhythms and Basic Syncopations

As you will remember from your previous studies, a dot following a note adds another half of the original note's value. Thus, a dotted-half note is the same duration as a half note and quarter note together. A dotted-quarter note is the same duration as a quarter note and an eighth note together. A syncopation occurs when a longer note value begins on a normally unaccented location in the rhythmic pattern contradicting the conventional accentuation.

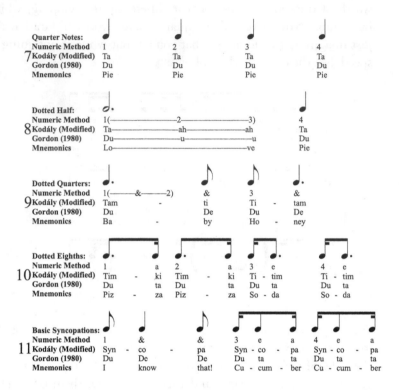

Quarter Notes:				
Numeric Method	1	2	3	4
7 Kodály (Modified)	Ta	Ta	Ta	Ta
Gordon (1980)	Du	Du	Du	Du
Mnemonics	Pie	Pie	Pie	Pie

Dotted Half:				
Numeric Method	1(———————2———————3)			4
8 Kodály (Modified)	Ta————————ah————————ah			Ta
Gordon (1980)	Du————————u			Du
Mnemonics	Lo————————————————ve			Pie

Dotted Quarters:				
Numeric Method	1(——&——2)	&	3	&
9 Kodály (Modified)	Tam -	ti	Ti -	tam
Gordon (1980)	Du	De	Du	De
Mnemonics	Ba -	by	Ho -	ney

Dotted Eighths:				
Numeric Method	1 a	2 a	3 e	4 e
10 Kodály (Modified)	Tim - ki	Tim - ki	Ti - tim	Ti - tim
Gordon (1980)	Du ta	Du ta	Du ta	Du ta
Mnemonics	Piz - za	Piz - za	So - da	So - da

Basic Syncopations:					
Numeric Method	1	&	&	3 e a	4 e a
11 Kodály (Modified)	Syn - co -	pa	pa	Syn - co - pa	Syn - co - pa
Gordon (1980)	Du De		De	Du ta ta	Du ta ta
Mnemonics	I know		that!	Cu - cum - ber	Cu - cum - ber

Exercise F.13.   Practice each pattern, contradicting the conventional accentuation in the figure above. Start with the quarter notes (no. 7), and move to the dotted half (no. 8), considering the subdivision of the dotted half into three quarters. Unless you are already very familiar with dotted rhythms, you may wish to practice constant eighths (no. 2 in the rhythmic syllable chart) before moving on to the dotted quarter (no. 9). As you work down to the syncopations (no. 11), continue tapping the quarter notes with one hand while speaking the other rhythms.

Exercise F.14.   Make up your own mnemonic devices for each rhythmic pattern, keeping the emphases found in the mnemonics we have provided.

Exercise F.15.   *Audiation*: in order to practice *internalizing* the rhythmic patterns, start singing or playing any rhythmic pattern above. Then, take a single duration (such as a dotted eighth) and perform it differently (try tapping, whistling, or humming). Now leave that duration out altogether, just imagining the durations that you left out while maintaining the same speed.

Exercise F.16.   *Simon says*: have a friend or your instructor play or sing one of the rhythmic patterns above. Sing or play the rhythmic pattern in imitation, and then identify which pattern it was. Now expand to two different rhythmic patterns and try imitating, and then identifying, them both. Try mixing all the rhythms from nos. 1 through 11 above. How many rhythms can you identify in a row?

Rhythmic Improvisation Two

Exercise. F.17.   Have a friend or your instructor point to nos. 7–11 above. Try a random order at first, and then attempt to build a longer rhythmic phrase (a complete musical idea, with a beginning, middle, and end) by stringing together several rhythmic patterns. Which patterns tend to sound more like beginnings and endings? Which are more climactic? Try mixing patterns 1–11 above.

Exercise F.18.   Now, build a rhythmic phrase as in Exercise F.17, and then add text, using the example of the mnemonic devices you created in Exercise F.14. Try to create a short story in rhythm. Pay particular attention to retaining the rhythmic emphases in the mnemonic devices provided. Be prepared to perform this in class.

Meter: Conducting Simple Meters

As you are already aware, the durations and rhythmic patterns of Western music are organized according to repeating patterns of accents, as indicated by a meter signature (or time signature) and which we notate in measures. Being able to conduct simple metric patterns while singing or playing is essential to the internalization of pulse and accent, and it will lead to more fluent rhythmic understanding. We start with three simple metric patterns: duple (two beats per measure, first beat accented), quadruple (four beats per measure, first and third beats accented), and triple (three beats per measure, first beat accented). The basic conducting patterns are diagramed below. They are typically executed with the right hand. Your instructor can demonstrate in class, or you can find many video examples online.

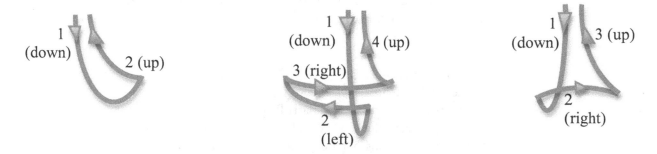

Exercise F.19.   Learn the basic conducting patterns for simple duple, triple, and quadruple meters (shown above). Practice conducting whenever possible, so that your physical connection to meter may become automatic. Start by conducting yourself while counting straight quarter notes, and then try speaking or singing each of the rhythmic subdivisions shown above while conducting. Note that each rhythmic pattern above (nos. 1–11) fits a single quadruple meter measure. When practicing duple conducting, you may simply use two duple conducting patterns for each of the rhythmic patterns (nos. 1–11). When practicing the triple meter conducting patterns, you may simply leave off the final quarter note's worth of duration.

Exercise F.20.   Now, do the same exercise as in Exercise F.19, but add accents for all strong beats (1 and 3 in quadruple meter; beat 1 in triple and duple meters). Feel free to exaggerate at first, but then find a more musically nuanced way to accent the strong beats.

Exercise F.21.   Variation for different values of the beat: if the meter signature is 2/4, 3/4, or 4/4, each line of the conducting pattern will equal one quarter note in duration. That is, the quarter note will be the basic beat. In meter signatures such as 2/2, 3/2, and 4/2, however, each line of the conducting pattern will equal one half note in duration. In meter signatures such as 2/8, 3/8, and 4/8, each line of the conducting pattern will equal one eighth note in duration. Practice conducting rhythmic patterns 1–11 with all three conducting patterns, imagining that the beat is either a half note or an eighth note. Adjust the rhythmic patterns as required in order to fit them into your newly defined meters. You will also want to alter your tempo to ensure that your rhythms can remain completely accurate and that you can use the appropriate syllables (as requested by your instructor). Finally, maintain the light accents you practiced in Exercise F.20.

Exercise F.22.   The website linked with this textbook (www.auralskillsincontext.com) has a number of recordings available for the many contextual listening assignments found in later chapters. For now, visit the website and find the recordings for the following excerpts and practice (a) finding the beat, (b) tapping the beat, (c) conducting along with the recording, and (d) conducting along with the recording while imagining accents on the appropriate beats. Note that some of these excerpts start on the downbeat (the first beat of the measure), while others start with an upbeat anacrusis (they start on the final or penultimate beat of the measure). Which of these excerpts start with an anacrusis?

• Contextual Listening F.3 "Call Me Maybe" (quadruple)
• Contextual Listening 1-1 "Ode to Joy" (quadruple)
• Contextual Listening 4-2 Scarlatti Piano Sonata (triple)
• Contextual Listening 4-3 "The Holly and the Ivy" (triple)
• Contextual Listening 5-1 Beethoven String Quartet (duple)
• Contextual Listening 6-3 Leopold Mozart, Bourrée (quadruple)
• Contextual Listening 8-5 "Where Is the Love" (quadruple)
• Contextual Listening 12-2 "My Funny Valentine" (duple)
• Contextual Listening 15-1 Beethoven quintet (triple)
• Contextual Listening 16-3 "Amazing Grace" (triple)
• Contextual Listening 18-1 Mozart Piano Sonata (duple)
• Contextual Listening 22-4 "There's No Business" (duple)

Be prepared to conduct these excerpts in class.

Singing Scales with Rhythm and Meter

Exercise F.23.   Practice singing major and minor scales in even note values while conducting (all quarter notes, all eighth notes, etc.). Sing each note for a full quarter-note duration but on the even rhythmic division you've selected. As a challenge, add accents for all strong beats. Alternate between singing scale-degree solmization syllables and rhythmic syllables. Try this in duple, triple, and quadruple meter. In order to accommodate various meters, always start the scalar ascent on the tonic (first degree of the scale), and on the downbeat. When you get to the top of the scale, sing the upper tonic until you get to the next downbeat; then descend with the upper tonic on the new downbeat. See the example below:

Exercise F.24.   This exercise is similar to the previous one, except that now you will sing the scales with one pitch of the scale for each duration. Be sure to continue conducting and to choose a tempo that will allow you to sing accurately. Sing using rhythmic syllables and scale solmization. Only scale solmization is shown in the example that follows (with rhythm no. 10 from the earlier rhythm syllable chart):

Exercise F.25.　　*Audiation variation*: try Exercises F.23 and F.24, but leave out every other pitch of the scale. At first, just tap the rhythm of the missing pitch, but then just *think* the rhythm *and* pitch of the notes you leave out.

Exercise F.26.　　*Singing in parts variation*: now try singing Exercises F.23 and F.24 as a round, as discussed in Exercises F.2 and F.3. Be sure that you conduct together. You may also wish to try singing the audiation variation (F.25) in a round.

Excerpts from the Chapters as Rhythmic Exercises and Rhythmic Improvisations

Any excerpt (and indeed, any piece of notated music) can be used as a purely rhythmic exercise, even when there are notated pitches. This is typically the best way to practice a rhythmically challenging excerpt, at least until you are a proficient rhythm reader. Take this excerpt from Chapter 1, for instance:

Exercise F.27.　　Speak the rhythm only, using rhythmic syllables. It should sound something like this:

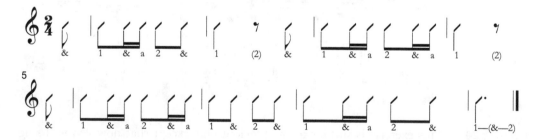

Exercise F.28.　　Count the number of rhythmic patterns found within an entire measure, ignoring the anacrusis (pickup), but not the final dotted quarter (imagine there is an eighth rest there to complete the measure). You should find only five rhythmic patterns:

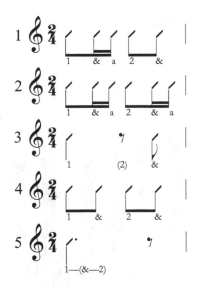

Practice each of these rhythmic patterns separately until you can chant them fluently.

Exercise F.29.   *Rhythmic improvisation*: as in rhythmic improvisation F.11, have a friend or your instructor point to nos. 1–5 above. Try a random order at first, and then attempt to build a longer rhythmic phrase (a complete musical idea, with a beginning, middle, and end) by stringing together several rhythmic patterns.

Exercise F.30.   *Meter, rhythm, and text*: because we are all familiar with the natural accents of language, setting music with new texts is an excellent exercise for linking meter, rhythm, and accent. In addition, performing the new texts reinforces the fluency of rhythmic/metric understanding. Briefly examine the text setting in the original tune. Note the placement of the strong syllables "dame," "lame," "crane," "pray," "Jane," and "home." Note that such weak syllables as "my," "that was," "oh," and "had a" are *never* placed on the stronger parts of the beats in the measure (that is, they never fall directly on the beat *and* beat 1 typically gets the strongest syllable). Try replacing the text above with one of your own creation, making sure that weak syllables are never placed on beat 1 and that strong syllables are never placed off the beat (never on the "and" or "a").

Exercise F.31.   *Rhythmic improvisation with text*: now, build a rhythmic phrase as in Exercise F.29, and then add a completely new text, following the guidelines found in Exercise F.30. Consider making a short video of yourself performing your work, and feel free to add dance moves! You may be asked to share this on a class website or YouTube page. At the very least, be prepared to perform this in class.

Exercise F.32.   Try Exercises F.21 through F.31 above with Examples 1.2, 1.3, and 1.4 of Chapter 1. You will be asked to do something similar with Example 1.22 at the end of that chapter.

Geography of the Keyboard

As stated earlier, playing, singing, listening, and thinking from the keyboard are critical skills for all musicians, even for those who have little experience with a piano. Remember, technical limitations should not get in the way of slow, but fluid and rhythmic practice at the keyboard.

Exercise F.33.   As you may be aware from your previous musical studies, the keyboard is laid out in an ascending scalar pattern, such that playing the white notes from C to C will generate a C major scale, while playing the white notes from A to A will result in a minor scale (natural) with the lowered sixth and seventh scale degrees. Practice both of these scales until you can play them at a steady tempo. Don't worry about technique; instead, focus on keeping a slow but consistent pace. Be sure you can easily and quickly identify the note name of any key on the piano.

Exercise F.34.   Since you should already be familiar with major and minor key signatures from your previous studies, try playing several major and minor scales on a piano. You may wish to focus particularly on C, D, F, and G for major. Use A, C, E, and D for minor, exploring all the alterations of scale degrees $\hat{6}$ and $\hat{7}$. As before, your playing should be fluid but not necessarily rapid.

Exercise F.35.   *Sing and play*: start by playing one of the scales suggested in Exercise F.34, and then sing the same scale. Now, sing and play simultaneously, making sure to match each pitch.

Exercise F.36.   *Sing, play, and audiate*: now play and sing your scales, alternating each note between the piano and the voice. This drill is very good for developing audiation skills. As an additional challenge, alternate between singing, playing, and audiating.

Exercise F.37.   Now play and sing a scale canon with yourself (singing and playing simultaneously), as in Exercise F.3. Feel free to choose *any* steady tempo.

Exercise F.38.   Play the scales in rhythms as in Exercises F.23 and F.24.

Exercise F.39.   *Piano scales in rhythms audiation exercise*: play the scales in rhythms, singing alternating pitches (as in Exercise F.25).

Exercise F.40.   *Piano scales in rhythms in canon*: as in Exercise F.26, sing and play your rhythm scales in canon with yourself (singing and playing simultaneously).

Geography of the Piano: Whole Steps and Half Steps

The distance between any two immediately adjacent keys on the keyboard is a half step (other names: semitone, minor second). The distance between any two keys that are two half steps apart is a whole step (other names: whole tone, major second). That is, the distance between any two white keys separated by a black key is a whole step; likewise, the distance between any two black keys separated by a white key is also a whole step. The following exercises draw on your knowledge of the placement of pitches on the keyboard while reinforcing both the sound and physical placement of whole and half steps.

Exercise F.41.   Start by identifying all naturally occurring half steps on the white notes of the piano between C4 and C5 ("middle C" to the octave above). There should be two of them! If you've already learned the interval patterns of the major scale, you'll already know which two. Play and sing a C major scale, singing only the notes that are a semitone apart and playing the remainder.

Exercise F.42.   Now identify all the naturally occurring whole steps on the white notes of the piano. Play and sing a C major scale, singing only the notes that are a whole step apart and playing the remainder.

Exercise F.43.   Now try the same exercises (F.41 and F.42) for G major, D major, F major, A minor, C minor, E minor, and D minor scales (all versions of minor).

Exercise F.44.   *Sing-a-path improvisation*: How many ways can you get from point A to B?

 • Start by choosing two notes (at relatively close proximity) on the piano (or have your instructor or a peer do this for you). For instance:

- Now, identify a possible path from the lower note to the higher, always ascending by whole or half step only. Repeat it until you can play it the same way every time. For instance:

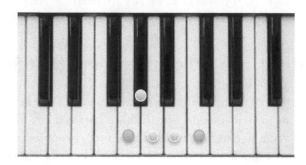

- Practice singing the resulting path from the lowest note to the highest in two ways:

1. With note names (thus, G–G#–A–B–C, in the example above)
2. Starting with the first note name, but thereafter focusing on the distance between notes (thus, G–half–half–whole–half, in the example above).

Exercise F.45.   Try the sing-a-path game with your peers (Exercise F.44). Start by announcing the starting and ending pitches; then play your whole- and half-step path between the two. Have your peers sing the path back to you using the two methods above. The person who selects the path verifies its accuracy by playing the path at the piano. You may also wish to have someone pointing to a keyboard drawn on a chalkboard. Once all paths between the selected notes have been exhausted, choose another set of two notes.

Singing Intervals in the Context of the Scale

Exercise F.46.   Sing major and minor scales starting with the first note name, but thereafter focusing on the distance between notes (thus, a C major scale would start as follows: "C–whole–whole–half . . . ").

Exercise F.47.   *Master interval drill, minor seconds*: this drill will be used to explore all intervals contained within the context of the major scale, while establishing their relationship with specific scale-degree function. For now, we will start with the minor seconds (additional intervals will be added in later chapters). Start by singing the major scale to give yourself a context; then, always conducting, sing the two pairs of half-step-related pitches in the major scale following the pattern in the following example. If you have trouble getting from $\hat{4}$ (fa) to $\hat{7}$ (ti), you may re-sing the major scale between them until you can get from one minor second to the other without needing to sing the scale.

3 - 4   mi - nor se - cond,   7 - 8   mi - nor se - cond.
mi   fa   mi - nor se - cond,   ti   do   mi - nor se - cond.

Exercise F.48.   *Master interval drill, major seconds*: following the directions for Exercise F.47, conduct while singing the major seconds in the major scale as shown below. Again, start by singing the major scale. If you get lost, for now, you can re-sing the scale at any point in the exercise. Continue practicing this drill until you can perform it successfully without needing to re-sing the scale.

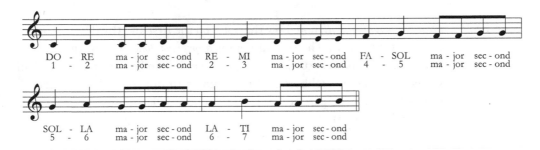

DO - RE   ma - jor sec - ond   RE - MI   ma - jor sec - ond   FA - SOL   ma - jor sec - ond
1 - 2   ma - jor sec - ond   2 - 3   ma - jor sec - ond   4 - 5   ma - jor sec - ond

SOL - LA   ma - jor sec - ond   LA - TI   ma - jor sec - ond
5 - 6   ma - jor sec - ond   6 - 7   ma - jor sec - ond

Exercise F.49.   *Audiation and the master interval drill*: sing the two intervals of the master interval drill, audiating (thinking, but not singing) every other pitch. Make sure to continue conducting.

Exercise F.50.   *Aural memory and the scale*: have a peer or your instructor play or sing a short (one-measure) scalar melodic fragment; then you and your peers should repeat the exact fragment, singing first with syllables, then by singing the syllable of the first note, and finally the distance (whole or half step) between subsequent notes. Now try imitating at the keyboard. Examples:

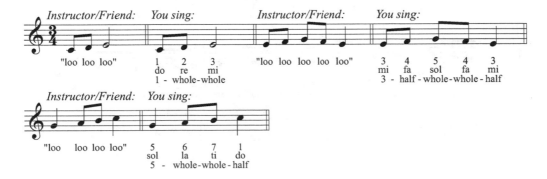

Instructor/Friend: *You sing:*   *Instructor/Friend:*   *You sing:*

"loo loo loo"   1   2   3   "loo loo loo loo loo"   3   4   5   4   3
                 do   re   mi   mi   fa   sol fa   mi
                 1 - whole - whole   3 - half - whole - whole - half

Instructor/Friend: *You sing:*

"loo   loo loo loo"   5   6   7   1
                        sol la   ti   do
                        5 - whole - whole - half

Exercise F.51.   *Rhythmic telephone*: this is an improvisation variation of Exercise F.50. Have a peer or your instructor play or sing a short (one-measure) scalar melodic fragment in rhythm and then sing the fragment back, changing one or two rhythms of the fragment; sing the fragment again. Have another peer add an additional rhythmic variation, and so on, until the fragment comes all the way around the room.

Melodic Hierarchy: Neighbor Tones and Passing Tones

Just as there are strong and weak beats in a metric context, certain pitches will seem to have greater weight than the ones around them. This is particularly common in a stepwise context, such that some passages of stepwise notes appear to be "passing through" one pitch to get to another, or may feature a pitch that seems to function as a "neighbor," returning immediately to the stepwise-related pitch that preceded it. The following drills are designed to build familiarity with the notion of melodic hierarchy within the context of the scale. Chromatic versions of these exercises will be included in later chapters.

Exercise F.52.   *Diatonic neighbor drill*: note how the notes on the first and third beats (eighth notes) are the same. The second note is a *neighbor tone*, which, though important to the musical surface, carries a lower hierarchical weight. The drill starts with lower neighbors and then moves to upper neighbors. Practice the drill in just one part at first, and then have a classmate sing the second part (as in a canon).

Exercise F.53. Now try playing the second part of the diatonic neighbor drill on the piano while singing the first part. Pick any tempo that is comfortable, but steady.

Exercise F.54. *Audiation variation*: start by audiating only the neighbor tones (the tones in the middle); then audiate the outer notes, singing only the neighbor tones.

Exercise F.55. *Diatonic passing-tone drill*: the notes on the first and third beats (eighth notes) carry more hierarchical weight than the middle "passing tone." This drill works nicely in minor, but it may also be performed in major (see if you can figure out how to transform it). Practice the drill in just one part at first, and then have a classmate sing the second part (as in a canon).

Exercise F.56.   Now try playing the second part of the diatonic passing-tone drill on the piano while singing the first part. Pick any tempo that is comfortable, but steady.

Exercise F.57.   *Audiation variation*: start by audiating only the passing tones (the tones in the middle); then audiate the outer notes, singing only the passing tones.

Exercise F.58.   *"Melismating,"* improvising with neighbor tones: similar to the tradition of melismatic embellishment, you will explore ornamenting a given set of notes using whole and half-step neighbors. Start with a short fragment in half notes, which may be provided by the instructor or another student. For instance:

Sing the scale to which they belong (C major, in this case), and then sing the four half notes. Now, embellish the half notes with diatonic (within the scale) upper or lower neighbors using an "eighth–eighth–quarter" rhythm. For instance:

Exercise F.59.   *Piano variation* of Exercise F.58: start by playing the half-note fragments on the piano, and then sing the embellished version, playing only the first and fourth notes of each measure (your original half notes).

Harmony, Triads, and Arpeggiation

There is a centuries-old debate about whether harmony or melody has priority in Western music. The argument follows the same lines as the old chicken-and-egg paradox: Which came first? Suffice it to say for now that harmony and melody are dependent on one another. Although at its surface music appears to be driven by melody, Western melodies of the past four centuries make sense only insofar as they are supported by typical harmonic motion (whether implicit or explicit). Thus, a great deal of the present text is focused on developing your familiarity with typical harmonic patterns. By placing musical excerpts within a harmonic context, we hope that you will be able to fluently internalize this connection between melody and harmony. You may be learning about tonal harmony from other sources in more detail than can be provided by this book. Instead, what we provide is a musically oriented approach to *experiencing* harmony.

As you will no doubt recall from your previous musical studies, there are four qualities of triads (major, minor, diminished, and augmented). Building triads on each of the scale degrees of the major and minor scales will result in a variety of chord qualities. For now, we will focus on the tonic triad (the "home" triad of any particular key), which is built on the tonic scale degree (scale degree 1̂) of any scale. Being able to hear the arrival on the tonic triad in any piece of music will help you know "where you are" in the musical landscape. Being able to arpeggiate the tonic triad no matter where in the piece you are will help you understand any particular harmony because of its relationship to the tonic.

Exercise F.60.   Sing a major scale in its entirety; then sing it again, audiating all pitches except for 1̂, 3̂, and 5̂. These are the notes of the tonic triad, with 1̂ acting as the *root* of the triad, 3̂ acting as the *third* of the triad, and 5̂ acting as the *fifth* of the triad.

Exercise F.61.   Practice Exercise F.60 with a number of major *and* minor scales. The tonic triad for the minor scales is a *minor* triad, while the tonic triad for the major scales is a *major* triad.

Exercise F.62.   Now, practice *arpeggiating* the tonic triads of several keys, by singing the scales in their entirety and then singing just 1̂, 3̂, and 5̂, without audiating the pitches in between. Sing the scales using your regular solmization syllables, but sing the triad as follows: "root," "third," "fifth."

Exercise F.63.   *Piano variation*: now complete Exercises F.60 through F.62 on the piano, just touching the keys (without sound) for the pitches you would have audiated. Remember that to play any major or minor arpeggio (in *root position*, discussed below) you will play the first, third, and fifth notes of the scale.

Exercise F.64.   *Sing and play arpeggiations*: sing and play tonic triads for various scales, alternating between playing on the piano and singing. When singing, use the terms "root," "third," and "fifth" for the respective chord members. Try this with your instrument as well.

Exercise F.65.   *Inversion variation*: triads can be spaced such that the third, or sometimes the fifth, is in the lowest register. Practice audiating the scale and then singing the triad from different chord members, moving the lower chord members up an octave, as shown below. The smaller notes should be audiated or played only on the piano. Be sure to practice this in both major and minor.

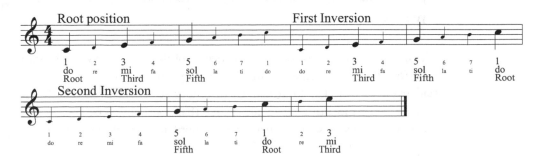

Exercise F.66.   *Playing a complete triad on the piano*: one advantage of the piano is that you can play multiple notes at the same time. Take advantage of this by adding another step to F.63 above: after arpeggiating the tonic triad of each scale you choose, play all the pitches of the tonic triad simultaneously. Practice this until you can play C major, G major, D major, F major, A minor, D minor, E minor, and C minor triads without playing the scale or arpeggiating them first.

Exercise F.67.   *Triad-minus-one improvisation*: the easiest way to start improvising is with a one-note solo! This exercise will help you locate triads at the piano, while simultaneously exploring concepts such as timbre, rhythm, articulation, and tone.

1. Play *only two* pitches of a triad at the piano in a constant quarter-note rhythm (or have a friend do this for you). For instance:

2. Now improvise (or have a friend do so) using the missing pitch (in this case an A-flat or A-natural). Start by using the rhythms and rhythmic syllables in Exercises F.7 and F.13. Pick a specific dynamic level, and choose from these articulation styles:

   • Staccato or disconnected and short
   • Legato or smooth and connected
   • Marcato or "marked," with each note accented

3. Have a friend or classmate identify the quality of triad, the rhythmic pattern you sang, the articulation you chose, and the dynamic level you used.

Exercise F.68.   *Other triads*: triads may be built on any degree of the scale following the same audiation strategy described above. As you may have learned elsewhere, each triad from a single key (drawn from that key's scale) is assigned a Roman numeral, which identifies the scale degree that constitutes the chord's root. The following exercise arpeggiates every chord in a single key. Because it includes the Roman numerals for each chord, is best sung using numbers (which offer an easy transfer to harmony). Start by singing all the notes, but emphasizing the notes of the chords (the larger noteheads). Then play this at the keyboard, singing only the notes of the chords. Finally, sing just the notes of the chords, audiating the smaller noteheads. Note that major triads are indicated using uppercase Roman numerals, while minor triads are indicated using lowercase. The final triad, the leading-tone chord, is actually a diminished triad. Unlike the major and minor triads, it is relatively unstable and can never act as a tonic chord.

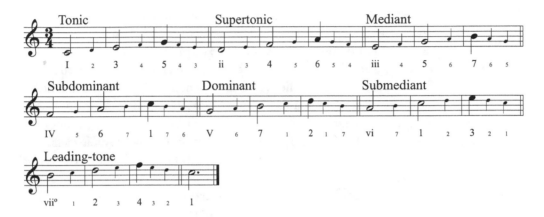

Exercise F.69.   Now complete Exercise F.68, but in minor. Note that the scale has been altered in ways that may seem counterintuitive but are necessary in order to render the most commonly used triadic qualities in minor and to avoid the awkward augmented second that occurs between the lowered scale degree $\hat{6}$ and the raised scale degree $\hat{7}$. The change in the capitalization of Roman numerals reflects the change in triad qualities between the major and minor scales. Tonic and subdominant harmonies are now minor, while mediant and submediant change to major. The dominant and leading-tone harmonies retain the raised $\hat{7}$, so they do not change in quality. Finally, the supertonic becomes diminished. Start by singing all the notes, emphasizing the members of the triads; then sing and play, as before. Finally, audiate all the smaller notes, singing only the notes of the triads out loud.

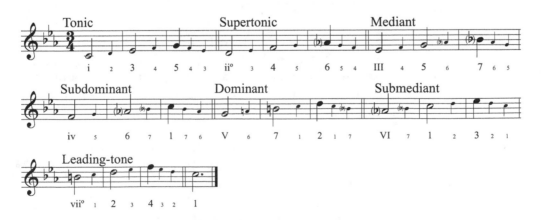

Exercise F.70.   *Play and listen*: have a friend or your instructor establish a key by playing an entire major or minor scale, and then have him or her arpeggiate a single triad from the scale in root position. Sing the arpeggiated triad yourself; see if you can identify the triad by quality and Roman numeral. This will present a significant challenge at first, but regular practice early on will help you greatly later, when you want to be able to identify chord progressions (changes) by ear.

Practice with Multiple Clefs

All the exercises so far in this chapter have used the treble clef, but most likely you have experience with such others as the bass clef. Treble and bass are certainly the two most common clefs, and both will be used in most of the excerpts found in this book. Many instruments, however, require the ability to read a C clef, which can be moved to several spots on the staff, always indicating middle C (C4) at its center. When a C clef is centered on the middle line of the staff, it is an alto clef (used by violists); when it is centered on the second-highest line of the staff, it is a tenor clef (used by bassoonists, trombonists, cellists, and double bassists). Understanding the principles of reading movable clefs, such as the alto clef, is very useful, but it is unlikely that you will become fluent in the C clefs unless you spend a great deal of time playing, reading, and notating in them. There are a number of excerpts in this book that require you to read the alto clef, but if you desire true fluency, practice reading viola scores or consider purchasing and practicing from a score-reading manual.[2]

The following exercises introduce the principles of bass and alto clef reading, starting with scales and moving onto scale segments. It is important that you do these exercises using both solmization syllables *and* pitch names.

Exercise F.71.   Sing the scales below using syllables and pitch names.

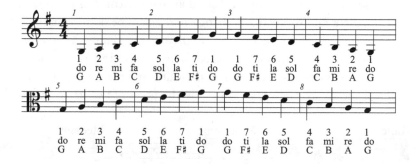

Exercise F.72.   Have an instructor or friend call out any of the eight measure numbers in the scales above, and sing that measure using pitch names. See how quickly you can switch between clefs.

Exercise F.73.   The exercise below spans two octaves in C major, all in stepwise motion. Sing the exercise below using note names. At first, call out the name of the

[2] A particularly useful score-reading manual is R. O. Morris and Howard Ferguson's *Preparatory Exercises in Score Reading* (Oxford University Press, 1968).

clefs between each measure; then resume singing as quickly as possible. Because the range is rather large, feel free to sing each scale in whichever octave is most comfortable for you.

Exercise F.74.   *Stepwise fragments and clef improvisation*: each of the following snippets presents a single-measure, stepwise fragment with no clef. Sing a complete C-major scale, and then practice each snippet separately, applying all three clefs (on the left) to each snippet and singing note names. Now, have a friend call out snippet numbers and clef names. See how quickly you can sing the correct pitches. You may need to reestablish the key of C major periodically by singing the scale. Finally, try to construct an entire phrase out of snippets and clefs. You'll want to end your improvised phrase on the tonic.

Clefs   Melodic Snippets

Exercise F.75.   *Transfer assignment:* list the tangible ways in which the aural skills that you will be acquiring can help you achieve your long-term goals in music study and beyond.

SmartMusic

Although there are no SmartMusic exercises in this chapter, if your curriculum requires the use of SmartMusic now is the time to purchase, download, and become familiar with the software.

1. Go to www.smartmusic.com and click "Students." SmartMusic has agreed to extend a discount price to institutions that adopt this textbook, which will be credited during the check-out process.

2. An external microphone is a recommended option for use with SmartMusic. It is possible to use your computer's internal microphone instead, but assessments are slightly more accurate with an external microphone. PC users may select any external microphone (although they are available for purchase at a discount on the SmartMusic website). Mac users will need a USB mic (also available at a discount).

3. Once you have installed the software, start the program and click "enroll for class." The program will ask you for some basic information and then will prompt you to find your school. If necessary, you may search for your institution by zip code.

4. On the following webpage, choose your correct course number and instructor.

5. At this point, you may search for assignments by clicking the "assignments" tab. Assignments will be assigned directly to your account on an ongoing basis. When you click "assignments," you will be asked to log in and will then receive a list of assignments that you have yet to complete. Be sure to pay attention to due dates and directions.

6. Feel free to complete the online tutorials. Should you encounter technical challenges, click the "support" link on their website.

7. If your instructor will be using the online gradebook, you will be able to view your grades and personalized feedback by clicking the "gradebook" tab in SmartMusic. You should check this regularly to see how your recordings and homework assignments have been assessed.

8. Many of the chapters have "suggested" SmartMusic assignments. Although any excerpt may be assigned in SmartMusic, the suggested assignments present a cross-section of skills, keys, and musical approaches. Be sure to check with your instructor to see if there are different assignments required for your course.

9. SmartMusic is also a wonderful practice tool. Simply click on the "Find Music" tab and you will be able to find accompaniments for almost any piece of standard repertoire for your instrument.

SmartMusic Pro Tips

- *SmartMusic tip no. 1*: you may practice an excerpt as many times as you like before completing an assessment. You may *also* redo an assessment as many times as you like *before submitting it* until you are content with your score. Once you have submitted the assessment, however, you cannot redo an assessment.

- *SmartMusic tip no. 2*: once you complete an assessment, study your results. You can see which notes and rhythms you missed (marked in red), while listening to your own singing. If you have trouble hearing your own mistakes, practice the excerpt while the "solo line" is playing. Exercises completed using the solo line cannot be submitted for a grade, but they can be a useful practice tool. Remember, though, that the eventual goal is for you to be able to read a melody at sight and audiate it in your head without having heard the music in advance.

- *SmartMusic tip no. 3*: to hear the starting pitch of an excerpt before the accompaniment starts to play, click P on your keyboard. Using the P key during an assessment is cheating! If you need help getting pitches, you need more practice before completing the assessment.

- *SmartMusic tip no. 4*: you can always change the key, tempo, and click options on your SmartMusic excerpt before completing an assessment.

The Six-Step Method of Dictation

The ability to hear an excerpt and notate it in its entirety not only is useful as a skill unto itself but also transfers directly to all other aspects of musicianship. The more finely tuned your ears are, the better you will be able to self-correct and teach others. As such, notating short excerpts of music (sometimes in multiple parts) is an important focus of this text. The Contextual Listening exercises in this chapter already ask you to identify pitches and rhythms by ear, and this will grow progressively more challenging throughout the course of this book.

The Six-Step Method aims to improve your dictation skills by breaking the dictation of an example into smaller, more manageable steps, while retaining a focus on the larger issues of harmonic context and musical landscape. When each example is performed six times, this method gives you a specific goal to achieve on each listening. It is always OK to write more than necessary on each hearing. Write down as much useful information as possible every time. *As you practice your dictations, you'll eventually want to work toward only five, or even four, hearings* (combining the third and fourth, as well as the fifth and sixth steps).

Preparation before getting started with the first hearing:

- Make sure your staff is set up in advance with the key signature, time signature, and number of measures (if you know this information ahead of time). Also, mark each beat with a "tick" mark (as we have done in the first long dictation in Chapter 1). In your first or second hearing, you can then just circle any tick mark where you hear a musical "attack" (the start of a new pitch), allowing you to easily fill in the rhythm during the break between playings.

- Audiate the starting pitch, as well as tonic and dominant.
  - Step 1. First hearing: big picture
    - When first starting dictation, it is important to practice listening intently without trying to notate any pitches. As you get better at remembering whole excerpts, you may want to start circling attack marks during the first hearing.
    - Conduct to maintain a steady beat and feel where downbeats are.
    - Pick out general helpful features: What is the contour of the melody? Does it start and end on the same pitch? Which measures are more rhythmically active? Where is the high point? The low point? Are there any repeated materials?
  - Step 2. Second hearing: rhythm and cadences
    - Listen to the example carefully and circle any tick marks where you hear a musical attack. Wait to fill in the rhythm during the break between playings.
    - Once the excerpt is over, sketch out the rhythm as accurately as possible.
    - If you are unsure of a measure, skip ahead to the next downbeat (keep time with your big toe or your finger) and continue from there.
    - If you are ready to do a harmonic dictation, identify the harmony implied in the first and last measure of each phrase. On the basis of your knowledge of cadences, the harmonies in these measures will be very predictable.
  - Step 3. Third hearing: tonics and dominants
    - As the example is played, fill in any tonics or dominants you hear. You can also fill in every time you hear the starting pitch repeat itself later on.
    - If you are ready to do a harmonic dictation, identify every tonic and dominant harmony. You can also fill in harmonies where a chord is arpeggiated in the melody or bass.
  - Step 4. Fourth hearing: stepwise motions and approaches to tonic and dominant
    - As the example is played, fill in all stepwise motion, as well as any approach to tonic and dominant.
    - Even if you can't identify an interval right away, you can always make helpful notes about whether the interval is ascending or descending, or large or small, or whether it leaps to a consonance or a dissonance.
  - Step 5. Fifth hearing: larger intervals and harmonic context
    - As the example is played, fill in the remaining pitches. You'll want to consider the harmonic context at this stage as much as possible. It will be helpful to look for larger lines and patterns, rather than just the single interval in question.
    - If some pitch is especially tricky, try audiating the tonic (or other often repeated pitch) from earlier in the example and comparing it to the mystery pitch in your head.
    - If you are attempting a harmonic dictation, you should try to complete it in this playing.
    - If you have time, it is a good idea to attempt to audiate what you have written at this point.
  - Step 6. Final hearing: checking
    - On this hearing, catch anything that is still incomplete. Check your work and ensure that there are enough (or not too many) notes in each measure. Do your rhythm and pitches make sense? Do your harmonies make sense with the melodic pitches?
    - Try audiating the example (sing it in your head). Do the notes you wrote sound like the example you heard?

Name: _____ Date: _____ Instructor: _____

CONTEXTUAL LISTENING F.1

Listen to the following song excerpts and start by identifying whether each is in major or minor. Then, underline the syllable(s) in the text where the singer arrives on the *tonic* pitch. In addition, indicate over the lyrics whether the pitches before *and* after the arrival on the tonic generally fall above that tonic or below it.

For example:

       above   *above*

"<u>Twinkle</u>, twinkle, little star, how I wonder what you <u>are</u>."

     below   *below*

"Here <u>comes the bride</u>, all . . ."

---

1. **"The Holly and the Ivy" (traditional English)**

    a. This excerpt is in (circle one):   Major   Minor

    b. Underline the syllable(s) in the text where the singer arrives on the *tonic* pitch:

    "Of all the trees that are in the wood, the holly bears the crown."

    c. Indicate over the lyrics whether the pitches before *and* after the tonic generally fall above the tonic or below it.

2. **"Scarborough Fair" (traditional English Ballad)**
    (sung by Paul Simon and Art Garfunkel; 00:00–00:40)

    a. The mode of this excerpt is more closely affiliated with (circle one):
    (Major)   Minor

    b. Underline the syllable(s) in the text where the singer arrives on the *tonic* pitch:

    before
    "Are you going to <u>Scarborough</u> Fair? Parsley, sage, rosemary and <u>thyme</u>,

    after
    Remember me to one who lives there, she once was a true love of <u>mine</u>."

    c. Indicate over the lyrics whether the pitches before *and* after the tonic generally fall above the tonic or below it.

3. **"Amazing Grace" (traditional)**

   a. This excerpt is in (circle one):   Major   ~~Minor~~

   b. Underline the syllable(s) in the text where the singer arrives on the *tonic* pitch:

   before   after   before

   "Amazing grace! How sweet the sound that saved a wretch like me!

   after   *before*

   I once was lost, but now am found, was blind, but now I see."

   c. Indicate over the lyrics whether the pitches before *and* after the tonic generally fall above the tonic or below it.

4. **Richard Rodgers (1902–1979), "My Funny Valentine," from *Babes in Arms* (1937)**

   a. This excerpt is in (circle one):   Major   ~~Minor~~ .

   b. Underline the syllable(s) in the text where the singer arrives on the *tonic* pitch:

   before   after   before   after

   "My funny valentine, sweet comic valentine, you make me smile with my heart"

   c. Indicate over the lyrics whether the pitches before *and* after the tonic generally fall above the tonic or below it.

5. **Harold Arlen (1905–1986), "Over the Rainbow"**
   (1938; sung by Judy Garland; 01:50–02:15)

   a. This excerpt is in (circle one):   ~~Major~~   Minor

   b. Underline the syllable(s) in the text where the singer arrives on the *tonic* pitch:

   before   after   before

   "If happy little bluebirds fly beyond the rainbow, why, oh why, can't I?"

   c. Indicate over the lyrics whether the pitches before *and* after the arrival on the tonic generally fall above the tonic or below it.

6. **Nirvana, "Smells Like Teen Spirit" (03:40–04:30)**

   a. This excerpt is in (circle one):   Major   ~~Minor~~

   b. Underline the syllable(s) in the text where the singer arrives on the *tonic* pitch:

   before   after

   "Here we are now, entertain us. I feel stupid and contagious"

   before

   "A denial."

   c. Indicate over the lyrics whether the pitches before *and* after the arrival on the tonic generally fall above the tonic or below it.

CONTEXTUAL LISTENING F.2

"First Call," "Reveille," and "Taps," military bugle calls

Bugle calls are musical signals that announce particular events or times of day in military settings. Naturally, the far-reaching, loud sound of trumpets and bugles are ideal for communicating in a battlefield or in military camps. You will notice that all bugle calls feature exclusively the notes of a single triad; this is because a bugle, which has no valves, can only play a very limited number of pitches.

1. Transcribe the following three bugle calls ("First Call," "Reveille," and "Taps") and answer the questions. The rhythm and several of the pitches are provided for you. All pitches for the excerpts below are drawn from a single triad.

"REVEILLE"

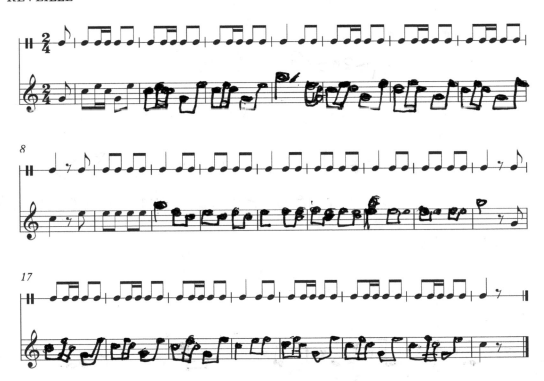

a. "Reveille" could be divided into three segments. What in the music helps delineate these segments? The change of rhythms

b. From the options below, choose the form that most closely matches the melodic design (note that an A–A–A design would suggest that the same music occurs three times, while an A–B–C design would suggest that all three sections were completely different):

A–A–A   A–B–A   A–B–B   A–B–C

"FIRST CALL"

a. If you were to divide "First Call" into segments, how many segments would you divide it into?

2

b. What in the music suggests such divisions?

measure 5 rest

c. What is the last note of each segment? Why are these notes appropriate for ending the respective segments?

1 ends in a 6, 2ends in
6, it's appropriate for a resolution

"TAPS"

a. "Taps" is performed at a slow tempo; as you can see in the score, it features a profusion of fermatas (which indicate that a note should be held for an indefinite period of time to be determined by the player or a conductor). Why are the tempo and numerous fermatas appropriate for this particular bugle call?

it's a military ceremony song,
specifically funerals

EXPANDING THE REPERTOIRE F.3

Carly Rae Jepsen, "Call Me Maybe"

This upbeat and catchy song sold more than fifteen million copies worldwide and was named Song of the Year in 2012 by MTV. Throughout the music video, Jepsen desperately (yet timidly) seeks the attention of an attractive neighbor, leading to a quite unexpected twist.

1. On the staff below, transcribe the melody of the song. The notes you will provide all belong to the *tonic* triad (notes that do not belong to the tonic triad are furnished). In addition, write out the scale degree numbers or solfège syllables for each melody note (some of these are given).

2. Even though the lyrics in the verse appear to be an internal monologue, the lyrics of the chorus seem to be trying to grab the boy's attention. How does the melody in the chorus achieve this? (Think in terms of register and range.)

the range goes upward to be more arrived

3. Recall how we explored the lower hierarchical status of a neighbor tone compared to the stabler tones around it in Exercises F.52 and F.55. This tune makes use of another type of less-hierarchical tone: an appoggiatura. It is similar to the neighbor tone, in that it resolves to a stabler tone by step, but it is different in that an appoggiatura is a dissonant (or less-stable) tone that is approached by leap but left by step. The neighbor $\hat{1}$–$\hat{3}$–$\hat{4}$–$\hat{3}$–$\hat{1}$ (do–mi–*fa*–mi–do) and appoggiatura $\hat{1}$–$\hat{3}$–$\hat{2}$–$\hat{2}$–$\hat{1}$ (do–*mi*–re–*re*–do) in "so here's my number, so call me maybe" instill a mellow and uncertain quality in the melody. Speculate how the neighbor tone and appoggiatura might highlight the girl's personal insecurities, or the fact that she is in a vulnerable position by offering her number. For instance, what is the effect of replacing the neighbor tone and appoggiatura with $\hat{1}$–$\hat{3}$–$\hat{5}$–$\hat{3}$–$\hat{1}$ (do–mi–sol–mi–do) and then $\hat{1}$–$\hat{3}$–$\hat{1}$–$\hat{1}$–$\hat{1}$ (do–mi–do–do–do)? Try singing the passage this way.

the sounds represent ∨ vunerability or weakness

4. As you already know, the singer navigates (almost exclusively) the notes of the tonic triad. Harmonically, however, the song never anchors on the stable (and so desirable) root position I, except very briefly while Jepsen is not singing (see the provided accompaniment). Speculate how this dichotomy musically maps the "uncertainty" of her getting a call (maybe!).

the root never stays to show tha the girl's insecurity

Chapter 1

The Tonic Triad and Its Melodies

As you discovered through the many exercises in the Foundations of Aural Skills chapter, singing musical materials based on the major and minor scales outside of a musical context is both fun and useful, but it is a fairly simple exercise. Likewise, the previous chapter's exploration of basic rhythmic patterns and metric designs, while avoiding the domain of pitch, is (and will continue to be) useful preparation. Ultimately, firmly locating every note of the scale and every rhythmic duration within a true musical and harmonic context will take some time and lots of practice. It is critical, however, that you grow fluent in your ability to find pitches and recognize rhythmic patterns, so that larger leaps, intervals, and complex rhythms will not lead you astray.

This chapter includes melodies that focus primarily on the first five notes of the scale, as well as the tonic in the upper octave, all in simple meter. Some of the harmony parts are also restricted in this manner. You are encouraged to sing harmony parts whenever possible, but you should also attempt to play the harmonies on an instrument while you (or your classmates) sing along.

This and all future chapters present a great number of useful drills and exercises that can help you better explore the concepts presented in the chapter excerpts. You may find it useful to work back and forth between the drills and exercises and the excerpts. In particular, a focus on rhythm reading is found in the exercises at the back.

Examples from the Repertoire

Example 1.1.   "Au Clair de la Lune" (traditional French)

* Be sure to practice singing the tenor line, since it is restricted to scale degrees $\hat{3}$, $\hat{4}$, and $\hat{5}$.

Example 1.2.   "Mary Had a Little Lamb" (traditional)

* Note the dotted rhythms. Be sure to conduct while you sing.

Example 1.3.   "There Was an Old Woman" (traditional)

Example 1.4.   "Wenn ich ein Vöglein Wär" (traditional German)

* Be sure to observe the performance markings.

Example 1.5.   "A Sailor Went to Sea" (traditional)

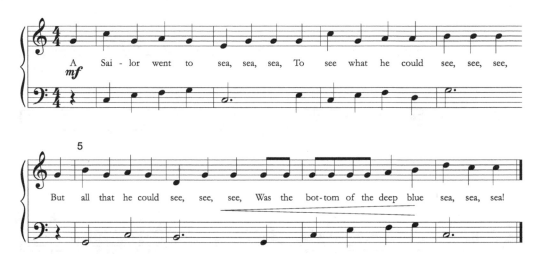

* Focus on the bass part and its use of very common harmonic paradigms. The well-known melody goes beyond the scale degrees that are emphasized in this chapter, but feel free to play the melody on the piano while you sing the lower part.

Example 1.6.   "Row, Row, Row Your Boat" (traditional round in four voices)

* This familiar round is typically notated in compound meter (6/8), which will be introduced at the end of Chapter 2. Be sure to alternate strong and weak measures to replicate a more typical metrical context. Also, see the Improvisation section at the end of this chapter for some additional ideas to spice up your round.

Example 1.7.   "Hey Tswana" (traditional African)

Example 1.8.   German canon (traditional round in four voices)

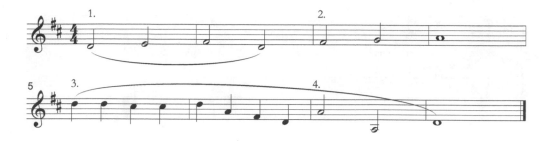

Example 1.9.   Philip Hayes (1738–1797), Round in three voices

* Note that this canon essentially follows the same pattern as the others (scale degrees $\hat{1}$–$\hat{5}$), but it has octave leaps that add to the level of difficulty. Start by practicing the tune without the octave leaps, instead maintaining all the pitches in the lower octave.

Example 1.10.   "Polly Wolly Doodle" (traditional)

For I'm goin' to Lou'-si-an-a for to see my su-sy-an-na, Sing pol-ly wol-ly doo-dle all the day.

Example 1.11.   "An die Freude" (traditional German)

Al - le Men - schen wer - den brü - der, wo dein sanf - ter Flü - gel weilt.

Example 1.12.   "Wishy Washy" (traditional)

Oh, we are two sail - ors come from o'er the sea, if you want to go a - way a-gain,

come a - long with me. Oh, wish - y wash - y, wish - y wash - y, wish - y wash - y wee!

If you want to go a - way a - gain, come a - long with me.

Example 1.13.   "Chanson du lépreux" (traditional Breton tune)

* *Translation*: Once you gave me your heart, gentle to the surprised eye. Do you think I have forgotten it?

Example 1.14.   "Pat-a-Pan" (traditional)

* Try playing the lower part while singing the melody. Observe how the lower part shifts between the lowered and raised seventh scale degree.

Example 1.15.   "Oh my Love" (traditional round in four voices)

Oh   my   Love,   Lov'st   thou   me,   then

Quick - ly   come   and   save   him   who   dies   for   thee.

* Scale degree $\hat{7}$ is briefly introduced here as a lower-neighbor-like departure from the tonic. Consider singing this excerpt in E minor instead of major, but retaining the D♯ as the leading tone.

Example 1.16. "The Bell doth Toll" (traditional round in three voices)

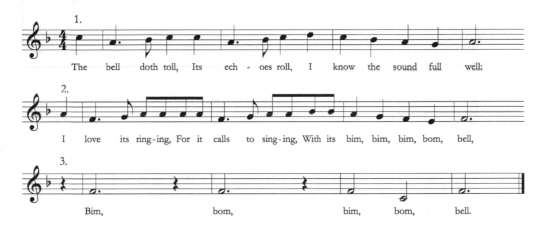

The   bell   doth toll,   Its   ech - oes roll,   I   know   the   sound   full   well;

I   love   its ring-ing, For it   calls   to sing-ing, With its bim, bim, bim, bom,   bell,

Bim,   bom,   bim,   bom,   bell.

* Scale degree $\hat{6}$ is introduced here as an upper neighbor to the dominant. This round is also quite lovely in minor, although you will want to employ the lowered version of the sixth scale degree.

Example 1.17.   Johann Kuhnau (1660–1722), *Biblical Sonata no. 5* (1700), section marked
                 "Gideon encouraged his soldiers"

* The tonic arpeggiation exercise will help prepare you for this excerpt. If necessary, feel free to sing
the upper parts down an octave. Do make a point to learn all three parts!

Example 1.18.   "The Crane" (traditional round in three voices)

Example 1.19.   Johann Sebastian Bach (1685–1750), "Ach, wie Flüchtig, Ach wie
                 Nichtig," BWV 26

* *Translation*: Ah, how fleeting, Ah how futile are the things of men!

    This excerpt in A minor from Bach's sacred cantata BWV 26 travels by step from the tonic to dominant and back again. The harmony, however, briefly suggests the major mode and then returns to minor while employing the raised sixth and seventh scale degrees. Try singing the melody while playing each of the other parts. Which of the other parts makes the best two-part counterpoint with the melody?

Example 1.20.   Bach, "Freuet euch, ihr Christen alle"

* As with the previous excerpt, the harmony here briefly suggests the major mode and then returns to minor. Again, try singing the melody while playing each of the other parts. All the accidentals here refer to typical alterations of the minor mode, except the A♮ in the tenor of m. 1. You may leave this as an A♭, if you like, or try playing the line with its brief chromatic passing tone.

Example 1.21.   Cécile Chaminade (1857–1944), "Berceuse" (1894)

Au de - hors   souff - le un vent gla - cé_____   Qui de sa der - niè - re pa - ru - re,

* *Translation*: Outside blows an icy wind that [strips nature] of its last finery.

Try singing all four voices. The tenor voice just moves down by a semitone to the leading tone and then up again. Try to feel the syncopation of the inner voices. How does Chaminade evoke harmonic motion with a repeating bass that includes an E pedal tone? (Note particularly the lack of a slur in m. 2.)

Example 1.22.   Antonín Dvořák (1841–1904), Sonatina for Violin op. 100, mvt. 2

* Practice all three rhythmic patterns or "shapes" in this excerpt separately before attempting to sing this excerpt. Then sing the melody while playing the bass.

CHORALE WORKSHOP

Play a major or a minor chord on the piano in your left hand, and try playing groups of three melodic notes in your right hand. You will find that passing tones bounded by members of the chord ($\hat{3}$–$\hat{2}$–$\hat{1}$/mi–re–do, or $\hat{3}$–$\hat{4}$–$\hat{5}$/mi–fa–sol, for example) work nicely. Other options include arpeggiations and neighbor tones ($\hat{1}$–$\hat{2}$–$\hat{1}$, for example).

IMPROVISATION: GAMES AND EXERCISES

1. Stand in a small group. The leader should improvise some sort of repeated and exaggerated bodily movement. The next student will then represent that movement in sound (using the voice or an instrument), while repeating the physical gesture. Each additional student will improvise additional sounds that contrast with but still somehow represent the movement of the leader. The goal of this exercise is to begin to free oneself from the notated page as well as the direct succession of pitches and instead to think in complete, creative gestures. In addition, it supports all manner of ensemble communication.

2. Refer to Example 1.17, the *Biblical Sonata* no. 5 by Kuhnau. Start by singing the excerpt as written with at least the outer two voices. Now, with the majority of your group singing the lower voice, choose one individual to improvise a new melody using only the scale degrees that Kuhnau himself used ($\hat{1}$, $\hat{3}$, $\hat{5}$, and $\hat{4}$ as a passing tone from $\hat{3}$ to $\hat{5}$). Start with exactly the same rhythms that Kuhnau used, and then slowly add new rhythmic configurations.

3. Improvise a melody using the three-note paradigms you discovered in the Chorale Workshop.

4. Improvise rounds over the tonic triad. Compose your own round based on a single triad, following the model of the rounds found in this chapter ("Row, Row, Row Your Boat," for example). You will want to employ the three-note paradigms found in the Chorale Workshop, being sure that members of the tonic triad fall on the strong beats of every measure.

5. Choose a very short fragment of a melody from one of the earlier examples (or perhaps one of the eight exercises in the "Short-Term Musical Memory" section that follows). Sing the passage, and then have a partner repeat what you have sung without looking at the notation. Now, have your partner add a single variation (try a neighbor note or a passing tone, or change one of the rhythms). Repeat the same passage, including the new variation. Then you should introduce a new variation. Continue passing the short excerpt back and forth, first repeating exactly and then adding a new variation.

IMPROVISATION: FOCUS ON RHYTHM AND METER

1. Experiment with singing "Row, Row, Row Your Boat." Try having one set of singers do their round at half the tempo of the rest of the class (creating a sort of

"augmented" *cantus firmus*, a slow melody over which faster contrapuntal might be sung). You can also add another set singing twice as fast!

Example 1.22 above presents three challenging rhythmic shapes:

2. Practice all three of the rhythmic shapes (each one measure long) and then compose a short rhythmic round (at least six measures long) that will be performed in class.

DRILLS: TONIC CHORD AND MAJOR/MINOR SECONDS

1. *Tonic chord arpeggiation drill*: try arpeggiating the tonic triad both upward (scale degrees $\hat{1}$–$\hat{3}$–$\hat{5}$–$\hat{1}$) and downward ($\hat{1}$–$\hat{5}$–$\hat{3}$–$\hat{1}$), starting on each of the successive notes ($\hat{1}$–$\hat{3}$–$\hat{5}$–$\hat{1}$–$\hat{5}$–$\hat{3}$–$\hat{1}$, $\hat{3}$–$\hat{5}$–$\hat{1}$–$\hat{3}$–$\hat{1}$–$\hat{5}$–$\hat{3}$, etc., or do–mi–sol–do–sol–mi–do, mi–sol–do–mi–do–sol–mi, etc.). Be sure to attempt this in both major *and* minor.

2. *More on the master interval drill*: learn both the minor and major seconds (see the following page). Practice distinguishing between the two.

3. Have a classmate play a three-note stepwise melody (up or down, and including either two major seconds or one minor and one major). Determine whether the intervals are major or minor seconds. Have the classmate identify the starting pitch, and then notate the pitches on staff paper.

MASTER INTERVAL DRILL

As you read in the previous chapter, this drill is designed to solidify one's familiarity with the diatonic intervals and their relationship to the degrees of the major scale. Practice this as you walk between classes, while you wait in line at the cafeteria, and whenever your roommate is sleeping. The seconds have already been introduced, but you should work on the remaining intervals at whatever pace your instructor suggests. We have notated through the minor third for you; the remaining intervals follow the same pattern. We have restricted the exercise to the octave; once you master this, feel free to expand beyond the octave to such intervals as the $\hat{7}$–$\hat{2}$/ti–re minor third and the $\hat{6}$–$\hat{2}$/la–mi perfect fifth.

| MI - FA | mi - nor sec - ond | TI - DO | mi - nor sec - ond |
| 3 - 4 | mi - nor sec - ond | 7 - 8 | mi - nor sec - ond |

| DO - RE | ma - jor sec - ond | RE - MI | ma - jor sec - ond | FA - SOL | ma - jor sec - ond |
| 1 - 2 | ma - jor sec - ond | 2 - 3 | ma - jor sec - ond | 4 - 5 | ma - jor sec - ond |

| SOL - LA | ma - jor sec - ond | LA - TI | ma - jor sec - ond |
| 5 - 6 | ma - jor sec - ond | 6 - 7 | ma - jor sec - ond |

etc.

| RE - FA | mi - nor third... |
| 2 - 4 | mi - nor third... |

The drill is sung strictly in tempo (with rhythm of quarter–quarter–eighth–eighth–quarter).

Minor thirds

$\hat{2}$–$\hat{4}$ re–fa
$\hat{3}$–$\hat{5}$ mi–sol
$\hat{6}$–$\hat{8}$ la–do

Major thirds

$\hat{1}$–$\hat{3}$ do–mi
$\hat{4}$–$\hat{6}$ fa–la
$\hat{5}$–$\hat{7}$ sol–ti

Perfect fourths

$\hat{1}$–$\hat{4}$ do–fa
$\hat{2}$–$\hat{5}$ re–sol
$\hat{3}$–$\hat{6}$ mi–la
$\hat{5}$–$\hat{8}$ sol–do

Tritone (augmented fourth/ diminished fifth)

$\hat{4}$–$\hat{7}$ fa–ti

Perfect fifths

$\hat{1}$–$\hat{5}$ do–sol
$\hat{2}$–$\hat{6}$ re–la
$\hat{3}$–$\hat{7}$ mi–ti
$\hat{4}$–$\hat{8}$ fa–do

Minor sixth

$\hat{3}$–$\hat{8}$ mi–do

Major sixths

$\hat{1}$–$\hat{6}$ do–la
$\hat{2}$–$\hat{7}$ re–ti

Minor seventh

$\hat{2}$–$\hat{8}$ re–do

Major seventh

$\hat{1}$–$\hat{7}$ do–ti

Perfect octave

$\hat{1}$–$\hat{8}$ do–do

SMARTMUSIC ASSESSMENTS

You may wish to review the "SmartMusic Tips" found in the introduction. Your instructor will choose which excerpts to assign for SmartMusic assessment. The assigned excerpts can be found in the "assignments" tab in SmartMusic. Your instructor may also provide a list. Important: although the notation may be available on-screen, it is best to complete your SmartMusic assessments by reading the music from your textbook, where the typesetting, spacing, and overall music-reading experience will more accurately replicate the group music making that you will be doing in class and elsewhere.

• *Suggested assignment 1*: start by practicing the excerpts listed below. Be sure that you can sing them smoothly and accurately on scale degrees or syllables (as required by your instructor) *and note names, while conducting.* Log into SmartMusic, click "assignments," and complete the assessments for these excerpts: 1.1 (both soprano and tenor parts), Examples 1.2, 1.4, 1.6, 1.8, 1.9, 1.11 (both melody and bass), and the master interval drill for minor and major seconds. Be sure to observe the performance markings.

• *Suggested assignment 2*: prepare excerpts using scale degrees or syllables *and note names,* and then complete SmartMusic assessments as follows (be sure to practice while conducting): Examples 1.12 (both parts); 1.13 (melody only), 1.14 (try singing while playing the lower part), 1.16 (you will be asked to sing and record the first part, while the computer plays the third and fourth voices), 1.17 (all parts), 1.20 (melody only), 1.21 (both parts), and 1.22 (melody only).

SHORT-TERM MUSICAL MEMORY

The brief musical passages referenced below are intended to be used in class or in practice as an exercise in short-term musical memory. As in future chapters, these passages are drawn from the examples in the previous pages. Taking them in dictation will help to train your musical memory and build a more immediate connection between your ear and musical notation. You should be able to notate the correct pitches and rhythms on hearing each one only once or twice.

Your instructor will announce which example is to be played. In addition, you will be told what key and which clef to use; the key and clef *may not be the same* as in the original example. Fill in the key signature and clef where indicated, and write in the initial note(s) according to the given pitch and rhythm information. Your instructor (or practice partner) will play a short progression to establish the key and then count off several beats to establish the tempo. Because of the brevity of each extract, you should have an overall impression of the rhythm, contour, and scale degrees after just one or two hearings. Write down the entire fragment. See whether you find it easier to grasp the pitches or rhythms, and devote extra practice to whichever you find more difficult.

1. Example 1.1, last two measures, top part. Starts on beat 1 (quarter note, scale degree $\hat{1}$).

Clef and key
signature

2. Example 1.4, first four measures, top part. Starts on beat 1 (quarter note, scale degree 1̂).

Clef and key
signature

3. Example 1.4, last three measures, top part. Starts on beat 1 (quarter note, scale degree 3̂).

Clef and key
signature

4. Example 1.5, first eight notes, top part. Starts on beat 4 (quarter note, scale degree 5̂).

Clef and key
signature

5. Example 1.13, last five measures, top part. Starts on beat 1 (eighth note, scale degree 1̂).

Clef and key
signature

6. Example 1.14, up to second downbeat, top part. Starts on beat 3 (quarter note, scale degree 1̂).

Clef and key
signature

7. Example 1.20, last two measures, top part. Starts on beat 1 (quarter note, scale degree 3̂).

Clef and key
signature

8. Example 1.22, up to third downbeat, top part. Starts on beat 1 (quarter note, scale degree 1̂).

Clef and key
signature

DICTATION OF LONGER EXAMPLES

The examples in this textbook feature many conventional patterns of melody, rhythm, and harmony, and they reinforce a variety of skills required for strong musicianship. This section of each chapter can be used for in-class dictation or for dictation practice outside of class. Doing so will help you link your sight reading and audiation skills with your musical memory, while also building your ability to connect written notation to musical sound.

We have provided a staff, guide pitches, and the bass part for the first of these excerpts, but for the remainder you will work on your own staff paper. Your instructor or a classmate will choose one of the examples listed below and inform you of the key, the clef, the meter, the first note (scale degree, rhythmic value, and metric placement) of one or more parts, and the total number of measures. The key and clef *may not be the same* as in the original example. On a separate piece of staff paper, write down the clef(s), key signature, time signature, first note(s), and bar lines. You will hear a short progression to establish the key of the example, and you will then hear the example several times with breaks between hearings. Listen first to the melody and notate it completely (you can begin by notating the rhythm and scale degrees separately, *off* the staff, if that is easier). Then notate accompanying part(s) if directed to do so.

For help with dictation, you may wish to reread the Six-Step Method for Dictation found in the introduction. You'll note that the primary goal of the method is to try to hear target points across the entire excerpt, rather than simply attempting to notate from left to right.

You may also wish to practice by having Smartmusic play the excerpts indicated (you will need to click the "my part" button in order to have Smartmusic play all the parts).

1. Example 1.14 ("Pat-a-Pan"), all.
   • For this excerpt only, we have filled in all the tonic and dominant pitches in the top voice, as suggested in step 3 of the Six-Step Method. Be sure to fill in all the blanks.

- The bass part has been supplied in order to reinforce the connection between melody and harmony.
- Before you even start listening, you may want to mark each beat with a tick mark (we have done this for you, just above the staff). In your first or second hearing, simply circle any tick mark where you hear a musical attack (the start of a new pitch). Then it will be easy to fill in the rhythm during the break between playings.
- Also during the first or second hearing, see if you can track any repetitions in the melody. Then note any contour peaks and valleys.
- Once you have the "landscape" of the melody and rhythm sketched out, you can start notating.

2. Example 1.3, all.

3. Example 1.8, all.

4. Example 1.9, all.

5. Example 1.10, ending on the downbeat of m. 8.

6. Example 1.11, all.

7. Example 1.15, all.

8. Example 1.16, ending on the downbeat of m. 8.

Name: _____ Date: _____ Instructor: _____

CONTEXTUAL LISTENING 1.1

Ludwig van Beethoven (1770–1827), "Ode to Joy"

This familiar melody is heard in many Christmas concerts, pageants, and carols. The text was written by the German poet Friedrich Schiller and appears in the final movement of Beethoven's "Choral" Symphony no. 9. Through this melody, Beethoven wished to convey joy, hope, and the universal brotherhood of humanity. How does he convey these ideas musically?

1. What is the meter of this excerpt?

   $\frac{2}{4}$ $\frac{3}{2}$ $\frac{6}{8}$ $\boxed{\frac{4}{4}}$

2. On the basis of your answer to the previous question and your listening, how many measures long is this excerpt?

   (a.) 8   b. 10   c. 12   d. 14   e. 16

3. The excerpt has three sections. What scale degree does each section begin and end on?

   Section 1:   a. $\hat{3}, \hat{1}$ b. $\hat{5}, \hat{3}$ (c.) $\hat{3}, \hat{2}$ d. $\hat{5}, \hat{1}$ e. $\hat{3}, \hat{3}$
   Section 2:   a. $\hat{1}, \hat{5}$ b. $\hat{2}, \hat{3}$ (c.) $\hat{2}, \hat{5}$ d. $\hat{1}, \hat{3}$ e. $\hat{2}, \hat{1}$
   Section 3:   a. $\hat{5}, \hat{3}$ (b.) $\hat{3}, \hat{1}$ c. $\hat{5}, \hat{1}$ d. $\hat{2}, \hat{3}$ e. $\hat{3}, \hat{2}$

4. Do any sections repeat? Please describe.

   Section 1 repeats after the first time

5. List the scale degrees for the melody of the first four measures (only). Hint: it does *not* begin on $\hat{1}$ (tonic).
   (Use the staff below. Don't forget to add bar lines.)

6. For extra credit, feel free to postulate how this excerpt's musical structure leads to the sentiments described in the text.

Use the following staff to help you fill in the missing pieces. For extra practice, use the second staff to write out the complete melody (all sections).

5. 3 3 4 5 5 4 3 2 1 1 2 3 3 2 2

Name: _____ Date: _____ Instructor: _____

CONTEXTUAL LISTENING 1.2

"Aiken Drum" (traditional)

Aiken Drum is a traditional Scottish tale of a man who lives "in the moon." It describes his face and clothes as made of cheese and other edible items. Folk music has been handed down by word of mouth and can sometimes paint a vivid picture of life as it once was. What do you think may have been the source of this song?

1. What is the simple meter of this excerpt?

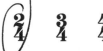

2. On the basis of your answer to the previous question and your listening, this excerpt lasts for how many measures? (Hint: it starts on beat 2.)

   a. 8   b. 10   c. 12   d. 14   e. 16

3. The excerpt has two sections. What is the relationship (similarities *and* differences) between the two sections?

   a. The first halves of the two sections are different, but the second halves are the same.

   b. The first halves of the two sections are the same, but the second halves are different.

4. On which scale degree does each section begin and end?

   Section 1:   a. $\hat{1}, \hat{1}$ b. $\hat{1}, \hat{2}$ c. $\hat{1}, \hat{5}$ d. $\hat{2}, \hat{2}$ e. $\hat{2}, \hat{5}$
   Section 2:   a. $\hat{1}, \hat{1}$ b. $\hat{1}, \hat{2}$ c. $\hat{1}, \hat{5}$ d. $\hat{2}, \hat{2}$ e. $\hat{2}, \hat{5}$

5. List the scale degrees or solmization syllables for the melody of the entire first section.

   (Use the staff below. Don't forget to add bar lines.)

6. Now notate the rhythm (without pitches, but with bar lines) for the second section. There is an accompanimental part that occurs periodically throughout the piece. *Mark an asterisk on the measures where the second part is also playing.*

Use the following staff to help you. Fill in the missing pieces. For extra practice, use the second staff to write out the complete melody (all sections).

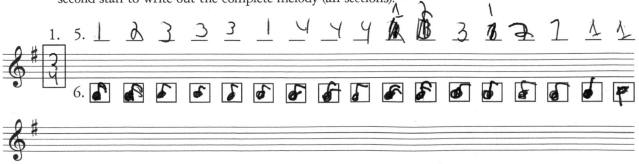

EXPANDING THE REPERTOIRE 1.3

Glen Hansard and Markéta Irglová, "Falling Slowly," from *Once* (2007)

This song appeared in the film *Once* (2007) and won the Academy Award for Best Original Song. In the movie, Hansard and Irglová play and sing the song; he sings the lead melody and she provides vocal harmony (also called backup vocals).

1. The song has four sections (introduction, verse, bridge, and chorus). How many measures are in each section?

   Introduction (0:00–0:15):   Verse (0:15–0:42):
   Bridge (0:42–1:00):   Chorus (1:00–1:31):

2. On the staff below, write out the melody of the verse and and chorus, following the rhythmic figuration provided and specifying scale degrees; for the bridge, only write out the rhythm. Write the notes and rhythms of the back-up vocals with a smaller print or different color. Do not forget to include the meter signature.

Scale Degree: *1*

Scale Degree: 1

3. Although the entire song is in C major, one section is strongly rooted in the relative minor key (A minor). Which section? How is that achieved?

   the chorus, with A minor chords

4. Most of the song features Irglová on backup vocals. At what interval(s) from the melody does she sing?

   minor 6th's and major 6th's

5. For extra credit, speculate about the locations and, to the extent that you can, the types of cadences (moments of phrase closure) used in this song and their effects.

6. *Optional assignment 1: compose* a new melody for the verse that fits well with the original harmonic progression, but employing the original rhythm. Make sure to specify the scale degrees. Hint: choose chord tones for strong beats.

Scale Degree:

7. *Optional assignment 2:* prepare to improvise on the harmonic progression of the verse using the backup track provided online. This recording features an accompaniment pattern on a twelve-string guitar; compare the sound to the acoustic guitar sound used on the commercial recording of *Once*.

Chapter 2

The Submediant Scale Degree and the Major Pentatonic

The excerpts and exercises in this chapter are devoted to the exploration of the submediant, or scale degree $\hat{6}$ (la). The submediant often functions as a neighbor note to the dominant (scale degree $\hat{5}$, sol), frequently moving directly to and/or from the dominant. Sometimes the connection between $\hat{5}$ and $\hat{6}$ is spread out, such that they are not immediately adjacent. This is particularly common when arpeggiating the subdominant harmony, which we will learn more about in Chapter 4. The submediant can also act as a passing tone between $\hat{5}$ and $\hat{7}$ (or even $\hat{5}$ and $\hat{8}$), as will be shown in Chapter 3. For now, you can always locate scale degree $\hat{6}$ by singing it as a neighbor to $\hat{5}$. Also in this chapter, we will be focusing on the scale-degree melodies that can be supported by the most common harmonic progression: I–V–I. Finally, the end of this chapter introduces compound meters through simple rhythmic exercises. Don't forget to move back and forth between the excerpts and the exercises at the end of the book.

The submediant is particularly prevalent in works based on major pentatonic scales, which can be created by eliminating the two semitones from the major scale. Several pentatonic examples are included later in this chapter. The most common form of the major pentatonic is as follows:

The second of these two examples shows the black-note or G♭ major pentatonic, easily played on the piano by striking only the black notes. Improvising with pentatonic scales (particularly by using the black notes of the piano) is simple, as you will discover in the improvisation exercises below.

The minor pentatonic scale also eliminates the two semitones and is found by identifying the relative minor of the pentatonic major scale (A minor pentatonic, and E♭ minor pentatonic from the examples above). Since the minor pentatonic includes lowered scale degree $\hat{7}$, it is explored in the next chapter.

Example 2.1.   "Oh, How Lovely Is the Evening" (traditional round in three voices)

* Note how the submediant moves immediately to the dominant, acting as a long-range neighbor to the C, with the A as an inserted consonant skip.

Example 2.2.   Wolfgang Amadeus Mozart (1756–1791), Twelve Variations on "Ah vous dirai-je, Maman," K. 265/300e (theme)

* What is the form of this excerpt? How does it differ from the popular children's tune "Twinkle, Twinkle, Little Star"? If you have studied some counterpoint, you may want to identify the intervals between the outer parts and describe how the voices interact contrapuntally.

Example 2.3.   "Chairs to Mend" (traditional round in three voices)

Example 2.4.   "Hymnus in Ioannem" ("Ut queant laxis")

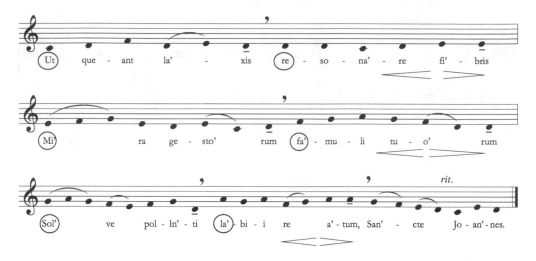

* *Translation*: So that your servants may, with loosened voices, resound the wonders of your deeds, clean the guilt from our stained lips, O Saint John.

The circled syllables were used by the monk Guido of Arezzo (c. 1032) to teach the scale, creating the first system of solmization. The syllable "Ut" was replaced by "Do" (from *Dominus)* in the seventeenth century, probably since the *U* was pronounced differently in so many languages. This tune is modal and, although the final of the mode is D, it can be sung with C as tonic, in order to place the solmization syllables in familiar spots. Just as you are doing, Guido's monks memorized this familiar song using solmization syllables so that they could adapt the syllables to any music that they were sight singing.

Example 2.5.   "Gaudeamus" (traditional round in three voices)

* The major scale segment in the second part travels from $\hat{1}$ to $\hat{6}$, as in the "Ut queant laxis" chant.

Example 2.6.   "Good-bye, Brother" (traditional American)

* This simple pentatonic melody skips the submediant altogether, focusing instead on tonic arpeggiations. Be particularly careful about the simple syncopations here. You may need to start your practice by counting eighth notes. This excerpt (and a number of others in this chapter) exhibits antecedent-consequent design, in a configuration that is called a parallel period. The first half comes to an inconclusive cadence on the dominant. The second half repeats the melodic material of the first, adjusted such that it comes to rest with an authentic cadence on the tonic.

Example 2.7.   Stephen Foster (1826–1864), "Oh, Susanna" (1848)

* Note how this famous tune emphasizes the minor third between $\hat{3}$ and $\hat{5}$. In fact, the first eight bars are completely pentatonic, only to be interrupted by the prominent A in the refrain. Why do you suppose Foster breaks out of the pentatonic collection at that spot?

Example 2.8.   "No More Rain Fall for Wet You" (traditional American)

Example 2.9.   Ada R. Habershon (1861–1918), "Will the Circle Be Unbroken" (1848)

* Both this and the following pentatonic excerpt go below the tonic to the fifth and sixth scale degrees. The eighth-note "fill" in the bass is optional.

Example 2.10.   "Go Tell It on the Mountain" (traditional)

* Note the dotted-eighth, sixteenth rhythm in this familiar tune. Be sure to practice this rhythm in advance. Why is the E♭ in m. 6 so hard to miss?

Example 2.11.   Florence Price (1887–1953), "Juba Dance," from Symphony in E Minor (1932)

* The upper two voices are completely pentatonic, with the violin's florid melody juxtaposed over the trumpet's simpler countermelody and the bass's standard progression. Like many of the excerpts in this text, this is excerpted from an instrumental work but intended to be sung. You may want to start by singing the trumpet and bass parts and then add the violin part (top line) very slowly, using syllables. Once you get up to tempo, you may wish to replace the syllables in the violin melody with a percussive syllable such as "ta."

Example 2.12.   "Early to Bed" (traditional round in three voices)

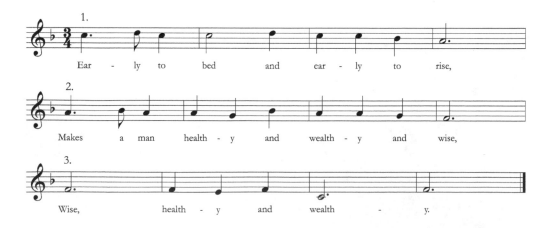

* Both this and the following excerpt emphasize the submediant as a neighbor to $\hat{5}$ but include scale degree $\hat{7}$ in a neighbor motion from the lower tonic.

Example 2.13.   "Auld Lang Syne" (traditional, text by Robert Burns)

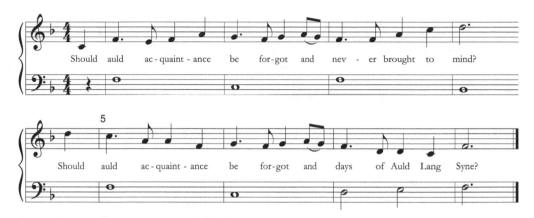

Example 2.14.   "Deus, miserere" (plainchant)

* *Translation*: God, have mercy. O good Jesus, do spare him. God, have mercy.

This chant is unmetered and sung without accompaniment. Breaths should be taken only where they are marked and at the double bar; otherwise the rhythm should be taken somewhat freely. Also, the chant is modal, but it may be sung as if it were A minor with a subtonic scale degree (the lowered $\hat{7}$). It may be sung in any octave.

Example 2.15.   Gabriel Fauré (1845–1924), "Libera me," from *Requiem*, op. 48 (1887–1890)

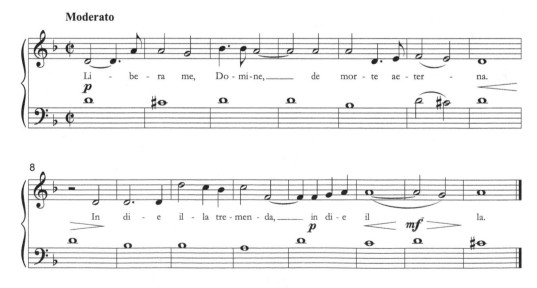

* *Translation*: Deliver me, O Lord, from eternal death.

Note the plaintive quality of the semitonal motion from $\hat{6}$ to $\hat{5}$ in this minor excerpt.

Example 2.16.   "Hanukkah Song" (traditional)

CHORALE WORKSHOP: ROOT-POSITION TONIC AND DOMINANT

The goal of the chorale workshops is for you to build a "vocabulary" of typical harmonic patterns along with their common melodic companions. It is important for you to reinforce these connections in your ear, with your voice, on your instrument, and on the keyboard (a fundamental driving force behind many harmonic/melodic constructions.)

Your primary focus should be on the counterpoint of the outer voices; hence we have laid out the exercises so that the left hand (represented by Roman numeral patterns) is on the left side of the page, while the melodic configurations of the right hand (represented by scale degrees) is on the right side of the page.

For each progression, first sing just the bass line. Then, working at a piano, try singing each soprano line while playing the bass line and singing each bass line while playing the corresponding soprano line. Make sure the soprano is always sounding in a higher register than the bass. You will then want to practice every progression with complete four-note chords in keyboard style (chords in the right hand) on the piano in a variety of simple keys. Try all the soprano lines in turn. Finally, arpeggiate the four-voice harmonies on your instrument or by singing. This will help to build a body-ear connection through harmony.

To reiterate, your focus should be on the outer voices, but you will still want to avoid parallel octaves and fifths between your inner and outer voices as much as possible, and you should attempt to resolve your leading tone to the tonic in the same voice in which you play it. In most cases, this will be easily achieved by maintaining smooth connections between notes in the inner voices. The simple "upshift" and "downshift" of fingers to the closest chord tone will often result in well-constructed inner voices. From this point forward, we will use the term *realize* when asking you to play a progression with four voices on the keyboard.

Because your ability to fluidly realize these progressions in many keys is a critical goal of the chorale workshops, we recommend that you work out your voices directly at the keyboard and *not* on a sheet of paper. If you are new to the piano, you may find that writing out all four voices of a progression provides a helpful crutch, but we urge you to move quickly away from the page, playing your outer parts and focusing only on the upshifting and downshifting of the fingers in the inner parts. If you build good habits from the beginning, you will find that the more complex patterns appearing later in the book can be learned with ease.

Once you've sung and played the outer voices as suggested above, play the following I–V–I (i–V–i) progressions in several simple keys. Be sure to practice placing all of the melodic patterns below in the soprano voice. As you can see, this progression can be played in either major or minor, so practice both.

Harmony (bass line in left hand)	Possible soprano scale degrees (right hand)
I V I	$\hat{5}$ $\hat{5}$ $\hat{5}$
or	$\hat{3}$ $\hat{2}$ $\hat{1}$
i V I	$\hat{3}$ $\hat{2}$ $\hat{3}$
	$\hat{1}$ $\hat{2}$ $\hat{3}$
	$\hat{1}$ $\hat{2}$ $\hat{1}$
	$\hat{1}$ $\hat{7}$ $\hat{1}$

For this chapter only, we have offered several realizations in a single key, only to demonstrate the upshifting and downshifting of fingers in the inner voices, as shown by the lines between inner notes. Be sure to practice these in several keys, and try to avoid looking at anything but the Roman numerals and soprano scale degrees above.

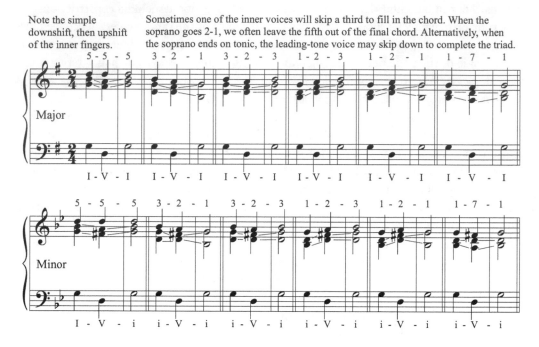

Note the simple downshift, then upshift of the inner fingers.

Sometimes one of the inner voices will skip a third to fill in the chord. When the soprano goes 2-1, we often leave the fifth out of the final chord. Alternatively, when the soprano ends on tonic, the leading-tone voice may skip down to complete the triad.

To complete this exercise by connecting directly to your voice and instrument, sing or play each realization on your instrument, arpeggiating the chords from the bottom up and then top down with the appropriate voice leading, such that one of the soprano lines is followed in the upper voice. For example:

IMPROVISATION: GAMES AND EXERCISES

1. *"Pass the triad member"*: sit or stand in a small group. One person establishes a key by singing tonic. Then, each individual audiates a single, sustained pitch in the tonic triad. On a signal from the group leader or instructor, each individual sings or plays his or her pitch out loud. The group leader or instructor will then signal a switch, and each member of the group will adopt the pitch of the person to the left. Once this is mastered, the group leader or instructor can begin to vary the directions of the switch (left, right, across). This exercise builds audiation skills, as you have to sing and listen simultaneously. It is particularly challenging if everyone sings in the same range, so you may wish to assign a range to each individual (soprano, alto, tenor, bass).

2. Improvise a melody over a tonic-dominant-tonic progression using the three-note melodies you discovered in the Chorale Workshop (see below for rhythmic variations).

3. Refer to Example 2.10, "Go Tell It on the Mountain." Start by singing the excerpt as written with the outer two voices. Now, with the majority of your group singing the lower voice, choose one individual to improvise a new melody using only the pentatonic scale degrees (1̂, 2̂, 3̂, 5̂, 6̂). Start with exactly the same rhythms as the original melody, and then slowly add new rhythmic configurations.

4. Try a similar exercise to that in 3 above, employing the bass part from Example 2.11 (Florence Price's Symphony in E Minor).

5. Improvise a round that alternates tonic and dominant harmonies, maintaining chord tones on the strong beats but employing passing tones on weak beats.

IMPROVISATION: FOCUS ON RHYTHM AND METER

1. *Rhythmic "feel" for improvisation*: below, you will find the first of many rhythmic "feels" that are a basis for improvisation and harmonic exploration for all the chapters that follow. The rhythmic feels are loosely based on various rhythmic repertoires, although they have been adapted to a much more flexible state for classroom practice. Practice the rhythmic feel (you are free to swing the rhythm), and be prepared to sing it in class. The harmonies can and should be changed to suit the exercise, but these rhythms should give you a nice basis for rhythmic and harmonic exploration.

Freely in the 50's style

Doo-wop doo doo-wop doo   doo-wop doo doo-wop doo   Doo-wop doo doo-wop doo   doo-wop doo doo-wop doo

2. *Pentatonic scat with the rhythmic feel*: start by playing (or having a friend sing) the rhythmic feel above, using a I–V–I or i–V–i progression (one harmony per measure). Now, improvise a tune using only the notes of the major pentatonic scale. Start by using scale-degree numbers or solfège syllables, and then replace them with nonsense scat syllables such as "ta" and "ba."

3. *Rhythmic improvisation*: try setting famous names in various meters using rhythmic patterns and metric placements that emphasize the appropriate syllables. For example, note the strong syllables in the well-known name **WOLF**gang Ama**DE**us **MOZ**art. All the strong syllables require a metric accent, and possibly a longer note value. One example (there are many possibilities) is as follows:

Wolf - gang   A - ma - de - us   Mo - zart

4. *Preparation for rhythm pieces*: the first three units of this textbook each conclude
with a complete rhythm piece originally composed for voices. Each chapter will
introduce short sections and rhythmic ideas from the rhythmic pieces at the end
of the unit. The goal is for you to be completely familiar with the individual
rhythmic shapes when you eventually put the pieces together in a small group.

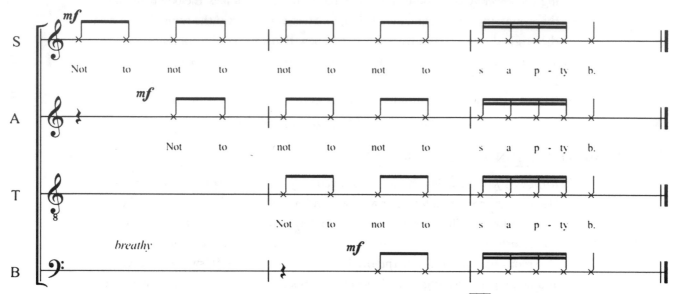

*S a p-ty b is an abbreviation of "Such a pretty bird" and is always set to the rhythm 𝅘𝅥𝅯𝅘𝅥𝅯𝅘𝅥𝅯𝅘𝅥
(The words must be spoken throughout--not the abbreviation!)

Start by practicing the two primary rhythms (m. 1, soprano; m. 3, soprano) separately, and then sing each of the parts individually. Now, make up new words,
being sure to retain the alternating strong-and-weak syllables of the original. You
might consider using names as you did in number 3 above.

INTRODUCTION TO COMPOUND METERS

You may have encountered compound meter in your other musical studies, but because
the beat is divided into groups of three rather than groups of two (as in the simple meters), it is instructive to practice the patterns of compound meter using rhythmic syllables
(as first introduced in the Foundations of Aural Skills chapter). In compound meter, a
dotted note will receive the beat. In the common compound meters of 6/8, 9/8, and 12/8,
the duration of the beat is a dotted-quarter note, which is subdivided into three eighth
notes. A number of excerpts in compound meter are introduced at the end of Chapter 3.

Conducting patterns: for 6/8 meter (as shown in the examples below), you will typically want to use the duple conducting patterns shown in the introductory chapter (there
are two beats in every measure, each lasting a dotted-quarter note). For 9/8, you should
use a triple conducting pattern, and for 12/8 a quadruple conducting pattern.

The syllables found in nos. 2 through 4 of the example below should also be used for
triplet divisions of beats that are more typically subdivided into twos.

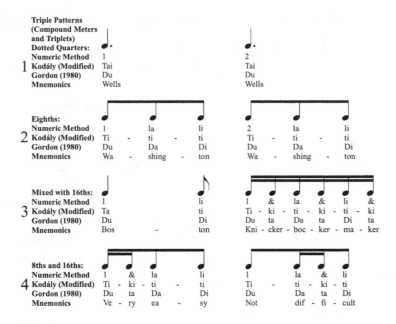

COMPOUND METER DRILLS

1. Practice each pattern above. Start with the dotted-quarter notes (no. 1), and, as you work down to the eighths and sixteenths (no. 4), continue tapping the dotted-quarter beat with one hand while speaking the given rhythms.

2. Make up your own mnemonic devices for the rhythmic patterns, keeping the emphases found in the mnemonics we have provided.

3. *Audiation*: in order to practice *internalizing* the rhythmic patterns, start singing or playing a rhythmic pattern above. Then take a single duration, or an entire beat's worth of durations, and perform it differently (try tapping, whistling, or humming). Now leave that duration out altogether, just imagining the durations you leave out while maintaining the same speed.

4. *Simon says*: have a friend or your instructor play or sing one of the rhythmic patterns above. Sing or play the rhythmic pattern in imitation, and then identify which pattern it was. Now expand to two rhythmic patterns and try imitating and then identifying them both. Try mixing all the rhythms from nos. 1 through 4 above. How many rhythms can you identify in a row?

RHYTHMIC IMPROVISATION WITH COMPOUND METER PATTERNS

1. Have a friend or your instructor point to nos. 1 through 4 above. Try a random order at first, and then attempt to build a longer rhythmic phrase (a complete musical idea, with a beginning, middle, and end) by stringing together several rhythmic patterns.

2. Now, build a rhythmic phrase as you did in 1 above, and then add text, using the example of the mnemonic devices you created in compound meter drill 2. Try to create a short story in rhythm. Pay particular attention to retaining the rhythmic emphases in the mnemonic devices provided. Be prepared to perform this in class.

DRILLS: MAJOR AND MINOR THIRDS, TONIC AND DOMINANT CHORDS

1. *Arpeggiation drill*: arpeggiate the tonic and dominant triads as found in the chorale workshop above. Be sure to try ascending and descending arpeggiations in both major and minor.

2. *More master interval drill*: learn the major and minor thirds. Practice distinguishing the two.

SUGGESTED SMARTMUSIC ASSESSMENTS

Start by practicing the excerpts listed below. Be sure you can sing them smoothly and accurately on scale degrees or syllables (as required by your instructor) while conducting the correct beat pattern. Log into SmartMusic, click "assignments," and complete the assessments *for all parts* as follows: 2.2, 2.6, 2.8, 2.11, 2.15, and 2.16. In addition, complete the assessment for the top voice of 2.10 (you might consider preparing the bass of 2.10 for class, perhaps for extra credit).

SHORT-TERM MUSICAL MEMORY

As in the previous chapter, we have provided brief musical passages intended to be used in class or in practice as an exercise in short-term musical memory. Taking them in dictation will help to train your musical memory and build a more immediate connection between your ear and musical notation. Fill in the key signature and clef as indicated by your instructor, and write in the initial note(s) according to the given pitch and rhythm information. Note that the key and clef *may not be the same* as in the original example. Your instructor (or practice partner) will play a short progression to establish the key and will then count off several beats to establish the tempo. Because of the brevity of the extracts, you should have an overall impression of the rhythm, contour, and scale degrees after just one or two hearings. Notate the entire fragment.

1. Example 2.4, fourth phrase ("*fa-mu-li tu-o-rum*"). Starts on beat 1 (quarter note, scale degree 3̂). Use an appropriate key signature even though the original does not have one.

Clef and key
signature

2. Example 2.5, mm. 6–8. Starts on beat 1 (quarter note, *high* scale degree 1̂).

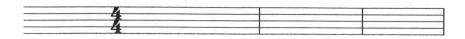

Clef and key
signature

3. Example 2.7, top part, first nine notes. Starts on beat 4 with pickup of two eighth notes (scale degrees $\hat{1}$ and $\hat{2}$).

Clef and key
signature

4. Example 2.10, first two measures, top part. Starts on beat 1 (half note, $\hat{3}$).

Clef and key
signature

5. Example 2.13, top part, last seven notes. Starts on beat 4 with pickup of two eighth notes (scale degrees $\hat{3}$ and $\hat{2}$).

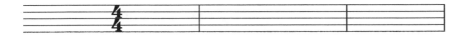

Clef and key
signature

6. Example 2.14 (in minor), first seven pitches, notated in quarters. Use key signature so that first note is treated as $\hat{1}$.

Clef and key
signature

7. Example 2.2, m. 4 to the downbeat of m. 6, both voices. Both start with quarter notes on beat 1 (scale degree $\hat{5}$ in top voice, scale degree $\hat{3}$ in bottom voice).

Clef and key
signature

8. Example 2.9, both voices, up to beat 3 of m. 2. Top voice starts on beat 4 (two eighth-note pickups, scale degrees $\hat{5}$ and $\hat{6}$); bottom voice has a quarter rest on beat 4 (quarter note on first downbeat, scale degree $\hat{1}$).

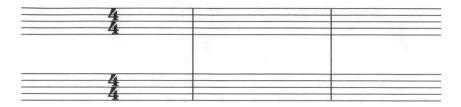

Clef and key
signature

DICTATION OF LONGER EXAMPLES

As suggested in the previous chapter, the excerpts in this section can be used for in-class dictation or for dictation practice outside of class. Your instructor or a classmate will choose one of the examples listed below and inform you of the key, clef, meter, first note (scale degree, rhythmic value, and metric placement) of one or more parts, and total number of measures. Use a separate piece of staff paper to write down the indicated information. You will hear a short progression to establish the key of the example, and then hear the example several times with breaks between hearings.

Don't forget to reread the Six-Step Method for Dictation found in the introduction. You may also wish to practice by having SmartMusic play the indicated excerpts.

1. Example 2.2, mm. 1–8, bass line (or you may be asked to take down both outer parts).
2. Example 2.5, mm. 17–24.
3. Example 2.8, pickup to m. 5 through m. 8, both outer parts.
4. Example 2.11, mm. 1–8.
5. Example 2.15, all.

CONTEXTUAL LISTENING 2.1

"Here We Come A-Wassailing" (traditional English)

This well-known Christmas carol comes from England. Wassail is a delicious spiced punch traditionally served during the winter months and Christmas season. Carolers would travel from door to door singing carols until the host offered to hand out wassail. This was a common practice in England and can be seen in other carols as well, where carolers demand "figgy pudding" and won't leave until they "get some." See if your instructor will give into your sung demands!

Note that there are three audio "mixes" of this excerpt: one with evenly balanced parts, one with the top voice louder than the others, and one with the bottom voice louder than the others. Feel free to use any of the recordings to answer the questions.

1. What is the meter of this excerpt?

    4/4   6/4   3/4   6/8   2/4

2. Does this excerpt begin on an anacrusis (upbeat) or downbeat?

   a. Anacrusis   b. Downbeat

3. On which beat does the excerpt start?

   a. 1   b. 2   c. 3   d. 4   e. 6

4. On the basis of your answer to the previous question and your listening, how many measures long is this excerpt?

   a. 8   b. 9   c. 10   d. 11   e. 12

5. This excerpt does begin with a tonic harmony, but the melody does not start on 1̂. What is the first scale degree in the melody?

   a. 6̂   b. 2̂   c. 5̂   d. 4̂   e. 3̂

6. Now, use the staff below to list the scale degrees of the entire melody.

6. 3 4 5 1 6 5 3 4 5 1 6 5 3 4 5 6 3 4

(continued) 2 1 7 1 2 3 1 4 3 4 5 6 3 4 2 1 5 1

7. What kind of scale is suggested by the melody?

   (a.) Major   b. Minor   c. Pentatonic

8. Now, notate the rhythm (without pitches but with bar lines). Note that, excluding the first and last measures, every measure draws from one of three rhythmic patterns. One pattern is repeated six times. Additionally, in one bar a single pitch is repeated, such that it does not match the exact rhythmic pattern.

9. You should already be thinking about harmonic design in these melodies, and for this question you may want to listen to the version in which the lowest voice is emphasized. The tonic pitch is found in the bass voice in all but four measures (including any partial measures). Circle the measures that do *not* include the tonic pitch in the bass voice. Try humming the tonic pitch while listening. (Hint: cross out any extra measures according to your answer to 4 above).

10. What are the first three scale degrees in the bass voice?

    (a.) $\hat{1}, \hat{2}, \hat{3}$ b. $\hat{3}, \hat{4}, \hat{5}$ c. $\hat{1}, \hat{7}, \hat{1}$ d. $\hat{3}, \hat{4}, \hat{3}$ e. $\hat{1}, \hat{2}, \hat{1}$

11. For fun and extra practice, notate as much of the bass as you can.

CONTEXTUAL LISTENING 2.2

"Amazing Grace" (Christian hymn)

Originally a Christian hymn, "Amazing Grace" crossed over from its gospel origin to more secular audiences with numerous recordings by popular artists (Elvis Presley, Maureen McGovern, Il Divo, et al.). It has become an icon of American culture.

1. What is the meter of this song?

   $\frac{9}{8}$ $\frac{6}{4}$ $\frac{12}{8}$ $\frac{4}{4}$ $\boxed{\frac{3}{4}}$

2. The melody is based on the major pentatonic scale. Il Divo's version of this hymn (included online) is in A♭ major. Transcribe the melody on the staff provided below, including scale-degree numbers for all the notes. Performance practice within this style permits the incorporation of melismatic as well as rhythmic variations. The rhythm below has been normalized for ease of reading. Please circle the notes on which the lead vocalist adds ornamentation.

3. The various stanzas of this hymn are set to the same music, yet performers vary the presentation of each stanza to add interest and shape to the entire piece. Listen carefully to Il Divo's version, and describe how they manipulate various parameters of the music from stanza to stanza. For instance, does this version stay in the same key throughout? How do the timbres of the lead vocalists change throughout the song? What instruments are incorporated as stanzas change? Are there other changes or sonic manipulations?

EXPANDING THE REPERTOIRE 2.3

Steve Miller Band, "Fly Like an Eagle" (1976)

The Steve Miller Band has been active in American rock music since the late 1960s and continues to produce albums today. The song "Fly Like an Eagle" topped the charts in 1977 and became one of the most recognizable songs from the seventies. It was used in the soundtrack of the 1996 hit movie *Space Jam* and continuously on advertisements for the U.S. Postal Service through the nineties. Listen to this well-known four-bar excerpt and answer the questions below.

1. What is the simple meter of this excerpt?

    2/4   3/4   4/4

2. On what beat does this excerpt start? ("I wanna . . .")

    a. "and" of 4   b. 2   c. "and" of 3   d. 3   e. "and" of 2

3. List the scale degrees for the melody of the *first three measures*. For fun, try the final measure (you may find a chromatic surprise).

*Required*_____ *Optional*_____

4. What scale degree begins and ends the excerpt?

    a. $\hat{5}$ b. $\hat{6}$ c. $\hat{3}$ d. $\hat{1}$ e. $\hat{2}$

5. Is this excerpt in major or minor?

    a. Major   b. Minor

6. For extra credit: In which measure and on which beat does an "altered" or nondiatonic note occur? Can you tell what it is or how it has been altered?

Chapter 3

Seventh Scale Degree and Minor Pentatonic

All of the excerpts in this chapter fall into one of two categories. The first includes excerpts in the compound meters that were introduced at the end of the previous chapter but are restricted to the scale degrees and patterns found in the earlier chapters. The majority of the chapter, however, is devoted to excerpts that explore the entire octave, including both the leading tone, which you experienced as a lower neighbor in the previous chapter, and the subtonic (the lowered seventh scale degree in minor), which you practiced, also as a lower neighbor, in the chant examples from the previous chapter and as part of the various adaptations of the minor scale. Some minor melodies that use the subtonic also omit the second and sixth scale degrees, in which case they are employing the minor pentatonic (see Chapter 2). Many of the melodies in this chapter include subdominant support, and you will be attempting to arpeggiate the common progression I–IV–V–I (i–iv–V–i) in the drill exercises below. You may wish to begin exploring the exercises at the end of the chapter before starting to sing the excerpts.

Example 3.1.   Traditional English round in four voices

* This round is a simple arpeggiation of the tonic triad, but it expands the range found in the earlier chapters. Once you have sung it in four voices, consider having various entrances in augmentation (doubling all the rhythmic values), or even in diminution (halving all the rhythmic values).

Example 3.2.   Michael Praetorius (c. 1571–1621), "Viva la Musica!" (round in three voices)

* The leap from $\hat{4}$ to $\hat{7}$ may present a challenge at first. If you have already practiced the tritone as part of the master interval drill, you might want to review that now. In addition, try practicing this passage without singing $\hat{7}$, since getting back to tonic is fairly straightforward. Then, imagine the leading tone immediately before the tonic in m. 6, and practice singing the final two measures together.

Example 3.3.   "Hear! The Cock Crows" (traditional Italian)

* *Translation*: Hear! The cock crows. It's break of day. Good-bye, my sweet; I must part.

Example 3.4.   "Shoo fly!" (traditional)

* The lower part here consists of arpeggiations of the tonic and dominant triads. This type of accompaniment is called "Alberti Bass." You should try singing the lower part while playing the melody. This will reinforce your sense of harmonic context (and of voice leading). Start slowly on solfège syllables or scale degrees, but as you speed up you may want to substitute rhythmic syllables, such as those demonstrated in the introductory chapter.

Example 3.5.   "Banbury Ale" (traditional English round in four voices)

Example 3.6.   Antonio Caldara (c. 1670–1736), round in three voices

Example 3.7.   "Shepherds Hark!" (traditional Austrian)

Hört, ihre Hir - ten, und lasst euch sag'n,   Was sich Neu's hat   zu - ge - trag'n:

Ei - ne Jung - frau   zart und rein   Hat ge - bor'n ein   Kin - de - lein,

Ei,___   ei,___   ei, ei, ei,   In dem Stall auf   ei - ner __ Streu.

* *Translation*: Hark, you shepherds, and let me tell you what news has occurred. A virgin tender and pure has given birth to a little child. Ei! In a stall on the straw.

   Note the expression marking, "Zart," which means "tender" or "delicate."

Example 3.8.   "Fox and Geese" (traditional seventeenth-century round in four voices)

There   was   an in - vi - si - ble   Fox   by   chance,

did   meet   with two   vi - si - ble,   vi - si - ble   Geese:

He   taught   them   a   fine   in - vi - si - ble   Dance

for a   Hun - dred,   Hun - dred   Crowns   a   piece.

Example 3.9.   "Nobilis humilis" (twelfth-century organum)

No-bi-lis, hu-mi-lis, Mag-ne mar-tyr sta-bi-lis, Ha-bi-lis, u-ti-lis, co-mes ve-ne-ra-bi-lis,

et tu-tor lau-da-bi-lis, Tu-os su-bi-tos ser-va car-nis fra-gi-lis___ mo-le po-si-tos.

* *Translation*: Noble, humble Magnus, steadfast martyr, skillful, helpful, worthy companion and de-fender. Protect thy servants who are weighed down by their weak, soft flesh.

This example employs the Lydian mode, but it may be sung with scale degrees/syllables with F as final (or tonic). Try it with B♭, and then try it in its native Lydian with a B♮. Watch out for the half-step between C and B when you sing it this way!

Example 3.10.   Bob Marley (1945–1981), "Stir It Up!" (1967)

Stir it up ___

* The rhythm staff here is added for fun and as a rhythm exercise. Practice all three parts, paying special attention to the I–IV–V progression in the bass (with its prominent leading tones). You will use this bass line (and, possibly, the rhythmic track) as the basis for improvisations.

Example 3.11.   Muzio Clementi (1752–1832), Sonatina, op. 36, no. 2, mvt. 1.

* As with all the excerpts, you should feel free to transpose this to a range you find comfortable.

Example 3.12.   Ludwig van Beethoven (1770–1827), String Trio, WoO 37, mvt. 3 (theme)

* Start slowly when learning the second violin part, and subdivide with eighth notes.

Example 3.13. George Gershwin (1898–1937) and Ira Gershwin (1896–1983), "Someone to Watch over Me" (1926)

* Try playing the second part while singing the melody.

Example 3.14. "Victimae paschali laudes" (tenth-century chant)

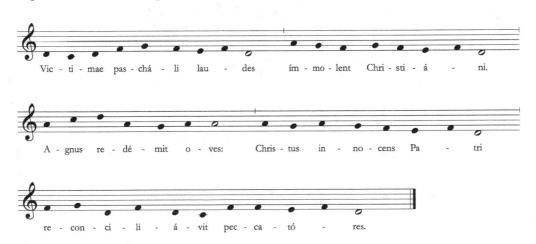

* *Translation*: To the victim of Easter, praises be offered (by) Christians. The Lamb has redeemed the sheep: Christ (the) innocent to the Father has reconciled sinners.

This chant example is actually in D Dorian mode but can be sung using the syllables for D minor, incorporating a lowered-seventh scale degree (subtonic). Like the previous chants, it should be sung freely with breaths only at the half bar lines.

Example 3.15.   "Land of the Silver Birch" (traditional Canadian round in four voices)

* This round uses the pentatonic minor. Note the absence of $\hat{2}$ and $\hat{6}$.

Example 3.16.   Florence Price (1887–1953), Symphony in E minor (1932), mvt. 1

* Focus primarily on the bassoon's opening tune (mm. 1–6) and the oboe's countermelody (starting in m. 7). These two melodies are entirely in the melodic pentatonic, except for a surprising pitch in mm. 5–6. Why did Price briefly depart from the minor pentatonic in these two spots? Florence Price was one of the first African-American symphonists. What might she be trying to evoke with these two minor-pentatonic tunes? See also Example 2.11.

Example 3.17.   Gabriel Fauré (1845–1924), "Libera me," from *Requiem*, op. 48 (1887–1890)

* *Translation*: Deliver me, o Lord, from eternal death. On that fearful day.

Example 3.18.   English canon no. 2 (traditional round for three voices)

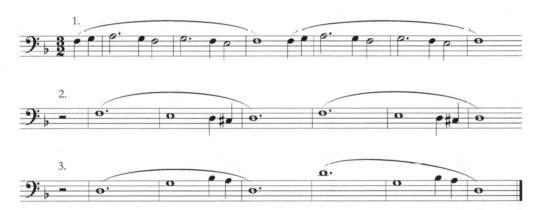

COMPOUND METER

All the remaining excerpts in this chapter are in compound meter. If you need to review the syllables and conducting patterns, please refer to the exercises at the end of the previous chapter (and the conducting patterns in the introductory chapter).

Example 3.19.   "Joan Glover" (traditional seventeenth-century round for four voices)

* Practice conducting the beat in two while singing. Remember: the dotted quarter receives the beat, of which there are two in each measure.

Example 3.20.   Fanny Mendelssohn Hensel (1805–1847), "Nachtwanderer," op. 7 no. 1 (1843)

* Practice conducting the beat in three while singing (there are three dotted-quarter beats per measure). Be sure to sing the bass part as well, with its single upper semitone neighbor to the minor submediant.

Example 3.21.   "Merrily, Merrily" (traditional round in four voices)

Example 3.22.   John Lennon (1940–1980) and Paul McCartney (b. 1942), "Oh! Darling"
                 (1969)

* This major pentatonic tune is in a quadruple compound meter. Conduct in four while subdividing the beat into three eighth notes.

Example 3.23. "Oh Dear, What Can the Matter Be?" (traditional)

CHORALE WORKSHOP: ROOT-POSITION TONIC, SUBDOMINANT, AND DOMINANT

As in the previous chapter, your primary focus should be on the counterpoint of the outer voices. For each progression, first sing just the bass line. Then, working at a piano, try singing the soprano line while playing the bass line and then singing the bass line while playing the corresponding soprano line. You should practice every progression with complete four-note chords in keyboard style (chords in the right hand) on the piano in a variety of simple keys. Try all the soprano lines in turn. Finally, arpeggiate the four-voice harmonies on your instrument or by singing.

As we explained in the previous chapter, you will still want to avoid parallel octaves and fifths between your inner and outer voices as much as possible, and you should attempt to resolve your leading tone to the tonic in the same voice in which you play it. In most cases, this will be easily achieved by maintaining smooth connections between notes in the inner voices. The simple upshift and downshift of fingers to the closest chord tone will often result in well-constructed inner voices.

Here, be particularly careful when voice-leading both the major and minor versions of this progression: I–IV–V–I (i–iv–V–i). The upper voices will always move in contrary motion with the bass when moving from IV to V (or from iv to V). Again, we recommend you work out your voices directly at the keyboard and *not* on a sheet of paper.

Harmony (bass line in left hand)	Possible soprano scale degrees (right hand)
I IV I	$\hat{5}$ $\hat{6}$ $\hat{5}$
or	$\hat{5}$ $\hat{4}$ $\hat{3}$
i iv i	$\hat{3}$ $\hat{4}$ $\hat{3}$
	$\hat{1}$ $\hat{1}$ $\hat{1}$
I IV V I	$\hat{5}$ $\hat{6}$ $\hat{5}$ $\hat{5}$
or	$\hat{5}$ $\hat{4}$ $\hat{2}$ $\hat{3}$
i iv V i	$\hat{5}$ $\hat{4}$ $\hat{2}$ $\hat{1}$
	$\hat{3}$ $\hat{4}$ $\hat{2}$ $\hat{3}$
	$\hat{3}$ $\hat{4}$ $\hat{2}$ $\hat{1}$
	$\hat{1}$ $\hat{1}$ $\hat{7}$ $\hat{1}$

Finally, attempt to sing or play the progressions on your instrument, arpeggiating each triad from the bottom up (and then top down), with the appropriate voice leading. Try this with all the progressions. For example:

IMPROVISATION: GAMES AND EXERCISES

1. Improvise a melody over a tonic-subdominant-tonic progression using the three-note melodies you discovered in the Chorale Workshop.

2. Continue to play "pass the triad member" as in the previous chapters, but, after the leader establishes a tonic pitch, an individual in the group should instead audiate a note in the dominant triad; then sing and pass the triad member to his or her neighbor when the group leader gives the signal.

3. Refer to Example 3.16, Price's Symphony in E Minor. Start by singing the excerpt as written, focusing on the bass and the two melodies (starting in the middle line, moving to the upper line). Now, with the majority of your group singing the lower voice, choose one individual to improvise a new melody using only the minor pentatonic scale degrees: $\hat{1}$, $\hat{3}$, $\hat{4}$, $\hat{5}$, $\downarrow\hat{7}$ (the down arrow denotes the subtonic, or lowered, version of the seventh scale degree in minor). Start with approximately the same rhythms as the original melody, and then slowly add new rhythmic configurations.

4. Improvising with scale degrees 1̂–8̂: start by singing the refrain from the famous song "Stir it Up," by Bob Marley (Example 3.10, above). A similar repeating bass line with a I–IV–V progression and rhythmic line are shown below.

Now, using the notes from Bob Marley's tune, improvise new rhythms over the bass and rhythm. Try improvising your own tune using different chord tones and rhythms. Finally, use different progressions drawn from the Chorale Workshop section and improvise a melody over the bass line.

IMPROVISATION: FOCUS ON RHYTHM AND METER

1. *Rhythmic feel for improvisation*: as in the previous chapter, here is a rhythmic feel that can supply a basis for improvisation and harmonic exploration. Practice the rhythmic feel and be prepared to sing it in class. The harmonies can and should be changed to suit the exercise. Keep in mind that the top line in a bossa nova is typically syncopated over the bar line.

2. *Minor pentatonic scat with the rhythmic feel*: start by playing (or having a friend sing) the rhythmic feel above (thinking now in minor, rather than major). Improvise a tune using only the notes of the minor pentatonic scale. Start by using scale-degree numbers or solfège syllables, and then replace them with nonsense scat syllables such as "ta" and "ba."

3. Try setting lines of famous poems in a rhythmic round (no pitch, just rhythmic chanting). Use 6/8 meter and be sure to give every strong syllable a metric accent, and possibly a longer note value. One candidate is from Matthew Arnold's famous sonnet *West London*. An initial excerpt is furnished as an example:

> She will not ask of aliens, but of friends,
> Of sharers in a common human fate.
> She turns from that cold succour, which attends
> The unknown little from the unknowing great,
> And points us to a better time than ours.

4. Preparation for rhythm pieces: start by practicing the three primary rhythms separately (m. 2, soprano; upbeat to m. 2 through the downbeat of m. 3, alto; m. 4,
   soprano), and then sing the parts individually. Now, make up new words, being
   sure to retain the alternating strong-and-weak syllables of the original.

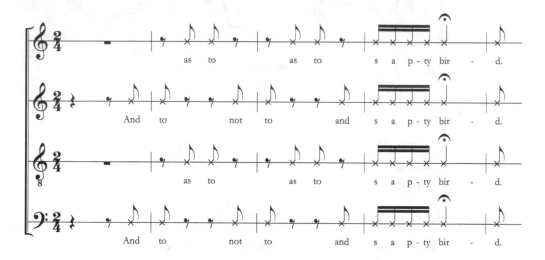

DRILLS: MAJOR AND MINOR THIRDS, TONIC AND DOMINANT CHORDS

1. *Arpeggiation drill*: arpeggiate triads as suggested in the Chorale Workshop above.
   Be sure to try ascending and descending arpeggiations in both major and minor.

2. More on the master interval drill: learn fourths and the tritone. Practice distinguishing between the two.

SUGGESTED SMARTMUSIC ASSESSMENTS

1. Practice the following excerpts until you can sing them fluently and accurately on
   syllables/scale degrees while conducting. Then complete SmartMusic assessments
   3.1, 3.2, 3.3 (both parts), 3.4 (both parts), 3.5, 3.6, 3.7 (both parts), and 3.14 (no
   accompaniment).

2. Prepare and complete SmartMusic assessments as follows: 3.12 (melody), 3.13 (upper two parts), 3.15, 3.16 (all parts), 3.17 (both parts), and 3.20 (melody).

3. Prepare and complete SmartMusic assessments 3.9, 3.11 (both parts), 3.18, 3.19,
   and 3.23 (both parts).

SHORT-TERM MUSICAL MEMORY

Fill in the key signature and clef as indicated by your instructor, and write in the initial
note(s) according to the given pitch and rhythm information. Note that the key and clef
may not be the same as in the original example. Your instructor (or practice partner) will
play a short progression to establish the key and then count off several beats to establish
the tempo. Because of the brevity of each extract, you should have an overall impression of the rhythm, contour, and scale degrees after just one or two hearings. Notate the
entire fragment.

1. Example 3.1, mm. 5–6. Starts on beat 1 (eighth note, scale degree 1̂).

Clef and key
  signature

2. Example 3.10, mm. 1–2, bass line. Starts on beat 1 (quarter note, scale degree 1̂).

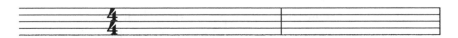

Clef and key
  signature

3. Example 3.18, mm. 15–17 (third vocal entrance, first five notes). Starts on beat 1 (dotted whole note, scale degree 1̂).

Clef and key
  signature

4. Example 3.19, mm. 3–4. Starts on beat 1 (dotted eighth note, scale degree 1̂).

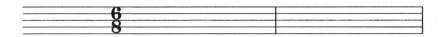

Clef and key
  signature

5. Example 3.3, mm. 7–8. Notate both voices on the same staff, using upward and downward stems. Both voices start with quarter notes on beat 1 (scale degree 7̂ in the bottom voice, and a minor sixth higher in the top voice).

Clef and key
  signature

6. Example 3.7, mm. 9–10. Notate both voices on the same staff, using upward and downward stems. Both voices start with quarter notes on beat 1 (scale degree $\hat{7}$ in the bottom voice, and a minor third higher in the top voice).

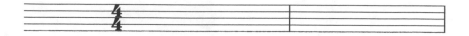

Clef and key
signature

7. Example 3.22, m. 6 to beat 2 of m. 7, outer parts. Both parts start on beat 1 (dotted quarter note and scale degree $\hat{6}$ in the top voice, dotted half and scale degree $\hat{2}$ in the bottom voice).

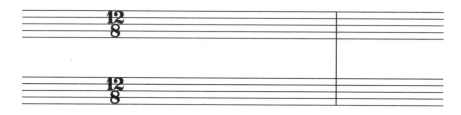

Clef and key
signature

DICTATION OF LONGER EXAMPLES

Your instructor or a classmate will choose one of the examples listed below and inform you of the key, clef, meter, first note (scale degree, rhythmic value, and metric placement) of one or more parts, and total number of measures. Use a separate piece of staff paper to write down the indicated information. You will hear a short progression to establish the key of the example, and you will then hear the example several times with breaks between hearings.

1. Example 3.2, all.
2. Example 3.9, from the rest to the end, notated in 4/4.
3. Example 3.11, mm. 1–4, bass.
4. Example 3.16, m. 7 to the end, oboe melody.
5. Example 3.17, m. 8 to the end (possibly with bass line as well).
6. Example 3.20, entire excerpt, both parts.
7. Example 3.23, mm. 5–8 (not including final eighth note), both parts.

Name: _____ Date: _____ Instructor: _____

CONTEXTUAL LISTENING 3.1

Beethoven, Trio, WoO 37, mvt. 3, variation 4

This trio for piano, flute, and bassoon was written in 1786. The third movement presents seven variations of progressive rhythmic challenge. The fourth variation breaks from the prevailing mode and meter of the theme (found earlier in the chapter), presenting a variation in the style of the siciliano, a pastoral dance of the Baroque period.

1. What is the meter of this eight-bar excerpt?

   $\frac{3}{4}$ $\frac{9}{8}$ $\frac{4}{4}$ $\frac{6}{8}$ $\frac{2}{4}$

2. Map out the structure of this excerpt. Where does musical material repeat? Where is it different?

   Measures _1–2_ are repeated in mm. _5–6_ .
   Measures _7_ and _8_ have new musical material.

3. Listen to the top two parts alone. With only a pair of exceptions, the top parts move in parallel motion. What interval separates the two upper parts for all but the brief exceptions?

   a. Unison   (b. Third)   c. Fifth   d. Sixth   e. Octave

4. There are ties from a weak beat to a strong beat in the upper two parts. Two of them occur between measures, and two occur in the middle of a measure. In one additional spot, the same pitches (again in the upper two parts) are repeated (rearticulated) over the bar line, creating a similar effect. List the locations of these ties and the "rearticulation."

   Ties: mm. _2_–_3_ , mm. _5_–_6_ , m. _7_ , and m. _8_ .
   Rearticulation: m. _3_ .

5. For extra credit, explain how these ties and repeated pitches might affect your performance of this excerpt.

6. In the staff on the next page, see if you can notate the rhythm of the top two voices in the first four bars.

7. In the staff on the next page, list the scale degrees used by the top two parts (remember that the second voice follows in parallel motion).

8. Listen to the outer parts alone. Pay careful attention to the *first* bass pitch in each measure and attempt to notate it in the staff at the bottom of the page.

9. What is the penultimate (the one before the last) scale degree in the bass?

   a. $\hat{1}$ b. $\hat{3}$ c. $\hat{4}$ d. $\hat{5}$ (e. $\hat{6}$)

10. Listen carefully to the bass line. Given the outlined harmonies, what is the general harmonic structure of the excerpt? (Hint: the excerpt divides into two halves, with two primary harmonies outlining the first half, and three outlining the second.)

    a. I–IV–I–V–I   b. I–V–I–V–I   (c. I–IV–V–I–V)   d. V–I–IV–V–I

11. In bars 1 and 3, what type of motion generally describes the relationship between outer parts?

    a. Contrary motion   (b. Parallel motion)   c. Oblique motion

12. Compare this excerpt with the "theme" from the same trio movement (which can be found earlier in this chapter). How did Beethoven vary the theme here? What did he retain? List at least four aspects that Beethoven changed and four aspects that he retained (be more specific than the general ideas suggested in the preface to this exercise).

    Changed: the rhytnm

    Retained: overall notes and melody

Use this staff to answer questions 6, 7, and 8.

CONTEXTUAL LISTENING 3.2

"Old Blue" (traditional)

Like most traditional songs, "Old Blue" exists in hundreds of variations. It has been recorded by many artists over the years. Peter, Paul, and Mary's three-part rendition is particularly noteworthy. It is unclear when the song first became popular, but a very similar poem appeared in *The Mother Goose; Containing All the Melodies the Old Lady Ever Wrote*, edited by Dame Goslin (1850).

1. What is the meter of this sixteen-measure excerpt?

$\frac{3}{2}$ $\frac{4}{4}$ $\frac{6}{8}$ $\frac{6}{4}$ $\frac{9}{8}$

2. This excerpt includes a number of internal repetitions. Map them out.

Repetition 1: mm. _1–2_ = mm. _5–6_ .
Repetition 2: _3–4_ = _7–8_ .
Repetition 3: _9–10_ = _13–14_ .
Repetition 4: _11–12_ = _15–16_ .
Repetition 5. _4_ = _8_ .
Repetition 6: _12_ = _16_ .

3. Comment on how the first and second halves of the song are differentiated by changing the length of music between repetitions (pay special attention to the dynamics). _there's different dynamics_

4. In the staff on the next page, notate both the rhythm and the pitches of the melody in F major on the staves below. Try to do this within six hearings. You should consider following the Six-Step Method of Dictation outlined in Chapter 1.

5. Now notate the rhythm and pitches of the lower part. You may wish to listen to the recording with the amplified bass.

6. Finally, underneath each measure, label the implied harmonies as either I or V. There is only one harmony per bar, except in mm. 11, 12, 15, and 16, where there are two.

CONTEXTUAL LISTENING 3.2

EXPANDING THE REPERTOIRE 3.3

Harold Arlen (1905–1986), "Over the Rainbow" (1938)

This famous song from *The Wizard of Oz* was voted the twentieth century's number one song by the Recording Industry Association of America and the National Endowment for the Arts. The soaring leaps of the chorus are suggestive of the hopeful heights of the rainbow that Dorothy believes will deliver her to a better place.

1. What is the meter of this eight-measure excerpt?

$$\frac{4}{4} \qquad \frac{6}{8} \qquad \frac{3}{2} \qquad \frac{9}{8} \qquad \frac{4}{8}$$

2. Listen to the bass line in the two-part version online. List the scale degree of the bass note on the first beat of every measure. *Also* include the scale degree of the penultimate (next to last) bass note.

3. There are three large motivic *ascending* leaps in the melody of this excerpt; each successively smaller than the preceding one. Identify the scale degrees of both pitches in all three leaps, and then identify the three intervals.

   Leap 1: _____ to _____ . Interval: _____ .

   Leap 2: _____ to _____ . Interval: _____ .

   Leap 3: _____ to _____ . Interval: _____ .

4. Now you should attempt to notate both the rhythm and the pitches of the melody in E♭ major. Try to do this within six hearings. You may have already established a strategy for this, but if not, then consider following the Six-Step Method for Dictation outlined in Chapter 1.

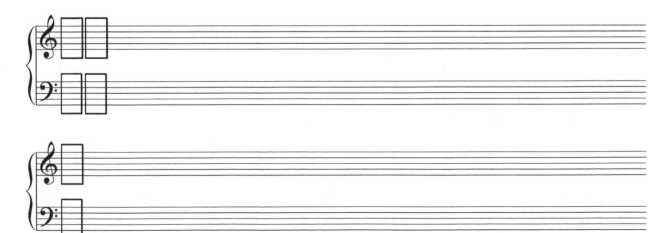

EXPANDING THE REPERTOIRE 3.4

Cee Lo Green, "Forget You" (2010)

This song in the style of sixties Motown was aimed at the music industry and appeared in several versions (with more explicit or more censored versions of the lyrics).

1. What is the meter of this song?

   $\frac{9}{8}$ $\frac{6}{4}$ $\frac{12}{8}$ $\frac{4}{4}$ $\frac{3}{4}$

2. The song is based on a harmonic progression of four chords that repeats through most of the song. There is, however, one section that diverges harmonically by outlining a different progression. Although you might not be aware of the chords used, can you aurally identify the section that differs? (Timings for the various sections are provided.)

   ____ Intro   ____ Chorus   ____ Verse 1   ____ Chorus

   ____ Verse 2   ____ Chorus   ✓ Bridge   ____ Chorus

   (0:06–0:14)   (0:14–0:44)   (0:44–1:14)   (1:14–1:44)

   (1:44–2:15)   (2:15–2:44)   (2:44–3:15)   (3:15 end)

3. Does the melody of the chorus begin on an anacrusis (upbeat) or downbeat?

   a. Anacrusis   b. Downbeat

4. The melody of the chorus is based on the major pentatonic scale. Write out the complete melody of the chorus. A small melodic gesture performed by the backup vocals is included in parentheses.

Chapter 4

Plagal Melodies I

In Chapters 4 and 5 you will begin singing an entire octave, focusing on the fourth below the tonic to the fifth above, from the lower dominant to the upper dominant. This space is called the "plagal" range, and it stems from early organizations of plainchant. Many of the melodies that you have already sung include extensions to the lower dominant, but now we will focus on filling in this space. The newest challenge will be the incorporation of the submediant scale degree, particularly as it leads to both the lower dominant and up through the leading tone to the tonic. Rhythmic activity will remain relatively stable. As you proceed in this dimension, however, you should consider the basic rhythmic "shapes" that occur in any one measure, motive, or musical idea. In the improvisation section, you will be encouraged to improvise rounds and melodies that explore a single rhythmic pattern. In addition, you will be working on extensions of a previous harmonic paradigm (I–IV–I/i–iv–i) through the addition of first-inversion triads. From this point forward, and as your understanding of harmony becomes more sophisticated, you will see more paradigms included in each chapter. The paradigms provide important harmonic "frameworks," which, when learned fluidly, will give your musical mind easy access to possible melodies, harmonization, and pattern continuations. This is a critical element of the kinds of musicianship you are beginning to develop.

Example 4.1.   Michael Praetorius (c. 1571–1621), round in three voices

Example 4.2.　　Traditional English round in four voices

Example 4.3.　　"Joan, Come Kiss Me" (traditional round in three voices)

Example 4.4.　　Joseph Haydn (1732–1809), round in three voices

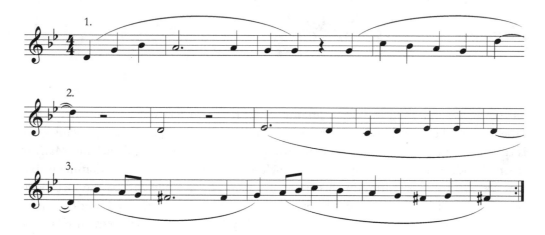

* Note that this round begins with a three-beat anacrusis. Practice conducting and singing, aiming for important melodic arrivals, rather than for the initial pitch of the anacrusis.

Example 4.5.　　Haydn, round in four voices

Example 4.6.   Traditional German round in four voices

Example 4.7.   "Hey, Ho! Nobody Home" (traditional round in three voices)

* The use of the subtonic in this and the following round gives them a very folk (modal) flavor.

Example 4.8.   "Shalom chaverim" (traditional Hebrew round in three voices)

* *Translation*: Goodbye friends, Goodbye friends, Goodbye, Goodbye! Until we meet again, Goodbye, Goodbye!

Example 4.9.   "En roulant ma boule" (traditional Canadian)

* *Translation*: While rolling my ball . . . Behind our house there is a pond. Three beautiful ducks are going swimming. Roll-on, roll, my rolling ball.

Example 4.10.   "An die Freude" (traditional German)

* *Translation*: Be embraced, millions! This kiss to the entire world! Brothers, above the starry canopy . . . (must a loving father dwell).

Example 4.11.   "The Prisoner" (traditional Spanish)

* *Translation*: Month of May, when the days are warm, when the wheat fields are in flower.

Example 4.12.   Henry Purcell (1659–1695), "Now We Are Met" (round in three voices)

* All of the Purcell rounds in this and later chapters are "catches," short rounds that were meant to be sung informally at social occasions. Frequently, the combined voices in the catches bring out words or phrases that are hidden in the single lines. Catches are always meant to be sung through in unison, followed by typical round singing, wherein each of the three groups starts at the number one and sings all the way through the three lines. The second group starts at the beginning when the first group reaches number two, and so forth.

Example 4.13.   "Good King Wenceslas" (traditional English)

Example 4.14.   Felix Mendelssohn (1809–1847), "Hark! The Herald Angels Sing" (1840)

* Note the consistent rhythmic pattern that starts in m. 1. What is the effect of the shifting of the dotted rhythm in m. 17?

Example 4.15.   Wolfgang Amadeus Mozart (1756–1791), String Quartet in D minor, K. 421, mvt. 3

* Notice how Mozart uses all the chromatic manipulations of the minor scale in the bass part to achieve a chromatic descent from tonic to dominant. Be sure to practice both of the outer parts.

CHORALE WORKSHOP: THREE-CHORD TONIC EXPANSIONS USING IV (iv) AND INVERTED TRIADS

Working at a piano, play the following paradigms in simple major and minor keys. Try placing the listed melodic pattern in the soprano voice. Note that the four-voice versions of many of these paradigms will use doublings that are different from their root-position equivalents. In most cases, simply avoiding parallel octaves and fifths will simplify the process. In addition to playing in four voices, try playing in two or three voices while singing the soprano pattern. It is important to build this connection between the harmony and the melody. Finally, as in the previous chapters, attempt to sing the progressions, arpeggiating each triad from the bottom up (and then top down), with the appropriate voice leading.

Expansions of tonic through the subdominant:

Harmony (bass line in left hand)	Possible soprano scale degrees (right hand)
I IV I^6 or i iv i^6	$\hat{5}$ $\hat{6}$ $\hat{5}$ $\hat{3}$ $\hat{4}$ $\hat{5}$ $\hat{1}$ $\hat{1}$ $\hat{1}$
I^6 IV I^6 or i^6 iv^6 i^6	$\hat{5}$ $\hat{6}$ $\hat{5}$ $\hat{1}$ $\hat{1}$ $\hat{1}$
I^6 IV I or i^6 iv i	$\hat{5}$ $\hat{6}$ $\hat{5}$ $\hat{5}$ $\hat{4}$ $\hat{3}$ $\hat{1}$ $\hat{1}$ $\hat{1}$
I IV^6 I^6 or i iv^6 i^6	$\hat{3}$ $\hat{4}$ $\hat{5}$ $\hat{1}$ $\hat{1}$ $\hat{1}$

IMPROVISATION: GAMES AND EXERCISES

1. Continue to play "pass the triad member" as in the previous chapters, but after the leader establishes a tonic pitch groups members should instead audiate a note in the subdominant triad and then sing and pass the triad member to their neighbor when the leader gives the signal. When the leader gives a special signal, switch to audiating a note of the tonic triad, and then pass it again. Switch back and forth between tonic and subdominant triads, following the leader's signals.

2. Copy the harmonic patterns above to notecards. Choose four cards, and arrange them in a row for a partner. Now, with your partner or team singing or playing the lower three voices of the harmonies, sing an appropriate set of soprano lines. Then branch out and attempt to switch soprano lines while your partner or team continues singing or playing the lower three voices.

3. Refer to Example 4.9. Retaining the same bass and harmonic structure, improvise a new melody with the same rhythms as the original melody, placing chord tones on the first eighth note of every dotted-quarter beat. A good place to start would be to try inverting (flipping upside-down) the contours within each beat of the melody. Eventually, you may want to add new rhythmic configurations.

IMPROVISATION: FOCUS ON RHYTHM AND METER

1. Practice the dotted rhythmic patterns from "Hark! The Herald Angels" (Example 4.14, m. 1 and m. 17) and the Praetorius round (Example 4.1, m. 1). Now string the patterns or "shapes" together to set a poetic text of your choosing. Be sure to

place the syllables that you most want to accent on the dotted quarter notes. Try performing your rhythmic setting straight, and then as a round.

2. Compose a melody for the rhythmic setting created above. Use the harmonic paradigms in this chapter (or earlier chapters).

3. *Rhythmic feel for improvisation*: use this feel as a basis for improvisation and harmonic exploration. Practice the rhythmic feel, and be prepared to sing it in class. The harmonies can and should be changed to suit the exercise. Try using the harmonies from the chorale workshop in your improvisations.

4. *Preparation for rhythm pieces*: start by practicing each part separately, paying close attention to the meter change in the third measure. Make sure that you emphasize the change in strong-weak beat patterns. Then try singing all four parts together. Finally, make up new words, being sure to retain the pattern of strong-and-weak syllables from the original.

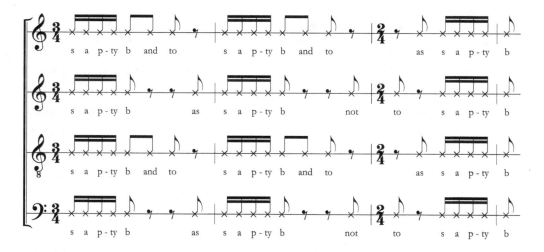

DRILLS: INTERVALS AND ARPEGGIATIONS

1. *Arpeggiation drill*: arpeggiate triads as suggested in the Chorale Workshop above. Be sure to try ascending and descending arpeggiations in both major and minor.

2. *More on the master interval drill*: complete the master interval, learning the fifths, sixths, and sevenths. Practice distinguishing between the intervals in their various contexts.

SUGGESTED SMARTMUSIC ASSESSMENTS

Practice the following excerpts until you can sing them fluently and accurately on syllables/scale degrees while conducting, and then complete SmartMusic assessments 4.1, 4.4, 4.5, 4.8, 4.9 (both parts), 4.10 (both parts), 4.11 (both parts), 4.12, 4.13 (bass), and 4.15 (bass). Earn extra credit if you can sing the melody of 4.14 while you play the bass on the piano.

SHORT-TERM MUSICAL MEMORY

Fill in the key signature and clef as indicated by your instructor, and write in the initial note(s) according to the given pitch and rhythm information. Note that the key and clef *may not be the same* as in the original example. Your instructor (or practice partner) will play a short progression to establish the key and then count off several beats to establish the tempo. Because of the brevity of each extract, you should have an overall impression of the rhythm, contour, and scale degrees after just one or two hearings. Notate the entire fragment.

1. Example 4.1, mm. 1–2. Starts on beat 1 (dotted quarter note, *high* scale degree 1̂).

Clef and key
   signature

2. Example 4.3, up to downbeat of m. 3. Starts on beat 1 (dotted quarter note, scale degree 1̂).

Clef and key
   signature

3. Example 4.5, mm. 1–4. Starts on beat 1 (dotted quarter note, scale degree 1̂).

Clef and key
   signature

4. Example 4.8, up to beat 3 of m. 2. Starts on beat 4 (quarter note, low scale degree 5̂).

Clef and key
   signature

5. Example 4.9, mm. 1–2, top line. Starts on beat 1 (quarter note, scale degree 3̂).

Clef and key
   signature

6. Example 4.12, mm. 1–2. Starts on beat 1 (quarter note, scale degree 1̂).

Clef and key
signature

7. Example 4.13, mm. 1–2, both voices. Starts on beat 1 (eighth note and scale degree 1̂ in top voice, half note and scale degree 3̂ in bottom voice).

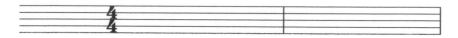

Clef and key
signature

8. Example 4.15, up to downbeat of m. 3, top line, along with viola part transposed down an octave. Top voice starts on beat 3 (dotted eighth note and sixteenth note, both scale degree 1̂); bottom voice starts with same rhythm one measure later (a major sixth lower than the top voice started).

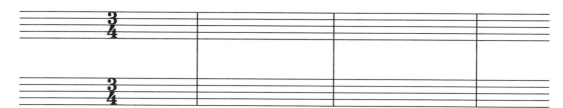

Clef and key
signature

DICTATION OF LONGER EXAMPLES

Your instructor or a classmate will choose one of the examples listed below and inform you of the key, clef, meter, first note (scale degree, rhythmic value, and metric placement) of one or more parts, and total number of measures. Use a separate piece of staff paper to write down the indicated information. You will hear a short progression to establish the key of the example, and you will then hear the example several times with breaks between hearings.

1. Example 4.2, all.
2. Example 4.6, through beat 3 of m. 6.
3. Example 4.10, all, melody.
4. Example 4.11, up to m. 8, melody (or both voices).
5. Example 4.15, all, bass line.

CONTEXTUAL LISTENING 4.1

"My Bonnie Lies over the Ocean" (traditional Scottish)

This traditional Scottish song speaks nostalgically of "Bonnie Prince Charlie," a very handsome eighteenth-century Scottish prince who was exiled to France after leading a failed Jacobite takeover of the English throne.

1. It is possible to understand this excerpt in either simple or compound meter, but the questions will assume that it is notated in a compound meter. Which compound meter can be used to notate this excerpt?

$$\frac{9}{8} \qquad \frac{3}{4} \qquad \frac{6}{8} \qquad \frac{2}{4} \qquad \frac{12}{8}$$

2. How many measures are in this excerpt?

   a. 8   b. 10   c. 12   d. 14   e. 16

3. Does the excerpt begin on an anacrusis?

   Yes   No

4. In which measure might you find a fermata?

   a. 6   b. 7   c. 8   d. 12   e. 14

5. Which scale degree is held during the fermata?

   a. $\hat{1}$ b. $\hat{2}$ c. $\hat{3}$ d. $\hat{5}$ e. $\hat{6}$

6. Describe the structure of the first eight measures (first two phrases). Are there any similarities between the first two phrases? What is different?

7. Each of the first two phrases starts with a familiar harmonic paradigm (with the melody slightly embellished). What harmonies are found in mm. 1–2 and 5–6?

8. What harmony ends the first phrase? The second phrase?

9. Which phrase ending sounds more "conclusive"? If you recall the terms *half cadence* and *authentic cadence* (as mentioned in Chapter 2), you may wish to use them here.

10. Transcribe the pitch and rhythm of the soprano and bass for the first eight measures in the key of B♭ major. Attempt to follow the Six-Step Method of Dictation.

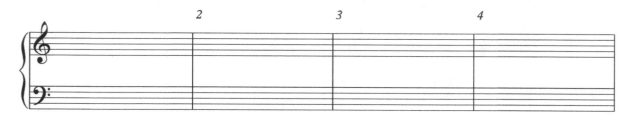

11. The second section begins in m. 9. What is the relationship between what happens melodically in m. 9 and what happens in m. 10?

12. Which scale degrees appear on the downbeats of mm. 9, 10, 11, and 12?

    a. $\hat{5}, \hat{5}, \hat{6}, \hat{7}$ b. $\hat{1}, \hat{7}, \hat{6}, \hat{5}$ c. $\hat{5}, \hat{5}, \hat{6}, \hat{6}$ d. $\hat{1}, \hat{2}, \hat{3}, \hat{4}$ e. $\hat{5}, \hat{6}, \hat{7}, \hat{1}$

13. Can you describe what is happening on the downbeats of mm. 9–12? Does this motion continue any further? Describe.

14. Note the bass line in m. 9. What chord is suggested here? Does it change inversions during the measure?

CONTEXTUAL LISTENING 4.2

Domenico Scarlatti (1685–1757), Piano Sonata, K. 32

The eighteenth-century Italian composer Domenico Scarlatti wrote 555 keyboard sonatas during his years of service to the Portuguese and Spanish royal families. His late-Baroque compositions looked forward to the balanced structure, simple melodic writing, and harmonic exploration of the Classical era. The large leaps in this excerpt's melody hide a simpler underlying long-range melodic motion from the submediant to the tonic.

1. What is the meter of this excerpt?

6/8   3/4   2/2   9/8   12/8

2. For how many measures does the excerpt last?

   a. 7   (b. 8)   c. 11   d. 11   e. 12

3. The final note of the excerpt in both parts is a D. What key is this excerpt in? Is it in major or minor?

   Major   (Minor)

4. What is the size and quality of the leap in m. 6?

   (a. P5)   b. m6   c. M3   d. m3   e. P8

5. What two scale degrees are involved in the large leap in m. 2? (The ↓ indicates the lowered $\hat{6}$ and $\hat{7}$ in minor, while the ↑ indicates the raised $\hat{6}$ and $\hat{7}$ in minor.)

   (a.) ↑$\hat{6}$ and ↑$\hat{7}$ b. 3 and ↑$\hat{7}$ c. ↓$\hat{6}$ and $\hat{1}$ d. ↓$\hat{6}$ and ↓$\hat{7}$
   e. ↓$\hat{6}$ and ↑$\hat{7}$

6. In which two measures does the melody include the leading tone?

   a. 2 and 4   b. 5 and 7   c. 2 and 7   d. 4 and 7   (e. 2 and 5)

7. In which two measures does the bass include the dominant (scale degree $\hat{5}$)?

   a. 2 and 5   b. 3 and 7   c. 5 and 7   (d. 3 and 5)   e. 2 and 3

8. The melody presents a three-note rhythmic motive in m. 1. Which two of the following measures start with the same motive (now starting on different pitches), and which pitches do they start on?

3↓2   5↓7 (leading tone)

9. On the basis of your answers to the above questions, transcribe both the soprano and bass following the Six-Step Method outlined in the preceding chapters.

CONTEXTUAL LISTENING 4.3

"The Holly and the Ivy" (traditional English)

This traditional Christmas carol is referenced in some form or another as early as 1710. Long associated with the sacred (by early pagans, then by Romans, and finally by Christians), this carol compares the attributes of the plant and its hearty winter fruit with the events surrounding the birth of Jesus Christ.

1. What is the simple meter of this excerpt?

$\frac{2}{4}$ $\frac{6}{8}$ $\left(\frac{3}{4}\right)$ $\frac{9}{8}$ $\frac{4}{4}$

2. For how many measures does the excerpt last?

a. 6   b. 7   c. 8   ~~d. 9~~   e. 10

3. Does the excerpt start on an upbeat or a downbeat?

(Upbeat)   Downbeat

4. What is the relationship between the melody in mm. 1–2 and in mm. 3–4?

a. Transposition by _____

b. Similar contour

c. Repetition

d. Contrary motion

5. This excerpt is arranged as a duet. What is the relationship between the two parts when the second part starts? When does this relationship change?

the relationship between the two is the drum acts as a sense of tempo

6. The first leap in the melody decorates a more important structural pitch that falls on the first beat of the second measure. What scale degrees are used here? Does a similar decoration of the same structural pitch happen elsewhere in the melody (excluding exact repetition)?

a. Leap 1: scale degrees __1__, __6__, and __5__

b. Similar leap: scale degrees __1__, __6__, and __5__

7. Accurately transcribe *both* parts of this duet with G as tonic. Attempt to transcribe each part within six hearings.

EXPANDING THE REPERTOIRE 4.4

Ritchie Valens, "La Bamba" (1958), Mexican folk song

The Beatles, "Twist and Shout" (1964), written by Bert Russell

These great songs are strikingly similar in harmonic structure, harmonic rhythm, melodic gestures, instrumentation, etc. In fact, they are so similar that in 1964 Johnny Rivers covered both songs in a medley on his album *At the Whisky à Go Go.*

1. What is the simple meter of both songs?

   $\mathbf{\frac{9}{8}}$ $\quad$ $\mathbf{\frac{6}{4}}$ $\quad$ $\mathbf{\frac{12}{8}}$ $\quad$ $\mathbf{\frac{4}{4}}$ $\quad$ $\mathbf{\frac{3}{4}}$

2. What is the key of each song as performed on the versions provided online? (You may use your instrument or a keyboard to figure this out.)

   "La Bamba": C $\qquad\qquad$ "Twist and Shout": D

3. What pickup melodic gesture introduces both songs?

   a. $\hat{4}$-$\hat{3}$-$\hat{2}$-$\hat{1}$ $\quad$ b. $\hat{5}$-$\hat{6}$-$\hat{7}$-$\hat{1}$ $\quad$ c. $\hat{5}$-$\hat{5}$-$\hat{5}$-$\hat{1}$ $\quad$ d. $\hat{4}$-$\hat{5}$-$\hat{2}$-$\hat{1}$

4. The initial phrases in the lead melodies of both songs are quite similar as well. In both, the melodies start on the same scale degree, and the melodies end on the same scale degree. Choose the starting and ending scale degrees from the options below:

   a. $\hat{5}$/$\hat{1}$ $\quad$ b. $\hat{4}$/$\hat{3}$ $\quad$ c. $\hat{4}$/$\hat{1}$ $\quad$ d. $\hat{2}$/$\hat{1}$

5. The instrumental intro is four measures long in both songs and in both cases sets up the harmonic pattern (and harmonic rhythm) for the entire song. Choose the correct harmonic pattern and harmonic rhythm among the proposed options:

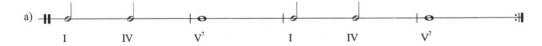

a) I — IV — V⁷ — I — IV — V⁷

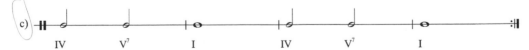

b) I — IV — V⁷ — I — IV — V⁷

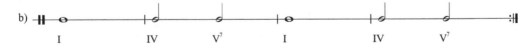

c) IV — V⁷ — I — IV — V⁷ — I

d) V⁷ — IV — I — V⁷ — IV — I

6. *Optional assignment*: prepare to improvise on the harmonic progression of these songs. The practice tracks provided online are in C major, D major, and B♭ major.

EXPANDING THE REPERTOIRE 4.5

Taio Cruz, "Telling the World," from *Rio* (2011)

This midtempo song features (almost exclusively) a repeating I–I^{sus4}–vi^7–I harmonic progression that avoids the dominant. The more typical I–vi–IV–I progression (which also excludes a dominant harmony) can be heard in countless pop songs (such as in Bruno Mars' *Just the Way You Are*).

1. What is the meter of this song?

$$\frac{9}{8} \qquad \frac{6}{4} \qquad \frac{12}{8} \qquad \boxed{\frac{4}{4}} \qquad \frac{3}{4}$$

2. Even while repeating a single harmonic paradigm, the song builds toward the chorus. Describe how the texture, melody range, dynamic level, and other parameters contribute to this effect. *the building is based on the dynamics*

3. Write the chords symbols and the corresponding notes for the harmonic progression in E♭, and play it at the piano while hearing the song:

4. The melody of the chorus (0:44–1:00) is based on four pitches, scale degrees $\hat{1}$ through $\hat{4}$. Write out the complete melody of the chorus, and add the Roman numerals in the boxes below the melody.

5. *Optional assignment 1*: prepare to improvise on the progression of "Telling the World" using only scale degrees $\hat{1}$ through $\hat{4}$. Similarly to the original song, the backup track found online features a layering of textural elements that helps create momentum.

6. *Optional assignment 2*: same as above, but in alternative keys, D major and F major.

Chapter 5

Plagal Melodies II

This chapter continues a focus on the plagal melody (from the lower dominant to the upper dominant) while introducing new rhythmic and multipart singing challenges. The melodies include a greater incidence of syncopation, changing meters, and generally increased rhythmic activity. Continue to focus on repeated rhythmic patterns or shapes. You will also be working on extensions of a previous harmonic paradigm (I–V–I, i–V–i) through the addition of first-inversion triads. More possibilities for expanding the tonic will be introduced in later chapters. If you have already discussed them in written theory, however, you may also want to employ two paradigms that include the leading-tone and passing-six-four chords: I–vii^6–I^6 and I–P$^6_4$–I^6. Don't forget to work on the exercises in the back of the chapter while exploring the excerpts.

Example 5.1.   Traditional seventeenth-century round in three voices

Example 5.2.   Traditional English round in three voices.

Example 5.3.   Edmund Nelham (d. 1646), "Come Follow Me" (round in three voices)

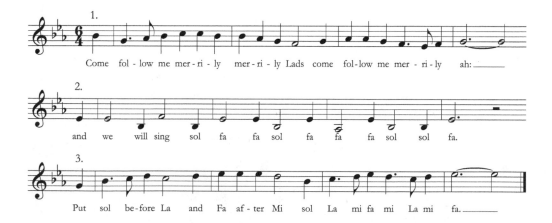

* Note the clever play with solmization syllables. It is based on a form of solfège that is used in the Sacred Harp tradition, and it should not be confused with the system used in this text.

Example 5.4.   Henry Purcell (1659–1695), "Once in Our Lives" (round in three voices)

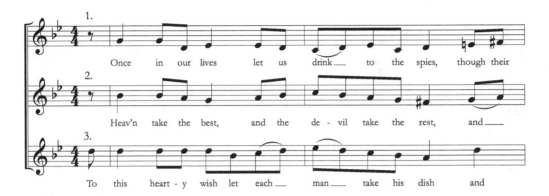

Once   in   our   lives   let   us   drink___   to   the   spies,   though   their

Heav'n   take   the   best,   and   the   de - vil   take   the   rest,   and ___

To   this   heart - y   wish   let   each ___   man ___   take   his   dish   and

num - ber ___ be ___ but ___ small. _____ *to line 2*

so   we   shall   get   rid ___   of   them   all. _____ *to line 3*

drink,   drink   'til   he   fall. _____ *da capo*

* This Purcell catch follows the catch tradition introduced in the previous chapter. All groups should start by singing the entirety in unison. Then, on the next time through, the second group starts when the first group reaches the "2" in the score, and so forth, as in a regular round.

Example 5.5.   Purcell, "Under This Stone" (round in three voices)

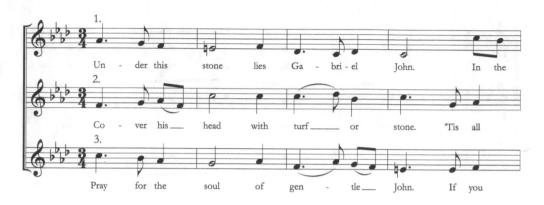

* This catch by Purcell provides useful rhythmic variety. Practice each of the one-measure rhythmic patterns individually before singing it. Then, use the rhythmic shapes in the improvisation activity below.

Example 5.6.   George Frideric Handel (1685–1759), "Heroes, When with Glory," from *Joshua*, HWV 64

* Note the unusual voice leading in the final measures of this operatic ritornello. This foreshadows the end of the aria, where all of the instruments double the singer to provide a truly emphatic and heroic ending.

Example 5.7.　"On the Grass" (traditional Belgian)

* *Translation*: We are here in a dance, all full of young folks. What displeases me the most, my love, is not in it. On the grass, a diddle dum day. Come lambkins, a diddle dum day.

Example 5.8.　Ludolf Waldmann (1840–1919), "Mit Sing und Sang" (excerpt 1)

* *Translation*: I wander through the lands, only a simple singer, and praise in word and music nature's majesty!

Example 5.9.   La Cucaracha (traditional Mexican).

* Note the syncopations and the distinct articulations. The harmonies here should be familiar. Practice improvising new melodies over the bass line. This folk song was originally sung in $\frac{5}{4}$ meter in order to imitate the awkward gate of a cockroach missing its sixth leg.

Example 5.10.   Waldmann, "Mit Sing und Sang" (excerpt 2)

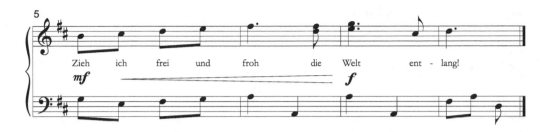

* *Translation*: With singing and song and the sound of Lieder, free and happy I travel the entire world! Be mindful of the balance between parts, particularly the bass and the upper voices.

Example 5.11.   Michael Praetorius (c. 1571–1621), "Lo, How a Rose" (1609)

* This tune was originally written without a notated meter. The shifting meters notated here are an editorial tradition but present certain challenges to the singer. Start by underlining those notes that should be accented (here, the text acts as an excellent guide), and then sing in two parts (or sing and play), while slightly emphasizing the changing accents and the rhythmic disagreement between the parts.

Example 5.12.   George Gershwin (1898–1937), "I Got Rhythm," from *Girl Crazy* (1930)

* The syncopated rhythm here may require practice (and, for those with jazz experience, may be swung). Note how the measures are divided into groupings of eighth notes (twos and threes). For instance: m. 1 goes 2+3+3 whereas m. 2 goes 3+3+2. Practice the groups of twos and threes, conducting them slowly at first. Then conduct in four while listening to or playing the bass. Finally, explain below why the relationship between rhythm and meter becomes more regular in m. 7.

Example 5.13.   Wolfgang Amadeus Mozart (1756–1791), Serenade no. 1, K. 250, Trio

* Sing this in three parts. The chromatic passing tone in m. 5 is optional but is simple and lovely. Pay close attention to the structure of this excerpt. How long are the phrases and subphrases? Do any repeat?

Example 5.14.   Burt Bacharach (b. 1928), "I Say a Little Prayer for You" (1967)

* Note that m. 10 might also be notated as two quarter-note triplets (three quarter notes in the space
of two). If you are familiar with this sort of triplet, try singing it this way. The shifting meter in this
excerpt (and in this song as a whole) is very clever. Try clapping along with a steady beat, and see how
the metric shifts and syncopations move the clapping to the off-beat and back again. Why do you suppose that this is a fairly common feature of Bacharach's music?

Example 5.15.   Joseph Haydn (1732–1809), String Quartet no. 31, op. 20, no. 1, mvt. 1

* Pay especially close attention to the use of the alto clef in the viola line. You may want to review the clef exercises in the Foundations of Aural Skills chapter of this book before trying this line.

Example 5.16.   Franz Schubert (1797–1828), "Der Lindenbaum," from *Winterreise* (1828)

Ich musst' auch heu-te wan-dern vor-bei in tie-fer Nacht, da

hab' ich noch im Dun-kel die Au – gen zu-ge-macht.

* *Translation*: Also today I had to wander past it in the deep night, even in the darkness I had to close my eyes.

CHORALE WORKSHOP: THREE-CHORD TONIC EXPANSIONS USING INVERTED V TRIADS

Play the following progressions on the piano in simple major and minor keys. Try placing each listed melodic pattern in the soprano voice. Note that the four-voice versions of many of these paradigms will use doublings that are different from their root-position equivalents. In most cases, simply avoiding parallel octaves and fifths will produce the desired results. In addition to playing in four voices, try playing in two or three voices while singing the soprano pattern. Finally, as in the previous chapters, attempt to sing and play the progressions, arpeggiating each triad from the bottom up (and then top down), with the appropriate voice leading.

Harmony (bass line in left hand)	Possible soprano scale degrees (right hand)
I V^6 I	$\hat{5}$ $\hat{5}$ $\hat{5}$
or	$\hat{3}$ $\hat{2}$ $\hat{3}$
i V^6 i	$\hat{1}$ $\hat{2}$ $\hat{3}$
	$\hat{3}$ $\hat{2}$ $\hat{1}$
	$\hat{1}$ $\hat{2}$ $\hat{1}$
I^6 V^6 I	$\hat{5}$ $\hat{5}$ $\hat{5}$
or	$\hat{1}$ $\hat{2}$ $\hat{3}$
i^6 V^6 i	$\hat{1}$ $\hat{2}$ $\hat{1}$
I V i^6	$\hat{5}$ $\hat{5}$ $\hat{5}$
or	$\hat{3}$ $\hat{2}$ $\hat{1}$
i V i^6	$\hat{1}$ $\hat{2}$ $\hat{1}$
	$\hat{1}$ $\hat{7}$ $\hat{1}$
I^6 V I	$\hat{5}$ $\hat{5}$ $\hat{5}$
or	$\hat{1}$ $\hat{2}$ $\hat{3}$
i^6 V i	$\hat{1}$ $\hat{2}$ $\hat{1}$
	$\hat{1}$ $\hat{7}$ $\hat{1}$

IMPROVISATION: GAMES AND EXERCISES

1. *"Pass the triad" variation*: once the group leader has hummed a tonic, have him or her indicate whether you are to audiate a dominant or subdominant triad member. Sing the pitch and then pass the pitch to your neighbor for a while. When the group leader gives the signal, audiate a note in the tonic triad. Then sing and, on the signal, pass the pitch to your neighbors again.

2. Refer to Example 5.9 ("La Cucaracha"). Retaining the same bass and harmonic structure, improvise a new melody using a single rhythmic value. Now, try the same thing retaining the rhythms from the original melody. Eventually, you will want to add new rhythmic configurations.

IMPROVISATION: FOCUS ON RHYTHM AND METER

1. Improvise a melody over a progression using the three-note paradigms you discovered in the Chorale Workshop. Adopt the following rhythmic feel and then try using some from the earlier chapters.

2. Practice the syncopated rhythms found in the examples in this chapter and summarized below. Then compose/improvise a rhythmic round setting a text of your choosing, using each of the syncopated rhythmic shapes. What meter do they represent?

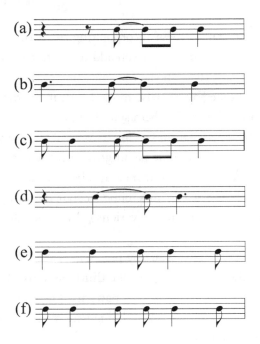

3. Now you can create a larger musical structure combining the harmonic paradigms with the rhythmic patterns above. Melodies tend to contain certain notes that are more important than others. These *structural* pitches act like the skeleton of the melody, giving it a basic shape. If you took them away, the melody would no longer be recognizable. Other pitches add to this basic shape and "embellish" it, heightening interest.

   For an example, look at the first phrase of "Good King Wenceslas," Example 4.13, and play I^6–IV–I^6 with $\hat{1}$–$\hat{1}$–$\hat{1}$ (then $\hat{1}$–$\hat{1}$–$\hat{5}$) in the soprano. See if you can hear a hint of "Good King Wenceslas" as you play this progression. Next, examine the example below, where the most important structural pitches appear

as regular-size noteheads and the others have been reduced in size. Do you recognize the I⁶–IV–I⁶ progression you've just played?

Festively

I⁶   IV   I⁶   IV   vii°⁶ I⁶

This is how you can go about incorporating the harmonic paradigms into
your compositions. The pitches that you add to the framework can be other notes
from the chord, such as the E in the first measure, or they may be other pitches,
connected to chord tones by stepwise motion. Just make sure that your "skeletal"
pitches have features that make them sound important: longer duration, sounding
on the strong beat, repetition, and so forth. Most of all, use your ears!

Activity: apply these harmonic paradigms with one chord per measure. Use the
soprano patterns above to give your melody a basic structure, but feel free to embellish. Stick strictly to the rhythms found in your rhythm piece.

4. Try a similar exercise, but using the various $\frac{3}{4}$ rhythmic "shapes" found in Example
   5.5 (Purcell round).

5. Preparation for rhythm pieces: start by practicing each part separately, paying
   close attention to the meter change in the third measure. Make sure that you emphasize the change in strong-weak beat patterns. Then try singing all four parts
   together. Finally, make up new words, being sure to retain the pattern of strong-
   and-weak syllables from the original.

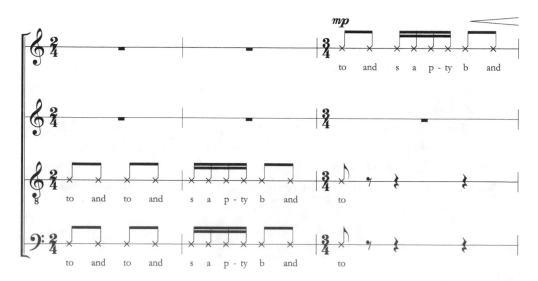

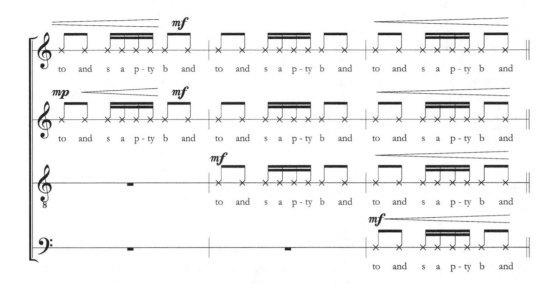

DRILLS: INTERVALS AND ARPEGGIATIONS

1. *Arpeggiation drill*: arpeggiate triads as suggested in the Chorale Workshop. Be sure to try ascending and descending arpeggiations in both major and minor.

2. *Up-down interval drill*: practice the up-down interval drill from the tonic pitch (we'll be expanding to the dominant scale degree in Chapter 8). This drill follows the same pattern and principle as seen in the master interval drill, however here you will be finding all the intervals from a single degree of the scale. Like the master interval drill, this one is designed to solidify familiarity with the diatonic intervals and their relationships to the degrees of the major scale. This drill pushes beyond the octave, linking scale degrees both above and below any particular scale degree. The drill is sung strictly in tempo. Practice this as you walk your dog, sit in the bath, or do your biology homework. Feel free to sing the drill in any key that is practicable.

UP-DOWN INTERVAL DRILL

SUGGESTED SMARTMUSIC ASSESSMENTS

Practice the following excerpts until you can sing them fluently and accurately on syllables/ scale degrees while conducting. Then complete Smartmusic assessments for the excerpts in Examples 5.2, 5.6 (outer parts), 5.7 (both parts), 5.8 (top voice), 5.9 (bass only), 5.10 (bass only), 5.11 (melody), 5.16 (both parts), and 5.15 (viola part only)—for 5.15, we encourage you to sing note names instead of scale degrees or syllables. Watch out for the alto clef!

Optional additional singing: work with a trio or quartet to prepare one of these excerpts for "performance" in class: 5.3, 5.4, 5.5, 5.13, or 5.15. Your instructor may assign the excerpts so that not everyone is doing the same one. Performances like these should be *very well prepared musically*!

SHORT-TERM MUSICAL MEMORY

Fill in the key signature and clef as indicated by your instructor, and write in the initial note(s) on the basis of the given pitch and rhythm information. Note that the key and clef *may not be the same* as in the original example. Your instructor (or practice partner) will play a short progression to establish the key and then count off several beats to establish the tempo. Because of the brevity of each extract, you should have an overall impression of the rhythm, contour, and scale degrees after just one or two hearings. Notate the entire fragment.

1. Example 5.2, last two notes of m. 2 through m. 4. Starts on beat 6 (two sixteenth notes, scale degrees $\hat{3}$ and $\hat{4}$).

Clef and key
signature

2. Example 5.3, last two measures with upbeat. Starts on beat 6 (quarter note, scale degree $\hat{5}$).

Clef and key
signature

3. Example 5.5, top voice, up to downbeat of m. 4. Starts on beat 1 (dotted quarter note, scale degree $\hat{3}$).

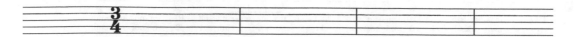

Clef and key
signature

4. Example 5.7, from just *after* the downbeat of m. 10 ("Venez, moutons") to the end, top voice. Starts on the third eighth note of the measure (scale degree î).

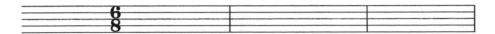

Clef and key
signature

5. Example 5.16, up to the downbeat of m. 4, top voice. Starts on an eighth-note upbeat (scale degree 5̂).

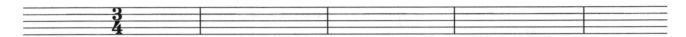

Clef and key
signature

6. Example 5.8, from upbeat to m. 9 to downbeat of m. 12, both voices. Top voice starts on eighth-note upbeat (low scale degree 6̂); bottom voice starts with a quarter note on the first downbeat (scale degree 7̂).

Clef and key
signature

7. Example 5.13, last four measures, outer voices. Both start on beat 1 (dotted half note and high scale degree 3̂ in top voice, half note and low scale degree î in bottom voice).

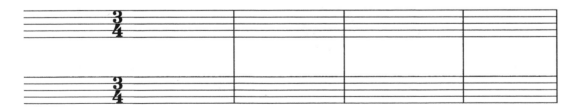

Clef and key
signature

DICTATION OF LONGER EXAMPLES

Your instructor or a classmate will choose one of the examples listed below and inform you of the key, clef, meter, first note (scale degree, rhythmic value, and metric placement) of one or more parts, and total number of measures. Use a separate piece of staff paper to write down the indicated information. You will hear a short progression to establish the key of the example, and then the example several times with breaks between hearings.

1. Example 5.4, mm. 1–8.
2. Example 5.6, all, outer voices.
3. Example 5.10, all, outer voices.
4. Example 5.15, up to beat 3 of m. 3, top two parts. Both start with quarter notes on beat 1 (a high scale degree $\hat{5}$ in top voice and a minor third lower in the middle voice).

Name: _____   Date: _____   Instructor: _____

CONTEXTUAL LISTENING 5.1

Ludwig van Beethoven (1770–1827), String Quartet in G major, op. 18, no. 2, mvt. 4

Beethoven's String Quartet op. 18 no. 2 in G major was written between 1798 and 1800. It is one of the most traditionally classical of the composer's quartets. The fourth movement juxtaposes two motives, one based on simple arpeggiations and the other on a more stepwise filling in of an ascending fifth, or its inversion, a descending fourth.

1. How many measures are in this duple-meter excerpt?

   a. 6   b. 8   c. 10   d. 12   e. 16

2. The melody starts with an arpeggiation of which harmony?

   a. V   b. IV   c. V⁷   d. I

3. What harmony is arpeggiated in the melody beginning in m. 5?

   a. V   b. IV   c. V⁷   d. I

4. What harmony supports m. 1? In which measure does this initial harmony change? When does the original harmony finally return in root position?

   Harmony in m. 1: _____.

   New harmony begins in m. _____.

   Initial harmony returns in m. _____.

5. Accurately transcribe the melody (only) in G major. You will find two recordings, one of a simplified arrangement and the other of an actual string quartet. Attempt to complete the transcription within six hearings.

Name: _____ Date: _____ Instructor: _____

CONTEXTUAL LISTENING 5.2

"Great Tom Is Cast" (traditional round)

This traditional English round tells of the casting of the seventh, and largest, bell in the Tom bell tower in Oxford, England.

1. How many voices are in this round? (Start by counting entrances.)

   a. 2   (b. 3)   c. 4   d. 5   e. 6

2. Only one voice performs the entire melody in its entirety without any repeats. Which voice is it?

   a. 1   b. 2   (c. 3)   d. 4   e. 5

3. Describe what happens in the other voices. When do they come in? How much do they repeat, or where do they get cut off?

   they come in at the beginning of the second bar of the melody. they repeat the melody

4. Not counting any repeats, how many measures are in the entire melody (in common time)?

   a. 2   b. 4   (c. 5)   d. 6   e. 8

5. The first note in the melody is an F♯4 and lasts a half note. Accurately transcribe the melody and rhythm in the appropriate key (with the appropriate key signature). There is no need to notate the additional voices or any repeats of the melody.

6. In order to experience the intersection between rhythm and meter in a different domain, try writing an appropriate text for this round. Make sure that you do not accent any normally unaccented syllables. Then prepare to sing this round in class.

   great tom is cast, and christ church
   bells ring 1, 2, 3, 4, 5, 6 and tom
   comes last

149

EXPANDING THE REPERTOIRE 5.3

Beethoven, "Für Elise," Bagatelle no. 25 in A minor (1810)

Nas, "I Can" (2003)

"Für Elise" is one of Beethoven's most instantly recognized pieces. Although generally known by that name, this piece is a *bagatelle*, which is a short, light, and mellow piece. Nas uses part of "Für Elise" as background for his song "I Can."

1. What is the simple meter of this piece?

$$\mathbf{\frac{9}{8}} \quad \mathbf{\frac{6}{4}} \quad \mathbf{\frac{12}{8}} \quad \mathbf{\frac{4}{4}} \quad \mathbf{\frac{3}{4}} \quad \boxed{\mathbf{\frac{3}{8}}}$$

2. Transcribe the first thirteen measures of "Für Elise" (melody and accompaniment) following the rhythmic figuration provided. Make sure to include the meter signature, and write in the Roman numerals in the blanks below the staff. The piece is in A minor.

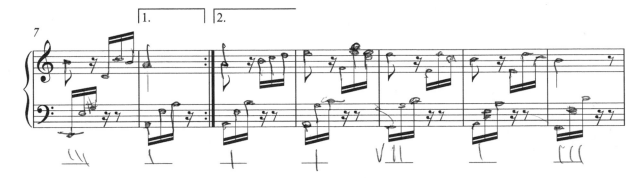

3. *Expanding the Repertoire question*: listen to Nas's "I Can." This song adjusts "Für Elise" to accommodate an alternative meter and key. What meter? How did the arranger achieve this? In what key is this arrangement?

4/4 and C major the arranger

F# minor/a major the arranger achieved this by moving it up a 6th

4. *Optional assignment 1*: compose a new melody, keeping the exact same rhythmic figuration, harmonic progression, and accompaniment pattern (in A minor). Copy the Roman numerals from above in the blanks below the staff.

5. *Optional assignment 2*: try to transpose and play the piece in any key up to two sharps or two flats. Start with the accompaniment, and then, once you feel confident, attempt to transpose the melody. It is quite helpful to recognize the scale degree (or solfège syllable) for each note. Take any tempo that feels comfortable.

EXPANDING THE REPERTOIRE 5.4

Elton John, "Rocket Man" (1972)

This song, by Elton John and Bernie Taupin, recounts a world in which a career as an astronaut is rather humdrum. The lyrics, based loosely on a short story by Ray Bradbury, reflect the thoughts of a Mars-bound man who is taking leave of his family. The rhythm of this excerpt, characteristic of the John/Taupin songs of this period, is particularly syncopated.

1. In what meter is this seven-measure excerpt?

$$\frac{9}{8} \qquad \frac{6}{4} \qquad \frac{12}{8} \qquad \frac{4}{4} \qquad \frac{3}{4}$$

2. Map out the overall structure of the chorus in as much detail as possible, focusing on repetition versus new material.

3. The melody of this excerpt is quite syncopated. Notate the rhythm of the melody's *first measure* only.

4. List the scale degrees used in the melody.

5. Now, listen to the reduced version. Transcribe the pitches and rhythm of the entire bass part for the reduced version in the key of F major.

6. *For extra credit,* try to identify, and write beneath the staff, the Roman numerals of the harmonies underlying each bass note.

Chapter 6

The Octave and Beyond

The excerpts in this chapter include all the diatonic scale degrees. There are a number of rounds, canons, and catches in this chapter, and you will want to use them as an opportunity to refine your multipart singing. Be sure to work on balance and independent pitch control. As you have in previous chapters, you will want to continue practicing basic rhythmic shapes. At this point, you should also be carefully considering the harmonic context of the melodies (particularly, but not exclusively, for the excerpts in a homophonic texture). Take the time to label the Roman numerals before singing. As you do this, examine the overall shape of the phrases. Do they have *internal* inconclusive closure (cadences)? Do they *end* conclusively or inconclusively? You will see a number of periods (pairs of phrases in an antecedent-consequent relationship) in this chapter, wherein the antecedent (the first half of the period) comes to an inconclusive cadence and the second half, the consequent, restarts the material of the first half but then brings it to a conclusive cadence. Try improvising consequents to a particular antecedent. You can start by improvising parallel consequents, which start very similarly to their antecedents, but then branch out to contrasting consequents that do not begin the same as their antecedents, usually by manipulating a motive or expanding the approach to the cadence. Finally, you will be working on the harmonic paradigms that often support phrases of the type described above: extensions of the I–IV–V–I (i–iv–V–i) through the addition of first-inversion triads.

Example 6.1.   Henry Purcell (1659–1695), "Upon Christ Church Bells in Oxford" (round
                in three voices)

Example 6.2.   Traditional English round in three voices

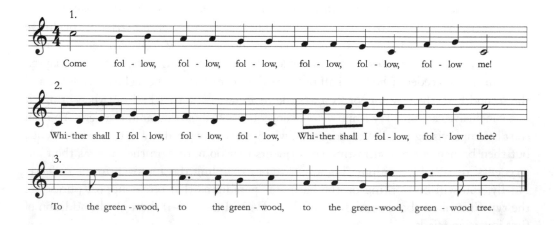

Example 6.3.   Traditional English round in three voices (eighteenth century).

Now, now we are met and hu - mours a - gree, Call,

Fill, fill it a - bout, to me let it come, Fill the

A health to the King, round, round let it pass, Fill it

call for wine, and lose no time, but let's mer - ry be;   *to line 2*

glass to the top: I'll drink ev-'ry drop su - per - na - cu - lum.   *to line 3*

up, and then drink it off like men, ne - ver balk your glass.   *da capo*

* This catch (round) is set up in the traditional way, with multiple staves so that you can easily see the harmonies created by the coincidence of the three parts. All groups start by singing the entirety in unison. Then one group starts at the beginning and sings all three lines in sequence, with the second group starting from the beginning when the first group reaches the "2" in the second line of the score, and so forth. Note the clever internal rhymes in this jovial text. This type of word play is characteristic of the catch genre.

Example 6.4.   Purcell, "When V and I" (round in three voices)

* Can you figure out Purcell's math? Note the play with the Roman numerals. Also note the direct motion from the subtonic (or lowered-seventh scale degree) to the leading tone (raised-seventh scale degree) in m. 4. Practice singing a C minor scale with both a lowered and a raised seventh.

Example 6.5. Wolfgang Amadeus Mozart (1756–1791), round in three voices

Example 6.6.   Johannes Ockeghem (c. 1410–1497), "Benediktiner Munklikör," also known
as "Hava Nashira" (round in three voices)

* This round was originally devoted to Ockeghem's favorite drink, "Benediktiner Munklikör" (Bene-
dictine monk liquor). More recently, Hebrew lyrics have been added and the tune has become an (unlikely) liturgical hit.

Example 6.7.   Traditional round in three voices

Example 6.8.   Traditional seventeenth-century round in four voices

Example 6.9.   Traditional round in three voices

* Note the literal and filled-in arpeggiations throughout this round. Try identifying each of them with a Roman numeral. How are these harmonies supported in the other parts?

Example 6.10.   Traditional round in three voices

Example 6.11.   "The Orchestra," traditional round in five voices

* Many of the longer rounds in the book are set up in multiple staves so that you can easily discern the
harmonies created by the coincidence of the different lines of the round. Be sure each group sings all
five lines all the way through. For fun, try imitating the sound of the various orchestral instruments.

Example 6.12.   "Sumer is icumen in," traditional Scottish round with two-voice ostinato
(fourteenth century)

* *Translation*: Summer is coming in, loudly sings the cuckoo, cuckoo, cuckoo. . . .

      The seed grows; the meadow blossoms, and the woods alivens anew.

      The ewe bleats after the lamb; the cow lows after the calf;

      The bull leaps; the goat capers; merrily sing cuckoo!

      Well sing you, cuckoo—don't ever stop now.

      Sing cuckoo, now. . . .

      [A is the sound of the vowel in "day"

      I is the sound of the vowel in "bee"

      O is the sound of the vowel in "throw"

      U is the sound of the vowel in "spoon"]

Practice the round in parts before adding the repeating ostinato.

Example 6.13.   Clara Schumann (1819–1896), "Romance," from *Quatre pièces caractéristiques,*
                 op. 5 (1835)

* Note the beautiful harmonization of this descending scale.

Example 6.14.   Sergei Prokofiev (1891–1953), "Lieutenant Kijé" Suite, op. 60 (1934)

* Be sure to identify the arpeggiations before singing this excerpt.

Example 6.15.   Richard Rodgers (1902–1979), "If I Loved You," from *Carousel* (1945)

* The chromatic harmonies in the bass clef should be played while the melody is sung.

Example 6.16.   "Ploughman" (traditional French)

* *Translation*: Little ploughman, your furrows are not straight. Don't tell our master
                that the oxen are mine, olé!
        Ah, pull down, léo, olé!
Take special care with the changing meters in this duet.

Example 6.17.   Anonymous (fourteenth century), "Nato nobis hodie"

* *Translation*: Born to us this day of the Virgin Mary.
        For the eternal king of glory, with grateful jubilation let us give thanks to God.

Practice the rhythm of mm. 6, 7, and 15 separately before singing this duet. This duet was originally in the Lydian mode. Try singing the two B♭s as B♮s.

Example 6.18.   Robert Cornysh (1465–1523), English partsong

A dew, a dew, my har-tis lust, A dew my joy and my sol-ace. wyth du-byl so-row com-playn I must, Un-tyl I dye_____ a-las, a-las.

Example 6.19.   Josquin des Prez (c. 1450–1521), "Et incarnatus est," from *Missa Pange lin-gua* (c. 1515)

Et in-car-na-tus est de Spi-ri-tu san-cto ex Ma-ri-a Vir-gi-ne: Ex ho-mo fac-tus est.

* *Translation*: And (he) was incarnate by the Holy Ghost, from the Virgin Mary: and was made man
   This mass was originally written without a notated meter, which results in the irregular meter of the excerpt above. You will want to start by determining how many half notes are in each measure, and then mark the syllables and metric spots that require additional accent. Be sure to learn all four parts. Also, try singing one part while playing the others.

Example 6.20.   Ludwig van Beethoven (1770–1827), Trio, WoO 37, mvt. 3 (1786)

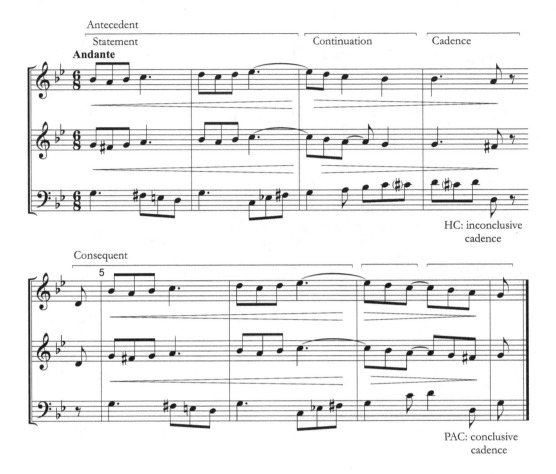

* Note the antecedent-consequent (parallel period) design of this and the following excerpt. The arrival on a root-position V as well as scale degree $\hat{2}$ in the upper voice signals a half cadence. A restart of the melodic material leads to a compressed cadential section in the consequent, followed by a root-position V to I motion (a perfect authentic cadence or PAC). Beethoven has included a chromatic passing tone in m. 3 and a chromatic neighbor in m. 4. You may choose to sing C-naturals here, but the C-sharps add a nice bit of spice. Use the syllables "raise" or "fi" for the C-sharps.

Example 6.21.   Robert Schumann (1810–1856), "Knecht Ruprecht," op. 68, no. 12 (1848)

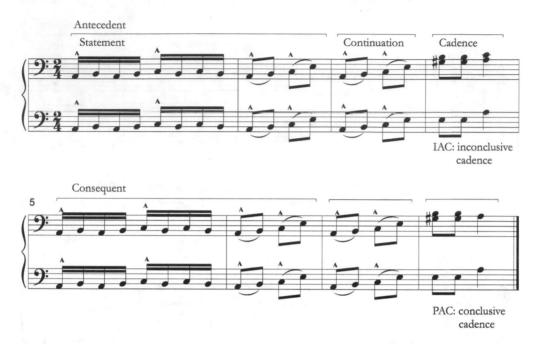

* This is another parallel period, but here, the inconclusive cadence at the end of the antecedent is an imperfect authentic cadence (IAC), signaled by the root position V–I arrival, accompanied by scale degree $\hat{3}$ in the top voice.

Example 6.22.   Joseph Haydn (1732–1809), Piano Sonata in C, Hob. XVI: 35 (1780), mvt. 1

* Although the first half of this excerpt looks like a typical antecedent, the initial arrival on V in m. 3 is "too early" for a proper half cadence. Indeed, try singing the rhythm by itself and decide where you would imagine the arrival of V (probably on the downbeat of m. 4). What follows is quite contrasting, further evidence that this is no typical period! Try improvising a parallel consequent in the final four measures (that is, starting with the same material as the antecedent, but coming to a PAC on the tonic). Why do you suppose Haydn chose not to write a typical period here?

Example 6.23. Haydn, Symphony no. 95 (1791), mvt. 3

* Note how the tonic pedal point (repeated tonic) in the first four measures precludes any sense of arrival in m. 4, thwarting what otherwise might have been conceived as an antecedent.

CHORALE WORKSHOP: TONIC-SUBDOMINANT-DOMINANT PROGRESSIONS USING INVERTED TRIADS

Working at a piano, play the following progressions in simple major and minor keys. Try placing the listed melodic patterns in the soprano voice. Note that the four-voice versions of many of these progressions cannot be used in close position on the piano and may use doublings that are different from their root-position equivalents. You should do your best to avoid parallels, doubled leading tones, and augmented seconds (in minor); in order to achieve this, you may need to leave the fifth off of some root-position chords. Since the voice leading here is complicated, your focus should be on the relationship of the outer voices. Be sure that you can play the outer voices correctly and that you can sing one of the outer voices while playing the other. Finally, attempt to sing the progressions or play them on your instrument, arpeggiating each triad from the bottom up (and then from the top down). Again, do your best with the voice leading, but focus on the outer voices.

Harmony (bass line in left hand)	Possible soprano scale degrees (right hand)
I IV^6 V I	$\hat{5}$ $\hat{4}$ $\hat{2}$ $\hat{3}$
or	$\hat{5}$ $\hat{4}$ $\hat{2}$ $\hat{1}$
i iv^6 V i	$\hat{3}$ $\hat{4}$ $\hat{2}$ $\hat{3}$
	$\hat{3}$ $\hat{4}$ $\hat{2}$ $\hat{1}$
	$\hat{1}$ $\hat{1}$ $\hat{7}$ $\hat{1}$

I IV⁶ V I⁶	$\hat{5}$ $\hat{4}$ $\hat{2}$ $\hat{1}$
or	$\hat{3}$ $\hat{4}$ $\hat{2}$ $\hat{5}$
i iv⁶ V i⁶	$\hat{3}$ $\hat{4}$ $\hat{2}$ $\hat{1}$
	$\hat{1}$ $\hat{1}$ $\hat{7}$ $\hat{1}$
I IV V I⁶	$\hat{5}$ $\hat{6}$ $\hat{5}$ $\hat{5}$
or	$\hat{5}$ $\hat{4}$ $\hat{2}$ $\hat{1}$
i iv V i⁶	$\hat{3}$ $\hat{4}$ $\hat{2}$ $\hat{1}$
	$\hat{1}$ $\hat{1}$ $\hat{7}$ $\hat{1}$
I IV⁶ V⁶ I	$\hat{5}$ $\hat{4}$ $\hat{2}$ $\hat{3}$
or	$\hat{5}$ $\hat{4}$ $\hat{2}$ $\hat{1}$
i IV⁶ V⁶ i*	$\hat{3}$ $\hat{4}$ $\hat{2}$ $\hat{3}$
(bass: $\hat{1}$ ↑$\hat{6}$ ↑$\hat{7}$ $\hat{1}$)	$\hat{3}$ $\hat{4}$ $\hat{2}$ $\hat{1}$
	$\hat{1}$ $\hat{4}$ $\hat{2}$ $\hat{3}$
	$\hat{1}$ $\hat{4}$ $\hat{2}$ $\hat{1}$
	$\hat{1}$ $\hat{1}$ $\hat{2}$ $\hat{3}$
	$\hat{1}$ $\hat{1}$ $\hat{2}$ $\hat{1}$

* The i–IV⁶–V⁶–i progression in minor makes use of the raised sixth scale degree, producing a major subdominant chord.

Harmony (bass line in left hand)	Possible soprano scale degrees (right hand)
I⁶ IV V I	$\hat{5}$ $\hat{6}$ $\hat{5}$ $\hat{3}$
or	$\hat{5}$ $\hat{4}$ $\hat{2}$ $\hat{3}$
i⁶ iv V i:	$\hat{5}$ $\hat{4}$ $\hat{2}$ $\hat{1}$
	$\hat{1}$ $\hat{1}$ $\hat{7}$ $\hat{1}$
I⁶ IV V I⁶	$\hat{5}$ $\hat{6}$ $\hat{5}$ $\hat{3}$
or	$\hat{5}$ $\hat{4}$ $\hat{2}$ $\hat{1}$
i⁶ iv V i⁶	$\hat{1}$ $\hat{1}$ $\hat{7}$ $\hat{1}$

IMPROVISATION: GAMES AND EXERCISES

1. *"Pass the pitch"*: as with "pass the triad," you will sit or stand in a small group. Then, without any particular tonic established, each individual audiates a single, sustained pitch. On a signal from the group leader or instructor, each individual sings or plays his or her pitch out loud (the resulting harmony is likely to be dissonant). The group leader or instructor will then signal a switch, and each member of the group will adopt the pitch of the person on the left. Once this is mastered, the group leader or instructor can begin to vary the directions of the switch (left, right, across). You may wish to assign a range to each individual (soprano, alto, tenor, bass).

2. Improvise a melody over a progression using the paradigms you discovered in the Chorale Workshop. Consider adopting a rhythmic feel from the earlier chapters.

3. Improvise (or compose) parallel and contrasting consequents to the antecedents found in Examples 1.2, 1.4, 2.6, 2.7, 2.9, 2.10, 3.11, 4.9, 4.11, 6.20, 6.21, 6.22, and 6.23.

IMPROVISATION: FOCUS ON RHYTHM AND METER

1. Improvise a melody over a progression using the harmonic patterns you discovered in the Chorale Workshop. Adopt the following rhythmic feel and then try using some from the earlier chapters. Note that, like many of the rhythmic feels, the pattern has been slightly simplified. Once you have the rhythm as notated, consider tying each sixteenth to the following eighth.

Rhumba (fast)

2. Practice the triplet rhythms from Example 6.17 above (mm. 6, 7, and 15). Now compose or improvise a rhythmic round, setting a text of your choosing. Each measure should include a single eighth-note triplet, but the triplet should not fall on the same beat in successive measures. All three of the triplet rhythms from Example 6.17 should be incorporated at least once.

3. Now apply the harmonic paradigms above to your rhythmic piece, with one chord per measure. Use the soprano patterns to give your melody a basic structure, but feel free to embellish. Stick strictly to the rhythms found in your rhythm piece.

4. *Preparation for rhythm pieces*: start by practicing each of the three lines below by itself. Watch the tricky changes of meter across the line breaks. Now take the three lines below and reorder them (say, line two, then three, then one), using each line twice in each of *two* separate voices so that you can construct a fourteen-measure, two-voice rhythmic canon. Make up new words, being sure to retain the strong-and-weak syllables of the original. Finally, perform your rhythmic canon with a partner.

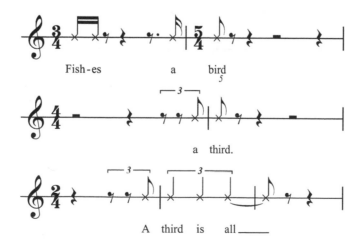

DRILLS: INTERVALS AND ARPEGGIATIONS

1. *Arpeggiation drill*: arpeggiate triads as suggested in the Chorale Workshop. Be sure to try ascending and descending arpeggiations in both major and minor.
2. *Up-down interval drill*: once you have mastered the up-down interval drill from the tonic pitch, you may attempt it from the dominant. This will be formally introduced in Chapter 8.
3. Make certain you have *mastered* all the intervals in the master interval drill.

SUGGESTED SMARTMUSIC ASSESSMENTS

1. Prepare all parts of the excerpts in this chapter to be sung on scale degrees or syllables in class (you may prefer to play the lower parts of Example 6.15 while singing). Don't forget any performance markings and consider the harmonic underpinnings where possible. Then complete SmartMusic assessments as follows: 6.1, 6.3, 6.4, 6.7, 6.10, 6.15 (melody), 6.20 (all three parts), and 6.21 (both parts). *Note*: extra sight-singing credit may be given for any group that prepares and records itself singing one of the rounds from Chapter 6. Consider posting the recording online on a public or class-only website.
2. Complete SmartMusic assessments as follows: 6.12 (just the round, not the ostinato), 6.13 (outer parts), 6.16 (outer parts), 6.18 (outer parts), 6.22 (outer parts), and 6.23 (all three parts).

SHORT-TERM MUSICAL MEMORY

Fill in the key signature and clef as indicated by your instructor, and write in the initial note(s) on the basis of the given pitch and rhythm information. Note that the key and clef *may not be the same* as in the original example. Your instructor (or practice partner) will play a short progression to establish the key and then count off several beats to establish the tempo. Because of the brevity of each extract, you should have an overall impression of the rhythm, contour, and scale-degree numbers after just one or two hearings. Notate the entire fragment.

1. Example 6.1, last two notes of m. 6 through m. 8. Starts on beat 4 (two eighth notes, scale degrees $\hat{5}$ and $\hat{4}$).

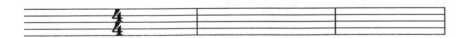

Clef and key
   signature

2. Example 6.3, middle staff, last two notes of m. 7 through m. 10. Starts on beat 3 (two eighth notes, scale degrees $\hat{3}$ and $\hat{4}$).

Clef and key
signature

3. Example 6.7, up to beat 4 of m. 2. Starts on beat 1 (quarter note, high scale degree $\hat{1}$).

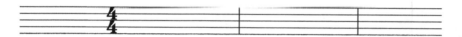

Clef and key
signature

4. Example 6.8, m. 5 up to downbeat of m. 7. Starts on beat 1 (dotted quarter note, scale degree $\hat{5}$).

Clef and key
signature

5. Example 6.12, mm. 5–8. Starts on beat 1 (quarter note, scale degree $\hat{1}$).

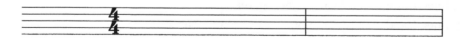

Clef and key
signature

6. Example 6.15, mm. 3–4, top voice. Starts on beat 1 (quarter note tied to a triplet-eighth, high scale degree $\hat{1}$).

Clef and key
signature

7. Example 6.14, mm. 1–2, both voices. Starts on beat 1 (dotted quarter note on low scale degree $\hat{5}$ in top voice; whole note a perfect fifth or perfect twelfth lower in bottom voice).

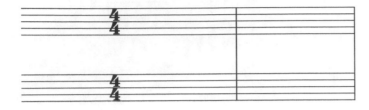

Clef and key
signature

8. Example 6.16, mm. 3–4, both voices. Both voices start with quarter notes on beat 1 (scale degree $\hat{3}$ in top voice, and a minor tenth lower in bottom voice).

Clef and key
signature

DICTATION OF LONGER EXAMPLES

Your instructor or a classmate will choose one of the examples listed below and inform you of the key, clef, meter, first note (scale degree, rhythmic value, and metric placement) of one or more parts, and total number of measures. Use a separate piece of staff paper to write down the indicated information. You will hear a short progression to establish the key of the example, and then the example several times with breaks between hearings.

1. Example 6.2, mm. 1–8.
2. Example 6.4, all, lines 1 and/or 3 (separately or together).
3. Example 6.6, all, lines 1 and 2 together. Notate line 2 above line 1.
4. Example 6.9, lines 2 and 3 together (transpose line 3 down an octave). Both voices start with dotted half notes on beat 1 (scale degree $\hat{5}$ in top voice, and a perfect twelfth lower in bottom voice).
5. Example 6.12, mm. 11–18.
6. Example 6.13, all, outer voices.
7. Example 6.18, last four measures, outer voices.

Name: _____ Date: _____ Instructor: _____

CONTEXTUAL LISTENING 6.1

Orlando di Lasso (1532–1594), "Célébrons sans cesse" (1576)

Lasso was a Franco-Flemish composer of the late Renaissance, known for his master of polyphonic contrapuntal vocal works. This multivoice canon has a wonderful syncopation that reflects the text: "Celebrate without ceasing the gift of God!"

1. How many voices are in this canon (start by counting entrances)?

    a. 2   b. 3   c. 4   d. 5   e. 6

2. Accurately transcribe the principal melody and rhythm in the key of F major (cut time), by filling in the blanks in the staves below. Note that the other voices sometimes reach over the main melodic line, so use the notes below to help you.

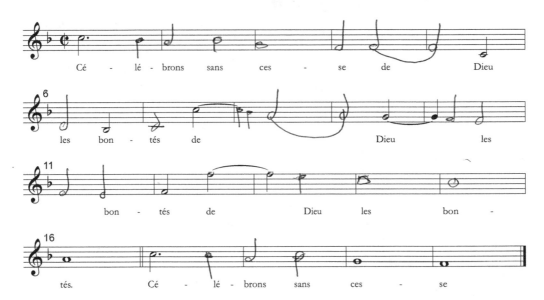

3. Describe what happens in the other voices. When do they come in? How much do they repeat or where do they get cut off?

    the other voices come after the first phrase of the melody is over, then repeat the first two lines

4. Be prepared to sing this canon in class. Note that you may add one additional voice when performing in class.

175

CONTEXTUAL LISTENING 6.2

Leopold Mozart (1719–1787), "Bourrée," from the
Notebook for Wolfgang Amadeus Mozart

Leopold Mozart, father of Wolfgang Amadeus Mozart, was an accomplished composer
and respected teacher in Salzburg. This excerpt features a familiar eighteenth-century
dance type, the bourrée.

1. How many measures are in this common-time excerpt?

   (a. 8)   b. 12   c. 14   ~~d. 16~~   e. 20

2. Does it start on an upbeat or downbeat (circle one)?

   ↘ (Upbeat)   ~~Downbeat~~

3. This dance is divided into two-measure units, several of which return in this excerpt. Assign each two-measure unit a lowercase letter (giving similar melodic
   material the same letter), and map out the structure of the excerpt by describing
   the order in which the two-measure units occur. Be sure to identify any cadences.

   a. ab cd   *they happen in order with clear change in the bassline and dynamics*

4. The harmonic rhythm is essentially two harmonies per bar, except in one two-
   measure unit that emphasizes a single harmony (this two-measure unit is repeated). Using Roman numerals or notating the bass part in the key of G minor
   (on the staves on the next page), attempt to identify which two harmonies are
   present in each measure. You are not responsible for identifying inversions.

5. Now, accurately transcribe the melody (both pitches and rhythm) in the key of G
   minor (4/4 time) on the staves on the next page.

6. For extra credit, describe how this excerpt exemplifies the dance type known as the bourrée.

CONTEXTUAL LISTENING 6.3

Wolfgang Amadeus Mozart (1756–1791), "Eine kleine Nachtmusik," K. 525, mvt. 2

Although W. A. Mozart's 1787 chamber work is very famous today, it was not published until 1827. The title is often translated as "a little night music," but a more proper translation is "a little serenade." The second movement is a "Romanze" in a rondo form (ABACA), from which this excerpt is the refrain.

This excerpt is in C major, and the opening anacrusis lasts a single half-note beat (in cut time), with the rhythm eighth, eighth rest, eighth, eighth rest. The rhythm for the entire excerpt is tricky, so you may want to jot that down separately.

1. How many measures are in this cut-time excerpt?

   a. 7   b. 8   (c. 9)   d. 10   e. 11

2. Map out the overall structure of the excerpt in as much detail as possible, showing any cadences and repeated musical material. You should include all of this vocabulary in your excerpt map: half cadence, PAC, antecedent, consequent, period. You may want to review Example 6.21.

   A – B – B – A

3. Accurately transcribe the melody (both pitches and rhythm) in the key of C major on the staves on the next page.

4. The cello voice (the bass) is relatively subtle (since it holds a tonic pedal) and becomes more active only in the measure(s) before the cadence(s). Notate just the bass voice in the measure(s) leading up to any cadence(s), and, of course, notate the arrival pitch at the cadence(s).

5. For extra credit, where possible identify with a Roman numeral the harmony underlying each bass note.

EXPANDING THE REPERTOIRE 6.4

> Cole Porter (1891–1964), "Wunderbar," from *Kiss Me, Kate* (1948),
> mm. 1–16 of refrain

Kiss Me, Kate was Cole Porter's most successful musical, winning the Tony Award for Best Musical in 1949 and surprising many critics who claimed he had passed his prime. In the musical, Fred, the egotistical director of a Broadway show, sings this song with Lilli, an old flame. They are remembering an operetta they performed together years earlier. Porter references the operetta through the song's recall of the Viennese waltz as well as its German keyword and title.

   You may wish to listen to the original Broadway recording (Sony, with Alfred Drake and Patricia Morrison singing), starting at 0:33. This recording takes a number of interesting liberties with Porter's notated melody.

1. What type of meter is found in this excerpt?

   a. Simple duple   b. Simple triple   c. Simple quadruple   d. Compound

2. Porter cleverly avoids the tonic pitch in the melody until a very critical point (on the word "Wunderbar"). List two ways in which he avoids the tonic pitch in the melody.

   he avoids this by dancing over the tonic with using different scale degrees

3. In what measure does the melody's tonic pitch finally arrive? When does it appear above a tonic harmony? Speculate as to why he may have treated the melody's tonic in this way.

   mm. most likely to bring importance to the specific measure

4. Accurately transcribe the melody (both pitches and rhythm) in the key of G major (starting in the octave directly above middle C).

5. Now, consider the harmonic structure of the excerpt. Each measure supports only a single harmony, either tonic or dominant. Underneath your melody, supply the accurate Roman numeral, either I or V. Do not worry about inversions. Note that both mm. 5 and 6 could be heard to have a harmonic shift on the final beat of the measure, so concentrate on the downbeats in these measures.

6. For extra credit, do some research and list at least two important ways in which the excerpt refers musically to the Viennese waltz.

EXPANDING THE REPERTOIRE 6.5

Andrew Lloyd Webber (b. 1948), "Memory," from *Cats* (1981),
first complete phrase (ends with "live again")

In Webber's award winning musical *Cats,* Grizabella sings this song while she recalls her glamorous past with nostalgia. In this excerpt, she sings of the current state in her upper range, dropping into the lower range to sing of the "old days" when she was "beautiful."

1. This excerpt is in *compound quadruple* meter. Be sure to listen for the larger beat; don't get thrown off by the smaller subdivisions. Which note value represents the beat? How many beats are in a measure?

   a. ♪ (eighth), twelve beats   b. ♩ (half), four beats
   c. o (whole), three beats   d. ♩. (dotted quarter), four beats

2. From your answer to question 1, what is the time signature for this excerpt?

3. How many measures are in this excerpt?

   a. 4   b. 8   c. 10   d. 12   e. 16

4. The same basic rhythmic motive is used three times in the excerpt. List the places where the rhythmic motive is used. Notate the rhythm of the motive.

   1: MM 1 ♩. ♩♩♩♩ , 2: MM 2 ♩. ♩♩♩ , and 3: MM 3 ♩.♩ ♩♩♩ .

5. The bass supports the use of the rhythmic motive, which is replayed at three different pitch levels (this is called a descending-third sequence). On which three scale degrees in the bass does the rhythmic motive start?

   a. $\hat{1}, \hat{7}, \hat{6}$ b. $\hat{5}, \hat{4}, \hat{3}$ c. $\hat{5}, \hat{3}, \hat{1}$ d. $\hat{1}, \hat{6}, \hat{4}$ e. $\hat{3}, \hat{2}, \hat{1}$

6. Webber uses some nonstandard counterpoint between the outer voices in mm. 3–4. Describe the relationship between the voices as they move from m. 3 to m. 4. The text here is: "Memory, all alone in the moonlight, I can smile at the old days. **I was beautiful then.**" (The text from mm. 3–4 is in bold.) How might Webber's unusual counterpoint reflect the text here?

   to convey this by using the specific intervals

7. Accurately transcribe the melody (both pitches and rhythm) in the key of C major, with the melody starting on C5 (i.e., the C one octave above middle C).

Chapter 7
Complete Examples from the Repertoire

This chapter presents several complete examples from the repertoire to be used as a supplement to the materials in other chapters. As such, there are no additional exercises or drills. Although the shorter examples are similar in length to some you have found earlier, all the arrangements in this chapter should be prepared to a performance standard, either in small groups or as a class. Some of these examples may include some simple chromatic motions in the lower parts. Do your best to learn them without the piano, and then check for accuracy. As explained earlier in the book, you may wish to use the syllable "raise" for a sharp and "low" for a flat. In solfège, you may add some adjusted syllables when ascending chromatically: *di, ri, fi, si, li*. When descending, use the adjusted syllables *te, le, se, me* ("may"), *ra*. The two rhythm pieces at the end of the chapter are quite involved and will require some practice. Be sure to follow the performance directions carefully. As always, focus on the basic rhythmic shapes.

Example 7.1.   Henry Bishop (1786–1855) and John Howard Payne (1791–1852), "There's No Place Like Home," from *Clari, Maid of Milan* (1823)

Example 7.2.   Henry Purcell (1659–1695), "At the Close of the Evening" (round in three voices)

* Remember that, as before, each voice sings all three parts. Start by singing the entirety in unison, and then begin your round as usual.

Example 7.3.   "The Snowstorm Is Blowing," traditional Russian

* *Translation*: The Snowstorm is blowing down the street. My sweetheart is walking there. (Stop, don't walk, my darling. Let me look at you, my joy!)

Note the arrivals on natural $\hat{7}$ in mm. 8 and 16, where it temporarily functions as V of G (or III).

Example 7.4. Jerome Kern (1885–1945), "Look for the Silver Lining," from *Sally* (1920)

* This song by the famous Broadway composer Jerome Kern essentially presents a large-scale parallel period (with variations, of course). The first sixteen measures present a large antecedent and the following sixteen measures present a large consequent. Note though, as with many of the songs of this era, the arrival on the V is in m. 15, and the arrival of I is in m. 31 (both arrivals are one measure "too early"). How does Kern manipulate the two halves of the period so that they present even sixteen-measure units?

Example 7.5. Franz Schubert (1797–1828), "An die Musik," op. 88 no. 4, D. 547 (1817)

* *Translation*: You hallowed art, in how many gray hours, while into life's wild circle I am hurled,
        Have you my heart to warm love reignited, to transport me into a better world!
        Often has a sigh from your harp drifted, a sweet, holy chord from you,
        To heaven's better times my soul uplifted, you hallowed art, my thanks to you for this.

Example 7.6.   "The First Noël" (Traditional, arr. John Stainer, 1871)

* Once you can sing the familiar melody with appropriate syllables, try singing each of the other parts. The tenor part is often sung in the octave above the melody as a descant; try playing the melody while singing the tenor line this way.

Example 7.7.   John Dowland (1563–1626), "Humour Say" (1597)

1st Voice:	O I am as heavy as earth; Say then, who is Humour now?
2nd Voice:	I am now inclined to mirth, humour I as well as thou.
1st Voice:	Why then 'tis I am drowned in woe.
2nd Voice:	No, no, Wit is cherished so.
Refrain:	But never humour yet was true, but that which only pleaseth you.

1st Voice:	Mirth then is drowned in Sorrow's brim. O in sorrow all things sleep.
2nd Voice:	No, no, fool, the light'st things swim, heavy things sink to the deep.
1st Voice:	In her presence all things smile.
2nd Voice:	Humour frolic then awhile.
Refrain:	But never humour yet was true, but that which only pleaseth you.

The bottom part was originally for lute but should be sung for this arrangement.

Example 7.8.   Ludwig van Beethoven (1770–1827), "La Marmotte," op. 52 no. 7

Translation: I have already come through many a land, with nothing but my Marmot,
and always found something to eat, with nothing but my Marmot.
With nothing here, with nothing there, with nothing but my Marmot.
A marmot is a large ground squirrel similar to a groundhog. They were typical companions for traveling organ grinders and hurdy-gurdy street performers. How does Beethoven's setting reflect on this constant companion while evoking the sound of a street organ or hurdy-gurdy? (Note that this was originally written with piano accompaniment, so the answer has to do with rhythm and harmony, rather than instrumentation.)

Example 7.9.   Thomas Fredrickson, "Such a Pretty Bird" (text by Gertrude Stein), from
Impressions for Mixed Chorus (1974)

*S a p-ty b is an abbreviation of "Such a pretty bird" and is always set to the rhythm ♪♪♪♪ ♩.
(The <u>words</u> must be spoken throughout--not the abbreviation!)

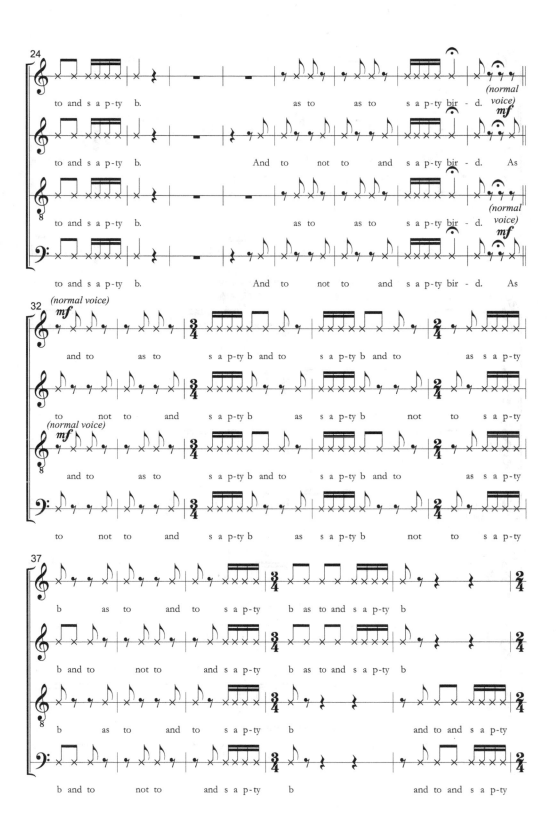

Slow (♩ = c. 46)

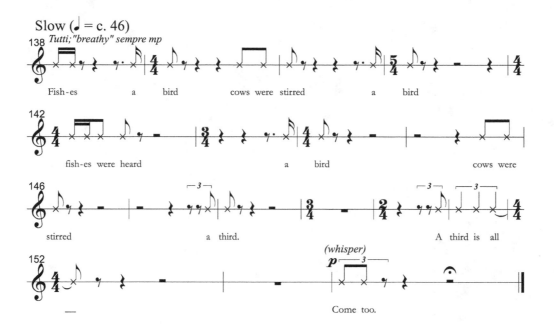

Fish-es   a   bird   cows were stirred   a   bird

fish-es were heard   a   bird   cows were

stirred   a   third.   A   third   is   all

—   Come   too.

Unit II Diatonic Contexts and Introduction to Chromatic Pitches

Chapter 8

Diatonic Sequences I

Now that you know and are comfortable with all of the diatonic scale degrees, Unit II will explore the various ways they are used in a diatonic context. This unit expands on your current understanding of phrases, moving toward larger forms. The excerpts in this chapter introduce the diatonic sequence, a frequently used technique for organizing pitches and harmonies. A sequence is simply the repetition of a musical idea at a different pitch level from the original (typically with at least two and a half iterations of the idea). Sequences can be fundamentally harmonic, melodic, or both. In a harmonic sequence, a regular interval is maintained between the chord roots of several subsequent harmonies that occur with a consistent harmonic rhythm. Typical examples include the falling-third sequence (I–vi–IV . . .) and the falling-fifth sequence (vi–ii–V–I). Melodic sequences are often accompanied by a recognizable harmonic sequence, but not always; some melodic sequences are purely linear in design. Melodic sequences typically maintain a consistent contrapuntal relationship with the bass; however, creating a repeating intervallic pattern (10th-5th and 10th-8ve between the outer voices are common possibilities). What follows in Table 8.1 are the sequence types found in this and the following chapter. You may want to look ahead to the end of Chapter 9, where you will be playing two-voice models of all these sequence types on the piano.

Sequence Type (with common variations)	Typical Root Motion	Typical Intervalic Patterns (repeated pattern of intervals between outer voices)
Descending 5ths	Down by 5th: I–IV–vii° . . .	10-8; 5-10; 8-5
Descending 5ths with initial chord in 6/3 inversion	As above, but with every other chord in first inversion: I6–IV–vii°6 . . .	6-5; 10-10; 6-8
Descending 5ths with second chord in 6/3 inversion	As above, but with the first chord in root position: I–IV6–vii° . . .	10-6; 5-6; 8-10
Descending 3ds (Pachelbel sequence!)	Down by 4th, then up by step, which yields a descending third every other chord: I–(V)–vi–(iii) . . .	10-5; 8-10; 5-8
Descending 3ds with second chord in 6/3 inversion	As above, but with every other chord in first inversion: I–(V6)–vi–(iii6) . . .	10-10; 5-6; 8-6
Ascending 2nds (5-6 sequence)	Up by step, but with intervening (but non-functional) first-inversion triads.	5-6; 8-6; 10-10
Ascending 2nds with second chord in root position	Up by step, but with intervening root-position triads: I–(vi)–ii–(vii°)–iii . . .	8-10; 10-5; 5-8
Ascending 5ths	Up by 5th: I–V–ii . . .	10-5; 5-8; 8-10

What is most important at this stage in your learning, however, is recognizing when a sequence has started or finished and using this to your advantage as you attempt to sight-sing accurately. In this chapter, not only will you want to learn all the parts of the excerpts, but you will also want to practice the excerpts carefully, singing one part while playing the other on the piano. When you are practicing, be sure to bracket all occurrences of the sequence, as well as its model (the musical idea on which the sequence is based).

Example 8.1.   "Angels We Have Heard on High" (traditional French)

* This example presents a clear descending-fifth sequence. Be sure to sing all four voices and practice singing the melody while playing the bass. Note that the melodic sequence starts earlier than the harmonic sequence in order to allow the passage to begin on tonic. Thus, the true linear pattern (10-8) doesn't become clear until the second measure. In m. 4, the bass line continues the sequential motion, moving to E, but this isn't a true continuation of the harmonic sequence. Why not?

Example 8.2.   George Frideric Handel (1685–1759), "For Unto Us a Child Is Born," from *Messiah*

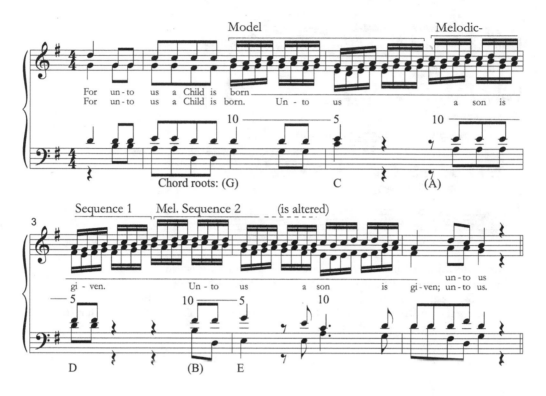

* This famous excerpt includes an ascending-second sequence with intervening root-position chords. The 10-5 intervallic pattern is marked between the staves. How does Handel break off the sequence?

Example 8.3.   Johann Sebastian Bach (1685–1750), Fugue in G major, BWV 860

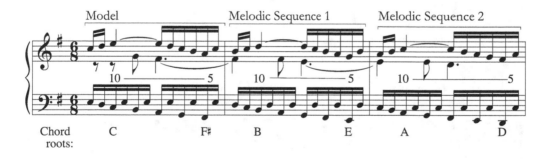

* Although the chord roots and the intervallic pattern are somewhat obscured by the figuration in the contrapuntal lines, the melodic sequence and underlying descending-fifth pattern in the bass are easily discernable. Be sure to sing the outer lines at a tempo that feels comfortable.

Example 8.4.   Bach, Little Prelude in C major, BWV 924 (transposed for ease of singing)

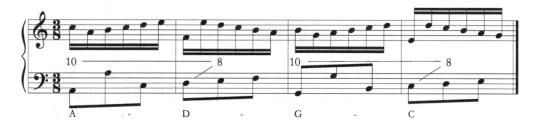

* The simple ascending-fifth harmonic sequence outlines four independent voices and includes a 10-5 intervallic pattern between the outer voices. The sequential motion causes the succession of harmonies to defy the most common harmonic practice here (with preference for descending fifths). Also, note how Bach delays the arrival of the top chord tone in the right hand. The diagonal lines show the displacement of the counterpoint, while the brackets show the iterations of the melodic sequence.

Example 8.5.   Bach, Invention no. 4 in D minor, BWV 775 (transposed)

* The intervallic pattern between outer voices and the descending-fifth-related chord roots are all marked for you. Note how the arrival on the "acting" soprano pitch is displaced in the even-numbered measures.

Example 8.6.   Bach, Invention no. 8 in F major, BWV 779 (transposed)

* The compound melody in this excerpt presents a significant challenge. You will want to start by singing this very slowly. Also, try singing the excerpt without the high G, F♯, and E upper line. How does Bach adjust this extensive descending-fifth sequence so that it stays within diatonic boundaries? Note that the chord roots are labeled for you.

Example 8.7.Johann Pachelbel (1653–1706), Canon in D Major

* This very familiar excerpt is includes a repeating ground bass with a special harmonic sequence. The harmonic motion is broken up by a descending fifth to each even numbered harmony: I–(V)–vi–(iii), and so forth. What is the relationship between the upper two parts? Can you add a fourth voice?

Example 8.8.Burt Bacharach and Hal David, "I'll Never Fall in Love Again," from *Promises, Promises* (1968)

* Despite the rhythmic variation and syncopations, the melodic and harmonic sequence is fairly evident. Also note the intervallic pattern between the two voices.

Example 8.9.   Bach, Prelude in B♭ Major, BWV 866, from *The Well-Tempered Clavier*, Book I

* This sequence outlines three independent voices. Does it sound familiar? Be sure to take this excerpt very slowly.

Example 8.10.   Wolfgang Amadeus Mozart (1756–1791), Piano Concerto, K. 488, mvt. 1

* Note how the outer parts move at different times. Some affectionately call this an "inchworm" sequence, but most label it by the pattern of intervals; what is the pattern?

Example 8.11.   Mozart, Rondo for Horn and Orchestra, K. 371 (transposed)

Example 8.12.   Bach, Prelude from Cello Suite no. 2 in D minor, BWV 1008

* Label the model and its melodic sequences. See if you can trace the harmonic progression here. You may observe as well that the movement is in D minor but the passage is in a different, though related, key.

Example 8.13.   François-Joseph Gossec (1734–1829), *Des Solfèges* no. 41

Example 8.14.   Claudio Monteverdi (1567–1643), "Perchè se m'odiavi"

* *Translation*: Why, if you despised me [did you] pretend to love me, only to deceive me? Alas, a star made you so beautiful, so cruel, so haughty, to destroy [my] soul.

The intervallic pattern for both of the included sequences is marked. Pay special attention to how Monteverdi plays with our expectations when he breaks out of the sequence. Why did he need an extra beat in the first complete measure of the second half? (Hint: consider the text "Alas, a star made you so beautiful.")

Example 8.15.   Ludwig van Beethoven (1770–1827), "Waldstein" Sonata, op. 53, mvt. 3 (transposed)

CHORALE WORKSHOP: FURTHER EXPANSIONS OF TONIC, SEQUENCE MODELS TO BE INTRODUCED IN CHAPTER 9

Although sequences seem to be centered on harmonic progression, they actually serve to expand only one or two harmonies, usually by way of departure and arrival points. This is very similar to the way in which treading water results in no actual forward motion. Though sequences are frequently used to expand a single harmony, such as tonic, other harmonies can be used to achieve a shorter expansion of the tonic (or other harmony). The harmonic paradigms in this chapter will complete our exploration of short harmonic patterns that expand tonic. Longer expansions (including sequences) will be addressed in subsequent chapters.

1. Working at a piano, play the harmonic patterns below in simple major and minor keys. Try placing the listed melodic patterns in the soprano voice. Note that the motion from vii°⁶ to I⁶ allows unusual voice leading in the upper voices: the diminished fifth may move to a perfect fifth because the resolution of $\hat{4}$ in the top voices arrives in the strong bass voice on the very next beat. Many of these progressions (including the one realized below) expand the tonic harmony by harmonizing a passing tone in the bass between I and I⁶. These harmonized passing tones may result in a second-inversion triad (a.k.a. "passing $^6_4$"). For these types of progressions, all voices should move by step or maintain a single pitch.

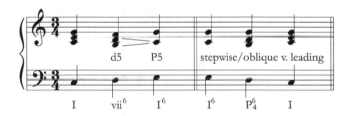

As you play, attempt good voice leading. As always, your focus should be on the outer voices (soprano and bass), but do your best to avoid parallel octaves and fifths with the inner voices. As the progressions get lengthier, it may become a greater challenge to arpeggiate the harmonic patterns on your instrument. That said, there is still much benefit to be gained from giving it a try!

Harmony (bass line in left hand)	Possible soprano scale degrees (right hand)
I vii°⁶ I⁶ or i vii°⁶ i⁶	$\hat{5}\ \hat{4}\ \hat{5}$ $\hat{3}\ \hat{2}\ \hat{1}$ $\hat{1}\ \hat{7}\ \hat{1}$
I⁶ vii°⁶ I or i⁶ vii°⁶ i	$\hat{1}\ \hat{2}\ \hat{3}$ $\hat{1}\ \hat{7}\ \hat{1}$
I⁶ P$^6_4$ I or i⁶ P$^6_4$ i	$\hat{5}\ \hat{5}\ \hat{5}$ $\hat{1}\ \hat{2}\ \hat{3}$ $\hat{1}\ \hat{7}\ \hat{1}$

2. Expansions of the tonic through the dominant-seventh chord. Note that many of these bass and soprano lines, when paired, form idiomatic motions.

Harmony (bass line in left hand)	Possible soprano scale degrees (right hand)
I V$^6_5$ I or i V$^6_5$ i	$\hat{3}$ $\hat{4}$ $\hat{3}$ $\hat{3}$ $\hat{2}$ $\hat{1}$ $\hat{5}$ $\hat{4}$ $\hat{3}$ $\hat{1}$ $\hat{2}$ $\hat{1}$ $\hat{5}$ $\hat{5}$ $\hat{5}$
I V$^4_3$ I or i V$^4_3$ i	$\hat{1}$ $\hat{7}$ $\hat{1}$ $\hat{3}$ $\hat{4}$ $\hat{3}$ $\hat{5}$ $\hat{5}$ $\hat{5}$
I V$^4_3$ I^6 or i V$^4_3$ i^6	$\hat{3}$ $\hat{4}$ $\hat{5}$ $\hat{1}$ $\hat{7}$ $\hat{1}$ $\hat{5}$ $\hat{5}$ $\hat{5}$
I V$^4_2$ I^6 or i V$^4_2$ i^6	$\hat{3}$ $\hat{2}$ $\hat{5}$ $\hat{3}$ $\hat{2}$ $\hat{1}$ $\hat{1}$ $\hat{7}$ $\hat{1}$ $\hat{5}$ $\hat{5}$ $\hat{5}$
I^6 V$^4_3$ I or i^6 V$^4_3$ i	$\hat{5}$ $\hat{4}$ $\hat{3}$ $\hat{1}$ $\hat{7}$ $\hat{1}$ $\hat{5}$ $\hat{5}$ $\hat{5}$

3. Now, review all the three-chord tonic expansions that you learned in the previous chapters. Practicing with a partner, try to distinguish them by ear. Start by notating outer voices. Then, you will want to think about possible harmonic functions, using your brain to confirm what your ear may be hearing. Distinguishing among V$^6_5$, vii^{o6} and P$^6_4$ may seem like a challenge at first, but pretty soon you'll hear the tritone (or absence thereof) in the upper voices.

IMPROVISATION: GAMES AND EXERCISES

1. *Sing and play*: improve your scales and arpeggios by alternating between singing them and playing them on your instrument or a piano. The goal is for you to make a direct connection between the placement of pitches in your voice and the physical manifestation of those pitches on your instrument. This will also build audiation skills and pitch accuracy. Try it with the excerpts in this book as well.

2. Using the repeating sequential ground bass from Pachelbel's Canon in D Major (see Example 8.7), create your own additional voices above the bass. Finally, improvise a melody over the top, using chords tones, complete neighbors, and passing tones.

IMPROVISATION: FOCUS ON RHYTHM AND METER

1. Improvise a melody over a progression using the harmonic patterns you discovered in the Chorale Workshop. Adopt the rhythmic feel of the Tango bass line below, and then try using some from the earlier chapters.

2. Practice the rhythmic patterns from Examples 8.4 and 8.9. Now compose or improvise a rhythmic round using those patterns, setting a text of your choosing. Be sure to keep the rests crisp and in tempo.

3. Now, apply the harmonic paradigms above to your rhythmic piece, with one chord per measure. Use the soprano patterns that correspond to your chosen harmonic paradigm to give your melody a basic structure, but feel free to embellish. Stick strictly to the rhythms found in your rhythm piece.

4. The rhythmic line shown below is from a piece by Ernst Toch entitled *Geographical Fugue*, the entire score for which is reproduced in Chapter 14. In order to prepare for quartet performances of the complete work, Chapters 8 through 13 will focus on one of the five basic rhythmic paradigms (patterns) that Toch uses. You may wish to start by marking in the $\frac{4}{4}$ meter and then subdividing according to the eighth note (since every eighth note is divided into a sixteenth-note triplet). Trade off between measures of straight eighth notes and the actual pattern below. It is recommended that you practice with a metronome, slowly increasing the tempo until you can move fluidly at a quarter note = 60.

5. Once you can sing the rhythm fluidly, create a three-voice rhythmic round employing a combination of the rhythmic pattern below and two other rhythmic patterns of your choosing (complete $\frac{4}{4}$ measures, please). Be prepared to perform it in class.

Can - a - da Ma - la - ga Ri - mi - ni Brin - di - si   Can - a - da Ma - la - ga Ri - mi - ni Brin - di - si

DRILLS: INTERVALS AND ARPEGGIATIONS

1. *Arpeggiation drill*: arpeggiate triads as suggested in the Chorale Workshop. Be sure to try ascending and descending arpeggiations in both major and minor.

2. Review the up-down interval drill as described in Chapter 5. Make sure that you can sing it fluently and without error from the tonic pitch.

3. Now, practice the up-down interval drill from the dominant. Be sure to start by establishing the tonic and then proceed as shown below.

SUGGESTED SMARTMUSIC ASSESSMENTS

Start by practicing the excerpts listed at the end of this paragraph—be sure that you can sing them smoothly and accurately on scale degrees or syllables, *while conducting* the appropriate meter. Log into SmartMusic, click "assignments," and complete the assigned assessments for the excerpts. Be sure to try to identify (1) harmonies, when possible; (2) types of harmonic sequences, where applicable; and (3) types of linear intervallic patterns, when applicable. The excerpts are Examples 8.1 (outer parts), 8.2 (outer parts), 8.4 (bass only), 8.5 (bass only), 8.7 (outer parts), 8.9 (bass only), 8.10 (outer parts), 8.12 (melody), 8.13 (both parts), and 8.15 (both parts).

Note that you will be assessed by the computer but can repeat the exercise until it is done to your own satisfaction. In addition, your instructor may choose one or two of the recordings to evaluate directly. Remember these SmartMusic tips:

1. To hear your starting pitch for an excerpt before the accompaniment starts to play, press P on your computer. Avoid doing this more than once during your actual assessment, as this constitutes cheating!

2. You can always change the key, tempo, and click options for your SmartMusic excerpt before completing an assessment.

SHORT-TERM MUSICAL MEMORY

Fill in the key signature and clef as indicated by your instructor and write in the initial note(s) on the basis of the given pitch and rhythm information. Note that the key and clef *may not be the same* as in the original example. Your instructor (or practice partner) will play a short progression to establish the key and then count off several beats to establish the tempo. Because of the brevity of each extract, you should have an overall impression of the rhythm, contour, and scale degrees after just one or two hearings. Notate the entire fragment.

1. Example 7.2, middle staff, last eighth note of m. 9 to beat 3 of m. 11. Starts on eighth-note upbeat (high scale degree $\hat{5}$).

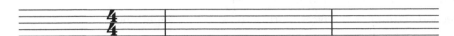

Clef and key
signature

2. Example 8.4, up to downbeat of m. 4, bass line. Starts on beat 1 (quarter note, low scale degree $\hat{1}$).

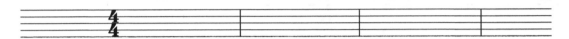

Clef and key
signature

3. Example 8.7, up to downbeat of m. 3, bass line. Starts on beat 1 (quarter note, scale degree $\hat{1}$).

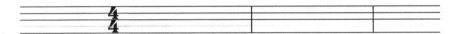

Clef and key
signature

4. Example 7.1, last four measures with upbeat, both voices. Top voice starts with eighth-note upbeat (scale degree $\hat{5}$); bottom voice starts a minor tenth lower with a quarter note on the downbeat.

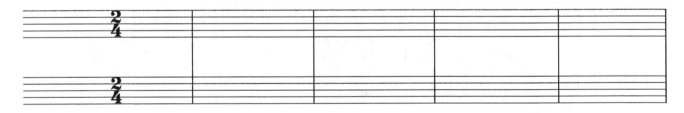

Clef and key
signature

5. Example 7.3: two possibilities.
   a. mm. 1–4, both voices. Both start on beat 1 (quarter note and scale degree $\hat{2}$ in top voice, half note a perfect twelfth lower in bottom voice).
   b. mm. 13–16 (second ending), both voices. Both start on beat 1 (eighth note and scale degree $\hat{1}$ in top voice, half note an octave lower in bottom voice).

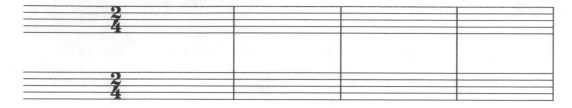

Clef and key
signature

6. Example 7.8, last four measures with upbeat, outer voices. Top voice starts with two sixteenth-note upbeats (scale degrees $\hat{1}$–$\hat{2}$); bottom voice starts with $\hat{1}$ (either one or two octaves lower) with a dotted quarter note on the downbeat.

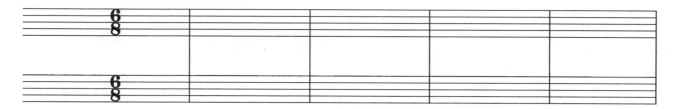

Clef and key
signature

DICTATION OF LONGER EXAMPLES

Your instructor or a classmate will choose one of the examples listed below and inform you of the key, clef, meter, first note (scale degree, rhythmic value, and metric placement) of one or more parts, and total number of measures. Use a separate piece of staff paper to write down the indicated information. You will hear a short progression to establish the key of the example, and then hear the example several times with breaks between hearings.

1. Example 7.2, up to beat 3 of m. 4, lines 1 and 3. Notate line 3 above line 1, but on the same staff.
2. Example 7.5, mm. 3–9, outer voices.
3. Example 7.7, last four measures, outer voices. Treat as if starting on beat 2 in a consistent $\frac{4}{4}$ meter.
4. Example 8.7, mm. 3–9, upper voice.
5. Example 8.13, up to downbeat of m. 9, both voices.

CONTEXTUAL LISTENING 8.1

George Frideric Handel (1685–1759), "Musette," from *Concerto Grosso*, op. 6, no. 6

Handel was a German-born composer who studied in Italy and became famous in London as the court composer of King George I. Among other things, he was famous for introducing the Italianate style to the English public through his well-known operas and oratorios. This excerpt is drawn from the "Musette" movement of one of Handel's many instrumental works. A musette is a dancelike piece in a pastoral style that recalls a bagpipe instrument known as a musette. They were often characterized by simple harmony and a drone pitch.

1. What is the meter of this eight-measure excerpt? (Hint: it ends on the downbeat of the eighth measure.)

   $\frac{12}{8}$ $\frac{9}{8}$ $\frac{3}{4}$ $\frac{6}{8}$ $\frac{4}{4}$

2. The first two bars of the excerpt present a model. How many times is it sequenced (not counting the model)? Hint: you might find that the final sequence is fragmented (cut in half).

   a. 1½   b. 2   c. 2½   d. 3   e. 6

3. How often does this sequential excerpt change harmonies (i.e., what is the harmonic rhythm)?

   a. Twice per measure   b. Every measure   c. Every two measures

4. Accurately transcribe the bass (both pitches and rhythm) for the entire excerpt in G minor on the staves provided on the reverse. Be sure to leave plenty of room for the spacing of the sixteenth-note melodic figuration in the staff above.

5. Now transcribe the melody (both pitches and rhythm of all melodic figuration) for the entire excerpt. Be sure to write neatly.

6. The excerpt alternates between root-position and first-inversion triads. Underneath the measures, label any root-position chords ROOT.

7. On the basis of your answer to question 6, what type of harmonic sequence controls this excerpt?

   a. descending thirds

   b. ascending step

   c. descending fifths

   d. ascending fifths

8. What is the intervallic pattern that controls the sequence? It is probably best to measure from the lowest bass note to the highest melodic note in each measure.

   a. 8–5   b. 10–6   c. 5–10   d. 5–8   e. 6–10

9. Now, circle every spot at which Handel makes a small alteration in the sequence, rather than following the model strictly.

EXPANDING THE REPERTOIRE 8.2

Jerome Kern and Oscar Hammerstein, "All the Things You Are" (1939)

A jazz standard from the 1930s, "All the Things You Are" has been recorded by dozens of the twentieth century's most famous recording artists, and was cited by Charlie Parker as being among his favorite songs. It is quite unusual in structure and is enjoyed by many.

1. What is the meter of this seven-measure (!) excerpt?

    $\frac{12}{8}$ $\frac{9}{8}$ $\frac{3}{4}$ $\frac{6}{8}$ $\frac{4}{4}$

2. The excerpt starts on an F-minor harmony, and the melody starts on A♭. On which pitch does it end? What is the root of the chord that underlies the final measure?

    Ending melodic pitch: _____ .   Root of the final chord: _____ .

3. How often does this sequential excerpt change harmonies (i.e. what is the harmonic rhythm)?

    a. Every measure   b. Every two measures   c. Twice per measure

4. Accurately transcribe the bass (both pitches and rhythm) for the entire excerpt on the staves provided on the reverse.

5. Now transcribe the melody (both pitches and rhythm) for all the measures except for m. 6, which starts and ends on an F.

6. Note that the second pitch in m. 6 is a chromatic alteration. What is the interval of the leap in m. 6? See if you can guess the second pitch in m. 6 (notate on the staff).

    a. M3   b. A4   c. P5   d. P4   e. d5

7. Underneath the staves, label the roots of the harmonies implied in each measure. Note that all the harmonies are in root position.

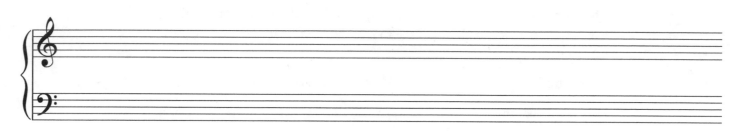

8. What quality of chord is implied in m. 6?

9. What type of harmonic sequence controls this excerpt? Note that the iterations of the melodic sequence are longer than the rate of harmonic change. Try bracketing the model and the subsequent sequences in your transcription.

    a. Descending thirds

    b. Ascending step

    c. Descending fifths

    d. Ascending fifths

EXPANDING THE REPERTOIRE 8.3

Leonard Bernstein (1918–1990), "America," from *West Side Story* (1957)

Leonard Bernstein was one of the most influential figures in twentieth-century music. Aside from writing the widely known musical *West Side Story*, he was one of the New York Philharmonic's most famous conductors and pioneered children's education programs in music. He also created a volume of works that are now part of the standard classical repertoire, including three symphonies and the choral masterwork *Chichester Psalms*.

1. What is the meter of the excerpt? (Hint: the rhythm of the first and third bars will indicate the meter. Measures 2 and 4 suggest a different meter or a syncopation of the initial meter.)

$\frac{12}{8}$ $\frac{4}{4}$ $\frac{9}{8}$ $\frac{3}{4}$ $\frac{6}{8}$

2. What meter might be suggested in mm. 2 and 4?

$\frac{12}{8}$ $\frac{4}{4}$ $\frac{9}{8}$ $\frac{3}{4}$ $\frac{6}{8}$

3 How many measures are in this excerpt?

a. 2   b. 4   c. 8   d. 12   e. 16

4. What is the primary motivic idea? (Hint: some might consider it as two separate ideas.) Describe in prose, and provide a musical example.

5. Notate the rhythm and outer parts of the first four bars *only*.

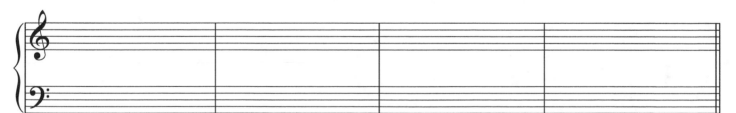

EXPANDING THE REPERTOIRE 8.4

Gloria Gaynor, "I Will Survive" (1978)

This song reached number one on the Billboard Hot 100 in 1979 and quickly became a disco anthem. Unlike other disco hits of the time, Gloria Gaynor's recording was not heavily produced (i.e., no addition of backup vocals, no adjustments in pitch and tempo, no overdubs, etc.).

1. The piece starts with an arpeggio of an extended dominant chord in the key of A minor. Specify the notes and choose the label that best describes them, keeping in mind that the ninth and eleventh simply specify an additional interval above the bass beyond the typical pitches of the dominant-seventh chord.

   a. Dominant ♭9   b. Dominant ♯9   c. Dominant ♯11

2. The implied bass and chord progression (in A minor) repeats throughout the entire song. Transcribe the implied bass and chord progression below; make sure to include the corresponding Roman numerals. The first two chords are provided.

Am   Dm

i   iv

3. The pattern transcribed above illustrates a sequence. Circle the correct name for this sequence type:

   a. Descending fifths   b. Descending thirds

   c. Ascending seconds   d. Ascending fifths

4. Transpose the bass pattern and chord progression to these keys.

   a. D minor:

Dm

i

   b. E minor:

Em

i

5. *Optional assignment 1*: perform the bass line at the piano while listening to the song.

6. *Optional assignment 2*: improvise a new melody for this progression. For practice, use the backup track provided online.

EXPANDING THE REPERTOIRE 8.5

Vitamin C, "Graduation (Friends Forever)" (2000)

Black Eyed Peas, "Where Is the Love" (2003)

Belle and Sebastian, "Get Me Away from Here, I'm Dying" (1998)

"Graduation," the biggest hit of American pop singer Vitamin C, is often played at high school graduations. "Where Is the Love" is the Black Eyed Peas' first top-ten hit, featuring additional vocals by Justin Timberlake. Similar to pieces in continuous variation form (from the Baroque period and beyond), both of these songs feature a single harmonic progression that repeats throughout. In contrast, "Get Me Away from Here, I'm Dying" steers away from this characteristic harmonic progression during the chorus.

1. Listen to "Graduation" and answer these questions.

    a. What key is it in?

    b. What particular sequence does it resemble? What Baroque composer (in the excerpts above) used a very similar progression?

    c. Transcribe the chord progression of "Graduation" with its corresponding Roman numerals and the implied bass line below.

    d. The progression transcribed above differs in just one chord from the progression featured in Pachelbel's Canon. Write the progression of the Canon in the key of C:

C

𝄢 o

I

e. Many popular songs feature a similar adjustment. Listen to Belle and Sebastian's "Get Me Away from Here, I'm Dying," and notate the chord progression below. The first note is not given, so you'll have to find it on your instrument.

2. Listen to "Where Is the Love" and answer these questions:

a. What key is it in?

b. What particular sequence does it resemble? How complete is it?

c. After introducing the primary chord progression, a melodic line on synthesized strings begins. Complete the melody below, and specify the chord progression with corresponding Roman numerals.

3. Listen closely to "Graduation" and "Where is the Love," paying particular attention to metric alterations and slight changes in phrase rhythm that help outline the various verses and the chorus. Answer these questions:

a. How many extra beats are introduced before the first chorus in "Graduation" (approx. 1:00 in the online video)? Does this happen before introducing *every* chorus?

b. In "Where Is the Love," are there any extra beats when the first chorus is introduced (approx. 1:00 in on the online video)? How many measures are added before the introduction of the second chorus? Why does it sound like "added measures" rather than part of the original pattern? (Listen closely to the harmonic rhythm.)

4. *Optional assignment*: improvise a new popular-style or jazz-style melody based on the progression from Pachelbel's Canon. For practice, use the various backup tracks provided online.

Chapter 9

Diatonic Sequences II and New Rhythmic Configurations

This chapter expands on the previous one, working to further your familiarity with diatonic sequences. As before, you should practice singing each one of the parts while playing one of the other parts on the piano in order to understand how the models and their sequences work as units. The chapter ends with two excerpts that display characteristics of sequences but may or not be classified as sequences. It will be up to you to argue your case. In addition, you will be asked to improvise both bass and melody from sequential models in this chapter. Finally, you will have the opportunity to play models of all the sequences on the piano.

Example 9.1.   George Frideric Handel (1685–1759), Bourrée, from *Royal Fireworks Music* (1749)

* You might consider using this sequence as a warm-up. Be sure you can play all three voices. Identify the harmonies as well as the intervallic pattern between outer voices.

Example 9.2.   Wolfgang Amadeus Mozart (1756–1791), Piano Sonata in C Major, K. 545, mvt. 1

* What is the relationship between the material in the right and left hands?

Example 9.3.   Michael Praetorius (1571–1621), "Der Lautenspieler" (1612)

* Identify the linear pattern between outer voices. How does Praetorius decorate the sequence?

Example 9.4.   Johann Sebastian Bach (1685–1750), Invention no. 13 in A minor, BWV 784

* You will want to sing this slowly in two parts and practice while playing the other part on the piano. Be sure to mark each iteration of the sequence. Study how Bach shortens the model as it progresses. You will also see how he cleverly uses just a very small number of melodic and rhythmic patterns.

Example 9.5.   Arcangelo Corelli (1653–1713), Allemanda, from Trio Sonata, op. 4 no. 5

* Be sure to practice all three voices. How is closure avoided in m. 2?

Example 9.6.   Josquin des Prez (c. 1450–1521), "Ave Maria"

* *Translation*: [Hail to thee, whose conception] full of solemn rejoicing, should fill heaven and earth with new joy.

Note that the voices overlap in order to preserve the integrity of the sequence. Be sure to identify the intervallic patterns.

Example 9.7.   Handel, Concerto Grosso, op. 6 no. 12, mvt. 1

Example 9.8.   Handel, Chaconne in G, Variation 11

* Try to identify both the harmonies and the intervallic pattern between outer voices. Then compare this with the excerpt below. How does this excerpt exemplify the Chaconne?

Example 9.9.   Handel, Chaconne in G, Variation 12

* Compare this with Variation 11 above. What has Handel changed? What did he retain?

Example 9.10.   Corelli, Allemanda, from Trio Sonata, op. 4 no. 8 (transposed)

Example 9.11.   Johannes Brahms (1833–1897), "Sommerabend," op. 85, no. 1

(schimmern...)

Translation: There, alone by the brook, bathes the beautiful nymph;
       Arm and neck, white and lovely (shimmer in the moonlight)
    Be sure to practice the bass triplets while singing the melody. If you are feeling particularly up to the challenge, try playing and singing the two lower parts together (two against three). Note that Brahms compresses the sequence toward the end (arriving back on tonic "too soon"). What happens to the G♯ in the inner voice of m. 6?

Example 9.12.   Fanny Mendelssohn Hensel (1805–1847), "Neue Liebe, neues Leben" (1836)

* *Translation*: Heart, my heart, what could this mean? What is plaguing you so?

Example 9.13.   Johannes Brahms, "Blinde Kuh," op. 58, no. 1

* *Translation*: Little child, have pity and come here!

Identify both the root motion and the contrapuntal pattern before practicing this excerpt in two parts. Observe the leaps to the accented incomplete neighbors (lower appoggiaturas) in the melody.

Example 9.14.   Johannes Brahms, "Es hing der Reif," op. 106, no. 3

* *Translation*: So spring warm and wonderful: then I noticed in the same greeting (that it was frost and winter).

Be sure to look for the sequential contrapuntal pattern between the outer voices. You may wish to sing the first half (through the downbeat of m. 4) using the syllables of A major, switching to the syllables of F♯ minor on beat 3 of that measure. Why do you suppose Brahms shifts to the minor mode here? Also, what is the lovely romantic harmony in m. 7?

Example 9.15.   Dietrich Buxtehude (1637–1707), "Man fragt nach Gott" from *Das jüngste Gericht*

* Although this excerpt is not strictly sequential (why is it not?), it does include a repeated melodic pattern in the melody. How does Buxtehude juxtapose the upper three voices with the bass? Take a particularly close look at the voice leading.

Example 9.16.   Buxtehude, *"Bedenke Mensch, das Ende"*

Chord roots: E   A   D   G   (A)

* There is a consistent root progression in this excerpt (which one?), but is it truly sequential? Why or why not?

CHORALE WORKSHOP: PLAYING AND IMPROVISING SEQUENCES USING FOUR-VOICE CHORALE PROGRESSIONS

Listed here are four-voice schematic models for the most common types of sequence. The Chorale Workshop and improvisation sections of this chapter will focus on these paradigmatic models. First, begin by playing all possible permutations. You will notice that each sequence has been laid out into four separate voices. Although the bass remains fixed, any one of the upper three voices could be found in the soprano, so it is important that you practice playing all the permutations. (i.e., bass plus soprano, bass plus alto, bass plus tenor). Second, improvise short sequential melodies based on the sequences in order to solidify your understanding of these musical sequences.

1. *Descending fifths.* The given soprano and bass yield a 10-8 intervallic pattern. Placing the alto part in the soprano yields a 5-10 intervallic pattern; placing the tenor part in the soprano yields an 8-5 intervallic pattern. Try this in minor as well, using the lowered $\hat{7}$ (the subtonic) and lowered mediant throughout *except* for the final leading tone (soprano, m. 7).

2. *Descending thirds.* The given soprano and bass yield a 10-5 intervallic pattern. Placing the alto part in the soprano yields an 8-10 intervallic pattern. Placing the tenor part in the soprano yields a 5-8 intervallic pattern.

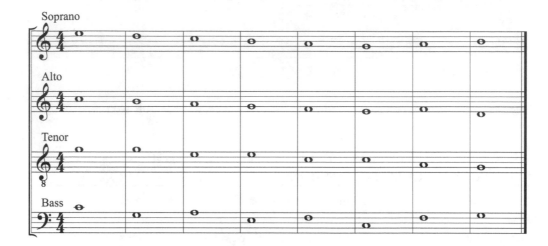

3. *Ascending seconds.* The given soprano and bass yield a 10-10 intervallic pattern (ascending by step every two chords). Placing the alto part in the soprano yields an 8-6 intervallic pattern. Placing the tenor part in the soprano yields a 5-6 intervallic pattern, and it is often referred to as the 5-6 sequence.

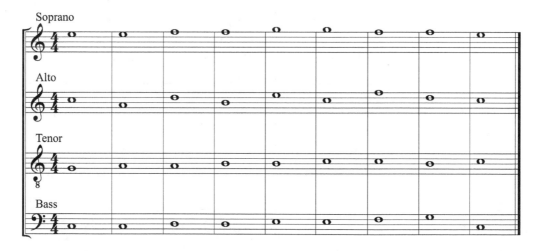

4. *Ascending fifths.* The given soprano and bass yield a 10-5 intervallic pattern. Placing the alto part in the soprano yields a 5-8 intervallic pattern. Placing the tenor part in the soprano yields an 8-10 intervallic pattern.

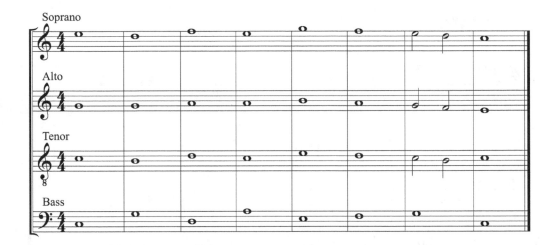

5. *Descending fifths* (first chord in $\frac{6}{3}$ inversion). What intervallic patterns are yielded by placing the various upper voices in the soprano? Mark your intervallic patterns before playing/singing.

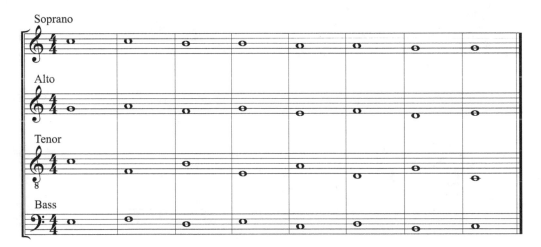

6. *Descending fifths* (second chord in $\frac{6}{3}$ inversion). Try this one in minor, using the lowered scale degree $\hat{7}$ (the subtonic) and lowered mediant throughout *except* for the final leading tone (soprano, m. 7).

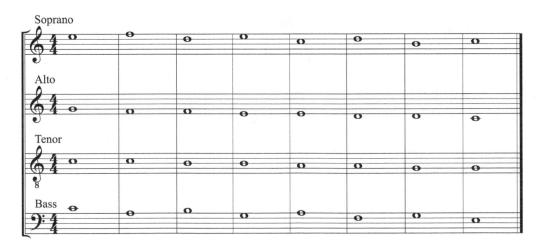

7. *Descending thirds* (second chord in $^6_3$ inversion).

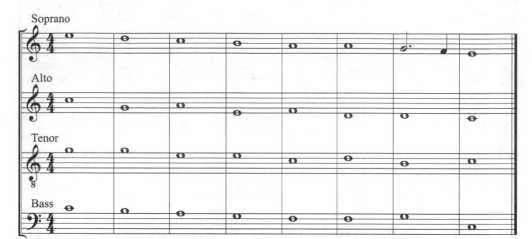

8. *Ascending seconds* (second chord in root position).

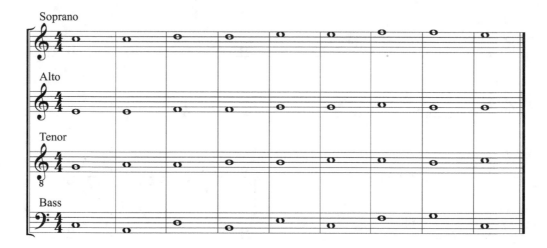

IMPROVISATION: GAMES AND EXERCISES

1. Have a partner or your instructor choose any four-note sequential melodic gesture as found in the patterns above. Now choose an appropriate sequential harmonization by (1) observing the relationship between the first and third notes of a given melodic fragment and then (2) choosing from these models to find an appropriate sequential "fragment." For instance, the melodic fragment $\hat{3}$–$\hat{2}$–$\hat{4}$–$\hat{3}$ must be harmonized with an ascending fifths sequence for two reasons:

   a. The relationship between the first and third notes is an ascending step, ruling out any of the descending sequences.

   b. The relationship between the first and second notes is a descending step, ruling out the possibility of harmonizing it with an ascending-step sequence.

2. Now start with one of the sequential patterns above. Play the bass line repeatedly, and sing one of the possible upper voices. Next, you may begin to embellish the upper voice, starting with simple neighbor tones, but moving on to chordal skips that will shift you between any of the upper three voices in the paradigms above. To begin with, you will want to return to the initial pitch before the bass shifts to the next measure so that you do not have to worry about the chord-to-chord voice leading.

3. After completing the contextual listening on the Handel Chaconne and examining the two variations above (Examples 9.8 and 9.9), improvise your own variation over one of the repeating bass lines, starting simple and moving toward a more typical Baroque texture (as found in the Handel variations).

IMPROVISATION: FOCUS ON RHYTHM AND METER

1. Adopt the rhythmic feel in the Lindy bass line below and apply it to one of the sequences above. Improvise a simple melody, and then embellish it.

2. The excerpt below shows the opening measure from the *Geographical Fugue* by Ernst Toch (found in Chapter 14). You may wish to start by marking the $\frac{4}{4}$ meter and then subdividing into sixteenths. Trade off between measures of straight eighth notes and the actual pattern below. It is recommended that you practice with a metronome, slowly increasing the tempo until you can move fluidly at a quarter note = 60.

Note how each beat presents a slightly different rhythm. Once you can sing each beat fluidly, create a short rhythm piece, employing each of the beat divisions three times (but in an order other than that found below), creating three $\frac{4}{4}$ measures. Now write a text for your piece, being sure to place accented syllables in the right spot.

DRILLS: SEQUENCES

Attempt to sing the outer voices of the sequences described in the Chorale Workshop, switching between the bottom and top notes as in the model below. Be sure to use scale degrees or solfège syllables, and choose a key that will allow you to feel comfortable singing both parts. The model shows one of the upper three voices (descending stepwise from the mediant), over the bass in a descending-third sequence. You might recognize this from the Pachelbel excerpt in Chapter 8. Be sure to practice all three of the upper voices with the bass lines.

SUGGESTED SMARTMUSIC ASSESSMENTS

Practice the following excerpts and then complete SmartMusic assessments: 9.1 (outer voices), 9.2 (outer voices), 9.3 (soprano and alto voices), 9.4 (outer voices); 9.5 (all three voices), 9.8 (outer voices), 9.11 (outer voices), and 9.13 (melody). Don't forget that you may choose your own tempo and key for these exercises.

SHORT-TERM MUSICAL MEMORY

Fill in the key signature and clef as indicated by your instructor and write in the initial note(s) on the basis of the given pitch and rhythm information. Note that the key and clef *may not be the same* as in the original example. Your instructor (or practice partner) will play a short progression to establish the key and then count off several beats to establish the tempo. Because of the brevity of each extract, you should have an overall impression of the rhythm, contour, and scale degrees after just one or two hearings. Notate the entire fragment.

1. Example 9.4, beat 4 of m. 3 to beat 3 of m. 4, bottom voice. Starts with scale degree 1̂ as the first of several sixteenth notes.

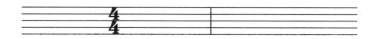

Clef and key
  signature

2. Example 9.7, up to second downbeat, top voice. Starts on beat 1 (sixteenth note, scale degree 3̂).

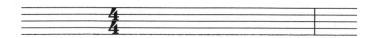

Clef and key
  signature

3. Example 9.9, m. 3 to downbeat of m. 4, lower voice, but start with a sixteenth rest on the first downbeat. First pitch after the rest is scale degree $\hat{3}$, the first of several sixteenth notes.

Clef and key
signature

4. Example 9.12, up to third downbeat, top voice. Starts on beat 3 (quarter note, scale degree $\hat{3}$).

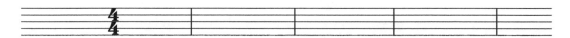

Clef and key
signature

5. Example 9.16, up to fourth downbeat, bass line. Starts on beat 3 (half note, scale degree $\hat{1}$). Optional change when playing for listener(s): allow the second-to-last note to resolve less surprisingly.

Clef and key
signature

6. Example 9.1, all, outer voices. Both voices start with quarter notes on beat 4 (scale degree $\hat{5}$ in the top voice, and a perfect fifth or a perfect twelfth lower in the bottom voice).

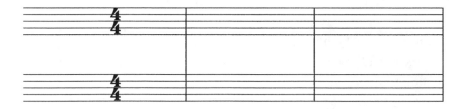

Clef and key
signature

7. Example 9.6, beat 4 of m. 5 to downbeat of m. 8, tenor and bass voices. Both start with a quarter note (bass starts on scale degree 3̂; tenor starts a minor sixth higher and is tied into the downbeat).

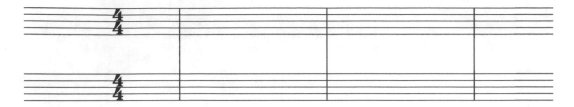

Clef and key
  signature

8. Example 9.15, all, outer voices. Both voices start with a half note on beat 3, both on scale degree 5̂ an octave apart (top voice is tied into the downbeat).

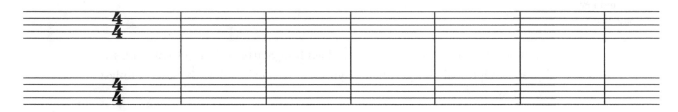

Clef and key
  signature

DICTATION OF LONGER EXAMPLES

Your instructor or a classmate will choose one of the examples listed below and inform you of the key, clef, meter, first note (scale degree, rhythmic value, and metric placement) of one or more parts, and total number of measures. Use a separate piece of staff paper to write down the indicated information. You will hear a short progression to establish the key of the example, and then the example several times with breaks between hearings.

1. Example 9.4, up to beat 4 of m. 2, both voices.
2. Example 9.5, beat 4 of second full measure to the end, outer voices.
3. Example 9.6, beat 3 of m. 9 to end, outer voices.
4. Example 9.8, up to third downbeat, top voice.
5. Example 9.11, all, top voice.

CONTEXTUAL LISTENING 9.1

Handel, Chaconne in G, Variation 9 and Variation 13

A chaconne is a type of Baroque instrumental piece wherein a repeated harmonic pattern is treated to successive variations. This contextual listening contains excerpts from two more variations of Handel's Chaconne (variations 11 and 12 are found earlier in this chapter). Both excerpts are in the same meter ($\frac{3}{4}$) and key (G minor).

1. How long are the two excerpts?

    a. Two measures   b. Four measures   c. Six measures   d. Eight measures

2. Variation 9 has a simplified bass and includes a single major-seventh leap in the soprano. Accurately notate the outer parts (both bass and melody) of Variation 9.

3. Now, using that as a model, see if you can accurately notate the melody (only) of Variation 13.

4. Bracket the model and its sequences in each variation. Also, see if you can identify the intervallic pattern between the outer voices in each of the variations.

5. List at least three musical features that are retained between the two variations. List at least three musical features that are varied (be as specific as possible).

6. Now, compare them to the two variations earlier in the chapter (Examples 9.8 and 9.9, Variations 11 and 12). How do Variations 9 and 13 differ from what you sang earlier? How are they similar? Be specific.

Features retained:

1. _____

2. _____

3. _____

Features varied:

1. _____

2. _____

3. _____

EXPANDING THE REPERTOIRE 9.2

Paul McCartney and John Lennon, "You Never Give Me Your Money" (1969)

The opening number from side two of the landmark album *Abbey Road*, this number showcases McCartney's natural songwriting style. *Abbey Road* was the Beatles' most successful album, sitting in number one spots worldwide for eleven weeks.

1. The harmonic rhythm of this excerpt is one chord per measure, *with a single exception* (where there are two chords in a single measure). How many measures are in this excerpt?

    a. Four   b. Five   c. Seven   d. Eight   e. Fourteen

2. What is the meter of this excerpt?

    $\frac{6}{8}$ $\frac{4}{4}$ $\frac{3}{4}$ $\frac{12}{8}$ $\frac{6}{4}$

3. For how many measures does the melodic sequence last (including the model)? Is it varied at all?

4. In which measures does the harmonic rhythm increase? Why do you think the harmonic rhythm increases here?

5. Accurately transcribe the outer parts (bass and melody) for the entire excerpt on the staves below in the key of A minor. Watch out for the *four* syncopated arrivals of the melody before beat 3.

6. What is the intervallic pattern that controls the sequence? What is the pattern of root motion that controls the sequence?

EXPANDING THE REPERTOIRE 9.3

Michel Legrand, "The Windmills of Your Mind" (1968)

This song by French composer Michel Legrand was used as the main theme for the film *The Thomas Crown Affair* and won the Academy Award for Best Original Song in 1968.

1. Listen closely to the first verse of the song, and answer the following:

   a. The first three chords of the song strongly establish E minor as the main key. What progression is used?

   ii^{o6}–V–i   i–V–i   i–iv–i   Cadential $^6_4$–V–i

   b. Having established E minor as the key, the rest of the verse embarks on a sequence. Choose the harmonic motion that most nearly sounds like what happens in the song:

   - E^7–Am–D7–G^{maj7}–C^{maj7}–F$\sharp$m$^{7(\flat5)}$–B^7–Em
   - Em^7–B^7–C–G–Am^7–F$\sharp$m$^{7(\flat5)}$–B^7–Em

   c. What is the name of the sequence you chose? What intervallic pattern do the roots of the chords outline?

   d. Which chord in the progression is not diatonic? Why does it work well within the progression?

   e. Because of the intervallic pattern outlined by the roots of chords, many scholars identify this sequence with the word "circle." How does this word relate to the title of the song, "The Windmills of Your Mind," and to the visuals as presented in the scene from *The Thomas Crown Affair* where the song is introduced? (Watch the video posted online.)

Chapter 10

Motivic Development and the Sentence

This chapter explores the extended use of motives, particularly in relation to the phrase type commonly known as the sentence. In addition it includes excerpts in which the phrase has been expanded (internally) or extended (the phrase is somehow continued beyond the final cadence). The sentence phrase type departs somewhat from the balance of the parallel period in favor of a full-scale drive toward a single, phrase-ending cadence. The typical sentence opens with a presentation, wherein a two-measure musical idea is repeated (often on the tonic, then on the dominant), followed by the continuation, which consists of smaller one-measure units (often fragments or motives from the opening musical idea) that appear two to three times, and a cadential section, typically two measures long. This cadential section can conclude with either a half cadence or an authentic cadence. Note that you will eventually encounter larger parallel periods (usually sixteen measures) made up of two sentences separated by a half cadence.

Several examples in this chapter will depart from the common eight-measure layout. A phrase that is "too long" typically incorporates an internal expansion or a postcadential extension. The most common ways to expand a phrase are to prolong the pre-dominant or to repeat a motive or fragment one or more extra times. The last section of this chapter will present a new set of harmonic progressions based on the expansion of the tonic through the combination of various pre-dominants along with inversions of vii° or V^7.

Example 10.1. Ludwig van Beethoven (1770–1827), Piano Sonata in F minor, op. 2, no. 1, mvt. 1 (transposed for ease of singing)

* This excerpt presents a prototypical sentence, as described in the introduction to this chapter. The "musical idea" is made up of two separate motives. Which of the motives appears more prominently in the "fragmentation" section? How is the *other* motive also referenced in the fragmentation section? What intervallic pattern between the outer voices controls the continuation of this sentence? What unusual voice leading does it allow?

Example 10.2. Beethoven, *Variations on God Save the King*, WoO 78, Theme

* Note the repeated musical idea of the presentation. How does Beethoven vary and develop the motive of m. 2 in mm. 5 and 6 (and even m. 7)? At what point does this phrase turn toward a cadential progression? (The first-inversion tonic is typically a good indicator.) This part of the phrase is typically called the cadential section.

Example 10.3.   Joseph Haydn (1732–1809), Piano Sonata in G major, Hob. XVI/27, mvt. 1 (transposed)

* Be sure to identify the parts of this sentence before singing. Avoid the turns and trills on your first attempts, but when you feel comfortable, give them a try! What motivic ideas return here?

Example 10.4.   Beethoven, Piano Sonata no. 8 in C minor, op. 13, mvt. 3 (transposed)

* Is this excerpt a sentence? What features might suggest sentential structure? (Hint: consider the motivic fragments starting in m. 5.) By contrast, are there any features that might suggest period-type organization? Which section does Beethoven repeat? Why do you suppose he does that?

Example 10.5.   Meredith Willson (1902–1984), "Goodnight My Someone," from *The Music Man* (1957)

* Note that the scale of this phrase is roughly double that of the previous examples. The bass voice may be sung without the optional chromatic pitches that are indicated in parentheses.

Example 10.6.   Wolfgang Amadeus Mozart (1756–1791), Piano Sonata in G, K. 283, mvt. 1

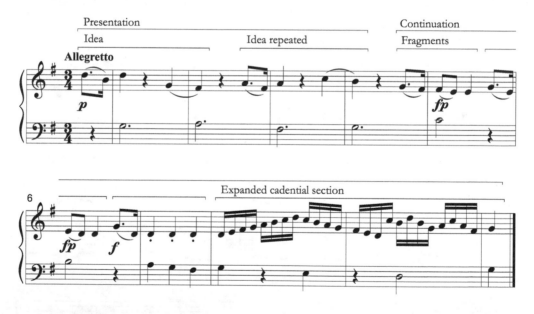

* This excerpt presents an expanded sentence. See if you can improvise an ending that would create a four-measure continuation to balance the presentation.

Example 10.7.   Mozart, "Dove Sono," from *Le Nozze di Figaro*, K. 492 (transposed)

* *Translation*: Where are the lovely moments, of sweetness and pleasure, where have they gone, the promises that came from those lying lips.

This excerpt includes two related phrases, separated by a half cadence. What kind of phrase type is suggested by the first eight measures? What are the differences between the first and second phrases? Are there any kinds of expansions? What kind of sequence is found in the second half of the excerpt? What kind of phrase type might be suggested by the larger eighteen-measure unit (hint: a very large antecedent/consequent)? The top voice (usually played by an oboe) plays an important structural role. How does it interact with the vocal melody?

Example 10.8.   REO Speedwagon, "Can't Fight This Feeling" (1984)

* This excerpt is similar in structure to the previous operatic one. The excerpt as a whole creates a large antecedent-consequent design, wherein each half presents its own phrase type. Be sure to identify the phrase types and any expansions. Try improvising a new melody over this typical 1980s bass line.

Example 10.9.   Johannes Brahms (1833–1897), "Sonntag," op. 47, no. 3

* *Translation*: The thousandfold beautiful young girl, the thousandfold beautiful heart; would God, I were with her today!

This excerpt presents a nearly standard eight-measure sentence. At the moment of the initial cadence, however, the melody does something slightly unexpected. What happens to it? What section of the phrase is repeated? How does it end?

Example 10.10. Giuseppe Verdi (1813–1901), *La Traviata* (1853), end of Act I

* The sentence found in the first eight measures starts off as a repeated two-measure cadential extension, which is then treated as a presentation. What follows is a series of codettas, or postcadential extensions of the phrase (sometimes called a "suffix").

Example 10.11. Haydn, Symphony no. 101 in D Major, mvt. 1 (transposed)

* This excerpt consists of a series of tonic-confirming short phrases found in the closing section of the movement after the cadence that closes the movement proper. Try mapping this out in detail. Notice how Haydn plays with a small number of motives.

Example 10.12. Antonín Dvořák (1841–1903), Symphony no. 8, op. 88, mvt. 3

* The continuation of this sentence is two measures "too long." Where is the phrase expanded? Try recomposing this excerpt as a more typical eight-measure phrase.

Example 10.13. Mozart, String Quintet in B-flat Major, K. 174, mvt. 4

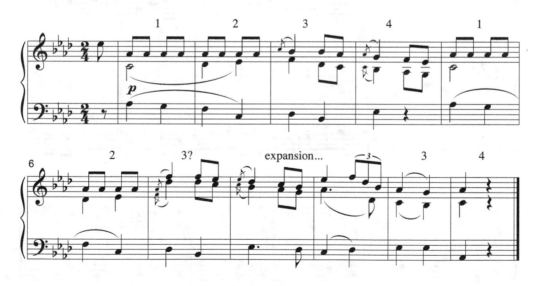

* Note how the first four bars present a normal-length antecedent (marked by the numbers 1 through 4 over the relevant measures). The register transfer in m. 7 ensures an expansion of the consequent. The "too late" arrival of the dominant in m. 8 could lead to a cadence in m. 9, but a passing tone in the bass and another upward leap in the melody helps the music evade closure. The normative cadential material appears only in the final two measures (notice how the numbers 1 through 4 are spread out over the second portion of the excerpt).

Example 10.14. Mozart, Clarinet Quintet in A, K. 581, mvt. 1

* See if you can determine what phrase type this is. Start by marking the cadences. What happens in m. 8? How does Mozart play with the phrase length?

Example 10.15. Johann Sebastian Bach (1685–1750), Cantata "Ach wie flüchtig, ach wie
nichtig," BWV 26 (1724)

* *Translation*: Ah how fleeting, ah how meaningless are the things of humankind.

Although the design here is based on the medieval bar form (AAB), it is similar to the sentences found earlier in the chapter with a repeated idea, followed by a continuation and a cadence.

CHORALE WORKSHOP: EXPANSION OF THE TONIC THROUGH THE COMBINATION OF PRE-DOMINANTS WITH INVERSIONS OF vii° AND V⁷

Working at a piano, play the following progressions in simple major and minor keys. Try placing the listed melodic patterns in the soprano voice. You should do your best to avoid parallels, doubled leading tones, and augmented seconds (in minor), but your focus should be on the relationship of the outer voices. In that light, be sure you can play the outer voices correctly and sing one of the outer voices while playing the other. Finally, as in the previous chapters, attempt to sing the progressions or play them on your instrument, arpeggiating each triad from the bottom up (and then top down).

Note that many of these progressions will include the raised submediant in minor in order to avoid the augmented second between $\hat{6}$ and $\hat{7}$. In these cases the subdominant chord will be major, even in the minor mode. From this point forward, the ↑ symbol will indicate a raised scale degree, while ↓ will indicate a lowered (or "unraised") scale degree.

We will use just a $\hat{7}$ to indicate the raised leading tone in minor, however, and $\downarrow\hat{7}$ if an unaltered scale-degree $\hat{7}$ is intended.

Harmony (bass line in left hand)	Possible soprano scale degrees (right hand)
I IV vii°⁶ I or i iv vii°⁶ i	$\hat{5}$ $\hat{6}$ $\hat{7}$ $\hat{1}$ (in minor: $\hat{5}$ $\uparrow\hat{6}$ $\hat{7}$ $\hat{1}$) $\hat{5}$ $\hat{4}$ $\hat{4}$ $\hat{3}$ $\hat{3}$ $\hat{4}$ $\hat{4}$ $\hat{3}$ $\hat{1}$ $\hat{1}$ $\hat{2}$ $\hat{3}$ $\hat{1}$ $\hat{1}$ $\hat{7}$ $\hat{1}$
I⁶ IV vii°⁶ I or i⁶ iv vii°⁶ i	$\hat{5}$ $\hat{6}$ $\hat{7}$ $\hat{1}$ (in minor: $\hat{5}$ $\uparrow\hat{6}$ $\hat{7}$ $\hat{1}$) $\hat{5}$ $\hat{4}$ $\hat{4}$ $\hat{3}$ $\hat{1}$ $\hat{4}$ $\hat{4}$ $\hat{3}$ $\hat{1}$ $\hat{1}$ $\hat{2}$ $\hat{3}$
I IV V$^4_2$ I⁶ or i iv V$^4_2$ i⁶	$\hat{5}$ $\hat{6}$ $\hat{7}$ $\hat{1}$ (in minor: $\hat{5}$ $\uparrow\hat{6}$ $\hat{7}$ $\hat{1}$) $\hat{3}$ $\hat{4}$ $\hat{5}$ $\hat{5}$ $\hat{1}$ $\hat{1}$ $\hat{7}$ $\hat{1}$
I IV vii°⁶ I⁶ or i iv vii°⁶ i⁶	$\hat{5}$ $\hat{6}$ $\hat{7}$ $\hat{1}$ (in minor: $\hat{5}$ $\uparrow\hat{6}$ $\hat{7}$ $\hat{1}$) $\hat{1}$ $\hat{1}$ $\hat{2}$ $\hat{1}$ $\hat{1}$ $\hat{1}$ $\hat{7}$ $\hat{1}$
I⁶ IV vii°⁶ I⁶ or i⁶ iv vii°⁶ i⁶	$\hat{5}$ $\hat{6}$ $\hat{7}$ $\hat{1}$ (in minor: $\hat{5}$ $\uparrow\hat{6}$ $\hat{7}$ $\hat{1}$) $\hat{1}$ $\hat{1}$ $\hat{2}$ $\hat{1}$ $\hat{1}$ $\hat{1}$ $\hat{7}$ $\hat{1}$
I IV⁶ V$^6_5$ I or i IV⁶ V$^6_5$ i (bass: $\hat{1}$ $\uparrow\hat{6}$ $\hat{7}$ $\hat{1}$)	$\hat{3}$ $\hat{4}$ $\hat{4}$ $\hat{3}$ $\hat{5}$ $\hat{4}$ $\hat{4}$ $\hat{3}$ $\hat{3}$ $\hat{1}$ $\hat{2}$ $\hat{1}$ $\hat{1}$ $\hat{1}$ $\hat{2}$ $\hat{1}$ $\hat{5}$ $\hat{4}$ $\hat{5}$ $\hat{5}$
I ii$^4_2$ V$^6_5$ I or i ii°$^4_2$ V$^6_5$ i	$\hat{1}$ $\hat{2}$ $\hat{2}$ $\hat{1}$ $\hat{5}$ $\hat{4}$ $\hat{4}$ $\hat{3}$ $\hat{3}$ $\hat{4}$ $\hat{4}$ $\hat{3}$ $\hat{3}$ $\hat{2}$ $\hat{2}$ $\hat{1}$

IMPROVISATION: GAMES AND EXERCISES

1. Start with any of the sentences among the excerpts above. Sing the presentation, and then attempt to improvise a new continuation. You may want to start by preserving the initial rhythms, while changing only the pitches. However, you should also try adapting and fragmenting a motive from the presentation in your continuation. Finally, you may wish to introduce a new motive, but preserve the

typical division of measures in the continuation: 1+1+2. Don't forget to aim for the cadence in the final two measures.

2. Start with any of the excerpts above. First, sing the phrase in a typical eight-measure structure. To do this, you may need to reduce out any expansions or extensions. Now, improvise your own expansions. You might try expanding the cadential section by adding predominant chords, or you may simply want to take a motivic fragment from the continuation of a sentence and treat and use it as the basis of a sequence. You may also add postcadential extensions as in Examples 10.10 and 10.11.

IMPROVISATION: FOCUS ON RHYTHM AND METER

1. Using the bass line from Example 10.8, improvise a new melody. You might start by preserving the original syncopated rhythms, but then you should try to incorporate rhythms from other excerpts in this chapter. See if your peers can figure out which excerpt provided the inspiration for your improvisation.

2. Improvise a melody over a progression using the harmonic patterns you discovered in the Chorale Workshop. Adopt the following rhythmic feel and then try using some from the earlier chapters.

Tango

3. Here is yet another rhythmic pattern from the *Geographical Fugue* by Ernst Toch. Start by marking the 4/4 meter and then subdividing into sixteenths. First practice singing just the eighth notes on "-bet." Then, crisply add the sixteenth notes that fall just before the beats. Finally, end with the resounding "yes!" that occurs on the first downbeat. Practice all three versions (with only eighths, with eighths and pre-beat sixteenths, as written) in sequence and write new words for your three-version sequence, being sure to place the accented syllables appropriately.

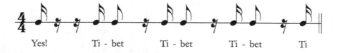

DRILLS: SEQUENCES AND PARADIGMS

1. *Arpeggiation drill*: arpeggiate the harmonies as suggested in the Chorale Workshop. Be sure to try ascending and descending arpeggiations in both major and minor. You should also practice playing and singing the outer voices.

2. Continue to master the sequence drill introduced in the previous chapter. Be sure you can sing the outer voices of all possible sequence permutations, based on the models provided there.

SUGGESTED SMARTMUSIC ASSESSMENTS

Complete the following SmartMusic assessments per the earlier directions. As much as possible, you will want to annotate your score with form and phrase markings: Exercises 10.1 (melody), 10.2 (outer parts), 10.3 (melody), 10.4 (melody), 10.5 (melody), 10.6 (melody), 10.7 (middle part and bass), 10.9 (melody), 10.12 (outer parts), 10.13 (melody), and 10.14 (melody).

SHORT-TERM MUSICAL MEMORY

Fill in the key signature and clef as indicated by your instructor, and write in the initial note(s) on the basis of the given pitch and rhythm information. Note that the key and clef *may not be the same* as in the original example. Your instructor (or practice partner) will play a short progression to establish the key and then count off several beats to establish the tempo. Because of the brevity of each extract, you should have an overall impression of the rhythm, contour, and scale degrees after just one or two hearings. Notate the entire fragment.

1. Example 10.4, beat 4 of m. 8 to end, top voice. Starts with two eighth-note upbeats (scale degrees $\hat{4}$–$\hat{5}$).

Clef and key
signature

2. Example 10.5, up to downbeat of m. 4, top voice. Starts on beat 3 (quarter note, scale degree $\hat{5}$).

Clef and key
signature

3. Example 10.9, up to end of m. 4, vocal line. Starts on beat 3 (quarter note, low scale degree $\hat{5}$).

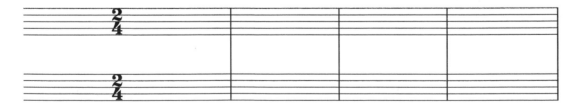

Clef and key
signature

MOTIVIC DEVELOPMENT AND THE SENTENCE

4. Example 10.7, mm. 1–4, melody and bass line. Both voices start on beat 1 (dotted quarter note and scale degree 1̂ in top voice, eighth note two octaves lower in bottom voice).

Clef and key
signature

5. Example 10.10, up to downbeat of m. 3, both voices. Both start on beat 1 (dotted quarter note and high scale degree 1̂ in top voice, eighth note a minor thirteenth below in bottom voice).

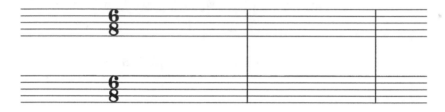

Clef and key
signature

6. Example 10.11, mm. 1–4, top two voices. Both start on beat 1 (quarter note and scale degree 5̂ in top voice, eighth note a minor third lower or a minor tenth lower in second voice).

Clef and key
signature

7. Example 10.13, up to beat 1 of m. 4, both voices. (Include two notes from top voice in m. 4.) Starts with eighth-note upbeat in top voice (high scale degree $\hat{5}$); bottom voice has eighth rest on upbeat and quarter note on downbeat a perfect twelfth below top voice entrance.

Clef and key
signature

8. Example 10.14, up to beat 2 of second full measure, both voices. Both start on beat 3 (quarter note and low scale degree $\hat{5}$ in top voice, half note a perfect fifth lower in bottom voice).

Clef and key
signature

DICTATION OF LONGER EXAMPLES

Your instructor or a classmate will choose one of the examples listed below and inform you of the key, clef, meter, first note (scale degree, rhythmic value, and metric placement) of one or more parts, and total number of measures. Use a separate piece of staff paper to write down the indicated information. You will hear a short progression to establish the key of the example, and then hear the example several times with breaks between hearings.

1. Example 10.2, all, outer voices.
2. Example 10.6, up to m. 8 downbeat, both voices.
3. Example 10.7, mm. 9–18, both voices.
4. Example 10.12, all, both voices.
5. Example 10.15, all, outer voices.

CONTEXTUAL LISTENING 10.1

Michael Praetorius (c. 1571–1621), *Tanzfolge* **no. 14**

Praetorius was a late Renaissance German composer and organist. He is most famous for his Advent carol "Es ist ein Ros entsprungen" (Lo, How a Rose E'er Blooming). This short sequential excerpt is drawn from a series of lovely dances.

1. This excerpt is six measures long, with a three-quarter-note anacrusis. What is the meter?

   $\frac{6}{4}$ $\frac{6}{8}$ $\frac{3}{4}$ $\frac{4}{4}$ $\frac{3}{2}$

2. The excerpt includes a prominent sequence. How long is the model, and how many times is it "sequenced"?

   a. One measure; 3½ times   b. Two measures; twice   c. One measure; once

3. There is a single chromatic neighbor (B♮) in the bass of the first complete measure. Within which beat does it fall?

   a. Beat 1   b. Beat 2   c. Beat 3   d. Beat 4   e. Beat 6

4. The melody employs essentially three different rhythmic shapes (each lasting three quarter notes). Notate these rhythmic patterns.

   a.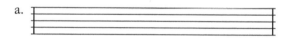

   b.

   c.

5. This excerpt ends in the key of F major and starts with a quarter-note E3 in the bass and G4 in the soprano. Accurately transcribe the outer parts (bass and melody) for the entire excerpt on the staves below.

6. The strong beats for the first two measures (and the anacrusis) suggest a consistent intervallic pattern. What is it? When does Praetorius break the pattern?

EXPANDING THE REPERTOIRE 10.2

John Williams, Theme from *Superman* (1978)

Through his recognizable scores for such movies as *Jaws*, *Star Wars*, and *Close Encounters of the Third Kind*, John Williams solidified himself as a powerhouse in film composition. Williams' scores for the *Indiana Jones* trilogy, the *Jurassic Park* movies, and *Schindler's List*, as well as his arrangement of the Olympic Fanfare for the 1984 Games, are familiar to all. The theme from *Superman*, seen here, exemplifies his control over orchestral textures and demonstrates his characteristic "touch," which makes his melody unmistakable.

This excerpt starts with the trumpet melody several measures into Williams' theme (which can be isolated using the online mixer). This eight-measure excerpt is in the key of C major and starts on C5.

1. Accurately transcribe the trumpet melody using the provided rhythmic configuration.

2. What type of phrase does this represent?

   a. Period   b. Consequent   c. Sentence   d. Subphrase   e. Antecedent

3. On your transcription, map out the phrasing as specifically as possible. You should use the following in your description: presentation, continuation, idea, fragment, cadential section.

EXPANDING THE REPERTOIRE 10.3

Freddie Mercury, "We Are the Champions" (1977)

"We Are the Champions" is one of the most well-known rock ballads performed by the band Queen. The popular song has been featured in numerous movie soundtracks. Think about some of the ways in which the music effectively mirrors the lyrics.

1. This familiar $\frac{6}{8}$ excerpt is in the key of F major and presents an interesting take on a common phrase type. The excerpt is based on a sixteen-measure model (rather than eight), meaning each of the units in a typical phrase of this type can be expected to last twice as long. How many measures are actually present in this example?

   a. Fourteen   b. Sixteen   c. Eighteen   d. Nineteen   e. Twenty

2. Map out the excerpt as carefully as possible, filling in the blanks in the diagram started for you below. Note that the "initial idea" a. is four measures long. The following portion of the phrase is also four measures long, but what are its origins?

   1. Four measures: initial idea (a)   6. _____: _____

   2. Four measures: _____   7. _____: _____

   3. Two measures: shorter motivic unit (b)   8. _____: _____

   4. Two measures: _____   9. Two measures: cadential section

   5. One measure: _____

3. Describe any expansions.

4. Although this excerpt represents a single phrase, imagine for a moment what phrase type would be represented if one started the phrase in measure 9.

   a. Sentence   b. Consequent   c. Subphrase   d. Period   e. Antecedent

5. What is the phrase type of the excerpt as a whole?

6. Accurately transcribe the outer voices of mm. 1–7 on the staves below.

Name: _____ Date: _____ Instructor: _____

EXPANDING THE REPERTOIRE 10.4

Joseph Kosma, "Autumn Leaves" (1945)

Although this was originally a French song featured in the film *Les Portes de la Nuit* of 1945, Johnny Mercer added lyrics to it for the American film *Autumn Leaves* from 1956, where it was sung by Nat King Cole. This song has become a jazz standard, both as an instrumental piece and as a song.

1. Transcribe the melody of the song, and include Roman numerals based on the chord symbols provided:

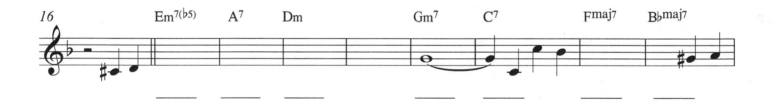

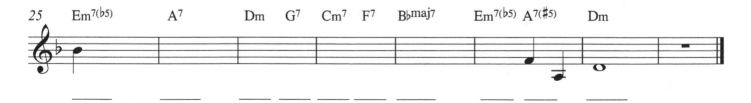

2. Observe the long notes in measures 1–2, 3–4, and 5–6. Each of these notes is first conceived as a chord member, but as the chord changes, so does its classification; choose the appropriate change of chord member from the options below. As you answer this question, realize that the thirds and the sevenths are the most

275

important notes to introduce in a melody, as the bass generally includes the root and the fifth; this notion will help your improvisations.

a. Third → seventh   b. Root → fifth

c. Seventh → third   d. Fifth → root

3. What characteristic sequence spans the first eight measures? How many times can you find the same exact sequence?

4. Now compare the sequence you chose for question 3 to the chord progression in mm. 27 to end, observing the root movement. How similar or different is it?

5. How would you describe the form of the entire song, on the basis of its melodic and harmonic design?

6. Why do you think the last dominant chord (m. 30) contains the $\sharp\hat{5}$ alteration?

7. *Optional assignment 1*: generally, this song is transposed to G minor when performed in a jazz instrumental ensemble. Transpose the entire song (including the chord progression) to G minor.

8. *Optional assignment 2*: prepare to improvise on the chord progression outlined in mm. 1–8, in the key of G minor. For practice, use the backup track provided online.

Chapter 11

Chromatic Neighbor Tones

This chapter introduces simple chromaticism, largely in the context of a complete neighbor tone. You have already encountered diatonic neighbor tones in the first chapter of this book, and it would be wise to review the diatonic exercises now. Chromatic neighbors typically add color to an otherwise diatonic musical line (recall the earlier exercises). Chromatic neighbors are sometimes supported by secondary harmonic functions (secondary dominants and leading-tone chords) and other times they are simply surface-level decoration. If you are employing scale degrees in your singing, you may wish to sing "raise" for notes that have been chromatically raised, such as chromatic lower neighbors, and "low" for notes that have been chromatically lowered, such as chromatic upper neighbors. In solfège (as explained previously) you may add the following adjusted syllables when ascending chromatically: di, ri, fi, si, li. When descending, you will use the following adjusted syllables: te, le, se, me ("may"), ra (see the drill section for chromatic scale drills; this may be a good place to start). Also in this chapter you will find a new set of harmonic paradigms, based on cadential progressions with vi, ii, and the cadential $\frac{6}{4}$.

Example 11.1.   Scott Joplin (c. 1867–1917), "Pineapple Rag" (1908)

* The chromatic lower neighbors here are nonfunctional and thus do not contribute to any change in harmony (use "raise," or in solfège "ri" and "fi," when singing). There are optional chromatic passing tones in the lower part. If you choose to try singing them, use the syllable "low" or "le" and "me." What sort of phrase type is found in each half of the excerpt? What is the structure of the entire excerpt?

If you are having trouble with the syllables for the chromatic neighbor, consider spending some time practicing the chromatic neighbor drill later in this chapter.

Example 11.2.   "There was an Old Woman Toss'd up in a Basket" (traditional)

* You should be able to sing this simple excerpt comfortably in three parts with little preparation. What is the function of the chromatic upper neighbor in m. 20? You will want to use "low," or in solfège "te," when singing that note. Map out the structure of this excerpt. What phrase types do you find here? Also, what is the relationship between the tenor and the melody in mm. 26–29?

Example 11.3.   "The Great Bells of Osney" (traditional round in three voices)

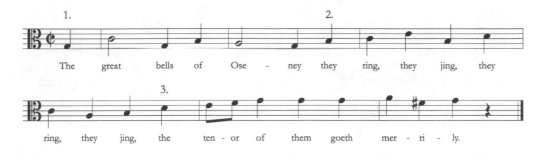

The great bells of Ose – ney they ring, they jing, they

ring, they jing, the ten – or of them goeth mer – ri – ly.

* This round presents a good opportunity to practice reading the alto clef. Sing using the names of the pitches as well as scale degrees. What is the function of the F♯? Note that it resolves up by semitone.

Example 11.4.   George Gershwin (1898–1937) and Ira Gershwin (1896–1983), "Someone to Watch over Me" (1926)

There's a some - bo - dy I'm long-ing to see,   I hope that he   turns out to be

There's a some - bo - dy I'm long-ing to see,   I hope that he   turns out to be

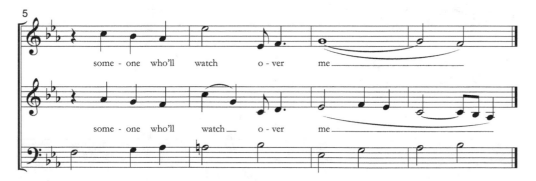

some - one who'll   watch   o - ver   me

some - one who'll   watch   o - ver   me

* You may remember this excerpt from an earlier chapter, where the focus was on the melody. Now you should concentrate on accurately singing the lower two parts. Be sure to use the correct syllables for the two chromatic lower neighbors, and give the two chromatic passing tones in the bass a try.

    This excerpt presents only the antecedent phrase. How do you think the consequent phrase goes?

Example 11.5.   Aleksandr Aliab'ev (1787–1851), *Grand Quatuor*, op. 4, mvt. 2

* What type of phrase structure does this excerpt present? Note how the first half is doubled in length, but the second half reverts to a more typical length for this type of phrase structure. Be sure to practice the syncopations before attempting the entire excerpt.

Example 11.6.   Henry Purcell (1659–1695), "I Gave Her Cakes" (round in three voices)

* Remember that, as in previous chapters, the longer catches and rounds are organized in staves in order to clarify the counterpoint and harmonic context. As before, catches are meant to be sung through
in unison, followed by typical round singing, wherein *all the groups (three of them) start at the number "1"
and sing all the way through the three lines.* The second group starts at the beginning when the first group
reaches the second line, and so forth.

   What is the effect of the chromatic upper neighbor?

Example 11.7.   Tomás Luis de Victoria, "O magnum mysterium"

* What is the relationship between the two voices here? Can you explain the E♭ upper neighbor in the lower part?

Example 11.8.   Ludolf Waldmann (1840–1919), "Mit Sing und Sang"

* *Translation*: Now open your doors, now open your house! Don't close your windows, but watch for me outside!

Example 11.9.   Joseph Haydn (1732–1809), "Grabschrift" (round in four voices)

* *Translation*: (Epitaph) Here lies Hans Lau with his wife. A cuckold was Hans Lau; What, then was his wife?

Example 11.10.   Felix Mendelssohn (1809–1847) "Entflieh' mit mir," op. 41, no. 1 (part song)

* *Translation*: Flee with me and be my wife, and rest by my heart;
            Far away let my heart be your country and your home.

Example 11.11. Joplin, "The Entertainer" (1902)

* There are two chromatic passing tones in this excerpt in m. 7. Use "raise" or "fi and ri" if you choose to sing them. There is a great deal of rhythmic richness and variety in this excerpt. Be sure to practice all eight different rhythmic "shapes" before attempting to sing this work in the ragtime style.

Example 11.12. Wolfgang Amadeus Mozart (1756–1791), Concerto for Flute, Harp and Orchestra, K. 299, mvt. 1

* Be sure to sing the solo line of the concerto as expressively as possible, paying particular attention to the large leaps and arpeggios in the solo line. It would be sensible to sing this one slower than its "Allegro" tempo marking. Also, note that the only true chromatic neighbor is the D♯ in m. 3. The remaining accidentals inflect the leading tone and the subtonic.

CHORALE WORKSHOP: CADENTIAL PROGRESSIONS WITH vi, ii, AND THE CADENTIAL $^6_4$

Working at a piano, play the following progressions in simple major and minor keys. Try placing the listed melodic patterns in the soprano voice. You should do your best to avoid parallels, doubled leading tones, and augmented seconds (in minor), but your focus should be on the relationship of the outer voices. In that light, be sure you can play the outer voices correctly and sing one of the outer voices while playing the other. Finally, as in the previous chapters, attempt to sing the progressions or play them on your instrument, arpeggiating each triad from the bottom up (and then top down). Note that root-position ii° is generally avoided in the minor mode.

Since the cadential $^6_4$ almost always falls on a point of metric strength, barlines have been indicated for the last of the progressions below. Perform the first chord as an upbeat so the cadential $^6_4$ arrives on beat 3 of the following measure.

Harmony (bass line in left hand)	Possible soprano scale degrees (right hand)
I⁶ ii⁶ V I or i⁶ ii°⁶ V i	$\hat{3}\ \hat{2}\ \hat{2}\ \hat{1}$ $\hat{1}\ \hat{2}\ \hat{2}\ \hat{1}$ $\hat{3}\ \hat{2}\ \hat{2}\ \hat{3}$ $\hat{3}\ \hat{2}\ \hat{7}\ \hat{1}$
I⁶ ii V I (in major only)	$\hat{1}\ \hat{2}\ \hat{2}\ \hat{1}$ $\hat{1}\ \hat{2}\ \hat{7}\ \hat{1}$
I⁶ ii⁶ V vi or i⁶ ii°⁶ V VI	$\hat{3}\ \hat{2}\ \hat{2}\ \hat{1}$ $\hat{1}\ \hat{2}\ \hat{2}\ \hat{1}$ $\hat{3}\ \hat{2}\ \hat{7}\ \hat{1}$
I⁶ ii $^6_5$ V $^{6-5}_{4-3}$ I or i⁶ ii°$^6_5$ V $^{6-5}_{4-3}$ i	$\hat{3}\ \hat{2}\ \hat{3}\ \hat{2}\ \hat{1}$ $\hat{1}\ \hat{1}\ \hat{1}\ \hat{7}\ \hat{1}$
I vi ii V I (in major only)	$\hat{3}\ \hat{3}\ \hat{2}\ \hat{2}\ \hat{1}$ $\hat{1}\ \hat{1}\ \hat{2}\ \hat{2}\ \hat{1}$ $\hat{5}\ \hat{6}\ \hat{6}\ \hat{7}\ \hat{1}$ $\hat{3}\ \hat{3}\ \hat{2}\ \hat{7}\ \hat{1}$
I vi ii⁶ V⁷ I or i VI ii°⁶ V⁷ i	$\hat{3}\ \hat{3}\ \hat{2}\ \hat{7}\ \hat{1}$ $\hat{3}\ \hat{3}\ \hat{4}\ \hat{4}\ \hat{3}$ in major only: $\hat{1}\ \hat{1}\ \hat{2}\ \hat{2}\ \hat{1}$
I⁶ ii⁶ V $^{8-7}_{6-5}_{4-3}$ I or i⁶ ii°⁶ V $^{8-7}_{6-5}_{4-3}$ i	$\hat{5}\ \hat{4}\ \hat{3}\ \hat{2}\ \hat{1}$ $\hat{1}\ \hat{2}\ \hat{1}\ \hat{7}\ \hat{1}$
I | vi ii⁶ V $^{6-5}_{4-3}$ | I or i | VI ii°⁶ V $^{6-5}_{4-3}$ | i	$\hat{3}\ \|\ \hat{3}\ \hat{4}\ \hat{3}\ \hat{2}\ \|\ \hat{1}$ $\hat{1}\ \|\ \hat{1}\ \hat{2}\ \hat{1}\ \hat{7}\ \|\ \hat{1}$

IMPROVISATION: GAMES AND EXERCISES

1. Have your friends sing or play the ragtime accompaniment from Example 11.1. Now, improvise a new melody, employing the exact same rhythmic configuration as in the original melody. Can you incorporate a few chromatic neighbors? Once you are comfortable, you may want to vary the rhythm.

2. *Sing and play arpeggios*: like the exercise at the very beginning of the book where you sang and played scales in a round, now sing and play arpeggiated harmonies in a round, starting the second voice when the first voice sings the second note. Once you have achieved success with the major triad, try minor triads, diminished

triads, various seventh chords, and, eventually, even more adventurous harmonies (augmented triads, augmented sixth chords, etc.).

IMPROVISATION: FOCUS ON RHYTHM AND METER

1. Improvise a melody over a progression using the harmonic patterns you discovered in the Chorale Workshop. Adopt the following rhythmic feel, and then try using some from the earlier chapters.

2. *Rhythmic improvisation*: practice eight of the more challenging rhythms from "Pineapple Rag" (11.1), "Someone to Watch over Me" (11.4), "Mit Sing und Sang" (11.8), "The Entertainer" (11.11), and Mozart K. 299 (11.12) (found below). Then compose or improvise a rhythmic round, setting a text of your choosing, using each of the rhythmic "shapes." Practice them until you are perfectly accurate. What is the meter?

3. Try a similar exercise, but using *at least* six of the $\frac{6}{8}$ rhythmic shapes (or patterns) found in the Purcell round (11.6). Practice your round until it is perfectly accurate.

DRILL

Chromatic neighbor drill: sing the following exercise as a round. Be sure to sing all the correct syllables. Aim for fluency and pitch accuracy. You might consider practicing with a chromatic tuner.

SUGGESTED SMARTMUSIC ASSESSMENTS

Complete the following SmartMusic assessments per the earlier directions. As much as possible, you will want to annotate your score with form and phrase markings: 11.1 (melody), 11.3 (second entrance), 11.4 (middle harmony), 11.6 (third entrance), 11.7 (lower part), 11.8 (melody), 11.9 (third entrance), 11.10 (melody, tenor, and bass), 11.11 (melody), and 11.12 (melody).

SHORT-TERM MUSICAL MEMORY

Fill in the key signature and clef as indicated by your instructor and write in the initial note(s) on the basis of the given pitch and rhythm information. Note that the key and clef *may not be the same* as in the original example. Your instructor (or practice partner) will play a short progression to establish the key and then count off several beats to establish the tempo. Because of the brevity of each extract, you should have an overall impression of the rhythm, contour, and scale degrees after just one or two hearings. Notate the entire fragment.

1. Example 11.2, beat 3 of m. 28 to end, top voice (starts with quarter note, scale degree $\hat{5}$).

Clef and key
signature

2. Example 11.3, up to downbeat of m. 4. Starts on beat 4 (quarter note, low scale degree $\hat{5}$).

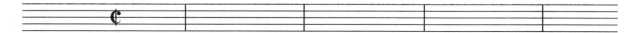

Clef and key
signature

3. Example 11.6, up to beat 4 of m. 2, middle staff. Starts on beat 6 (eighth note, high scale degree $\hat{5}$).

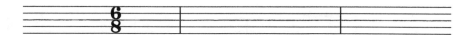

Clef and key
signature

4. Example 11.12, from upbeat to m. 3 until beat 2 of m. 4, top voice. Starts with eighth-note upbeat (scale degree $\hat{5}$).

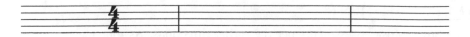

Clef and key
signature

5. Example 11.4, up to downbeat of m. 3, outer voices. Bottom voice starts on beat 1 (half note, scale degree 1̂); top voice has a quarter rest and then a dotted eighth note on beat 2, one octave higher than bottom voice entrance.

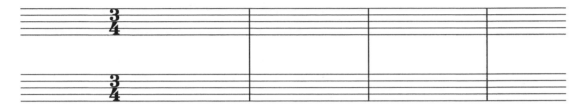

Clef and key
signature

6. Example 11.5, m. 5 up to downbeat of m. 8, outer voices. Both voices start on beat 1 (dotted quarter note and scale degree 1̂ in top voice, quarter note an octave lower in bottom voice).

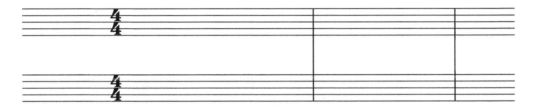

Clef and key
signature

DICTATION OF LONGER EXAMPLES

Your instructor or a classmate will choose one of the examples listed below and inform you of the key, clef, meter, first note (scale degree, rhythmic value, and metric placement) of one or more parts, and total number of measures. Use a separate piece of staff paper to write down the indicated information. You will hear a short progression to establish the key of the example, and then hear the example several times with breaks between hearings.

1. Example 11.1, all, both voices.
2. Example 11.4, up to downbeat of m. 7, outer voices.
3. Example 11.7, beat 2 of m. 6 to end, both voices.
4. Example 11.8, all, both voices.
5. Example 11.10, m. 5 to downbeat of m. 13, outer voices.

CONTEXTUAL LISTENING 11.1

Jean-Philippe Rameau (1683–1764), "Les Sauvages," from *Les Indes Galantes* (1735)

Rameau was a very influential composer, music theorist, and thinker of the Baroque period. His theories about fundamental bass are at the foundation of modern harmonic theory. *Les Indes Galantes* is an opera-ballet, an unusual combination of dance and singing. Each of the four acts tells a story set among different groups of indigenous peoples. The fourth and final act, from which this excerpt is drawn, is devoted to a story of love among the natives of the Americas.

1. How many measures are in this common-time excerpt?

    a. Eight   b. Sixteen   c. Twenty   d. Twenty-four   e. Thirty-two

2. The tonic of this excerpt is G. Is the excerpt major or minor?

    Major   Minor

3. What are the opening pitches in the right and left hands?

    Right hand: _____   Left hand: _____

4. Note that the first eight bars present one kind of theme type (made of two smaller phrases), while the entire excerpt combines smaller theme types into a larger, common theme type. Map out this excerpt as carefully as possible, describing all phrases, cadences, and repeated materials. You will want to use all of these terms: sentence, presentation, continuation, period, antecedent, consequent, half cadence, perfect authentic cadence.

5. Accurately transcribe the outer parts of the entire excerpt on the staves below.

CONTEXTUAL LISTENING 11.2

"Señoritas" (traditional)

This traditional tune is originally from Mexico, where the title is "Chiapanecas." Although the commonly heard English version includes quite different words, the original name is borrowed from a lively triple-time dance in which all participants clap. The anacrusis is one of the distinguishing features of the dance.

1. How long is the anacrusis for this $\frac{3}{4}$ excerpt?

   a. Quarter note   b. Eighth note   c. Two quarter notes   d. Two eighth notes

2. How many measures are in this excerpt?

   a. Fifteen   b. Sixteen   c. Twenty-four   d. Thirty-one   e. Thirty-two

3. Map this excerpt out as carefully as possible. Show all phrases, cadences, and repeated materials.

4. There are four chromatic lower neighbors in this excerpt. Where are they? What syllables or scale degrees would you use to sing them?

   Chromatic lower neighbor 1: _____. Syllable: _____.

   Chromatic lower neighbor 2: _____. Syllable: _____.

   Chromatic lower neighbor 3: _____. Syllable: _____.

   Chromatic lower neighbor 4: _____. Syllable: _____.

5. Accurately transcribe the outer parts of the entire excerpt in D major on the staves below.

EXPANDING THE REPERTOIRE 11.3

Cee Lo Green, "Forget You" (2010)

This song was presented in an earlier contextual listening example, where we explored the major pentatonic scale. Now we turn our focus to the idiomatic use of harmony here. The Lydian progression, which is quite prominent in popular music, uses a major version of the supertonic chord, hence its name "Lydian," which references the church mode with the raised-fourth scale degree. Indeed, the $\#\hat{4}$ is included in the supertonic chord here. You may be tempted to analyze this chord as a secondary dominant (or applied chord), namely V/V. In the context of a Lydian progression, however, it is best analyzed as "II" because this chord does not function in the same manner as its common-practice counterpart.

Songs featuring the Lydian progression include Queen's "It's a Kind of Magic," the Beatles' "Eight Days a Week", Lulu's "To Sir with Love," Blues Image's "Ride Captain Ride," Anne Murray's "You Won't See Me," and many others.

1. Write the chord symbols that correspond to a Lydian harmonic progression in C, and play it at the piano while listening to the song:

   I: II: IV: I:

2. The introduction (and most of the song) features a piano bass line that repeats a short-short-long rhythmic profile. Transcribe the bass line in the staff provided below.

3. How does the bass line fit the harmonic progression?

4. Earlier you identified that the melody of the chorus is based on the major pentatonic collection. Is the bass line drawn exclusively from the major pentatonic collection? Explain your answer.

5. *Optional assignment*: prepare to improvise on the Lydian progression using the notes of the major pentatonic scale. For practice, use the backup track provided online.

Chapter 12

Chromatic Passing Tones

This chapter continues exploring simple chromaticism, largely in the context of the passing tone. If you have not already reviewed the diatonic passing-tone exercises in the Foundations chapter of this book, you will want to go back and explore them now. As with the chromatic neighbor described in the previous chapter, this type of chromaticism can add color to an otherwise diatonic musical line. Chromatic tones sometimes indicate secondary harmonic functions (i.e., secondary dominants and secondary diminished-seventh chords) and, in certain cases, may lead to a change of key (none in this chapter). If you are employing scale degrees in your singing, you may wish to sing "raise" for chromatic alterations that include a half-step raising of a diatonic scale degree and "low" for chromatic alterations that involve a half-step lowering of a diatonic scale degree. In solfège (as explained previously), you may add adjusted syllables when chromatically raising a diatonic scale degree: di, ri, fi, si, li. When lowering a diatonic scale degree, you will use the adjusted syllables te, le, se, me, ra (see the drill section for chromatic scale drills). Also in this chapter you will find a new set of Chorale Workshop progressions based on the mediant triad and the subtonic triad (in minor).

Example 12.1.   Clara Wieck Schumann (1819–1896), "Romance," from *Quatre pièces carac-téristiques*, op. 5 (1835–36)

* Note how the melodic motive is transformed by the chromatic neighbor. Be sure to practice the chro-matic tones in the bass using the proper syllables.

Example 12.2.   Johannes Brahms (1833–1897), *Variations on a Theme by Haydn*, op. 56a (1873)

* Try mapping out the phrase structure. This certainly presents a familiar model, but observe how Brahms plays with the phrase lengths.

Example 12.3.   Ludwig van Beethoven (1770–1827), Quintet for Piano and Winds, op. 16 (1796), mvt. 3

* How does Beethoven vary the consequent phrase here?

Example 12.4.   William Hayes (1708–1777), "Wind, gentle evergreen" (round in three voices)

* What is the function of the C♯ in m. 5? What is the function of the G♯ in m. 12?

Example 12.5.   George Gershwin (1898–1937), "Bidin' my Time," from *Girl Crazy* (1930)

* What type of phrase structure is presented here? Also, why doesn't the D♮ resolve to E♭ as expected? Could there be a relation to the text?

Example 12.6.   Henry Purcell (1659–1695), "Ah! My Anna" (postlude)

* Be prepared to sing any voice in this four-part contrapuntal postlude. You may wish to attempt some Roman-numeral analysis to determine the function of the altered tones.

Example 12.7.   Wolfgang Amadeus Mozart (1756–1791), "Non so più," from *Le nozze di Figaro*, K. 492 (1786)

Translation: Simply at the name of love, of delight, I am disturbed, and my heartbeat alters
          And I am forced to speak of love, a desire I cannot explain.

    Be sure to practice singing one part while playing the other. Also, try to play the figured bass while singing the melody. Mapping this excerpt out and marking any phrase expansions reveals a much simpler structure (disregarding the expansions), which might make singing the excerpt easier.

Example 12.8.   Meredith Willson (1902–1984), "Goodnight, My Someone," from *The Music Man* (1957)

* What type of phrase structure is presented in each half of this thirty-two-measure song refrain?
What kind of phrase structure is presented by the entire thirty-two measures (note the half cadence in
the middle)? Some of the chromatic pitches in the lower part are incomplete neighbors. The compound
melody in the lower part obscures the otherwise direct neighbor motion (see, for example **D-(G)-C♯-D**
in mm. 3–4 and 19–20).

   If you are familiar with the rest of *The Music Man*, you will certainly notice a close connection between this melody and the signature tune of "76 Trombones."

Example 12.9.   Mozart, "Dies Bildnis ist bezaubernd schön," from *Die Zauberflöte*, K. 620
                (1791)

* *Translation*: Full of rapture, I would press her against this passionate bosom and forever would she
then be mine.

Feel free to sing this highly ornamented melody an octave lower. How does Mozart extend the
phrase (starting in m. 10)? Map out the many attempts at closure. Be sure to practice the rhythm here
slowly.

Example 12.10. Beethoven, Violin Sonata in D, op. 12 no. 1 (1797–98), mvt. 3

* Note how the G♯ in m. 2 is a chromatic passing tone from G♮ in the first measure.

Example 12.11. Mozart, "Sie wären gern bei ihm allein," from *Die Zauberflöte*, K. 620

* *Translation*: They would be happy to be with him alone. No, no, that cannot be.
   The phrase extensions here are similar to those in Example 12.7.

Example 12.12. Mozart, "Osanna in excelsis!" from *Requiem*, K. 626".

* *Translation*: Hosanna in the highest!
  Be sure to practice all four parts.

Example 12.13. Beethoven, Piano Trio in G, op. 1 no. 2 (1794–95), mvt. 2

* Identify the familiar phrase structure here. Also, note the sequence that controls part of the second half. Can you identify the linear pattern between outer voices as well as the root motion?

Example 12.14. Antonín Dvořák (1841–1904), Sonatina for Violin, op. 100, mvt. 2

* You may recall a portion of this excerpt from an earlier chapter, where you focused on the rather simple melody. Here, your focus should be on the bass line. What harmonies are suggested?

CHORALE WORKSHOP: PROGRESSIONS THAT INCLUDE iii (III) AND THE SUBTONIC IN MINOR

Working at a piano, play the following progressions in simple major and minor keys (except when major or minor is specified). Try placing the listed melodic patterns in the soprano voice. You should do your best to avoid parallels, doubled leading tones, and augmented seconds (in minor), but your focus should be on the relationship of the outer voices. In that light, be sure you can play the outer voices correctly and sing one of the outer voices while playing the other. Finally, as in the previous chapters, attempt to sing the progressions or play them on your instrument, arpeggiating each triad from the bottom up (and then top down).

As a reminder, the ↑ symbol will indicate a raised scale degree, while ↓ indicates a lowered (or unraised) scale degree. We will use just a $\hat{7}$ to indicate the raised leading tone in minor, however, and ↓$\hat{7}$ if an unaltered scale degree $\hat{7}$ is intended. The | symbol indicates a barline.

Harmony (bass line in left hand)	Possible soprano lines in scale degrees (right hand)
I | iii IV V or i | III iv V	1̂ 7̂ 6̂ 5̂ (in minor: 1̂ ↓7̂ 6̂ 5̂) 5̂ | 5̂ 4̂ 2̂ 3̂ | 3̂ 1̂ 7̂
I | iii ii⁶ V$^{6-5}_{4-3}$ | I or i | III ii°⁶ V$^{6-5}_{4-3}$ | i	3̂ | 3̂ 2̂ 1̂ 7̂ | 1̂ 5̂ | 5̂ 4̂ 3̂ 2̂ | 3̂ 5̂ | 5̂ 4̂ 3̂ 2̂ | 1̂ 1̂ | 7̂ 6̂ 5̂ 5̂ | 5̂ (in minor: 1̂ | ↓7̂ 6̂ 5̂ 5̂ | 5̂)
I | iii vi ii⁶ V⁷ | I or i | III VI ii°⁶ V⁷ | i	3̂ | 3̂ 3̂ 2̂ 2̂ | 1̂ 5̂ | 5̂ 6̂ 6̂ 4̂ | 3̂ 1̂ | 7̂ 1̂ 2̂ 2̂ | 1̂ (in minor: 1̂ | ↓7̂ 1̂ 2̂ 2̂ | 1̂)

Remaining progressions in minor only

i VII III ii°⁶ | V$^{6-5}_{4-3}$ i	3̂ 4̂ 5̂ 4̂ | 3̂ 2̂ 1̂ 1̂ 2̂ 3̂ 2̂ | 1̂ 7̂ 1̂
i VII⁶ III iv | V$^{6-5}_{4-3}$ Hold this cadential ⁶₄ for two beats.	3̂ 4̂ 5̂ 4̂ | 3̂ 2̂ 1̂ ↓7̂ ↓7̂ 6̂ | 5̂ 5̂ 5̂ 4̂ 3̂ 1̂ | 1̂ 7̂
i | VII V⁶₅ i	3̂ | 4̂ 4̂ 3̂ 1̂ | 2̂ 2̂ 1̂
i | VII iv⁶ V	1̂ | 2̂ 1̂ 7̂ 3̂ | 4̂ 4̂ 5̂ 5̂ | ↓7̂ 1̂ 2̂

IMPROVISATION: GAMES AND EXERCISES

1. *Group arpeggios*: sit or stand in a small group. The leader names a quality of triad (or seventh chord) and then plays or sings a sustained pitch. Each successive player/ singer adds one pitch to the arpeggio. If singing, the student should chant the chord member he or she is singing ("third," "fifth," or "seventh").
2. Improvise a melody over a progression using the harmonic patterns you discovered in the Chorale Workshop.

IMPROVISATION: FOCUS ON RHYTHM AND METER

1. Adopt the following rhythmic feel and improvise a tune that works with the rhythm/harmonic configuration found here. Now try applying one of the progressions found in the chorale workshop.

Foxtrot or Charleston (quick)

2. Practice the rhythm of Example 12.13 (the Beethoven Trio excerpt) at various tempos. Now, compose or improvise a *rhythmic* round (no pitches), reordering the measures of the Beethoven example, but using the rhythm from each measure's melody at least once. Then apply a text of your choosing, setting the text carefully. Practice your round, and see how fast you can perform it with perfect accuracy!

3. Below is another rhythmic pattern from the *Geographical Fugue*. Start by marking the $\frac{4}{4}$ meter and then subdividing into sixteenths. First practice singing just the second half, audiating the first part of the beat at the eighth rest. Then, practice only the second beat (starting on the sixteenth rest), being sure to subdivide. Now put it all together. See how fast you can speak this accurately, and then add new words, being sure to place the accented syllables appropriately.

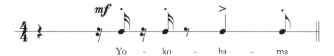

DRILLS

1. Continue practicing the chromatic neighbor-tone drill from the previous chapter.
2. *Chromatic passing-tone drill*: sing the following exercise as a round. Be sure to sing all the correct syllables. Aim for fluency and pitch accuracy. You may consider practicing with a chromatic tuner.

SUGGESTED SMARTMUSIC ASSESSMENTS

Complete the SmartMusic assessments per the earlier directions. As much as possible, you will want to annotate your score with form and phrase markings, while identifying harmonies: 12.1 (tenor), 12.2 (bass), 12.4 (second entrance), 12.6 (soprano, alto), 12.7 (melody, bass), 12.8 (bass), 12.11 (soprano, bass), 12.12 (tenor and alto), 12.13 (melody), and 12.14 (bass).

SHORT-TERM MUSICAL MEMORY

Fill in the key signature and clef as indicated by your instructor, and write in the initial note(s) on the basis of the given pitch and rhythm information. Note that the key and clef *may not be the same* as in the original example. Your instructor (or practice partner) will play a short progression to establish the key and then count off several beats to establish the tempo. Because of the brevity of each extract, you should have an overall impression of the rhythm, contour, and scale degrees after just one or two hearings. Notate the entire fragment.

1. Example 12.1, up to downbeat of m. 4, top voice. Starts on beat 1 (quarter note, scale degree $\hat{5}$).

Clef and key
 signature

2. Example 12.11, up to beat 4 of m. 2, top voice. Starts with eighth-note upbeat (scale degree $\hat{5}$).

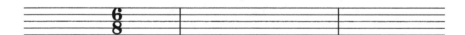

Clef and key
 signature

3. Example 12.13, m. 6 to downbeat of m. 7, top voice. Starts on beat 1 with first of several sixteenth notes (scale degree $\hat{6}$).

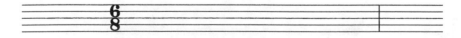

Clef and key
 signature

4. Example 12.5, up to downbeat of m. 3, both voices. Both start on beat 1 (half note and scale degree $\hat{3}$ in top voice, quarter note a major third or major tenth lower in bottom voice).

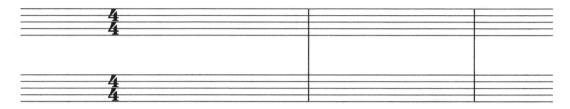

Clef and key
signature

5. Example 12.6, m. 2 to downbeat of m. 5, lower two voices. Both start with quarter notes on beat 1 (low scale degree $\hat{1}$ in bottom voice, and a minor tenth higher in other voice).

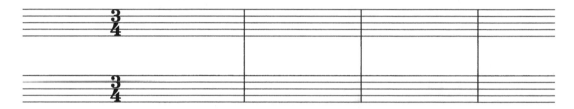

Clef and key
signature

6. Example 12.9, m. 5 through first half of m. 7, both voices (or just the melody). Both start on beat 1 with scale degree $\hat{1}$, one or two octaves apart (dotted sixteenth note in top voice, eighth note in bottom voice).

Clef and key
signature

7. Example 12.10, up to second beat (the fourth eighth-note) of m. 2, both voices (or just the melody). Melody starts with eighth-note upbeat (scale degree $\hat{5}$); bass line starts with eighth note on downbeat, a perfect twelfth lower than melody entrance.

Clef and key
  signature

8. Example 12.14, mm. 5–8, both voices (or just the melody). Both voices start on beat 1 (dotted eighth note and scale degree $\hat{3}$ in melody, half note a minor tenth below in bottom voice).

Clef and key
  signature

DICTATION OF LONGER EXAMPLES

Your instructor or a classmate will choose one of the examples listed below and inform you of the key, clef, meter, first note (scale degree, rhythmic value, and metric placement) of one or more parts, and total number of measures. Use a separate piece of staff paper to write down the indicated information. You will hear a short progression to establish the key of the example, and then hear the example several times with breaks between hearings.

1. Example 12.2, all, outer voices.
2. Example 12.3, all, outer voices.
3. Example 12.4, mm. 1–8.
4. Example 12.5, mm. 5–8, both voices.
5. Example 12.7, mm. 1–6, both voices.
6. Example 12.7, mm. 13–21, upper voice.

CONTEXTUAL LISTENING 12.1

Mozart, String Quintet in C Major, K. 406, mvt. 2

Scored for two violins, two violas, and a cello, Mozart's second string quintet was written in 1787 and is an arrangement of his Serenade for Wind Octet, K. 388. The second movement, marked *Andante*, starts with a wonderful series of properly resolving dissonances in the two violins (see question 7 below) and presents a typical eighteenth-century phrase structure.

1. How many measures are included in this ⅜ excerpt?

   a. 12   b. 16   c. 20   d. 24   e. 32

2. What type of cadence do you hear at m. 8? At m. 16?

   Cadence at m. 8: _____.

   Cadence at m. 16: _____.

3. What type of phrase structure is represented here? Be sure to use at least three appropriate labels to describe the structure.

4. There is a chromatic upper neighbor in mm. 7 and 8 that inflects the arrival on a half cadence (use "low," or in solfège "me," when singing). See if you can identify the final harmony of m. 7, which arrives as a consequence of the upper neighbor in the melody and the chromatic passing tone in the bass.

5. What type of sequence is used in the first and second halves of this excerpt?

   a. Descending thirds

   b. Ascending step

   c. Descending fifths

   d. Ascending fifths

6. Which type of nonchord-tone elaboration is found on the downbeats of mm. 4, 5, 6, 12, and 13?

   a. Accented passing tone   b. Appoggiatura   c. Suspension   d. Neighbor

7. Accurately transcribe the outer parts of the entire excerpt in E♭ major.

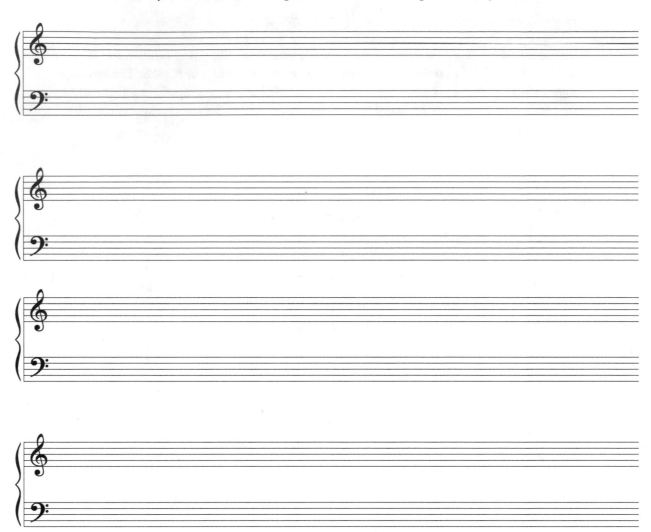

8. Prepare to sing the outer voices in class.

CONTEXTUAL LISTENING 12.2

Beethoven, Symphony No. 2 in D Major, op. 36 (1801–02), mvt. 2

No other composer has reached Beethoven's iconic status. His nine symphonies are regarded as quintessential cornerstones of the classical literature. This excerpt from his Second Symphony is drawn from the second movement, marked *Larghetto*, which shows clear pastoral and folk influences.

1. How many measures are in this $\frac{3}{8}$ excerpt?

   a. Four   b. Seven   c. Eight   d. Nine   e. Ten

2. What type of cadence ends this excerpt? Note that the final cadence is tonicized, such that the arrival chord acts as a temporary tonic.

   a. HC   b. Plagal cadence   c. Deceptive cadence   d. PAC

3. Map out the phrase structure as clearly as possible.

4. Beethoven uses the rhythm of a dotted sixteenth plus thirty-second in two spots. Where?

   1: _____.   2: _____.

5. What scale degree starts the melody?

   a. $\hat{1}$ b. $\hat{3}$ c. $\hat{4}$ d. $\hat{5}$ e. $\hat{6}$

6. Secondary harmonies are found in mm. 6 and 7. Attempt to provide Roman numerals. In m. 7, the secondary harmony is a rather standard embellishment; try to describe it.

7. Accurately transcribe the outer parts of the entire excerpt in the key of A major on the staves provided below.

EXPANDING THE REPERTOIRE 12.3

Richard Rodgers (1902–1979), "My Funny Valentine," from *Babes in Arms* (1937)

Richard Rodgers and Oscar Hammerstein co-wrote and produced hundreds of songs and nearly fifty Broadway productions, notably *South Pacific*, *The King and I*, and *The Sound of Music*, to name only a few. Their collaborations captivated America's audiences through the 1930s, '40s, and '50s. This tune's simple and classic structure has allowed it to be adapted and performed by many well-known artists, such as Frank Sinatra, Ella Fitzgerald, Miles Davis, and Chet Baker.

1. How many measures are in this cut-time excerpt?

   a. Four   b. Six   c. Seven   d. Eight   e. Ten

2. What interval does the voice leap between m. 5 and m. 6?

   a. Minor third   b. Diminished fifth   c. Perfect fifth

   d. Minor sixth   e. Perfect octave

3. What scale degree does the melody end on? What type of chord is found in the final measure? (Provide the Roman numeral and figure.)

   Scale degree: _____.   Chord: _____.

4. Accurately transcribe the outer parts of the entire excerpt in the key of C minor.

Chapter 13

Chromaticism Beyond the Stepwise Context

This chapter introduces a mixed variety of chromatic approaches, expanding on the excerpts found in the previous two chapters. Here, however, the chromaticism is not restricted to a stepwise approach, although the underlying basis will almost always be linear. The material here will help you see if you can connect chromatic tones to the pitches to which they would normally "resolve," even if they are not adjacent. As you will recall from the two previous chapters, when we encounter chromatic notes that seem to be playing an embellishing role (as opposed to any sort of harmonic role), we can relate them to nearby diatonic pitches in order to be able to perform them correctly or discern them by ear. Even in cases where these foreign tones are part of chromatic harmony, perhaps serving to temporarily "tonicize" a particular nontonic key center, one can usually hear them serving a linear embellishing role as well. In your performance as well as in your perception of chromatic melody, you can listen in both "directions" (melodically and harmonically) in order to understand the chromaticism and its role in the music. Finally, in this chapter you will find a new set of Chorale Workshop progressions that introduce secondary harmonies.

Example 13.1.   Johannes Brahms (1833–1897), "When, When?" (1885)

* *Translation*: When? When? When will heaven stop punishing [me] with albums and autographs? When?

(Written as a puzzle canon; see below)

* What is the function of the C♯ in m. 6? Although it is not a passing or neighbor tone like the chromatic pitches in the previous two chapters, it does resolve by step to D, while suggesting a chromaticized coloring of the motion to the dominant (see Chapter 22 on augmented-sixth chords for further explanation). The C♯ in m. 10 is approached by step, but it stays unresolved until the arrival of D in the final measure.

Try putting together the "puzzle canon" without looking at the realized answer above. In the Renaissance, puzzle canons were common compositional games wherein the performer would have to figure out where and on which pitch the second part would enter. Note the use of a movable C clef, with middle C (C4) on the lowest line (typically referred to as "soprano clef"). For a review of movable C clefs, refer to the Foundations of Aural Skills chapter.

Example 13.2.   Henry Purcell (1659–1695), "Come, Come!" (round in three voices)

* Note the function of the two sharps in m. 10. Although they appear to be descending, and thus defy-
ing the more normative "resolutions" of raised tones, the D♯ is actually the temporary leading tone to
vi (or E minor), which is established in m. 9. E minor (vi) is tonicized by its own dominant in m. 10
and then returns in m. 11, where vi is treated diatonically in the key of G major. The C♯ is the raised
submediant in the key of E minor, and thus both D♯ and C♯ should be sung with appropriate syllables
(raise, or fi and si).

Example 13.3.   Joseph Haydn (1732–1809), String Quartet in G, op. 64 no. 4 (1790), mvt. 2

* Be sure to identify the special harmony in m. 5. Also, map out the structure of the excerpt. The first
half presents a fairly typical antecedent phrase, but what happens in the second half?

Example 13.4.   Haydn, Symphony no. 87 in A (1785), mvt. 3

* What chord is tonicized in the first half of this excerpt? The structure of this excerpt is very
similar to a parallel period, except for one critical alteration: What has happened to the midperiod
half-cadence?

Example 13.5.   Bill Munro, "When My Baby Smiles at Me" (1920)

* The chromatic upper and lower neighbor of the opening creates an entire chromatic turn figure and mirrors the topsy-turvy feeling one gets when a loved one smiles in one's direction. The E♯ in m. 6

moves chromatically to the F♯ that follows but could be described as a chromatic passing tone from the E in the bass in that measure. In the parallel spot in m. 14 the initial tone (A, which moves to A♯) is actually in the top voice. The gradually higher registral placement of the words "me" and "love" eventually gives way to an emphasized high-point arrival on E, appropriately setting the word "heaven."

Example 13.6.   Ludwig van Beethoven (1770–1827), Quintet for Piano and Winds, op. 16, mvt. 1

* Before singing this excerpt, map out the overall phrase structure and identify the function of all chromatic tones.

Example 13.7.   Wolfgang Amadeus Mozart (1756–1791), Rondo in A minor, K. 511 (1787)

* Are any of these chromatic tones related to the harmony, or do they all provide exclusively "linear" color? Although Mozart used two B♭s here in his notation, what syllable might you use to sing them? In which direction do they resolve? What type of phrase structure is presented here? What is going on in the first three measures of each half?

Example 13.8.   Haydn, Symphony no. 104 in D Major ("London"), Hob. I:104 (1795), mvt. 3

* From which section of the movement do you think this excerpt is drawn? Provide a Roman-numeral analysis of m. 5 to the end, and identify the harmonic functions.

Example 13.9.   Beethoven, Octet, op. 103 (1792–93), mvt. 1

* Be sure to practice all four parts, although you may wish to concentrate on the bass, the melody, and the upper voice of the middle staff.

Example 13.10. Beethoven, Contredanse, WoO 14 (1795)

* Describe the phrase structure of this excerpt. Note how the arrival on the V of V in m. 9 tonicizes the arrival on V, creating a *tonicized half cadence.* How is this tonicization of V prepared in the first half of the excerpt?

Example 13.11. Mozart, Serenade no. 1, K. 439b, mvt. 1

* How has Mozart extended or expanded this phrase? Also, which chromatic notes are harmonically functional, and which are linear embellishments?

CHORALE WORKSHOP: PROGRESSIONS THAT INCLUDE $\frac{V^7}{V}$, $\frac{V^6_5}{V}$, AND DECEPTIVE CADENCES

Each of the following progressions can be realized in major and minor keys unless otherwise specified. For each progression, sing just the bass line, and then sing each chord as an arpeggio (up from its bass note and back down) or play it on an instrument. Then, working at a piano, try singing the soprano line while playing the bass line, and singing the bass while playing the soprano line. Make sure the soprano is always sounding in a higher register than the bass. Finally, practice every progression with every soprano line on the piano, in a variety of simple keys.

As a reminder, the ↑ symbol will indicate a raised scale degree, while ↓ indicates a lowered (or unraised) scale degree. We will use just $\hat{7}$ to indicate the raised leading tone in minor, however, and ↓$\hat{7}$ if an unaltered scale degree $\hat{7}$ is intended. The | symbol indicates a barline.

Harmony (bass line in left hand)	Possible soprano scale degrees (right hand)
I $\frac{V^7}{V}$ V	$\hat{5}$ ↑$\hat{4}$ $\hat{5}$
or	$\hat{3}$ ↑$\hat{4}$ $\hat{5}$ (only in major)
i $\frac{V^7}{V}$ V	$\hat{1}$ $\hat{1}$ $\hat{7}$
I⁶ ii⁶₅ $\frac{V^7}{V}$ | V	$\hat{5}$ $\hat{6}$ $\hat{6}$ | $\hat{5}$ (in minor: $\hat{5}$ $\hat{6}$ ↑$\hat{6}$ | $\hat{5}$)
or	$\hat{1}$ $\hat{1}$ $\hat{1}$ | $\hat{7}$
i⁶ ii°⁶₅ $\frac{V^7}{V}$ | V	
I $\frac{V^6_5}{V}$ V⁴₂ | I⁶	$\hat{1}$ $\hat{1}$ $\hat{7}$ | $\hat{1}$
or	$\hat{3}$ $\hat{2}$ $\hat{2}$ | $\hat{1}$
i $\frac{V^6_5}{V}$ V⁴₂ | i⁶	
I IV⁶ $\frac{V^6_5}{V}$ | V	$\hat{3}$ $\hat{4}$ $\hat{6}$ | $\hat{5}$
or	$\hat{1}$ $\hat{1}$ $\hat{2}$ | $\hat{2}$
i iv⁶ $\frac{V^6_5}{V}$ | V	$\hat{1}$ $\hat{1}$ $\hat{1}$ | $\hat{7}$
(unusual in minor)	
I vi $\frac{V^7}{V}$ V⁷ | I	$\hat{5}$ $\hat{5}$ ↑$\hat{4}$ ↓$\hat{4}$ | $\hat{3}$
	$\hat{3}$ $\hat{3}$ $\hat{2}$ $\hat{2}$ | $\hat{1}$
I vi $\frac{V^6_5}{V}$ V⁷ | I	$\hat{3}$ $\hat{3}$ $\hat{2}$ $\hat{2}$ | $\hat{1}$
	$\hat{1}$ $\hat{1}$ $\hat{1}$ $\hat{7}$ | $\hat{1}$

The following two patterns include deceptive cadences. Watch out for parallel fifths!

I $\dfrac{\text{V}^6_5}{\text{V}}$ V V^7 | vi $\qquad\qquad$ $\hat3$ $\hat2$ $\hat2$ $\hat2$ | $\hat1$

i^6 ii$^{\o6}_5$ $\dfrac{\text{V}^6_5}{\text{V}}$ V | VI $\qquad\qquad$ $\hat3$ $\hat2$ $\hat2$ $\hat2$ | $\hat1$

IMPROVISATION: GAMES AND EXERCISES

1. *Advanced group arpeggios*: sit or stand in a small group. The leader names a quality of triad (or seventh chord) and identifies the chord member he or she will be singing: root, third, fifth, or seventh. Then the leader plays or sings a sustained pitch. Each successive person adds one pitch to the harmony, announcing or chanting the chord member being sung or played.

2. Improvise a melody over the Chorale Workshop progressions.

3. Improvise your own puzzle canon (as in Exercise 13.1). Start with a harmonic alternation between tonic and dominant, and then create simple melodic lines with chord tones on the strong beats. See if a friend can imitate you directly without writing down the canon. You may wish to have a I–V vamp (a repeatedly sung or played pattern) going in the background.

IMPROVISATION: FOCUS ON RHYTHM AND METER

1. Improvise a melody over a progression using the rhythmic feel shown here, and then branch out to those harmonies you discovered in the Chorale Workshop.

2. Practice the rhythm of Example 7 at various tempos. Now, compose or improvise a *rhythmic* round (no pitches), using the rhythmic layout of each measure at least once. Then apply a text of your choosing, setting the text carefully. Practice your round, and see how fast you can perform it with perfect accuracy!

3. Try a similar exercise with the "two thirty-seconds, dotted-eighth" rhythm of Example 13.4.

4. Here is a summary of the rhythmic patterns from the *Geographical Fugue*, all but one of which you have already explored. In order to prepare for quartet performances of the complete work in the next chapter, you should review the five basic rhythmic paradigms (patterns) below. It is recommended that you practice each with a metronome until you can move fluidly at a quarter note = 60.

   Once you have learned the rhythmic patterns, practice performing them as a round in a group of 3 or 4. Be prepared to perform them this way in class. Also try a "chance" exercise, wherein each person picks a different random order for the patterns, and then you perform as an ensemble, with one individual entering at the beginning of each successive measure.

a.

Tri - ni - dad   and the big Miss-iss-ipp - i and the

b.

Can - a - da Ma - la - ga Ri - mi - ni Brin-di - si   Can - a - da Ma - la - ga Ri - mi - ni Brin-di - si

c.

Yes!   Ti - bet   Ti - bet   Ti - bet   Ti

d.

Yo - ko - ha - ma

e.

Yo - ko - ha - ma Hon-o - lu - lu

DRILLS: SINGING SECONDARY DOMINANTS

As you may already have sensed, when we sing secondary dominant chords and resolve them correctly we are momentarily replicating the motion from V^7 (and its inversions) to I within a "new key," without departing from the larger sense of the home tonic. The chords themselves contain a mixture of chromatic and diatonic scale degrees, temporarily acting in the new diatonic context. You may find it helpful to internalize the sound of a dominant seventh (a major-minor seventh chord), in order to associate this chord quality with the secondary dominants that you hear in your various musical endeavors. Before trying the exercises below, practice singing major-minor seventh chords, picking various chordal roots that lie comfortably within your range.[1]

Sing through the drills below without a piano. Label the scale degree or solfège syllables in m. 7 of each exercise. These are the scale degrees or solfège syllables associated with the various secondary dominants included here. With practice, you will learn to aurally associate particular scale degrees or solfège syllables with the corresponding secondary dominant. Try not to lose your sense of the overall tonic, and notice that the last six beats of every exercise reestablish the home key.

---

[1] Be sure to continue practicing the chromatic drills from the previous two chapters so that you can sing them with complete accuracy.

Secondary dominant drill no. 1:

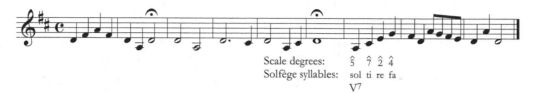

Scale degrees: $\hat{5}$ $\hat{7}$ $\hat{2}$ $\hat{4}$
Solfège syllables: sol ti re fa
V^7

Secondary dominant drill no. 2:

Scale degrees:
Solfège syllables: $V^7/$___

Secondary dominant drill no. 3:

Scale degrees:
Solfège syllables: $V^7/$___

Secondary dominant drill no. 4:

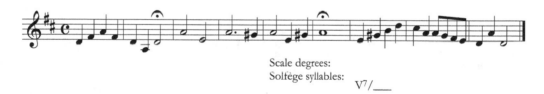

Scale degrees:
Solfège syllables: $V^7/$___

Secondary dominant drill no. 5:

Scale degrees:
Solfège syllables: $V^7/$___

Secondary dominant drill no. 6:

Scale degrees:
Solfège syllables: $V^7/$___

SUGGESTED SMARTMUSIC ASSESSMENTS

Complete SmartMusic assessments from Chapter 13 as follows:

1. Select secondary-dominant drills: 13.12, 13.13, and 13.15.
2. Examples 13.1 (lower part), 13.2 (second entrance), 13.5 (melody), 13.6 (melody, bass), 13.7 (melody), 13.9 (melody, bass, upper voice of middle staff), and 13.11 (melody, bass).

SHORT-TERM MUSICAL MEMORY

Fill in the key signature and clef as indicated by your instructor, and write in the initial note(s) on the basis of the given pitch and rhythm information. Note that the key and clef *may not be the same* as in the original example. Your instructor (or practice partner) will play a short progression to establish the key and then count off several beats to establish the tempo. Because of the brevity of each extract, you should have an overall impression of the rhythm, contour, and scale degrees after just one or two hearings. Notate the entire fragment.

1. Example 13.3, beat 3 of m. 4 to beat 2 of m. 6, top voice (starts with quarter note, low scale degree $\hat{5}$).

Clef and key
signature

2. Example 13.6, m. 6 to downbeat of m. 8, top voice. Starts on beat 1 (eighth note, high scale degree $\hat{1}$).

Clef and key
signature

3. Example 13.7, up to beat 4 of m. 2, top voice. Starts with eighth-note upbeat (high scale degree $\hat{5}$).

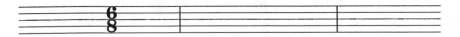

Clef and key
signature

4. Example 13.10, end of m. 2 to downbeat of m. 6, top voice. Starts with two six-teenth-note upbeats (scale degrees $\hat{1}$ and $\hat{7}$).

Clef and key
signature

5. Example 13.9, mm. 8–9, outer voices. Both start on beat 1 (dotted quarter note and scale degree $\hat{2}$ in top voice, eighth note a perfect twelfth lower in bottom voice).

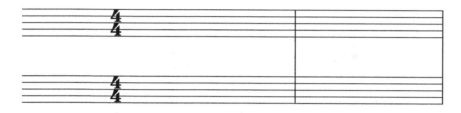

Clef and key
signature

6. Example 13.11, mm. 9–10, outer voices. Both start on beat 1 with scale degree $\hat{5}$ an octave apart (eighth note in top voice, quarter note in bottom voice).

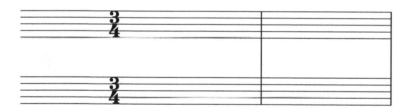

Clef and key
signature

DICTATION OF LONGER EXAMPLES

Your instructor or a classmate will choose one of the examples listed below and inform you of the key, clef, meter, first note (scale degree, rhythmic value, and metric placement) of one or more parts, and total number of measures. Use a separate piece of staff paper to write down the indicated information. You will hear a short progression to establish the key of the example, and then hear the example several times with breaks between hearings.

1. Example 13.1, m. 2 to downbeat of m. 8, both voices. Use either one or two staves.
2. Example 13.2, up to downbeat of m. 7, line 2.
3. Example 13.4, up to final downbeat, outer voices.
4. Example 13.6, m. 25 to end, outer voices.

CONTEXTUAL LISTENING 13.1

The French folk tune that is the basis of what you may know as "Twinkle, Twinkle, Little Star" was just as popular in eighteenth-century France as it is today. Mozart wrote a set of twelve variations based on this folk tune. Listen to Mozart's variations on this tune, and then consider how you might vary it in other ways.

1. Map out this excerpt in as much detail as possible. Note that each half of the excerpt is repeated and that sections of each half are also repeated with slight variations.

2. The tune on which this variation is based is quite familiar. What techniques does Mozart use to vary the tune?

3. The second half of the excerpt has a number of decorative chromaticisms, but the only one that is supported by a secondary chord is m. 21 (C♯). In the key of G major, what Roman numeral would you assign to this secondary chord?

4. A sequence can be found in mm. 4–7 (altered in m. 7 to bring the first half of the excerpt to a PAC). What intervallic pattern between outer voices controls the sequence starting in m. 7?

5. There are actually two notes in the right hand in mm. 4–8. Typically, the second (alto) voice moves in thirds below the top voice, but on three occasions the two upper voices make the interval of a second. Where does this occur?

6. Describe the relationship between mm. 9–12 and 13–16.

7. Now, accurately transcribe the entire excerpt (all parts) in the key of G major.

8. Finally, give a Roman-numeral analysis for the entire excerpt.

CONTEXTUAL LISTENING 13.2

Mozart, Piano Sonata in A Major, K. 331 (c. 1783), mvt. 1

Mozart's eleventh sonata is one of his most well-known works for solo piano. Its first movement entails a theme with six variations—an unusual way to begin a piano sonata. The compound time signature and *Andante grazioso* tempo marking are suggestive of the siciliano, a pastoral dance of the eighteenth century.

1. How many measures are in this $\frac{6}{8}$ excerpt?

   a. 6   b. 7   c. 8   d. 9   e. 10

2. Map out the overall structure of the excerpt in as much detail as possible, showing any cadences and repeated musical material. You should include all of this vocabulary in your excerpt map: half cadence, perfect authentic cadence, antecedent, consequent, period.

3. Now, accurately transcribe the melody (both pitches and rhythm) in the key of A major on the staves below.

4. Consider the structure of the bass voice. What is the typical relationship between the bass and the melody?

   a. Mostly contrary motion

   b. Mostly parallel motion

   c. Mostly oblique motion

5. Now, accurately transcribe the bass (both pitches and rhythm) in the key of A major on the staves below.

6. Identify the Roman numerals of the harmonies at the cadences.

EXPANDING THE REPERTOIRE 13.3

> **Frank Churchill (1901–1942), "Someday My Prince Will Come," from _Snow White_ (1937)**

Originally appearing in the 1937 Disney cartoon _Snow White_, this song quickly gained popularity. It has found its way into the jazz repertoire and has been recorded by such artists as Dave Brubeck, Herbie Hancock, and Miles Davis.

1. Map out this thirty-one-measure excerpt. What is repeated?

2. In what meter is this excerpt?

3. Accurately transcribe both parts in the key of F major.

Both melody and bass leap into a number of chromatic pitches. This will present a challenge, but try to imagine the pitch that is chromatically altered, as well as the pitch to which the chromatic note will eventually ("someday . . .") resolve.

Chapter 14

Complete Examples from the Repertoire

This chapter presents several complete examples from the repertoire to be used as a supplement to the materials found elsewhere in Unit II. As such, there are no additional exercises or drills. Although the shorter examples are similar in length to some you have found earlier, all the arrangements in this chapter should be prepared to a performance standard, either in small groups or as a class. Be sure to follow the performance directions carefully, and, as always, focus on basic rhythmic and melodic shapes. In addition, supply harmonic analyses, as this will help you link the various parts to the larger harmonic context.

Example 14.1.   Francesco Cavalli (1602–1776), "Tremulo spirito" from *La Didone* (1641)

scor - da - ti d'E - cu-ba, ve - do-va mi - se-ra.   Cau - sa-no

l'ul - ti-mo hor - ri-do e - si - ti-o Pa - ri-de e E - le-na.

* *Translation*: Tremulous spirit, weeping and languid, leave quickly;
        Fly, that turbid and greedy cupid, Erebo, awaits.
        Poor Priamus, forget about Hecuba, miserable widow.
        Causing the final horrible exile are Paris and Helen.

Note the fourfold repetition of the same bass line. How is the melody varied each time? We will see more examples of a "lament bass" (which involves descending by step from tonic) in Chapters 19 and 22.

Example 14.2.   Johannes Brahms (1833–1897), "Sonntag," op. 47 no. 3 (1859)

tau - send-schö - ne Her - ze - lein, woll-te Gott, woll-te Gott, ich wär' heu - te bei

ihr, woll-te Gott, woll-te Gott, ich wär' heu - te bei ihr!

* *Translation*:

Sunday

The entire week, I have not even
Seen my lovely sweetheart.
I saw her on a Sunday,
Standing right in front of the door:
The thousand-times beautiful girl,
The thousand-times beautiful little heart,
Would, God, I were with her today!

This entire week, my laughing
Cannot cease;
I saw her on a Sunday,
Going right into church:
The thousand-times beautiful girl,
The thousand-times beautiful little heart,
Would, God, I were with her today!

Each verse of this strophic song features a two-part phrase structure and a phrase extension. Study the phrase structure thoroughly before attempting to sing it.

Example 14.3.   Ludwig van Beethoven (1770–1827), Canon "Glück zum neuen Jahr" ("Happy new year"), WoO 165 (1815)

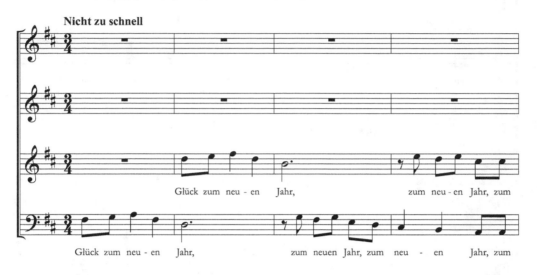

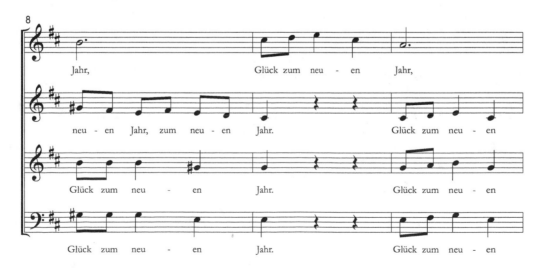

Example 14.4. Franz Schubert (1797–1828), "Das Wandern" from *Die schöne Müllerin*, op. 25, D. 795

14

Mül - ler — sein, dem nie - mals fiel das Wan - dern ein, das Wan - dern, das
Tag und Nacht, ist — stets auf Wan - der - schaft be - dacht, das Was - ser, das
stil - le — stehn, die sich mein Tag nicht mü - de — drehn, die Rä - der, die
mun - tern Reihn und wol - len gar noch schnel - ler — sein, die Stei - ne, die
Mei - ste - rin, laßt mich in Frie - den wei - ter - ziehn und wan - dern, und

18   *pp*

Wan - dern, das Wan - dern, das Wan - dern.
Was - ser, das Was - ser, das Was - ser.
Rä - der, die Rä - der, die — Rä - der.
Stei - ne, die Stei - ne, die — Stei - ne.
wan - dern, und wan - dern, und wan - dern.

pp

mf

22

2. Vom
3. Das
4. Die
5. O

* *Translation*: Wandering is the miller's joy, Wandering!
He must be a miserable miller,
who never likes to wander.
Wandering!

We've learned this from the water, From the water!
It does not rest by day or night,
It thinks always of journeying,
The water.

We see this also with the wheels, With the wheels!
They don't ever like to stand still,
And turn all day without tiring.
The wheels.

The very stones, heavy though they are,
The stones!
They join in the cheerful dance,
And want to go yet faster.
The stones!

Oh, wandering, wandering, my joy, Oh, wandering!
Oh, Master and Mistress,
Let me push on in peace,
And wander!

Example 14.5.   Wolfgang Amadeus Mozart (1756–1791), Canonic Adagio for Two Basset
Horns and Bassoon, K. 410 (1785)

* Examine how the top two lines compare to one another. What kind of canon is this? Prepare all three parts for performance (paying particular attention to the more chromatic sections).

Example 14.6. Henry Purcell (1659–1695), "Ye twice ten hundred deities," from *The Indian Queen* (1695)

* This excerpt features a total of five diminished fifths in the melody, all of which are immediately followed by a step or a third in the opposite direction. For practice purposes, try singing each diminished fifth as two minor thirds in a row. What kind of triad results?

The following examples present three approaches to the typical song form, which is usually thirty-two bars long and metrically "square" (4+4+4+4 or 8+8+8+8):

• One of the songs includes a phraseology that corresponds to A–A–B–A or A–A′–B–A′ (sometimes called quatrain form, sometimes compared to either binary or ternary form).

- Another of the songs divides into two similar sixteen-bar sentences with an inconclusive cadence in the middle, suggesting a large thirty-two-bar period, or A–B–A′–B′. Another example of this formal plan can be seen in Example 13.5.
- Finally, one song combines and expands the two models into an unusual forty-measure song: A–B–A′–B′–A″.
- See if you can tell which one is which and then label all the sections.

Example 14.7.   George Gershwin (1898–1937), "I Got Rhythm," from *Girl Crazy* (1930)

Example 14.8. Cole Porter (1891–1964), "Old Fashioned Garden," from *Hitchy-Koo* (1919)

Example 14.9.   James Hanley (1892–1942), "Second Hand Rose," from *Ziegfeld Follies* (1921)

Had the nerve to tell me he's been mar - ried be - fore___

Ev - 'ry one knows___ that I'm just se - cond hand Rose___ From

Se - cond A - ve - nue.___

Example 14.10. Ernst Toch (1887–1964), "Geographical Fugue" (1930)

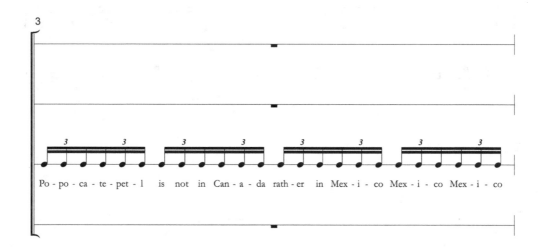

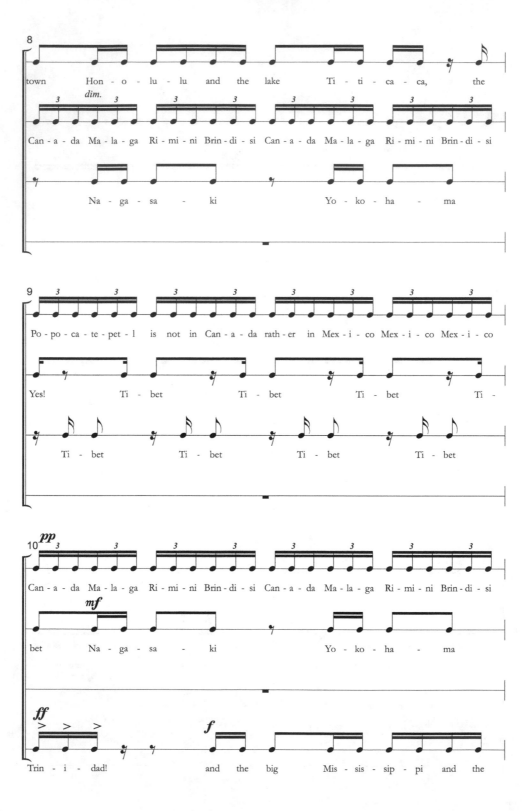

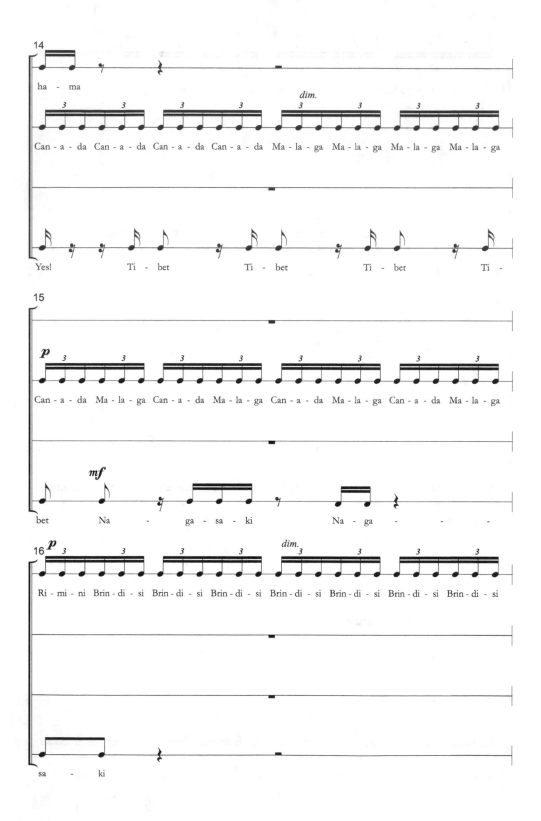

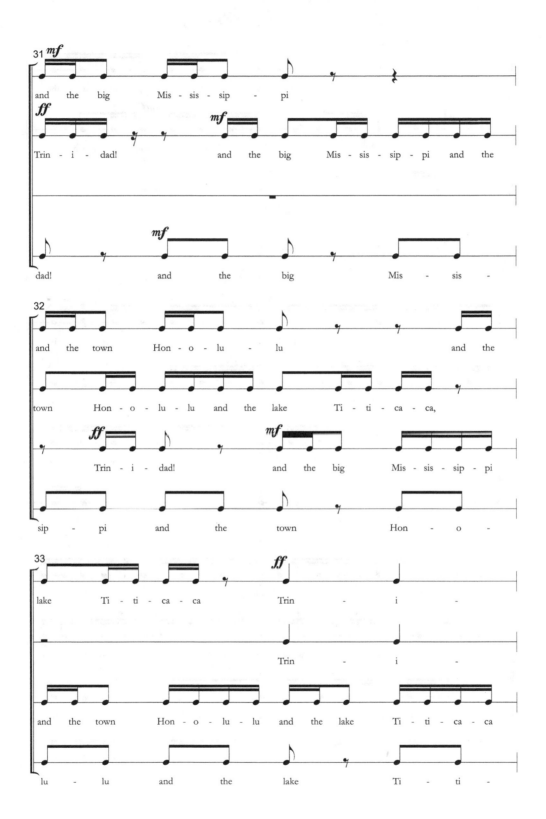

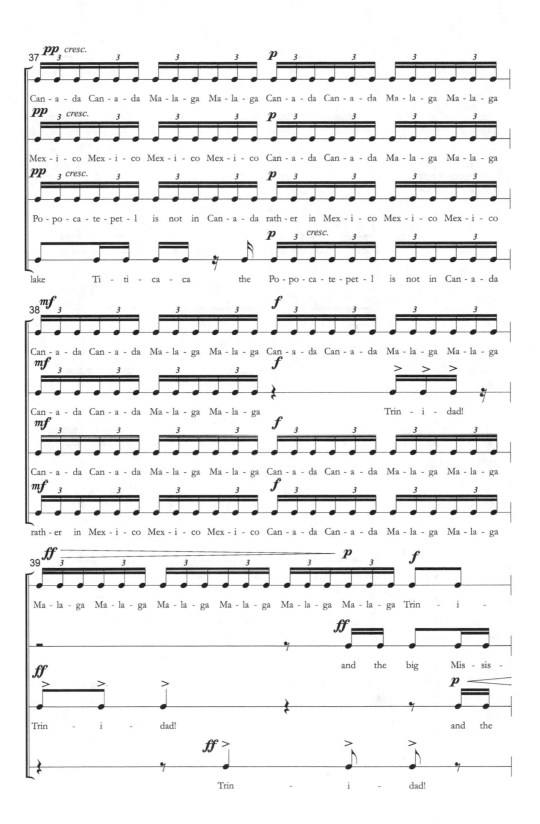

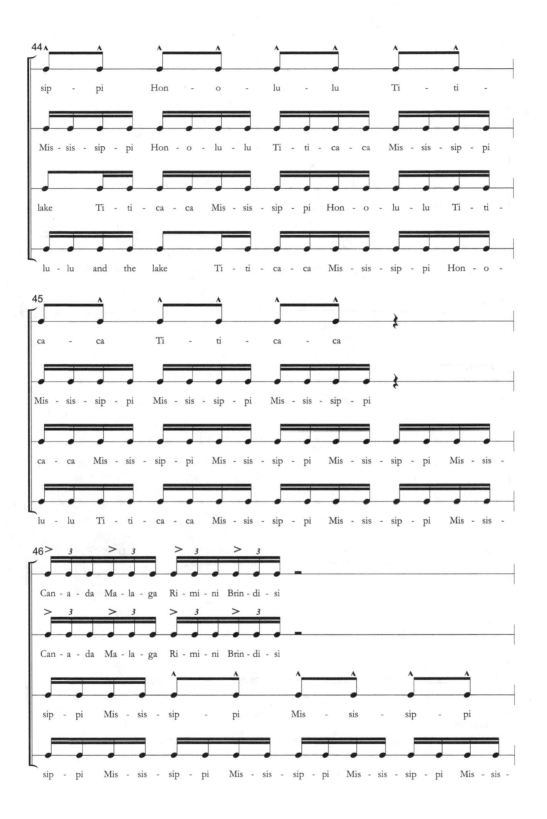

* By Ernst Toch

SUGGESTED SMARTMUSIC ASSESSMENTS AND GROUP SINGING

Depending on the speed with which your class works through this unit, you may have time to focus on all ten excerpts in this chapter. Or your instructor may instead wish to divide up the excerpts such that each group will be assigned two of the "complete works" in Chapter 14, with every individual responsible for all parts of the assigned pieces. You should prepare to perform your excerpts in class, and your performance should be confident and polished, so be sure to practice as a group.

In addition, every individual should complete SmartMusic assessments for *all voices* of the two works that have been assigned.

A useful division of works is as follows:

1. 14.1 and 14.6; 14.10 soprano
2. 14.2 and 14.7; 14.10 alto
3. 14.4 and 14.5; 14.10 tenor
4. 14.5 and 14.8; 14.10 bass

14.3 and 14.9 may be done as a class, or given to an additional group. 14.10 is the culmination of the rhythmic improvisations that have been completed over the entire course of this unit. This should be undertaken as an entire class, with each group assigned to a single voice, as indicated above.

UNIT III Advanced Melodies, Modulation, and Introduction to Musical Form

Chapter 15

Melodic Chromaticism

This chapter introduces a variety of chromatic melodies and bass lines in a wide range of music. It should prepare you for hearing and singing music that modulates, as well as hearing and singing complete musical forms, which is one of the main emphases of Units III and IV of this book. Remember to relate embellishing chromatic tones to nearby diatonic tones in order to be able to perform them correctly and discern them by ear. Also be sure to consider the possible harmonic bases for chromatic tones. Even when foreign notes are part of chromatic harmony (perhaps serving to temporarily "tonicize" a particular nontonic key center), they can often be heard as serving a linear embellishing role as well.

From this point forward, musical examples may exceed a normal vocal range. The goal is to help you read and sing music that (1) is not written for the voice and (2) includes ledger lines. You are encouraged to sing in whatever key and octave is comfortable, switching octaves where necessary.

As a reminder, if you are employing scale degrees in your singing, you may wish to sing "raise" for chromatic alterations that include a half-step raising of a diatonic scale degree and "low" for chromatic alterations that involve a half-step lowering of a diatonic scale degree. If using solfège, you may add adjusted syllables when chromatically raising a diatonic scale degree: di, ri, fi, si, li. When lowering a diatonic tone, use the adjusted syllables te, le, se, me ("may"), and ra (see the drills given in Chapters 12 and 13).

Example 15.1.   Joseph Haydn (1732–1809), Symphony no. 104 "London" (1795), mvt. 3

* Note the delightful ambiguity of the opening minor thirds (which suggest more than one possible key) and the cleverness of the phrase expansion. What type of cadence closes this excerpt?

Example 15.2.   Franz Schubert (1797–1828), "Lacrimoso," D. 131 (1815)

* The multiple confluences of B♭ and C♯ in this piece and the descending leaps from C to G♯ are very striking. How do these musical moments evoke the meaning of the text?

Example 15.3.   Aleksandr Aliab'ev (1787–1851), *Grand Quatuor* op. 4 (c. 1804), mvt. 1

* Be sure to supply Roman numerals for this excerpt before attempting to sing it. Note that it begins by tonicizing E minor but then moves through a large-scale sequence (what type?) toward G major.

Example 15.4.   Haydn, String Quartet in G, op. 54, no. 1 (1788), mvt. 3

* How does Haydn create balance between the two phrases?

Example 15.5.   Wolfgang Amadeus Mozart (1756–1791), Serenade no. 1, K. 439b

* Note how this excerpt starts by tonicizing the key of A minor but quickly moves through a sequence (what type?) to the dominant of the home key.

Example 15.6. Felix Mendelssohn (1809–1847), "Wedding March," from the incidental
music to *A Midsummer Night's Dream*, op. 61 (1842)

* Note the use of a secondary pre-dominant harmony to begin this excerpt. Prepare a Roman-numeral
analysis. (Further examples of secondary pre-dominants can be found in Examples 19.4, 21.3, and 22.3.)

Example 15.7.   Georges Bizet (1838–1875), "Habanera," from *Carmen* (1875)

est un oi-seau re-bel-le Que nul ne peut__ ap-pri-voi-ser,   Et c'est

bien en vain qu'on l'ap-pel-le,   s'il lui con-vient de__ re-fu-ser.   Rien n'y

fait, men-ace ou pri-è-re,   L'un par-le bien, l'au-tre se tait;   Et c'est

l'au-tre que je pré-fè-re   Il n'a rien dit;__ mais__ il me plaît.

* Practice making a distinction between triplets and duplets at both the eighth-note and sixteenth-note levels. Alternate back and forth between regular eighths and triplet eighths on a neutral syllable ("ta") while conducting. Aim for a perfectly even triplet rather than cutting the last of the three notes too short.

Example 15.8.   Heitor Villa-Lobos (1887–1959), *Bachianas Brasileiras* no. 5 (1938–1945)

* What type of sequence is suggested once the meter finally changes to common time ($\frac{4}{4}$) in m. 6?

Example 15.9.   Erroll Garner (1921–1977), "Misty" (1954)

* This melody features many leaps to dissonant notes, such as a seventh above the bass (on the first downbeat) and a ninth above the bass (the high C in m. 2, or the downbeat of m. 4). Practice all of these by leaping first to an octave above the bass and adjusting from there. Also make sure the quarter-note triplets are perfectly even.

DRILLS

1. *"Two-step" interval drill*: in the manner of the master interval drill and other drills from earlier chapters, sing stepwise ascending figures of three notes; then sing the qualities of both intervals. For a major scale, you would begin as follows: $\hat{1}$–$\hat{2}$–$\hat{3}$, $\hat{1}$–major–major; $\hat{2}$–$\hat{3}$–$\hat{4}$, $\hat{2}$–major–minor. . . ." Then after "$\hat{7}$–$\hat{1}$–$\hat{2}$, $\hat{7}$–minor–major," you should turn around and come back down the scale with descending figures ("$\hat{1}$–$\hat{7}$–$\hat{6}$, $\hat{1}$–minor–major, $\hat{7}$–$\hat{6}$–$\hat{5}$ . . .").

2. Listen to "On the Street Where You Live," from *My Fair Lady* (1956), by Alan Jay Lerner and Frederick Loewe. Compare the part of that tune that goes "All at once am I . . ." with the part of Example 15.9 that goes "I'm as helpless as. . . ." These fragments comprise different scale degrees, but they are intervallically identical. Try singing the beginning of one of these melodies on a neutral syllable and, when you get to the shared melodic fragment, pivoting into the other melody. Then start the melody you finished (in the same key as you have just used) and pivot back into the first melody. Were you able to get back to exactly the same key?

CHORALE WORKSHOP: SECONDARY LEADING-TONE TRIADS AND SEVENTH CHORDS

Each of the following progressions can be realized in major and minor keys unless otherwise specified. As a reminder, the $\uparrow$ symbol indicates a raised scale degree, while $\downarrow$ indicates a lowered or unraised scale degree. We will use just $\hat{7}$ to indicate the raised leading tone in minor, however, and $\downarrow\hat{7}$ if an unaltered scale degree $\hat{7}$ is intended. The | symbol indicates a bar line.

For each progression, first sing just the bass line and then each chord as an arpeggio (up from its bass note and back down), or play it on an instrument. Then, working at a piano, try singing the soprano line while playing the bass line, and singing the bass while playing the soprano line. Make sure the soprano is always sounding in a higher register than the bass. Finally, practice every progression on the piano, in a variety of simple keys, trying each soprano line in turn, and playing the inner voices in your right hand as well (rather than using block chords in your left hand).

Harmony (bass line in left hand)	Possible soprano scale degrees (right hand)
I | IV $\frac{\text{vii}^{\circ 7}}{\text{V}}$ V or i | iv $\frac{\text{vii}^{\circ 7}}{\text{V}}$ V	$\hat{5}$ | $\hat{6}$ $\hat{6}$ $\hat{5}$ (in minor: $\hat{5}$ | $\hat{6}$ $\uparrow\hat{6}$ $\hat{5}$) $\hat{3}$ | $\hat{4}$ $\downarrow\hat{3}$ $\hat{2}$ (in minor: $\hat{3}$ | $\hat{4}$ $\hat{3}$ $\hat{2}$) $\hat{1}$ | $\hat{1}$ $\hat{1}$ $\hat{7}$
I | IV $\frac{\text{vii}^{\emptyset 7}}{\text{V}}$ V (only in major)	$\hat{5}$ | $\hat{6}$ $\hat{6}$ $\hat{5}$ $\hat{3}$ | $\hat{4}$ $\hat{3}$ $\hat{2}$ $\hat{1}$ | $\hat{1}$ $\hat{1}$ $\hat{7}$

$$\text{I} \quad \text{IV}^6 \quad \frac{\text{vii}^{o6}}{\text{V}} \quad \text{V}_5^6 \mid \text{I}$$
or
$$\text{i} \quad \text{iv}^6 \quad \frac{\text{vii}^{o6}}{\text{V}} \quad \text{V}_5^6 \mid \text{i}$$

$\hat{5}$ $\hat{4}$ $\downarrow\hat{3}$ $\hat{2}$ | $\hat{1}$ (in minor: $\hat{5}$ $\hat{4}$ $\hat{3}$ $\hat{2}$ | $\hat{1}$)
$\hat{3}$ $\hat{4}$ $\uparrow\hat{4}$ $\downarrow\hat{4}$ | $\hat{3}$
$\hat{1}$ $\hat{1}$ $\hat{1}$ $\hat{2}$ | $\hat{1}$

$$\text{I} \mid \frac{\text{vii}^{o6}_5}{\text{V}} \quad \text{V}_5^6 \quad \text{I}$$
or
$$\text{i} \mid \frac{\text{vii}^{o6}_5}{\text{V}} \quad \text{V}_5^6 \quad \text{i}$$

$\hat{5}$ | $\uparrow\hat{4}$ $\downarrow\hat{4}$ $\hat{3}$
$\hat{3}$ | $\downarrow\hat{3}$ $\hat{2}$ $\hat{1}$ (in minor: $\hat{3}$ | $\hat{3}$ $\hat{2}$ $\hat{1}$)
$\hat{1}$ | $\hat{1}$ $\hat{2}$ $\hat{1}$

$$\text{I} \quad \text{V}^7 \quad \text{vi} \quad \frac{\text{vii}^{o6}_5}{\text{V}} \mid \text{V}$$
or
$$\text{i} \quad \text{V}^7 \quad \text{VI} \quad \frac{\text{vii}^{o6}_5}{\text{V}} \mid \text{V}$$

$\hat{3}$ $\hat{2}$ $\hat{1}$ $\hat{1}$ | $\hat{2}$
$\hat{1}$ $\hat{7}$ $\hat{1}$ $\hat{1}$ | $\hat{7}$
(only in major keys: $\hat{5}$ $\hat{4}$ $\hat{3}$ $\uparrow\hat{4}$ | $\hat{5}$)

IMPROVISATION: CHORALE WORKSHOP PRACTICE

As you encounter Chorale Workshop progressions that introduce a greater variety of chromatic chords and that may be longer than in previous chapters, keep the following practice strategies in mind:

1. In real time, practice improvising a variety of soprano melodies above the bass notes of a particular harmonic progression. The easiest way to do so would be at a slow tempo, with bass notes on the beat (played on the piano or sung by a classmate) and soprano notes on the offbeats.
2. Try improvising a melody against a given bass line at the same time as someone else is improvising over the same bass line.
3. While playing the outer voices of a given progression (or listening to someone else playing them), improvise an original inner voice or a descant voice.
4. Given a progression, several students or teams of students should each invent a viable soprano melody, write it down, and perform it for the other students, who will try to take dictation. See who is the more successful "dictator."

It will be useful to refer to these practice strategies throughout the rest of this book. You won't see them written out repeatedly, but you should nonetheless try them out in connection with all new sets of Chorale Workshop progressions that are introduced.

IMPROVISATION: GAMES AND EXERCISES

1. Refer to Example 15.2. Spend five minutes, individually or in a team, inventing a bass line of steady eighth notes to accompany the opening melody of this canon (six measures plus a downbeat). Your bass line should be original, not derived from a later part of the canon, and it should complement the melody without doubling very many of its notes. See if you (and any teammates) can achieve a bass line that sounds pretty believable. Then perform your bass line along with the given melody (mm. 1–7 only).

IMPROVISATION: FOCUS ON RHYTHM AND METER

1. Improvise a melody over a progression using the harmonic patterns you discovered in the Chorale Workshop. Adopt the following rhythmic feel, and then try using some from the earlier chapters.

2. The following excerpt is from "Story" by John Cage, the entire score for which is reproduced in Chapter 21. In order to prepare you for quartet performances of the complete work, each chapter will include activities to help you learn the basic rhythmic paradigms (patterns) that Cage uses in his creative and whimsical piece. Keep in mind that working with small chunks of larger repertoire is a great practice technique.

You may wish to start by marking in the beats (what is the meter?) and then subdividing into eighths. The arrows here show vocal inflection. That is, the downward arrow requires that you slide down in pitch, and the upward arrow requires that you slide upward. To make this clearly audible when you perform, you will need to exaggerate the inflections. This piece, however, is fundamentally rhythmic, and it is important that you keep the rhythms crisp, place the "d" consonant just before the beginning of the following eighth note, and give the rests their full length. You will want to aim for a performance speed with the quarter note somewhere around 65 beats per minute.

Start by practicing the two inflected rhythms by themselves: the quarter tied to the eighth with an eighth rest, and the two eighths. After practicing them in the order given below, arrange these two rhythms randomly, repeating each at least ten times. In Chapter 21 you will see that Cage manipulates these two rhythms in multiple ways.

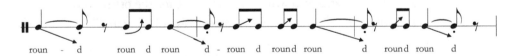

3. Write a ten-measure rhythm piece, employing vocally inflected words of your own devising. Use arrows to show inflections and use rhythms other than those found in the Cage. Be prepared to perform it in class.

SUGGESTED SMARTMUSIC ASSESSMENTS

Complete these SmartMusic assessments per the directions in earlier chapters: 15.1 (both parts), 15.2 (top line), 15.3 (all parts), 15.4 (all parts), 15.5 (all parts), 15.6 (all parts), 15.7 (top part), 15.8 (top part), and 15.9 (both parts).

SHORT-TERM MUSICAL MEMORY

Fill in the key signature and clef as indicated by your instructor and write in the initial note(s) on the basis of the given pitch and rhythm information. Note that the key and clef *may not be the same* as in the original example. Your instructor (or practice partner) will play a short progression to establish the key and then count off several beats to establish the tempo. Because of the brevity of each extract, you should have an overall impression of the rhythm, contour, and scale degrees after just one or two hearings. Notate the entire fragment.

1. Example 15.7, beat 2 of m. 4 to downbeat of m. 6, vocal part. Starts with two eighth notes (scale degrees Î–7̂).

Clef and key
  signature

2. Example 15.8, m. 7 to downbeat of m. 9, top voice. Starts on beat 1 (sixteenth note, scale degree 3̂).

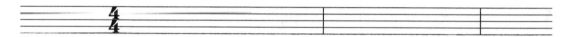

Clef and key
  signature

3. Example 15.8, mm. 11–12, top voice. Starts on beat 1 (sixteenth note, scale degree 3̂).

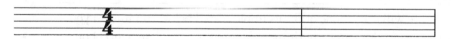

Clef and key
  signature

4. Example 14.1, m. 8 to downbeat of m. 12, vocal line and bass line. Both parts start on beat 1 (dotted half note and scale degree 3̂ in melody, half note a minor tenth lower in bass).

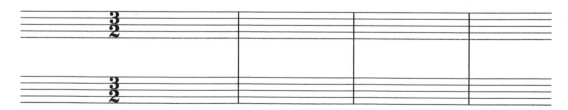

Clef and key
  signature

5. Example 15.6, up to downbeat of m. 4, outer voices (or just the top voice). Both voices start with half notes on beat 1 (high scale degree $\hat{1}$ in top voice, and scale degree $\hat{6}$ over two octaves lower in the bottom part).

Clef and key
signature

6. Example 15.9, m. 5 to downbeat of m. 7, both voices. Both start with quarter notes on beat 1 (scale degree $\hat{1}$ in bottom part; scale degree $\hat{3}$ a major tenth higher in top part, tied into beat 2).

Clef and key
signature

DICTATION OF LONGER EXAMPLES

Your instructor or a classmate will choose one of the examples listed below and inform you of the key, clef, meter, first note (scale degree, rhythmic value, and metric placement) of one or more parts, and total number of measures. Use a separate piece of staff paper to write down the indicated information. You will hear a short progression to establish the key of the example, and then hear the example several times with breaks between hearings.

1. Example 14.7, m. 25 to end, outer voices.
2. Example 14.8, m. 9 to downbeat of m. 16, both voices.
3. Example 15.2, up to downbeat of m. 7, top voice.
4. Example 15.3, m. 5 to end, violin 1 and viola parts (omit viola downbeat in m. 5). Establish the "destination key" before beginning dictation.

CONTEXTUAL LISTENING 15.1

Ludwig van Beethoven (1770–1827), Quintet for Piano and Winds, op. 16, mvt. 1 (Allegro)

This piece, written for oboe, clarinet, horn, bassoon, and piano, was inspired by Mozart's quintet for the same instrumentation and appears in the same key as its counterpart.

1. How many measures are in this $\frac{3}{4}$ excerpt?

2. What type of cadence ends this excerpt?

3. On what scale degree does the bass start?

4. Describe the harmonies in mm. 3–4 (both with Roman numerals and with a description of the motion in m. 4).

5. What Roman numerals would be appropriate for the final quarter of mm. 5 and 6?

6. There are three chromatic alterations, two in the melody and one in the bass. In which measures do they occur?

7. Accurately transcribe the outer parts of the entire excerpt in the key of C major.

CONTEXTUAL LISTENING 15.2

Corona Schröter (1751–1802), "Erlkönig"

This is the earliest known setting of Goethe's famous ballad. The Erlking (sometimes mistakenly referred to as the "Elf-King") is a common figure of German folklore, a malevolent being who lures travelers to their deaths. Goethe's ballad tells the tale of a father and son who are traveling; the son begins to see things that the father does not and is eventually attacked. His father races toward their destination but realizes too late that his son is already dead.

1. What meter does the composer use for this eight-measure excerpt?

2. Does the melody start on an upbeat or a downbeat? On what scale degree does the melody start?

3. On what scale degree does the bass start?

4. In which measure do we finally hear a root-position tonic chord on a downbeat?

5. There are two chromatic alterations in the middle voice of the piano—can you find them? What harmonies do they suggest?

6. What is the linear pattern between the outer voices that drives mm. 5–6?

7. Transcribe the outer parts of the entire excerpt in the key of A major.

8. Try to identify all the harmonies with Roman numerals.

9. Prepare to sing the outer voices in class.

EXPANDING THE REPERTOIRE 15.3

Michael Jackson, "Black or White" (1991)

The African-American musical tradition had (and still has) a great influence on the popular musical culture of the United States. Michael Jackson transcended many established boundaries of the music industry; for instance, his video for *Billie Jean* was the first video of an African-American artist to broadcast on MTV.

1. Listen from 2:38 to 3:10 of the "Black or White" official video. What typical chord progression (and musical form) do you hear?

2. With the aid of your instrument, can you identify the key? Make sure you can play the progression while hearing the song.

3. Provide the Roman numerals for the chord progression and notate the generic (simplified) bass line below:

4. Listen closely to the melody of the verse. Identify the one diatonic scale degree not present in the melody.

5. Speculate about what elements in this piece stem from the Rockabilly tradition and what elements are clearly drawn from the African-American musical culture.

6. On the basis of your answer to question 5, speculate how the title and lyrics of the song, Jackson's wardrobe, and the video as a whole (which suggests racial harmony) correlate with the music.

EXPANDING THE REPERTOIRE 15.4

"If We Ever Meet Again," Timbaland with Katy Perry (2010)

This song features rapper Timbaland with Katy Perry. As you will hear, a particular effect (Auto-Tune) is used on Timbaland's lead vocals. This pitch-shifting effect is sometimes used to correct out-of-tune notes, but it is also used aesthetically to achieve a particular sound.

1. Below, the timings for the various sections are outlined. Fill in the blanks by specifying the section of the song (e.g., intro, verse, bridge, chorus, outro, or other), and be prepared to discuss your perceptions in class. (The timings correspond to the version posted online.)

   0:00–0:18: No music

   0:18–0:28: intro

   0:28–0:58: verse

   0:58–1:29: _____

   1:29–1:38: _____

   1:38–2:08: _____

   2:08–2:38: _____

   2:38 3:08: _____

   3:08–4:09: _____

   4:09–4:39: _____

   4:09–5:13: _____

2. Similar to a common-practice *basso ostinato*, this song features a repeated ground bass, which is repeated throughout the entire piece. In common-practice classical music, the repetitive nature of the bass line is counterbalanced by variations in other parameters (melody, harmony, phrasing, etc.). In this song, however, texture is the most prominent tool for variation, though there is also a slight change in harmonic structure between the verse and the chorus. The following questions will guide your hearing as you listen.

   a. Transcribe the bass line that fits both the verse and chorus, with one note per measure:

b. Transcribe the first four measures of the verse according to the rhythm provided.

What's some-bod-y like   you   do-in' in   a   place like this?

c. Transcribe the first four measures of the chorus according to the rhythm provided.

I'll   ne - ver   be   the   sa - me,   (if   we   e - ver meet a - ga - in)

d. In the second measure of the chorus a chromatically altered note suggests a secondary function. What chord is suggested?

e. Write the Roman numerals for the progressions in the verse and chorus underneath the ground bass; play the progression while hearing the song. What happens if you attempt to exchange the chord progressions of the verse and chorus? Why do you think this sounds wrong?

Verse:

Chorus:

Chapter 16

Modulation

This chapter introduces the concept of "moving" from one key to another, whether by *tonicization* or *modulation*. Tonicization refers to the use of a secondary dominant or diminished chord so that the chord to which it resolves sounds temporarily like "tonic," but without actually changing key. Modulation refers to a change of key (by a variety of means, including the use of a pivot chord belonging to both old and new keys), and it typically leads to a cadential confirmation of the new key. If the new key is only temporary and there is no convincing cadential closure, then it is probably best understood as a tonicization.

Although a tonicization does not require you to change scale-degree numbers or solfège syllables, a modulation will require a change, corresponding to the change of key. You may need to experiment a little to find the most convenient place in a melody to change your numbers or syllables. It will usually make most sense to adjust syllables right before the dominant of the new key is introduced.

The study of modulation will prepare you for the perception and performance of complete musical forms, which usually feature both tonicizations and modulations. We will begin by exploring tonicizations of and modulations to the dominant, which is by far the most common destination when starting in a major key.

Example 16.1.   Ludwig van Beethoven (1770–1827), String Quartet op. 18, no. 5 (1801),
                 mvt. 3 (transposed)

* Which of this period's two phrases has been expanded beyond a four-measure norm, and how?

Example 16.2.   Wolfgang Amadeus Mozart (1756–1791), Piano Sonata K. 330/300h, mvt. 2

* Both of these phrases cadence on a C-major triad, but with different musical effects. What kind of
cadences are heard, and in what keys?

Example 16.3.   François Couperin (1668–1733), "Doux liens de mon coeur" (1701)

* *Translation*: Sweet bounds on my heart, pleasant pains, charming chains, from moment to moment, redouble my torment.

Notwithstanding the key signature, what key does this excerpt begin in? Where does the modulation occur?

Example 16.4.   Edvard Grieg (1843–1907), "In the Hall of the Mountain King," from *Peer Gynt Suite no. 1*, op. 46 (1875)

* This passage repeats several times in Grieg's composition. Feel free to conclude a performance with a final low-B downbeat.

    What kind of triad is heard on the downbeats of mm. 10, 12, 14, and 16? We will hear some more of this kind of triad in Examples 19.3, 20.5, 22.7, 22.10, and several examples in Chapter 24.

OTHER TONAL DESTINATIONS

Example 16.5.   Beethoven, Quintet for Piano and Winds, op. 16 (1796), mvt. 2

* Compare the four-note harmony implied by the second measure of this excerpt to the four-note harmony implied by the third measure, and comment on how the new key is introduced. Where will you change your numbers or syllables?

Example 16.6.   Mozart, Concerto for Flute and Harp, KV 299/297c (1778), mvt. 1

* This excerpt begins on the temporary tonic of G minor and then reaches the dominant of F minor after a sequential modulation. The sequence progresses by ascending thirds, with secondary dominant seventh chords tonicizing the triads (B♭ major, D minor, etc.). Mozart approaches each new dominant seventh chord from a fully-diminished seventh chord in the manner seen in Example 16.5.

Example 16.7.   Richard Wagner (1813–1888), *Die Walküre* (1854–1856), Act I, scene 2

Nun Weisse du fra - gen-de Frau,

wa-rum ich Fried - mund   nicht   heis - sel

* *Translation*: Now know'st thou, questioning wife, why "Peaceful" is not my name.

The lower two voices begin in the key of A♭ major. Where does the modulation occur? Does Wagner suggest any other keys along the way?

As you might guess, the full orchestral texture has a cadential six-four chord in m. 11 of this excerpt. How is the chord in m. 8 (also a six-four chord built on G in the bass) different in function?

Example 16.8.   Johann Sebastian Bach (1685–1750), Cantata no. 78 ("Jesu, der du meine
Seele"), tenor aria

und spricht mich frei, und spricht mich ___ frei.

Ruft mich der Höll - en Heer - zum Strei - te, zum

Strei - te, zum Strei - te, zum Strei -

- te, so ste - het Je - sus mir zur ___ Sei - te, dass

Strei - - - - te, so ste - - -

- - - - - - - het Je - sus,

so ste - het Je - sus mir zur____ Sei - te, das ich be herzt, be herzt

dass ich____ be herzt, ich be herzt und sieg haft sei.

* *Translation*: That blood that cancels my guilt
                 Makes my heart feel light again
                 And sets me free.
                 If hell's host calls me to battle,
                 Jesus will stand firm beside me,
                 So that I take heart and am victorious.

Before attempting this extended excerpt, examine the middle part of the piece for places where the vocal line has at least a whole measure of rest, and determine what key was attained just prior to each rest. Then work backward from these cadences and plan where it will be most convenient to change keys.

DRILLS

1. Continue practicing the two-step interval drill given in Chapter 15. If you haven't yet tried it in a minor key, do so. The melodic minor scale would work the best for this drill.

2. In preparation for Examples 16.5 and 16.6, arpeggiate a diminished seventh chord (by singing minor thirds up or down). Then lower one note by a semitone and arpeggiate the dominant seventh chord that results. Return to your original diminished seventh chord and lower another note to become a different dominant seventh chord. Do this with the other two notes in the diminished seventh chord as well. Ask a classmate to hold up one, two, three, or four fingers, and be ready to lower each one of the notes in a diminished seventh chord and arpeggiate the resulting dominant seventh chord.

CHORALE WORKSHOP: $\frac{V_2^4}{IV}$ AND $\frac{V_2^4}{V}$

The following progressions can all be realized in major and minor keys unless otherwise specified. For each progression, sing just the bass line, then sing the chord as an arpeggio (up from its bass note and back down) or play it on an instrument. Then, working at a piano, try singing the soprano line while playing the bass line and singing the bass while playing the soprano line. Make sure the soprano is always sounding in a higher register than the bass. Finally, practice every progression with every soprano line on the piano, in a variety of simple keys.

Harmony (bass line in left hand)	Possible soprano scale degrees (right hand)
I $\frac{\mathrm{V}^4_2}{\mathrm{IV}}$ IV⁶ V⁷ | I or i $\frac{\mathrm{V}^4_2}{\mathrm{iv}}$ iv⁶ V⁷ | i	$\hat{3}$ $\hat{3}$ $\hat{4}$ $\hat{4}$ | $\hat{3}$ (in minor: $\hat{3}$ ↑$\hat{3}$ $\hat{4}$ $\hat{4}$ | $\hat{3}$) $\hat{1}$ $\hat{1}$ $\hat{1}$ $\hat{7}$ | $\hat{1}$
I $\frac{\mathrm{V}^4_2}{\mathrm{IV}}$ IV⁶ P$^6_4$ | ii$^6_5$ V I or i $\frac{\mathrm{V}^4_2}{\mathrm{iv}}$ iv⁶ P$^6_4$ | ii°$^6_5$ V i	$\hat{5}$ $\hat{5}$ $\hat{4}$ $\hat{5}$ | $\hat{6}$ $\hat{5}$ $\hat{3}$ $\hat{3}$ $\hat{4}$ $\hat{3}$ | $\hat{2}$ $\hat{2}$ $\hat{1}$ (in minor: $\hat{3}$ ↑$\hat{3}$ $\hat{4}$ ↓$\hat{3}$ | $\hat{2}$ $\hat{2}$ $\hat{1}$)
I V$^6_5$ $\frac{\mathrm{V}^4_2}{\mathrm{IV}}$ IV⁶ | V or i V$^6_5$ $\frac{\mathrm{V}^4_2}{\mathrm{iv}}$ iv⁶ | V	$\hat{3}$ $\hat{2}$ $\hat{1}$ $\hat{1}$ | $\hat{7}$ $\hat{5}$ $\hat{4}$ $\hat{3}$ $\hat{4}$ | $\hat{2}$ (in minor: $\hat{5}$ $\hat{4}$ ↑$\hat{3}$ $\hat{4}$ | $\hat{2}$)
I $\frac{\mathrm{V}^4_2}{\mathrm{V}}$ V⁶ V⁷ | I or i $\frac{\mathrm{V}^4_2}{\mathrm{V}}$ V⁶ V⁷ | i	$\hat{3}$ ↑$\hat{4}$ $\hat{5}$ ↓$\hat{4}$ | $\hat{3}$ $\hat{1}$ $\hat{2}$ $\hat{2}$ $\hat{7}$ | $\hat{1}$ (in minor: $\hat{1}$ $\hat{2}$ $\hat{2}$ ↑$\hat{3}$ | $\hat{4}$ $\hat{2}$ $\hat{1}$)
I $\frac{\mathrm{V}^4_2}{\mathrm{V}}$ V⁶ $\frac{\mathrm{V}^4_2}{\mathrm{V}}$ | IV⁶ V I or i $\frac{\mathrm{V}^4_2}{\mathrm{V}}$ V⁶ $\frac{\mathrm{V}^4_2}{\mathrm{iv}}$ | iv⁶ V i	$\hat{3}$ ↑$\hat{4}$ $\hat{5}$ $\hat{5}$ | ↓$\hat{4}$ $\hat{2}$ $\hat{3}$ $\hat{1}$ $\hat{2}$ $\hat{2}$ $\hat{3}$ | $\hat{4}$ $\hat{2}$ $\hat{1}$
I I⁶ ii $\frac{\mathrm{V}^4_2}{\mathrm{V}}$ | V⁶ V⁷ I (only in major)	$\hat{5}$ $\hat{5}$ $\hat{4}$ ↑$\hat{4}$ | $\hat{5}$ ↓$\hat{4}$ $\hat{3}$ $\hat{3}$ $\hat{1}$ $\hat{2}$ $\hat{2}$ | $\hat{2}$ $\hat{7}$ $\hat{1}$

IMPROVISATION: GAMES AND EXERCISES

1. Try all four Chorale Workshop exercises listed under "Improvisation" in Chapter 15 for the progressions given in this chapter.

2. Refer again to Example 16.2, and sing the first four measures of the melody. Play the bass line on the piano or another instrument, or ask a low-voiced classmate to sing it. Instead of three Gs in m. 4, however, sing three Cs again (just like the upbeats to m. 1) and improvise a new answering four-measure phrase that reaches a perfect authentic cadence in F major. Once you are satisfied with your melody, work up a bass line (or ask your duo partner to do so) and perform the entire eight-measure period. See how yours is similar to or different from those of your classmates.

3. Refer to Richard Rodgers' song "My Funny Valentine," which you explored in Expanding the Repertoire 12.3 (in particular the first eight measures plus a downbeat):

    a. In five minutes or less, compose (and then perform) a melody with the same rhythm as the original tune. Your new melody should sound more or less compatible with the song's bass line, an approximation of which is shown below. You may start and end on the same note, but none of the interior pitches can be the same as those of the actual melody.

b. Now sing through the actual melody up to the downbeat of m. 8, and then improvise a new bass line—again retaining the same rhythm and the same first and last pitches, but this time changing every other pitch over those measures.

IMPROVISATION: FOCUS ON RHYTHM AND METER

1. As you will recall from the previous chapter, we are exploring small rhythmic patterns from "Story" by John Cage, the entirety of which you will perform in Chapter 21. The excerpt below shows three rhythmic patterns that Cage explores. You will recognize the second pattern, although the vocal inflections have been altered from the excerpts in the previous chapter. The first pattern is to be spoken half-voice, with a short "i" sound, as in "whisper." The third pattern requires a syncopated emphasis on the "-ce" sound of "once" (Cage marks this as "very sibilant").

Practice all three patterns until you can sing them confidently at 65 beats per minute.

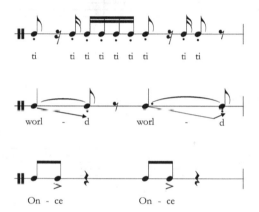

2. Now compose a three-voice rhythmic round using each pattern at least twice. Write your own words, focusing on the sounds of the vowels and consonants.

SUGGESTED SMARTMUSIC ASSESSMENTS

Complete these SmartMusic assessments per the earlier directions: 16.1 (both parts), 16.2 (all parts), 16.3 (both parts), 16.4 (top part), 16.5 (both parts), 16.6 (top part), 16.7 (all parts), and 16.8 (outer parts).

SHORT-TERM MUSICAL MEMORY

Fill in the key signature and clef as indicated by your instructor and write in the initial note(s) on the basis of the given pitch and rhythm information. Note that the key and clef *may not be the same* as in the original example. Your instructor (or practice partner) will play a short progression to establish the key and then count off several beats to establish the tempo. Because of the brevity of each extract, you should have an overall impression of the rhythm, contour, and scale degrees after just one or two hearings. Notate the entire fragment.

1. Example 16.2, from the middle of beat 2 in m. 6 to end, top voice. The first of six sixteenth notes heard before the first bar line is a high scale degree 1̂.

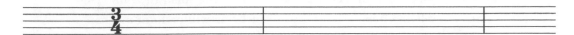

Clef and key
signature

2. Example 16.3, up to downbeat of m. 4, top voice. Starts on beat 2 (dotted half note, scale degree 1̂).

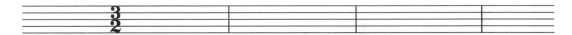

Clef and key
signature

3. Example 16.4, up to downbeat of m. 3, top voice. Starts on beat 1 (eighth note, scale degree 1̂).

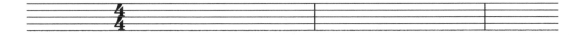

Clef and key
signature

4. Example 16.8, from beat 6 of m. 28 through m. 30, top voice. Starts with eighth-note upbeat (low scale degree 5̂).

Clef and key
signature

5. Example 16.8, from beat 6 of m. 32 to beat 5 of m. 34, top voice. Starts with eighth-note upbeat (high scale degree 1̂).

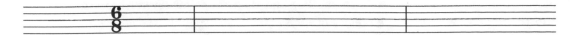

Clef and key
signature

6. Example 16.8, beginning through beat 4 of m. 2, outer voices. (Include only one note in bottom voice on beat 4 of m. 2.) Both voices start with eighth notes (low scale degree $\hat{1}$ in both, two octaves apart); top voice starts with upbeat eighth note; bottom part rests and then starts on second eighth of measure.

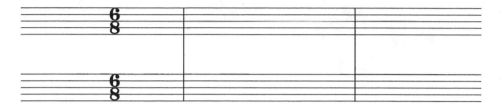

Clef and key
 signature

DICTATION OF LONGER EXAMPLES

Your instructor or a classmate will choose one of the examples listed below and inform you of the key, clef, meter, first note (scale degree, rhythmic value, and metric placement) of one or more parts, and total number of measures. Use a separate piece of staff paper to write down the indicated information. You will hear a short progression to establish the key of the example, and then hear the example several times with breaks between hearings.

Nonmodulating:

1. Example 16.6, m. 4 to downbeat of m. 7, top voice.
2. Example 16.8, beat 4 of m. 3 to beat 4 of m. 6, two accompanimental voices (include only one note in top voice on beat 4 of m. 6).

Modulating:

3. Example 16.1, all, both voices.
4. Example 16.2, up to beat 2 of m. 6, outer voices (include only one note in top voice in m. 6).
5. Example 16.5, all, top voice along with just the downbeats of the bottom voice (sustained throughout each measure).

CONTEXTUAL LISTENING 16.1

Name: _____ Date: _____ Instructor: _____

Bach, Fugue in B Minor, *Well-Tempered Clavier*, Book I, no. 24

Bach wrote two separate collections of contrapuntal works that contain preludes and fugues in all twenty-four major and minor keys. They are organized in pairs of parallel major and minor keys (C major and C minor, C♯ major and C♯ minor, and so on), ascending from C through B. This is the last fugue of Book I.

1. The subject (or main melody) of the fugue is three measures long (including the final downbeat). Complete a transcription of the entire subject below. Mark the spot where the subject changes keys, and indicate the key in which it cadences.

2. This subject is the most chromatic of all forty-eight fugues of the *Well-Tempered Clavier*. How many pitches (taking into account octave equivalence) does this subject use? Why do you think this is particularly important?

3. This fugue features four voices. Choose the graph below that best represents the entrances of the voices in the exposition (or opening of the fugue) in terms of register. Speculate about why one of the three designs might not be suitable for fugal expositions.

a.   b.   c.

4. On the termination of the initial subject of a fugue, a second voice will enter with an "answer," another version of the subject that most typically starts a fifth above the initial subject. The answer comes in two forms: a "real answer" (wherein the subject is transposed to another key, typically the dominant), or a "tonal answer" (in which the subject is altered so that it returns in the tonic, but with a different starting pitch).

Which type of answer does Bach use here in m. 4? Does it start the typical fifth above the initial subject?

List the first five scale degrees of the answer that starts in m. 4, and then describe what alterations Bach made from the initial subject.

5. What are the keys of all the subject-answer entrances? Does this fugue abide by the traditional four-voice fugue exposition model featuring a subject-answer-subject-answer?

6. Countersubject: the countersubject immediately follows the subject or answer and provides a counterpoint to the occurrence of a subject or answer in another voice. Here, Bach's countersubject is divided into multiple parts. In the space below, transcribe the first two measures (and sections) of the countersubject, starting in m. 4. Although the initial rhythms and contours have been supplied, be sure to provide any accidentals.

Note the surprising C♮ that has been marked for you. Where have we heard C♮ before in this fugue?

7. How does Bach contrast the first two sections of the countersubject (m. 3 compared with m. 4)?

EXPANDING THE REPERTOIRE 16.2

Astor Piazzolla, "Fuga y Misterio," from *María de Buenos Aires* (1968)

The music of Astor Piazzolla juxtaposes and navigates multiple genres (jazz, classical, rock, etc.) with one constant stylistic presence: tango.

1. As its name implies, this piece presents a contrapuntal design (similar to one that might be found in the Baroque era), with a clear fugal exposition (0:00–1:20 in the online recording).

    a. How many entrances of the subject and answer are there?

    b. What is the order of instruments entering?

    c. Choose the graph below that best represents the entrances of the exposition in terms of register.

    d. Transcribe the subject:

    e. What are the keys of the entrances? How does this compare with a traditional fugue exposition model in terms of subjects and answers?

EXPANDING THE REPERTOIRE 16.3

"Truck Driver's Gear Change" Modulation: Michael Jackson, "Man in the Mirror" (1988) and Maureen McGovern, "Amazing Grace" (1994)

The "Truck Driver's Gear Change" is an abrupt modulation generally found in popular music. Because of its colloquial name, it has the associations of being unimaginative and mechanical, yet popular musicians use this modulatory device profusely in order to increase the intensity of the listener's experience while achieving artistic and creative results.

1. Listen to Michael Jackson's "Man in the Mirror" and identify its initial key. Then, at about 2:50, there is an abrupt modulation. Answer the following:

   a. Does it modulate by whole step or half step? In which direction?

   b. Does it modulate after completing the chorus, toward the beginning of the chorus, or toward the end of it?

   c. Speculate about how the lyrics "take a look at yourself then make that . . . *Change!*" might help listeners correlate a structural event in the music with the lyrics.

2. Listen to "Amazing Grace" as sung by Maureen McGovern and answer the following questions:

   a. Complete the table below with the corresponding keys, and describe the texture of each segment.

Timings (for the video posted online)						
	0:00–1:44	1:44–2:22	2:22–3:00	3:00–3:35	3:35–4:38	4:38–5:49
Key	C Major					
Texture						

b. What type of sonority is introduced at the end of each stanza to initiate the modulation?

c. How would you describe the journey through the various keys? How does it help shape the form of the piece? How does this journey affect the mood of the piece?

EXPANDING THE REPERTOIRE 16.4

The Beatles, "Yesterday" (1965)

Originally recorded for their album *Help!* and featuring Paul McCartney on acoustic guitar backed by a string arrangement, this ballad remains very popular, as evidenced by numerous cover versions. It is common in jazz and in popular music to briefly navigate key areas by means of ii–V–I progressions (or a more extended progression: vi–ii–V–I). Given the length of complete pieces in these contemporary styles, this procedure treads a fine line between tonicization and modulation.

1. What is the form of the song?

   a. Verse–verse–chorus–verse
   b. Verse–chorus–chorus–verse
   c. Verse–chorus–verse–chorus

2. Transcribe the melody of verse 1, and analyze with Roman numerals, keeping in mind the proposed "key areas."

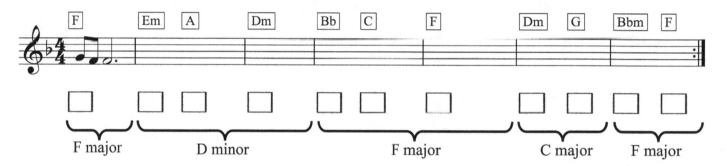

3. What type of cadence ends this segment?

4. Paying attention to metaphorical correlations between the lyrics and the harmonic progression, briefly speculate about the following:

   • What is the effect of moving to a foreign key area while the lyrics state "far away"?

   • What is the effect of the return to the home key as the lyrics state "here to stay"?

   • What is the effect of an unresolved progression when the lyrics state "I believe"?

5. Transcribe the rest of the song and analyze the chord progressions, noting how ii–V–I paradigms briefly establish secondary key areas.

Chapter 17

Simple Binary Form

Many familiar musical genres feature binary forms. Dance movements in Baroque suites (such as the allemande, courante, sarabande, and gigue) are invariably in binary form. In the Classical period, most sets of variations proceed from a theme in binary form. It is also typical to find that the second or third movement of a sonata or symphony is a pairing of two binary forms, entitled Minuet and Trio or Scherzo and Trio.

"Binary form" refers essentially to a movement with a two-part structure. (Since these parts are usually repeated, we will call them the first and second reprise.) The experience of binary form, however, involves more than simply sensing a formal division into two parts. There are two basic variables: whether or not the first reprise concludes with an authentic cadence in the home key (the second reprise will, of course, conclude that way, if the movement is to sound finished), and whether or not some or all of the first reprise will come back at the end of the second reprise. Careful attention to these and other "clues" can reveal a lot about the overall shape and drama of a piece in binary form and can inform a more effective performance.

If the first reprise ends with an authentic cadence in the home key (i.e., V to I in root position), we call it a *sectional* binary form. (This suggests that just this first "section" could be a completely independent little piece.) Otherwise, if it ends with a half cadence in the home key or modulates to a new key, we call it a *continuous* binary form, since the harmonic progression of structural harmonies and key areas "continues" from one reprise to the next.

This chapter presents a selection of so-called simple binary forms, those in which the second reprise features newly composed material rather than any literally repeated section. (Even in simple binary, however, the two halves will certainly resemble each other in terms of their musical character.) In Chapter 18, we will encounter some binary forms in which material from the first reprise returns in the second reprise.

SECTIONAL BINARY FORMS

Example 17.1.   Ludwig van Beethoven (1770–1827), Variations on "God Save the King," WoO 78 (1803)

* The first reprise is an unusual six-measure length, due to a repeated C–A–F–G . . . A–F–G contour in the bass line. Does this sound to you more like an expanded motion from I to vi (mm. 3–4) or an expanded cadential six-four (mm. 4–5)?

Example 17.2.   Leopold Mozart (1719–1787), Minuet in C major from *Notebook for Nannerl*
(1759–1764)

* What phrase structure is heard in each of the two reprises? Compare the C♯ in mm. 2 and 4 to the
F♯ in mm. 9 and 11; which are harmonically functional and which are merely embellishments?

CONTINUOUS BINARY FORMS

What follows are two continuous binary forms in which the first reprise does not modulate but instead ends on a half cadence in the home key. Even though no modulation occurs in the first reprise, the first reprise is still harmonically open, because it doesn't end
with a perfect authentic cadence.

Example 17.3.   Niccolò Paganini (1782–1840), Caprice no. 24 in A minor (1819), Theme
and Variations 2 and 3

* What kind of sequence is suggested by the first few measures after each of the repeat signs?

Example 17.4. Julius Fučík (1872–1916), "Entry of the Gladiators" (1899)

* What phrase structure is heard in each of the two reprises? Compare the two half cadences heard at
the end of the first reprise. The first ending tonicizes a surprise harmony (which harmony?) and then
emphasizes the leading tone instead of any kind of stable dominant chord, while the second ending
tonicizes the dominant.

What follows are two examples of continuous binary form in which the first reprise changes key.

Example 17.5.   From the notebook of Anna Magdalena Bach (1725), March in D Major, BWV Anh. 122

* Note how the "quarter-half" rhythm of mm. 1–2 is imitated in mm. 4–5 but how this conflicts with an expected phrase beginning in measure 5. Would you describe the metric breakdown of the first reprise as (4+1)+4, or 4+(4+1), or perhaps 3+3+3? This will certainly affect your performance.

Example 17.6.   Johannes Brahms (1833–1897), Waltz op. 39 no. 16 (1865)

* Here Brahms has simply written out the repeat of mm. 1–8 in a slightly varied way in mm. 9–16 (the top two voices of his texture exchange their material). Then the second reprise is enclosed within repeat signs as usual.

What key does this waltz begin in? What key is attained at the end of the first reprise, and which specific note undergoes enharmonic reinterpretation to get there?

FURTHER EXAMPLES AND ANALYTICAL QUESTIONS

Example 17.7.   Joseph Haydn (1732–1809), String Quartet op. 76 no. 3 "Emperor" (1797), mvt. 2, theme

Analytical questions:

1. Does the first reprise remain in the home key or modulate to a new key? If it modulates, what key does it go to? What kind of cadence concludes the first reprise?
2. The second reprise does not repeat in its entirety. What is the musical effect of this unusual scheme?
3. What prior thematic material (if any) is used in the second part of the second reprise? Is it heard in its entirety or in abbreviated form? Has it been changed?
4. On the basis of your answers to questions 1 and 3, name the precise type of binary form.

Example 17.8.   Johann Sebastian Bach (1685–1750), Air from Orchestral Suite no. 3, BWV
                 1068 ("Air on the G String")

Analytical questions:

1. What key (and what type of cadence) is attained at the end of the first reprise?
   Where does the modulation occur?
2. What keys are cadentially confirmed in the second reprise?
3. What type of binary form is this?

COMPOUND TERNARY FORM WITH NESTED BINARY FORMS

Example 17.9.   Bach, Gavottes 1 and 2 from Orchestral Suite no. 3, BWV 1068

Gavotte II

* What types of binary form are represented in this piece?

DRILLS

1. Continue practicing the two-step interval drill given in Chapter 15. When that drill is secure, try the next one (called the two-skip interval drill): sing stepwise ascending arpeggios of root-position triads, and then sing the qualities of both thirds. For a major scale, you would begin with "$\hat{1}$–$\hat{3}$–$\hat{5}$, $\hat{1}$–major–minor; $\hat{2}$–$\hat{4}$–$\hat{6}$, $\hat{2}$–minor–major. . . ." Don't forget to turn around at the top and come back down with descending arpeggios.

2. Refer to Example 17.3, specifically the beginning of the second reprise in the theme and both variations. Continue each sequential pattern for four more measures (ending on scale degree $\hat{1}$). Then start again from the high A and try the same pattern in major instead of minor.

3. With Example 17.3 in front of you, listen to the famous melody from the eighteenth variation of Rachmaninoff's *Rhapsody on a Theme by Paganini*. How do these melodies compare? Try singing the Rachmaninoff melody by ear while looking at the Paganini melody on the page. How is Paganini's descending-fifth sequence changed in Rachmaninoff's variation?

4. In mm. 14–15 of Example 17.5, the March from Anna Magdalena's Notebook, a different type of sequence begins. Continue the melodic pattern of this sequence for four more measures plus a final high-A downbeat. Then sing a continuation

of the bass-line pattern while someone else sings the complete melodic pattern, or continue the bass line on a piano or another instrument while singing the melodic pattern (or while someone else is singing).

CHORALE WORKSHOP: TONICIZING ii (ONLY IN MAJOR KEYS)

For each of the following progressions, sing just the bass line, and then sing the chord as an arpeggio (up from its bass note and back down) or play it on an instrument. Then, working at a piano, try singing the soprano line while playing the bass line and singing the bass while playing the soprano line. Make sure the soprano is always sounding in a higher register than the bass. Finally, practice every progression with every soprano line on the piano, in a variety of simple keys.

Since these progressions tonicize the supertonic triad, they can be realized only in major keys.

Harmony (bass line in left hand)	Possible soprano scale degrees (right hand)
I $\dfrac{\text{V}^7}{\text{ii}}$ ii V^7 $\vert$ I	$\hat{5}$ $\hat{5}$ $\hat{4}$ $\hat{4}$ $\vert$ $\hat{3}$ $\hat{3}$ $\hat{3}$ $\hat{2}$ $\hat{2}$ $\vert$ $\hat{1}$
I $\dfrac{\text{V}^7}{\text{ii}}$ $\dfrac{\text{V}^7}{\text{V}}$ V^7 $\vert$ I	$\hat{5}$ $\hat{5}$ $\uparrow\hat{4}$ $\downarrow\hat{4}$ $\vert$ $\hat{3}$ $\hat{3}$ $\hat{3}$ $\hat{2}$ $\hat{2}$ $\vert$ $\hat{1}$
I $\dfrac{\text{V}^6_5}{\text{ii}}$ ii V$^6_5$ $\vert$ I	$\hat{5}$ $\hat{5}$ $\hat{4}$ $\hat{4}$ $\vert$ $\hat{3}$ $\hat{3}$ $\hat{3}$ $\hat{2}$ $\hat{2}$ $\vert$ $\hat{1}$
I $\dfrac{\text{V}^6_5}{\text{ii}}$ $\dfrac{\text{V}^7}{\text{V}}$ V^7 $\vert$ I	$\hat{5}$ $\hat{5}$ $\uparrow\hat{4}$ $\downarrow\hat{4}$ $\vert$ $\hat{3}$ $\hat{3}$ $\hat{3}$ $\hat{2}$ $\hat{2}$ $\vert$ $\hat{1}$
I $\dfrac{\text{V}^6_5}{\text{IV}}$ IV $\dfrac{\text{V}^4_3}{\text{ii}}$ $\vert$ ii V^7 I	$\hat{1}$ $\downarrow\hat{7}$ $\hat{6}$ $\hat{5}$ $\vert$ $\hat{4}$ $\hat{4}$ $\hat{3}$ $\hat{1}$ $\hat{1}$ $\hat{1}$ $\uparrow\hat{1}$ $\vert$ $\hat{2}$ $\hat{7}$ $\hat{1}$
I $\dfrac{\text{V}^4_2}{\text{IV}}$ IV^6 $\dfrac{\text{V}^4_2}{\text{ii}}$ $\vert$ ii^6 V^7 I	$\hat{3}$ $\hat{3}$ $\hat{4}$ $\hat{3}$ $\vert$ $\hat{2}$ $\hat{2}$ $\hat{1}$ $\hat{1}$ $\hat{1}$ $\hat{1}$ $\uparrow\hat{1}$ $\vert$ $\hat{2}$ $\hat{7}$ $\hat{1}$

IMPROVISATION: GAMES AND EXERCISES

1. Try all four Chorale Workshop exercises listed under "Improvisation" in Chapter 15 for the progressions given in this chapter.
2. Refer to the second reprise of Example 17.4, "Entry of the Gladiators." Improvise a more interesting upper part to go along with the given bass-line melody over the entire second reprise. Your new melody should move in steady half notes throughout. Make sure your melody reinforces the $\dfrac{\text{vii}^{\circ 7}}{\text{V}}$ chord that the bass line outlines in mm. 27–28.

3. Refer to Example 17.8, the Air from Bach's Orchestral Suite no. 3 ("Air on the G String").

   a. Given just the melody over the last six bars (beginning with that gradually ascending sequential pattern) improvise a new bass line, aiming for fairly consistent eighth-note motion. (Your new bass line should still follow an ascending sequential pattern at first, since the melodic pattern is pretty clear.)

   b. Given just the melody and bass line over the first reprise, improvise a new inner voice. Feel free to shadow either the melody or bass in thirds or sixths some of the time, but consider filling in the "gaps" created by the long rhythmic values in the melody with something more florid, as Bach in fact did in the third and fourth measures. Feel free to wander up above the pitch level of the melody if you like.

4. Listen to the first reprise of Bach's Bourrée from Contextual Listening 17.2. Then try to sing its melody on solfège or scale degrees. Once you can sing the antecedent phrase (twenty-five melodic notes) with confidence, improvise a new consequent phrase that begins the same way but ends in the key of the (minor) dominant instead. Then commission a new bass line for your consequent phrase from a classmate, and perform as a vocal duo. (You should probably agree in advance where the new dominant and the new tonic should arrive.)

IMPROVISATION: FOCUS ON RHYTHM AND METER

1. As you will recall from the previous chapters, we are exploring small rhythmic patterns from "Story" by John Cage, the entirety of which you will perform in Chapter 21. The excerpt below shows four rhythmic configurations. Practice them, making sure they are clearly distinguishable. In particular, you will need to pay close attention to the placement of the final "t" consonance such that you don't cut the eighth notes too short or hold the sixteenths too long. Consider trying different words or sounds, and see if it is harder or easier to make the rhythms distinguishable.

2. Work with a partner to test your memories: start by singing one of the four rhythmic patterns, and then have your partner imitate it, adding another rhythmic pattern. Now, repeat the two rhythmic patterns and add a third. See how long you can go back and forth, keeping track to report to your instructor.

SUGGESTED SMARTMUSIC ASSESSMENTS

Complete SmartMusic assessments 17.1 (all parts), 17.2 (both parts), 17.3, 17.4 (both parts), 17.5 (both parts), 17.6 (all parts), 17.7 (all parts), 17.8 (all parts), and 17.9 (all parts).

SHORT-TERM MUSICAL MEMORY

Fill in the key signature and clef as indicated by your instructor and write in the initial note(s) on the basis of the given pitch and rhythm information. Note that the key and clef *may not be the same* as in the original example. Your instructor (or practice partner) will play a short progression to establish the key and then count off several beats to establish the tempo. Because of the brevity of each extract, you should have an overall impression of the rhythm, contour, and scale degrees after just one or two hearings. Notate the entire fragment.

1. Example 17.1, m. 3 to the downbeat of m. 6, bottom voice. Starts on beat 1 (quarter note, high scale degree 1̂).

Clef and key
signature

2. Example 17.3, Variation 2, m. 1 to downbeat of m. 3. Starts on beat 1 (sixteenth note, scale degree 1̂).

Clef and key
signature

3. Example 17.5, mm. 20–22, top voice. Starts on beat 1 (quarter note, high scale degree 5̂).

Clef and key
signature

4. Example 17.8, m. 15 to downbeat of m. 16, top voice. Starts on beat 1 (quarter note tied to a sixteenth note, low scale degree 5̂).

Clef and key
signature

5. Example 17.9, Gavotte II, up to downbeat of second full measure, top voice. Starts on beat 3 (eighth note, high scale degree 1̂).

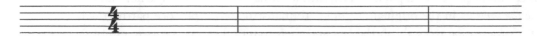

Clef and key
signature

6. Example 17.7, up to beat 2 of second full measure, top and middle voices. Both start with dotted quarter notes on beat 3 (scale degree 1̂ in top voice, and a minor sixth lower in middle voice).

Clef and key
signature

7. Example 17.9, Gavotte I, beat 3 of m. 22 to downbeat of m. 25, outer voices. Both start on beat 3 (quarter note and high scale degree 5̂ in top voice, eighth note a perfect twelfth lower in bottom voice).

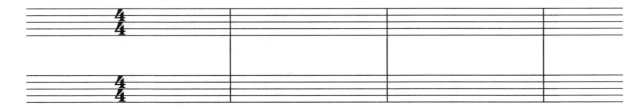

Clef and key
signature

8. Example 17.9, Gavotte II, beat 3 of m. 48 to downbeat of m. 50, outer voices. Both start on beat 3 (eighth note and scale degree 6̂ in top voice, quarter note scale degree 4̂ over two octaves lover in bottom part).

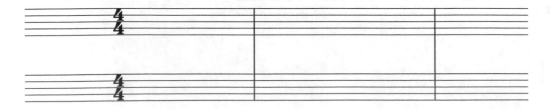

Clef and key
signature

DICTATION OF LONGER EXAMPLES

Your instructor or a classmate will choose one of the examples listed below and inform you of the key, clef, meter, first note (scale degree, rhythmic value, and metric placement) of one or more parts, and total number of measures. Use a separate piece of staff paper to write down the indicated information. You will hear a short progression to establish the key of the example, and then hear the example several times with breaks between hearings.

Nonmodulating:

1a. Example 17.2, mm. 1–8, both voices.
1b. Example 17.2, mm. 9–16, both voices.
 2. Example 17.4, m. 21 to downbeat of m. 35, bottom voice.

Modulating:

3. Example 17.5, up to downbeat of m. 8, both voices.
4. Example 17.6, up through end of m. 8, middle and bottom voices.
5. Example 17.9, Gavotte I, up to downbeat of m. 8, outer voices.

CONTEXTUAL LISTENING 17.1

George Frideric Handel (1685–1759), Minuet from *Water Music*, Suite in D major (1717)

This piece was commissioned by King George I, who had asked for music to accompany his court's trip on a barge down the Thames River. The resulting work was a collection of three orchestral suites that became collectively known as "Water Music."

The following questions refer to the *first reprise*:

1. Does the first reprise remain in the home key or modulate to a new key?

2. If it modulates, what key does it go to?

3. What kind of cadence concludes the first reprise?

Now for some questions about the *second reprise*:

4. What key(s) does the composer visit (and cadence in) in the second reprise before coming back to the home key?

5. What types of cadences are heard?

Concerning the entire movement:

6. On the basis of your answers to these questions, identify the type of binary form.

CONTEXTUAL LISTENING 17.2

Bach, Bourrée from Suite for Lute in E minor, BWV 996

Dance suites were frequently composed in the Baroque era. They consisted of a number of dances in different styles. A single dance suite could contain any number of the popular dances of the day: allemande, courante, sarabande, gavotte, minuet, or gigue, to name a few. This particular movement is a bourrée, a French dance with an anacrusis and in a quick double-time.

The following questions refer to the *first reprise*:

1. Does the first reprise remain in the home key or modulate to a new key?

2. If it modulates, what key does it go to?

3. What kind of cadence concludes the first reprise?

Now for some questions about the *second reprise*:

4. What key(s) does the composer visit (and cadence in) in the second reprise before coming back to the home key?

5. What types of cadences are heard?

Concerning the entire movement:

6. On the basis of your answers to these questions, identify the type of binary form.

CONTEXTUAL LISTENING 17.3

Wolfgang Amadeus Mozart (1756–1791), Theme from *Six Variations on "Hélas, j'ai perdu mon amant"* in G minor for violin and piano, KV 360

The title of the song from which this theme is taken is translated as "Alas, I have lost my love." The key of G minor was often used by eighteenth-century composers for dramatic subjects such as this.

The following questions refer to the *first reprise*:

1. Which of the two players has the principal melody? (This may suggest which of them has experienced romantic disappointment, as the title mentions.)

2. What kind of cadence concludes the first of the two phrases in the first reprise?

3. Does the second phrase stay in the home key or modulate to a new key? If you hear a modulation, what new key is reached?

4. What kind of cadence concludes the first reprise?

Now for some questions about the *second reprise*:

5. What change in harmonic quality occurs from the end of the first reprise to the beginning of the second reprise? (Hint: the same chordal root is heard on both sides of the repeat sign.)

6. Do you hear any thematic material from the first reprise returning in the second reprise? If so, describe it.

7. What closely related key is briefly tonicized near the end of the second reprise?

Concerning the entire theme:

8. On the basis of your answers to these questions, identify the type of binary form.

EXPANDING THE REPERTOIRE 17.4

> **Les Brown and Ben Homer, "Sentimental Journey," made famous by Doris Day**

This song was the number-one hit in 1945, when it became the unofficial homecoming song for World War II veterans. The lyrics speak of a metaphorical "journey" back to a loved one from the past. The chromatic descents of the A section, which describes the journey to the past, contrast with the chromatic ascents of the B section, a reflection of the singer's anticipation for "seven," when she will be "waiting up for heaven." This excerpt employs the quatrain form, first introduced in Chapter 14. Consider listening to Doris Day's original recording, focusing on the sung thirty-two-measure portion as a single statement of the form.

1. a. This song is famous for the two oscillating pitches that open the vocal melody and pervade the A sections. What is the interval? If the song were notated in C major, what would the two notes be?

   b. How many notes go by in the melody before we hear a new melodic pitch? What is the new pitch? What scale degree does it represent? What word does it set?

   c. The oscillation interval of the first section is altered in the second measure of the second section. What is changed? What is the resulting interval?

   d. This song is also famous for its syncopated rhythms. Notate the rhythm of the melody's first measure below. Note that it starts with an eighth rest (or a dotted-eighth rest, if notating the swung rhythms with dotted values).

2. As mentioned above, this song exhibits a common structure that is often considered to be a type of ternary form but that is more specifically described as quatrain form (or song form) with four distinct sections, the first two of which create a larger phrase type. Map out the thirty-two measures of this excerpt, filling in the blanks:

   A = Sections 1 and 2, mm. 1 through _____.

   Section 1 is mm. 1 to _____ and ends with an arrival on the
   _____ (harmony).

   Section 2 ends with a _____ cadence.

   The overall phrase structure of the A section can be described this way:

   _____ = Section 3, mm. _____ to _____ , ends with an arrival
   on the _____ (harmony).

   Section 3 highlights a semitonal motive, beginning with scale degrees
   _____ on the first "seven," scale degrees _____ on
   the second "seven," and then scale degrees _____ on the word "heaven."

The final melodic pitch of Section 3 is _____ .

_____ = Section 4, mm. _____ to _____ , ends with an arrival

on the _____ (harmony).

Section 4 is related to the _____ section. Describe the relationship.

3. On the staff lines below, notate the melody of entire A section in the key of C major. Below each staff line, provide Roman numerals for the measures that begin and end phrases (only) and label any cadences.

Bonus question: list at least two instances of word painting besides the one mentioned above.

Chapter 18

Rounded and Balanced Binary Form

In this chapter we encounter binary forms in which some (or all) musical material from the first reprise returns in the second reprise. Most commonly, the very beginning of the movement will return quite recognizably in the home key, somewhere near the middle of the second reprise. This gives the effect of having come "full circle" and is referred to as *rounded binary*. When material from the later part of the first reprise, instead of the beginning, returns in the second reprise, it is termed *balanced binary*.

Both of these scenarios are easy to recognize and distinguish by ear. Ask yourself whether you notice something substantial (a phrase or a theme, not just a motive or a cadential formula) returning from the first reprise, and where it originated (at the very beginning of the movement or at some later point). Although Example 17.5 featured the same fanfare figure at the end of both first and second reprises, it was classified as simple binary because cadential gestures recur quite frequently without affecting interpretations of musical form.

Simple, rounded, or balanced binary forms can be either sectional or continuous. Usually we label a binary form as simple, rounded, or balanced, and *then* specify whether it is sectional or continuous, even though, when you are hearing or performing a piece for the first time, you will discover it is sectional or continuous before you find out if it is simple, rounded, or balanced!

We will also be interested in studying the modulatory plans of these movements, as well as the proportional relationship between the first and second reprises. If the two sections are not the same length, the second reprise will usually be the longer one (as is often the case with rounded or balanced binary forms).

ROUNDED BINARY FORMS

Example 18.1.   Franz Schubert (1797–1828), Theme from Octet, D. 803 (1824), mvt. 4

* In singing the lower line, practice at first without the offbeat notes. Even when you add them back in, make sure you are thinking of the melodic connection between the notes on the beat.

Is this theme in sectional binary form or continuous binary form? What phrase structure is heard in the first reprise?

Although the melody from the first beat of m. 8 seems to recur in mm. 9 and 11, this theme is best understood as rounded binary rather than balanced binary, because of the unmistakable recall of the opening material in mm. 13–14. A balanced binary form recalls material from the end of the first reprise toward the *end* of the second reprise.

Example 18.2.   Joseph Haydn (1732–1809), Symphony no. 101 "Clock" (1794), mvt. 4

* Is this part of the movement in sectional binary form or continuous binary form?

   Provide Roman numerals from m. 1 to the downbeat of m. 16 (in D major for mm. 1–8, and then in A major after that). We will explore the type of chord that is implied at the end of m. 19 in Chapters 22 and 24.

BALANCED BINARY FORMS

Example 18.3.   Anton Diabelli (1781–1858), "Song"

* Is this piece in sectional binary form or continuous binary form?

Example 18.4.   Haydn, Theme from *20 Variations*, Hob. XVII/2 (1765)

* Is this theme in sectional binary form or continuous binary form?

There might be some reasonable concerns as to whether this is really "balanced enough" to be called balanced binary form. What do you think?

FURTHER EXAMPLES AND ANALYTICAL QUESTIONS

Example 18.5.   Johannes Brahms (1833–1897), Theme from *Variations on a Theme by Haydn*,
op. 56a (1873)

Analytical questions:

1. Does the first reprise modulate? What kind of period is it?
2. What is unusual about the phrase lengths? What kinds of cadences are heard?
3. What thematic material (if any) is reused in the second part of the second reprise?
   Is it heard in its entirety or in abbreviated form? Has it been changed?
4. What type of binary form is this?
5. What does the music at the end of the second reprise accomplish?

See the Improvisation section at the end of this chapter for further suggestions.

Example 18.6.   Johann Sebastian Bach (1685–1750), Courante from Partita no. 2 in C minor,
                 BWV 826 (1727)

Analytical questions:

1. Does the first reprise modulate or stay in the same key? What kinds of cadences are heard?
2. What thematic material (if any) is reused in the second part of the second reprise? Is it heard in its entirety or in abbreviated form? Has it been changed?
3. What type of binary form is this?

Example 18.7.   Domenico Scarlatti (1685–1757), Sonata in E Major, K. 380/L. 23 (1756–57)

Analytical questions:

1. Four quick half cadences are heard at the opening of the piece. To what key does the ensuing phrase modulate, and what type of cadence concludes the phrase?

2. Describe the character of the memorable theme that follows the fermata.

3. Prior to returning to the home key in the second reprise, we visit a new key whose dominant is prominently articulated but whose tonic is never cadentially confirmed; what key is this?

4. Which theme(s) from the first reprise, if any, coincide with the return to the home key toward the end of the second reprise?

5. How, then, would you identify the type of binary form?

Example 18.8.   George Frideric Handel (1685–1759), Air from *Water Music*, Suite in D major (1717)

This piece features two very similar binary forms, one after the other. What kinds of differences are there between the two binary forms?

Analytical questions:

1. Does the first reprise modulate or stay in the same key?
2. What kinds of cadences are heard?
3. What thematic material (if any) is reused in the second part of the second reprise in each binary form? Is it heard in its entirety or in abbreviated form? Has it been changed? (In particular, what is the musical effect of the harmony on the fifth downbeat in the second reprise in each binary form?)
4. How, then, would you identify the type of binary form in each case?

COMPOUND TERNARY FORM WITH NESTED BINARY FORMS

Example 18.9.   Wolfgang Amadeus Mozart (1756–91), Menuetto and Trio from "Eine kleine Nachtmusik," K. 525 (1787)

* What types of binary form are represented in this piece?

DRILLS

1. Continue practicing the two-step interval drill given in Chapter 15 and the two-skip interval drill given in Chapter 17. If you haven't yet tried the latter within a minor scale, then do so now; use a natural (unraised) scale degree $\hat{6}$, but use a raised leading tone when arpeggiating the V triad and the vii° triad.

2. Practice the rhythm of each measure of Example 18.1 separately (there are essentially eight one-measure rhythmic patterns). Now, with a partner, practice performing the rhythms for one another, asking each other to identify the rhythms that were performed. Then compose a rhythmic round with words, employing a text of your choosing or invention. Be sure that only the correct syllables are accented. Finally, practice performing the round in a trio or quartet until you can perform your round comfortably with only one person on a part.

CHORALE WORKSHOP: TONICIZING MEDIANTS AND SUBMEDIANTS, AND EVADED RESOLUTIONS

All of the following progressions can be realized in major and minor keys unless otherwise specified. For each progression, sing just the bass line; then sing the chord as an arpeggio (up from its bass note and back down) or play it on an instrument. Working at a piano, try singing the soprano lines while playing the bass line, and then singing the bass while playing the soprano lines. Finally, practice every progression with every soprano line on the piano, in a variety of simple keys.

Harmony (bass line in left hand)	Possible soprano scale degrees (right hand)
I $\frac{V^7}{iii}$ iii $\frac{V^7}{ii}$ | ii V^7 I (only in major)	$\hat{5}$ $\hat{6}$ $\hat{5}$ $\hat{5}$ | $\hat{4}$ $\hat{4}$ $\hat{3}$ $\hat{3}$ $\uparrow\hat{2}$ $\hat{3}$ $\hat{3}$ | $\hat{2}$ $\hat{2}$ $\hat{1}$
I $\frac{V^7}{iii}$ $\frac{V^7}{vi}$ $\frac{V^7}{ii}$ | $\frac{V^7}{V}$ V^7 I (only in major)	$\hat{5}$ $\hat{6}$ $\uparrow\hat{5}$ $\downarrow\hat{5}$ | $\uparrow\hat{4}$ $\downarrow\hat{4}$ $\hat{3}$ $\hat{3}$ $\uparrow\hat{2}$ $\hat{3}$ $\hat{3}$ | $\hat{2}$ $\hat{2}$ $\hat{1}$
i $\frac{V^6_5}{III}$ III ii^{o6} | V (only in minor)	$\hat{3}$ $\hat{4}$ $\hat{3}$ $\hat{2}$ | $\hat{2}$ $\hat{1}$ $\downarrow\hat{7}$ $\downarrow\hat{7}$ $\hat{6}$ | $\hat{5}$
I $\frac{V^4_3}{vi}$ vi $\frac{V^4_3}{IV}$ | IV V^7 I or i $\frac{V^4_3}{VI}$ VI $\frac{V^4_3}{iv}$ | [iv or IV] V^7 i	$\hat{5}$ $\uparrow\hat{5}$ $\hat{6}$ $\downarrow\hat{7}$ | $\hat{6}$ $\uparrow\hat{7}$ $\hat{1}$ (in minor: $\hat{5}$ $\hat{5}$ $\hat{6}$ $\downarrow\hat{7}$ | $\uparrow\hat{6}$ $\uparrow\hat{7}$ $\hat{1}$) $\hat{3}$ $\hat{3}$ $\hat{3}$ $\hat{3}$ | $\hat{4}$ $\hat{4}$ $\hat{3}$
I $\frac{V^7}{vi}$ IV $\frac{V^4_3}{IV}$ | IV^6 V^7 I or i $\frac{V^7}{VI}$ iv $\frac{V^4_3}{iv}$ | IV^6 V^7 i	$\hat{5}$ $\uparrow\hat{5}$ $\hat{6}$ $\downarrow\hat{5}$ | $\hat{4}$ $\hat{4}$ $\hat{3}$ (in minor: $\hat{5}$ $\hat{5}$ $\hat{6}$ $\hat{5}$ | $\hat{4}$ $\hat{4}$ $\hat{3}$) $\hat{3}$ $\hat{2}$ $\hat{1}$ $\hat{1}$ | $\hat{1}$ $\hat{7}$ $\hat{1}$
I V$^6_5$ $\frac{V^4_2}{IV}$ $\frac{V^7}{ii}$ | ii V^7 I (only in major)	$\hat{5}$ $\hat{5}$ $\hat{5}$ $\hat{5}$ | $\hat{4}$ $\hat{4}$ $\hat{3}$ $\hat{3}$ $\hat{4}$ $\hat{3}$ $\hat{3}$ | $\hat{2}$ $\hat{2}$ $\hat{1}$ $\hat{3}$ $\hat{2}$ $\hat{1}$ $\uparrow\hat{1}$ | $\hat{2}$ $\hat{7}$ $\hat{1}$

IMPROVISATION: GAMES AND EXERCISES

1. Try all four Chorale Workshop exercises listed under "Improvisation" in Chapter 15 for the progressions given in this chapter.

2. Consider the question in the comments below the Haydn excerpt in Example 18.4. The antecedent-consequent design of the A section would seem to lend itself to a typical rounded binary, but something about the B section gets in the way. Try improvising a new antecedent to begin the B section, coming to a half cadence, and then substitute the original consequent to convert this excerpt to a straight-forward rounded binary form. Then compare your results with Haydn's original.

3. Refer to Example 18.5, Brahms, *Variations on a Theme by Joseph Haydn*, op. 56a (also known as the "St. Anthony Chorale"). Given just the bass line over the first reprise, improvise a new melody along the lines of a fanfare or a familiar trumpet tune. (Make sure your melody cadences in the same measures as before.) Then listen to Brahms' variations on this theme.

4. Refer to the Menuetto from Mozart's Serenade K. 525, given in Example 18.9. Working under tempo, improvise either an inner voice or a descant part (moving at a steady quarter-note pace) for the whole Menuetto.

IMPROVISATION: FOCUS ON RHYTHM AND METER

1. Below you will find four more rhythmic patterns from "Story" by John Cage (the entire movement is found in Chapter 21). Start by marking in the beats, and then practice each one separately, being as precise as possible and following the given articulations. Now, take turns with a partner pointing at the rhythms and seeing how quickly you each can sing the given measure.

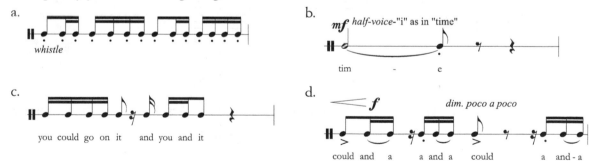

2. John Cage's "aleatoric" or chance music is well known. Following in his footsteps, you will compose an aleatoric duet by flipping two different coins (say, a nickel and a penny). Designate one of the two coins to indicate which rhythm you will use (penny), and the other (nickel) to indicate the voice of your duet where you will put the rhythm. Flip both coins at once, and if the rhythm coin (penny) is "heads" and the "voice" coin is "tails" then you will put rhythm (a) in the lower voice. For the second coin toss (and all "even" numbered tosses), you will use the row on the bottom, choosing between (c) and (d). The third toss (odd) will return to the upper row. Continue tossing and distributing rhythms until you have at

least five measures in *each* voice *and* you have used each rhythm at least twice.
Now, add new words and sounds, and prepare to perform in class!

SUGGESTED SMARTMUSIC ASSESSMENTS

Complete SmartMusic assessments 18.1 (both parts), 18.2 (all parts), 18.3 (both parts),
18.4 (top part), 18.5 (all parts), 18.8 (all parts), and 18.9 (Menuet both parts, Trio all parts).

SHORT-TERM MUSICAL MEMORY

Fill in the key signature and clef as indicated by your instructor, and write in the initial
note(s) on the basis of the given pitch and rhythm information. Note that the key and clef
may not be the same as in the original example. Your instructor (or practice partner) will play a
short progression to establish the key and then count off several beats to establish the tempo.
Because of the brevity of each extract, you should have an overall impression of the rhythm,
contour, and scale degrees after just one or two hearings. Notate the entire fragment.

1. Example 18.2, mm. 17–18, top voice. Starts on beat 1 (quarter note, scale degree $\hat{5}$).

Clef and key
  signature

2a. Example 18.6, up to downbeat of m. 2, top voice. Starts with eighth-note up-
    beat (scale degree $\hat{1}$).

Clef and key
  signature

2b. Example 18.6, last eighth note of m. 13 to downbeat of m. 15, top voice. Starts
    with eighth-note upbeat (low scale degree $\hat{5}$).

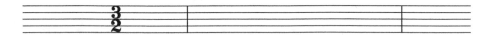

Clef and key
  signature

3. Example 18.7, mm. 77–78, upper voice. Starts on beat 1 with first of several
    sixteenth notes (high scale degree $\hat{1}$).

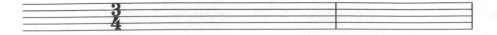

Clef and key
  signature

4.   Example 18.9, Trio section, m. 6 to downbeat of m. 8, top voice. Starts on beat 1 with first of several eighth notes (scale degree î).

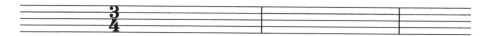

Clef and key
signature

5.   Example 18.1, up to beat 2 in m. 2, both voices (end where low note is heard in melody). Both voices start with an eighth note on beat 1 (both scale degree î, two octaves apart).

Clef and key
signature

6.   Example 18.5, m. 23 to downbeat of m. 25, upper and middle voices. Both start with dotted eighth notes on beat 1 (scale degree 3̂ in the middle voice and a minor sixth higher in the top voice).

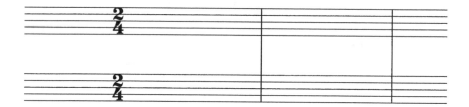

Clef and key
signature

7.   Example 18.8, up to downbeat of m. 2, outer voices. Both start on beat 1 (dotted eighth note and scale degree 3̂ in top part, quarter note a major tenth lower in bottom part).

Clef and key
signature

8. Example 18.9, Menuetto, m. 3 to downbeat of m. 5, outer voices. Both start with quarter notes on beat 1 (scale degree $\hat{3}$ in top part, scale degree $\hat{1}$ a major tenth lower in bottom part).

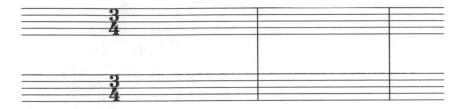

Clef and key
signature

DICTATION OF LONGER EXAMPLES

Your instructor or a classmate will choose one of the examples listed below and inform you of the key, clef, meter, first note (scale degree, rhythmic value, and metric placement) of one or more parts, and total number of measures. Use a separate piece of staff paper to write down the indicated information. You will hear a short progression to establish the key of the example, and then hear the example several times with breaks between hearings.

Nonmodulating:

1. Example 18.2, mm. 1–8, outer voices.
2. Example 18.4, downbeat of m. 8 to beat 2 of m. 12, top voice along with just the downbeats of the bottom voice (sustained throughout each measure).
3. Example 18.5, mm. 1–10, outer voices.

Modulating:

4. Example 18.6, beat 2 of m. 5 (i.e., half note as beat) to beat 2 of m. 7, outer voices. Both start on beat 2 (dotted quarter note and scale degree $\hat{3}$ in bottom voice, half note tied to eighth note a major tenth higher in top voice).
5. Example 18.7, mm. 12–18, both voices.
6. Example 18.8, mm. 23–26, outer voices.

CONTEXTUAL LISTENING 18.1

W. A. Mozart (1756–1791), Theme from Piano Sonata in D major, K. 284, mvt. 3

Mozart's sixth piano sonata, like all of his others, was intended to be played on either the harpsichord or the piano (which was invented only thirty years before Mozart was born).
   These questions refer to the *first reprise*:

1. Does the first reprise modulate? If so, to what key?

2. What type of period comprises the first reprise?

3. What types of cadences are heard at the end of the two phrases?

Now for some questions about the *second reprise*:

4. What type of cadence is heard at the midpoint of the second reprise? How does the composer emphasize the drama of this arrival?

5. What thematic material (if any) is reused in the second part of the second reprise? Is it heard in its entirety or in abbreviated form? Has it been changed?

Concerning the entire theme:

6. On the basis of your answers to these questions, identify the type of binary form.

CONTEXTUAL LISTENING 18.2

W. A. Mozart (1756–1791), Theme from Piano Trio in G major, K. 496, mvt. 3 (Allegretto)

A piano trio is a chamber group consisting of a violin, a cello, and a piano. How do you think Mozart's style creates a cohesive sound out of these instrumental partners?

These questions refer to the *first reprise*:

1. What kind of cadence is heard in the middle of the first reprise? What kind of cadence is heard at the end of the first reprise? What particular phrase structure makes up the first reprise?

2. Does the first reprise remain in the home key or modulate to a new key? If it modulates, what key does it go to?

Now for some questions about the *second reprise*:

3. What prior thematic material (if any) is used in the second part of the second reprise? How has it been changed?

Concerning the entire theme:

4. On the basis of your answers to these questions, identify the precise type of binary form.

CONTEXTUAL LISTENING 18.3

Baldassare Galuppi (1706–1785), Sonata in D major, mvt. 2 (Adagio)

Galuppi is particularly notable for his success as a composer of *opera buffa*, or comic opera. After the very poor reception of his first opera, he left Venice to study with Antonio Lotti and Antonio Vivaldi. This is one of his ninety sonatas. Do you hear any similarities to his teachers in this piece?

These questions refer to the *first reprise*:

1. How many phrases are in the first reprise? They are all the same length. Try counting along just a bit slower than one beat per second, and report the total number of pulses in each phrase. (Note that this consistent phrase length continues in the second reprise.)

2. What types of cadences conclude each phrase? If you hear a modulation within the first reprise, identify the new key and specify which phrase accomplishes the modulation.

Now for some questions about the *second reprise*:

3. What thematic material (if any) is used in the second part of the second reprise?

4. What is unusual about the lengths of the first and second reprises? (Try counting along through the second reprise at the same slow tempo you used before.)

Concerning the entire movement:

5. On the basis of your answers to these questions, identify the type of binary form.

EXPANDING THE REPERTOIRE 18.4

John Cage, *Sonatas and Interludes* for prepared piano (1946–1948)

John Cage composed several short works for "prepared piano," wherein objects are placed between and on the piano's strings in order to create unique timbres. In the *Sonatas and Interludes* for prepared piano, the influence of Indian music and philosophy is quite prominent, as these pieces are intended to express the rasa mental states or emotions.

1. Listen to Sonata no. 1 and provide a graphic representation of sonic events and textures in the timeline below. Note that sections are repeated. More than one listening is suggested.

2. On the basis of your aural perception of the piece, speculate about its formal design. Keep in mind that the formal designs in these pieces are outlined by means other than key or tonal centers. If you have chosen to look at the score, do not be misled by pitch information; ultimately, aural perception of the music should be the defining element.

Chapter 19

Modal Mixture

This chapter introduces the concept of modal mixture, which mainly refers to borrowing a chord from a minor key for use in a major key.[1] Especially when mixture chords are emphasized in some way, their use can have very expressive, colorful results. Predominant harmonies—iv, iv⁶, and ii°⁶, as well as iv⁷ and ii⁷ and all their inversions—have a darker quality than their diatonic (major-key) counterparts, as does the minor tonic triad (i) itself. Composers rarely use the root-position ii° ⁵₃ triad, however, for the same reasons that other root-position diminished triads (such as vii° ⁵₃) are avoided. Triads such as ♭III, ♭VI, and ♭VII are built on chordal roots that are a half-step lower than they would be in a major key (hence the flat to the left of the Roman numeral).

Once any of these chords appear in a phrase, a composer will typically continue to use mixture chords until the tonic is attained again (usually through the dominant). It would sound less convincing to move from a ♭VI triad to a (major) IV triad, since the lowered scale degree 6̂ has a strong tendency to descend toward scale degree 5̂, and a diatonic scale degree 6̂ would reverse this descent. Cadential six-four chords that follow a mixture

---

[1] Although a raised leading tone in a minor key may result in a V or a vii°⁶ that appears to have been borrowed from the parallel major mode, this is usually not referred to as modal mixture. Similarly, scale degree 6̂ can be raised in a minor key for contrapuntal reasons (when part of an ascending line, for instance), resulting in a major IV triad or something similar, but this is commonplace and does not have the same kind of coloristic effect as the use of a iv triad in a major key. However, the use of a "Picardy third" (a major tonic triad at the end of a piece in a minor key) might be described as modal mixture.

pre-dominant can be either major or minor. Mixture chords can be tonicized and even serve as modulatory goals.

In addition to the examples in this chapter, the third measure of Example 21.6 provides an archetypal example of modal mixture.

Example 19.1.   Schubert, "Der Wanderer" (excerpt), op. 4, no. 1 (D. 493)

* *Translation*: Where are you, where are you, my beloved land?
           Sought, imagined, and never known!

   Identify the mixture chord used in m. 7 of this excerpt. Note also that the cadential six-four in the next measure includes the lowered scale degree $\hat{3}$.

Example 19.2.   Schubert, "Lachen und Weinen" (excerpt), op. 59 no. 4 (D. 777)

ich nun wei - ne   bei   des   A - ben-des   Schei -

ne,   ist mir selb' nicht be - wußt, ist mir selb' nicht be - wußt.

* *Translation*: Laughter and tears at every hour
        Rest on love for so many reasons.
        In the morning I laughed for joy,
        and why I now weep in the evening's light
        is unknown to me.
    Note that F♭ is heard as a dissonance in m. 25, but then as a consonance in m. 27. Provide Roman
numerals for mm. 27–30.

Example 19.3.   Franz Schubert (1797–1828), "Tränenregen" from *Die schöne Müllerin*, op. 25, D. 795 (1824), no. 10

sprach: es kommt ein Re - gen, a - de,— ich geh' nach Haus.

* *Translation*: We sat so peacefully together under the cool shade of alders,
        We gazed so peacefully together into the murmuring brook.
        The moon was also out, the stars coming after,
        And we gazed so peacefully together into the silver mirror there.
        I looked for no moon, nor the stars' shine;
        I looked only at her reflection, at her eyes alone.
        And I saw them nodding and gazing up from the blessed brook,
        The little flowers on the bank, the blue ones, they nodded and gazed at her.
        And into the brook the entire heavens seemed sunken,
        And seemed to want to draw me into its depths.
        And over the clouds and stars, the brook happily murmured
        And called with singing and sound: friend, friend, with me!
        Then my eyes overflowed with tears, and made the mirror blurred;
        She said: "The rain is coming, goodbye, I am going home."

Notice the emphasis on E♯ and F♮ throughout this song. What kind of triad is heard on the upbeats to mm. 1, 3, 5, and 9? See Examples 16.4, 20.5, 22.7, 22.10, and several others in Chapter 24 for further instances of the same kind of triad.

What kind of cadence is heard in mm. 17–18, and what key does it suggest? How does Schubert portray the speaker's eyes filling up with tears, right after the repeat sign? How do the last four measures summarize the entire song?

The next three examples revisit the notion of the "lament bass," last heard in Cavalli's "Tremulo spirito" (Example 14.1). More generically, we can label any stepwise bass descent from scale degree Î toward scale degree 5̂ or lower as an instance of a lament bass. The bass line may descend diatonically or chromatically, and it may or may not repeat in the manner of Cavalli's ostinato. Lament basses in major keys often include at least one instance of mixture, most likely above a lowered scale degree 6̂ in the bass.

See also the first two examples in Chapter 22 for further instances of the lament bass.

Example 19.4.   Alexander Borodin (1833–1887), String Quartet no. 2 (1881), mvt. 3 "Notturno"

* What phrase structure is heard over the course of this theme? What is the function of the chromatic harmony in m. 5? What kind of six-four chord is heard in measure 6? What mixture chord is heard in m. 7?

At what point does the ensuing phrase diverge from the model of the earlier phrase? (Just as in Example 19.3, it involves the enharmonic equivalence of E♯ and F♮.) Examine and describe the chromatic sequence that follows. If mm. 16 and 18 sound like secondary V⁶ triads along the way, what Roman numerals would you use in mm. 15 and 17?

Example 19.5.   Ludwig van Beethoven (1770–1827), Symphony no. 7, op. 92 (1811–12)

* This passage approaches IV⁶ fairly conventionally but then introduces some more surprising harmonies in mm. 6–7. What is the chord on the downbeat of m. 7? Consider the function of both chords in m. 6, on the basis of how they resolve.

Example 19.6.   Antonín Dvořák (1841–1904), Cello Concerto, op. 104 (1894–95), mvt. 3,
              conclusion

* The harmonies in this short excerpt are not quite clear, as some of the triplet figurations lead into consonant eighth notes and some lead into dissonances. Considering only the melodic notes that are exactly coordinated with the last four chords, what kind of cadence is this, and what would be the Roman numerals?

Further examples of lament basses will be studied in Chapter 22.

MIXTURE AND TONICIZATION

The next three examples are all by Schubert, and all visit and return from the same distantly related modulatory goal—represented by the same Roman numeral with respect to each excerpt's home key. Identify what goal this is, and compare how Schubert attains it in each case. (Example 19.9 also visits a closely related key.)

Example 19.7.   Schubert, Waltz in F, op. 9 no. 33, D. 365 (1821)

* Identify the harmony on the downbeat of m. 13 with respect to both the opening key and the upcoming key.

Example 19.8.   Schubert, Impromptu op. 90, no. 1 (1827)

* What distantly related key is attained in the middle of this excerpt? How does Schubert get there and back?

Example 19.9.   Schubert, Octet, D. 803 (1824), mvt. 3 (Trio)

* Do you hear the cadence in m. 20 as an authentic cadence in G major or as a tonicized half cadence? With the F♮ right before and right after this cadence, it would be at least possible to stay in the home key. How does the tonic harmony change at the beginning of the second reprise, and to what key does Schubert then modulate?

What is the form of this piece?

Example 19.10. Engelbert Humperdinck (1854–1921), "Evening Prayer" from *Hansel and Gretel* (1893), Act II

* What key is attained (and cadentially confirmed) in m. 8? Examine and describe the two sequences heard in mm. 9–12 and mm. 13–17. Provide Roman numerals (with respect to the home of D major) for each tonicized triad in mm. 9–12.

DRILLS

1. Continue practicing the two-step interval drill and the two-skip interval drill. Along the same lines, turn back to Example 19.4 and sing the first two measures of the melody without the grace notes: "$\hat{1}$——$\hat{7}$–$\hat{6}$–$\hat{7}$–$\hat{5}$". Then sing it again, but with the names of the interval qualities ("$\hat{1}$——minor–major–major–major"). Since this melody moves down from a high scale degree $\hat{1}$, let's follow the direction of the tune and sing the same diatonic pattern at lower and lower points in a major scale ("$\hat{7}$——$\hat{6}$–$\hat{5}$–$\hat{6}$–$\hat{4}$, $\hat{7}$——major–major–major–major, $\hat{6}$——$\hat{5}$–$\hat{4}$–$\hat{5}$–$\hat{3}$ . . ."). Since this melodic fragment would sound pretty different upside down, there's no need to invert it and go back up. After singing "$\hat{3}$——$\hat{2}$–$\hat{1}$–$\hat{2}$–$\hat{1}$" and the sizes of those intervals, just sing a final "$\hat{1}$."

2. Refer to Example 19.5 and try the same thing. Sing the first five melodic notes ("$\hat{1}$–$\hat{5}$–$\hat{3}$–$\hat{6}$–$\hat{5}$"), and then sing them again with names for each interval size ("$\hat{1}$–perfect–minor–perfect–major"). Now move down step by step and do the same thing ("$\hat{7}$–$\hat{4}$–$\hat{2}$–$\hat{5}$–$\hat{4}$, $\hat{7}$–augmented–minor–perfect–major, $\hat{6}$–$\hat{3}$–$\hat{1}$–$\hat{4}$–$\hat{3}$, . . ."). Again, no need to go back up the scale; just sing a final "$\hat{1}$" as before.

3. Refer to Example 19.10, by Engelbert Humperdinck, specifically the sequence in mm. 9–12. Sing this progression as a series of arpeggios up from each bass note (in close position) and back down. Continue the pattern for four more measures. Then start again by arpeggiating the chords in m. 9, but this time transpose the initial one-measure pattern up by only a semitone—so that the secondary dominant on each downbeat has the same pitch in the bass as the triad just before. Which is easier?

CHORALE WORKSHOP: MIXTURE PRE-DOMINANTS

For each of the major-key progressions below, sing just the bass line; then sing the chord as an arpeggio (up from its bass note and back down) or play it on an instrument. Next, working at a piano, try singing the soprano lines while playing the bass line and singing the bass while playing the soprano lines. Finally, practice every progression with every soprano line on the piano in a variety of simple major keys.

Harmony (bass line in left hand)

I | iv V I

$I \dfrac{V^4_2}{IV}$ iv^6 V^7 | I

I | iv^6 iv^7 V$^{8-7}_{4-3}$ | I

Possible soprano scale degrees (right hand)

$\hat{1}$ | $\hat{1}$ $\hat{7}$ $\hat{1}$
$\hat{3}$ | $\hat{4}$ $\hat{2}$ $\hat{3}$
$\hat{5}$ | $\downarrow\hat{6}$ $\hat{5}$ $\hat{5}$

$\hat{3}$ $\hat{3}$ $\hat{4}$ $\hat{4}$ | $\hat{3}$
$\hat{1}$ $\hat{1}$ $\hat{1}$ $\hat{7}$ | $\hat{1}$

$\hat{5}$ | $\hat{4}$ $\downarrow\hat{6}$ $\hat{5}$ $\hat{4}$ | $\hat{3}$
$\hat{3}$ | $\hat{4}$ $\downarrow\hat{3}$ $\hat{2}$ $\hat{2}$ | $\hat{1}$
$\hat{1}$ | $\hat{1}$ $\hat{1}$ $\hat{1}$ $\hat{7}$ | $\hat{1}$

I | ii^{o6} V I $\hat{3}$ | $\hat{2}$ $\hat{2}$ $\hat{3}$
                                                         $\hat{1}$ | $\hat{2}$ $\hat{7}$ $\hat{1}$
                                                         $\hat{1}$ | $\hat{1}$ $\hat{7}$ $\hat{1}$

I | iv ii^{ø7} V$^{8-7}_{6-5}_{4-3}$ | I $\hat{5}$ | $\downarrow\hat{6}$ $\downarrow\hat{6}$ $\hat{5}$ $\hat{4}$ | $\hat{3}$
                                                         $\hat{3}$ | $\hat{4}$ $\hat{4}$ $\hat{3}$ $\hat{2}$ | $\hat{1}$
                                                         $\hat{1}$ | $\hat{1}$ $\hat{1}$ $\hat{1}$ $\hat{7}$ | $\hat{1}$

I | ii$^{ø}{}^{6}_{5}$ V^7 I $\hat{3}$ | $\hat{2}$ $\hat{2}$ $\hat{3}$

I $\dfrac{V^4_2}{IV}$ IV^6 ii$^{ø}{}^4_3$ | V $\hat{3}$ $\hat{3}$ $\hat{4}$ $\hat{4}$ | $\hat{5}$
                                                         $\hat{1}$ $\hat{1}$ $\hat{1}$ $\hat{1}$ | $\hat{7}$

I | ii$^{ø}{}^4_2$ V$^6_5$ I $\hat{3}$ | $\hat{4}$ $\hat{4}$ $\hat{3}$
                                                         $\hat{1}$ | $\hat{2}$ $\hat{2}$ $\hat{1}$

IMPROVISATION: GAMES AND EXERCISES

1. Try all four Chorale Workshop exercises listed under "Improvisation" in Chapter 15 for the progressions given in this chapter.

2. Improvise a straightforward rounded binary form with a partner. Have your partner improvise a four-measure antecedent phrase, coming to a half cadence, and then reply with a four-measure consequent, coming to an authentic cadence. Repeat. Now, have your partner improvise a new antecedent, again coming to a half cadence. Reply with your original consequent. Repeat. Once this is comfortable, try spicing it up by tonicizing the dominant at the end of the A section, adjusting it, of course, so that you come to a perfect authentic cadence at the end of the form.

IMPROVISATION: FOCUS ON RHYTHM AND METER

1. John Cage's "Story" (see Chapter 21) has a number of sections where triplets and sixteenths are immediately juxtaposed, as shown by the two rhythmic excerpts below. Mark the beats and practice the two lines *carefully*, subdividing into quarters. Be particularly careful to distinguish between the triplet eights and the nontriplet eighth and sixteenth in the first rhythmic excerpt. You will need to be able to sing each line comfortably at 65 beats per minute. Practice going back and forth and mix-matching the first measure of one with the second measure of the other.

2. Now, work with a partner to see if the two of you can sing the two lines simultaneously, switching back and forth between them. Finally, try tapping the rhythm of one while singing the rhythm of the other, then switch.

SUGGESTED SMARTMUSIC ASSESSMENTS

Complete SmartMusic assessments 19.1 (all parts), 19.2 (all parts), 19.3 (all parts), 19.4 (all parts), 19.5 (all parts), 19.6 (top part), 19.7 (all parts), 19.8 (all parts), 19.9 (all parts), and 19.10 (all parts).

SHORT-TERM MUSICAL MEMORY

Fill in the key signature and clef as indicated by your instructor, and write in the initial note(s) on the basis of the given pitch and rhythm information. Note that the key and clef *may not be the same* as in the original example. Your instructor (or practice partner) will play a short progression to establish the key and then count off several beats to establish the tempo. Because of the brevity of each extract, you should have an overall impression of the rhythm, contour, and scale degrees after just one or two hearings. Notate the entire fragment.

1. Example 19.1, up to downbeat of m. 3, outer voices. Top voice has eighth-note upbeat (scale degree $\hat{5}$); bottom voice enters on downbeat (quarter note a perfect twelfth lower than top voice entrance).

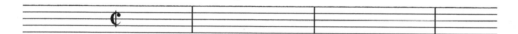

Clef and key
signature

2. Example 19.8, beat 4 of m. 5 to downbeat of m. 9, top voice. Starts with dotted eighth note (scale degree $\hat{1}$).

Clef and key
signature

3. Example 19.9, up to downbeat of m. 5, top voice. Starts on beat 3 (quarter note, scale degree $\hat{5}$).

Clef and key
signature

4. Example 19.2, up to beat 2 of m. 2, both outer voices (end on low notes in both parts). Both voices have an eighth-note upbeat (scale degree Î in top voice, and a minor sixth lower in bottom voice).

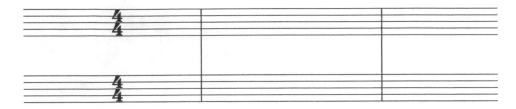

Clef and key
  signature

5. Example 19.3, beat 6 of m. 2 to beat 4 of m. 4, outer voices. Both start with eighth-note upbeat (low scale degree Î in bottom voice; scale degree 3̂ a major tenth higher in top voice, tied into downbeat).

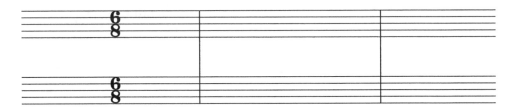

Clef and key
  signature

6. Example 19.6, mm. 3–5, middle and bottom voices. Both start with eighth notes on beat 1 (scale degree 3̂ in middle voice, low scale degree Î a major tenth lower in bottom voice).

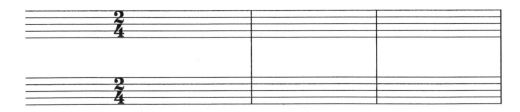

Clef and key
  signature

DICTATION OF LONGER EXAMPLES

Your instructor or a classmate will choose one of the examples listed below and will inform you of the key, clef, meter, first note (scale degree, rhythmic value, and metric placement) of one or more parts, and total number of measures. Use a separate piece of staff paper to write down the indicated information. You will hear a short progression to establish the key of the example, and you will then hear the example several times with breaks between hearings.

Nonmodulating:

1. Example 19.2, m. 17 to end, top and middle voices. Notate on one system with upward and downward stems.
2. Example 19.3, just after repeat sign until downbeat of m. 32, outer voices.
3a. Example 19.4, mm. 1–9, top voice along with just the downbeats of the bottom voice (sustained throughout each measure).
3b. Example 19.4, m. 32 to beat 3 of m. 43, middle voice (or middle and bottom voices).
4. Example 19.5, all, outer voices.

Modulating:

5. Example 19.7, mm. 9–16, top and middle voices.
6. Example 19.9, beat 3 of m. 32 to downbeat of m. 45, bottom voice.
7. Example 19.10, m. 13 to end, outer voices.

CONTEXTUAL LISTENING 19.1

> Wolfgang Amadeus Mozart (1756–1791), "Haffner" Serenade, KV 250, mvt. 3 (Menuetto)

This eight-movement work was commissioned for the wedding of a member of the Haffner family. In fact, most serenades during this time were "occasional music," written for an event or celebration. Can you think of any other Serenades and what they were written for?

1. Does the first reprise remain in the home key or modulate to a new key? If it modulates, what key does it go to?

2. The first reprise consists of four thematically distinct four-measure units, which can be labeled as A, B, C, and D. In what order do these four sections return in the second reprise (after the eight measures of dominant pedal)? Have any of them been transposed or otherwise changed from their earlier appearances?

3. On the basis of your answers to these questions, determine whether this is a sectional or continuous binary, and decide whether the unique thematic plan is more suggestive of rounded or balanced binary.

Name: _____ Date: _____ Instructor: _____

CONTEXTUAL LISTENING 19.2

Joseph Haydn (1732–1809), Piano Sonata in A major, Hob. XVI:26, mvt. 3
(Menuet al rovescio)

Haydn wrote fifty-one piano sonatas in all, often incorporating quite theatrical (and sometimes comedic) effects. This unique movement is also included in Haydn's Sonata in D major for Violin and Viola, Hob. VI:4, and his Symphony in G major, Hob. I:47.

1. Does the first reprise remain in the home key or modulate to a new key? If it modulates, what key does it go? What kind of cadence concludes the first reprise?

2. What very unusual relationship exists between the first and second reprise? (Hint: they are the same length.)

3. On the basis of your answer to these questions, determine whether this is sectional or continuous binary and whether you think the piece warrants any thematic descriptor other than simple binary. Defend your position.

CONTEXTUAL LISTENING 19.3

Jean-Philippe Rameau (1683–1764), "Le Rappel des Oiseaux" from Suite no. 2 (1724)

"Rappel des Oiseaux" means "Bird Calls." Listen to the way these voices interact. Do you think that the title is appropriate?

This piece sounds very continuous and spontaneous, but it is possible to hear the repetition of the first and second reprises of a binary form. (The first reprise is about thirty-five seconds long.)

1. What Roman numerals would describe the opening tonic expansion? (i–*something*–i)

2. Does the first reprise remain in the home key or modulate to a new key? If it modulates, what key does it go to? What kind of cadence concludes the first reprise?

3. Identify which closely related key is visited (abruptly) at the beginning of the second reprise. For extra credit, identify what type of sequence is employed to escape this key.

4. Which part of the first reprise—something from the beginning, or something from towards the end—seems to be recapitulated in some form upon the return to the home key in the second reprise? ("In some form" because it is not an exact thematic recall.) Describe the theme somehow, in terms of its rhythm or pitch contour or its motivic character; describe, if you can, how its two appearances are different.

5. On the basis of your answer to these questions, determine whether this is sectional or continuous binary, then decide whether a label of simple binary, quasi-rounded binary or quasi-balanced binary best applies.

EXPANDING THE REPERTOIRE 19.4

Queen, "Crazy Little Thing Called Love" (1979)

This song remained as a Billboard number-one hit song for four weeks. Although the song as a whole is in Rockabilly style, the melody features ♭3̂, which is reminiscent of the Blues, and the bass part is typical of Boogie-woogie!

1. The verse, which appears ten times in the song, is twelve measures long. Which of the following best describes the form of the verse?

   a. A B A   b. A B B   c. A A A   d. A A B

2. On the staff below, transcribe the melody of the verse and provide Roman numerals in the boxes according to the specified key. Then, circle the modal mixture chords.

3. The ♭VII–IV–I harmonic motion is called the "double plagal" cadence. Can you give a rationale for the name of this cadence?

4. *Optional assignment*: The *Aeolian cadence* (♭VI–♭VII–I) at the end of the verse is quite prominent in 1980s popular songs. Find one song that features this cadential gesture.

Chapter 20

Ternary Form

Ternary form refers to an A-B-A or A-B-A′ form in which an opening section returns—recognizably, if not identically—after a separate and distinct middle section. These may comprise one continuous piece (*simple* ternary) or they may be a pair of movements that alternate in this way (*composite* ternary). We have already encountered two examples of composite ternary at the ends of Chapters 17 and 18. Since the two Gavottes in Example 17.9 were themselves in binary form, as were the Minuet and the Trio in Example 18.9, these pieces are also examples of *compound* ternary form. This means that one or both of the sections are in binary or ternary form.

Whether simple or composite, ternary forms are defined by the contrast between their A and B sections and by the return of the A section. The returning A section may be modified from its first occurrence. Composers sometimes insert a transition into the B section, or more commonly a retransition from the B section back to the A section. There may also be an introductory section and/or a coda.

Further examples of ternary form are found in Chapter 24.

Example 20.1.   From the notebook of Anna Magdalena Bach (1701–1760), Musette in D
                 Major, BWV Anh. 126

* Although only two repeated sections are notated, this Musette is of course in simple ternary form
(note the "Da Capo" marking). What is a Musette, and why does the left hand have so much droning
to do? (Feel free to sing all of the octave leaps as unisons, instead.) How many scale degrees are heard in
the A section?

Example 20.2.   George Frideric Handel (1685–1759), "Lascia ch'io pianga" from *Rinaldo*
(1711), Act II scene 4

La - scia ch'io pian - ga   mia cru - da sor - te,

La - scia ch'io pian - ga   mia cru - da sor - te,

La - scia ch'io pian - ga   mia cru - da sor - te,

La - scia ch'io pian - ga   mia cru - da sor - te,_____

e che so - spi - ri   la li - ber - tà,

e che so - spi - ri   la li - ber - tà,

e che so - spi - ri   la li - ber - tà,

e che so - spi - ri   la li - ber - tà,

e che so - spi - ri,   e che so - spi - ri   la

e che so - spi - ri,   e che so - spi - ri   la

e che so - spi - ri,   e che so - spi - ri   la

e che so - spi - ri,   e che so - spi - ri   la

* *Translation*: Let me weep over my cruel fate,
And that I long for freedom!
Where does the B section begin? Where does the A section return?

Example 20.3. Robert Schumann (1810–1849), "Wild Rider," from *Album for the Young*, op. 68 (1848)

* How does Schumann transform the A section to become the B section? What factors help us to hear this piece as simple ternary form instead of rounded binary form?

Example 20.4. Johann Sebastian Bach (1685–1750), English Suite no. 3, BWV 808, Gavottes I–II

* What kinds of binary form are represented here? In what other ways do these two Gavottes contrast with each other?

Both Gavottes (indeed, all gavottes) begin on the middle of a duple or quadruple measure. Do some of the downbeats seem weaker than some mid-measure beats? Which downbeats sound the most stable?

Although you should feel free, as always, to change octaves as necessary for your voice, it would be best to preserve larger stepwise linear motions, such as the one found in mm. 26–32 of Gavotte I. You might consider singing this entire linear ascent in the lower octave.

Example 20.5.   Ludwig van Beethoven (1770–1827), Bagatelle op. 119, no. 1 (1822)

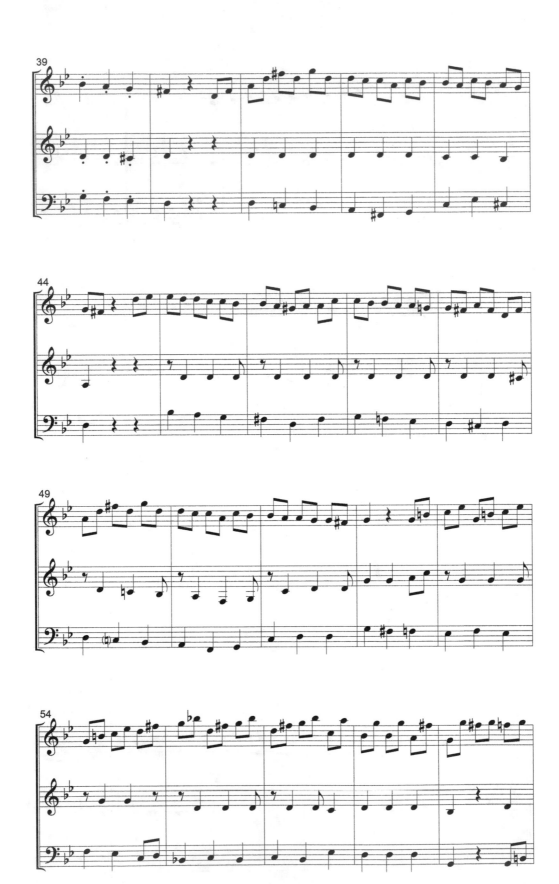

* Note the conjunction of E♭ and C♯ on the upbeat to m. 4, both heading toward D on the downbeat. This interval, an augmented sixth, characterizes a certain kind of chromatic pre-dominant (an augmented-sixth chord) that we will discuss further in Chapters 22 and 24.

Analytical questions:

1. What phrase structure is heard over the first eight measures? What phrase structure is heard over the first sixteen measures?

2. Between the A section (mm. 1–16) and its return in m. 37, we hear three subsections of eight measures, eight measures, and four measures in length. Is this a nested ternary form, or a transition plus a twelve-measure binary form, or a sixteen-measure binary form plus a retransition? Why?

3. Provide Roman numerals for mm. 17–20.

4. How is the returning A section different from what was originally heard? How would you describe the last sixteen measures of the piece?

Example 20.6.   Frédéric Chopin (1810–1849), Mazurka op. 30, no. 1 (1837)

poco riten.

Analytical questions:

1. Where does the B section begin and end?
2. Is the opening A section tonally closed?
3. Is the B section tonally closed?
4. At what point does the returning A section deviate from the opening A section?

Example 20.7. Leonard Bernstein (1918–1990), "Somewhere," from *West Side Story* (1957)

Analytical questions:

1. What key is this song in? What distantly related key is briefly tonicized in mm. 16–17?

2. What factors encourage us to hear a separate B section in this song, and where does it begin and end?

3. Comment on the nature of the final cadence (the last five measures of the song).

DRILLS

1. Review the two-step drill and the two-skip drill. Then try this "sliding $^6_3$" drill: in a major key, arpeggiate a tonic triad (high in your vocal range), and then sing the interval qualities ("$\hat{1}$–$\hat{3}$–$\hat{5}$, $\hat{1}$–major–minor"). Now do the same for first-inversion triads based on scale degrees $\hat{7}$, $\hat{6}$, $\hat{5}$, $\hat{4}$, $\hat{3}$, and $\hat{2}$. Finish with a root-position tonic triad.

2. Refer to Example 20.5, Beethoven's Bagatelle. Sing the melody to the downbeat of measure 4. Then sing the same pattern of diatonic intervals starting on scale degree $\hat{6}$, scale degree $\hat{7}$, and scale degree $\hat{1}$. Next, notice that the bass line moves in parallel tenths with the melody for these four measures. Sing the opening again (starting on scale degree $\hat{5}$), but insert the bass-voice notes into the melody as follows: "$\hat{5}$—$\hat{6}$ | $\hat{5}$–$\hat{3}$–$\hat{2}$–$\hat{4}$–$\hat{3}$–$\hat{1}$ | #$\hat{7}$—$\hat{2}$, $\hat{2}$—$\hat{4}$ | $\hat{3}$–$\hat{1}$–↓$\hat{7}$–$\hat{2}$–$\hat{1}$–$\hat{6}$ | $\hat{5}$—#$\hat{7}$" using eighth-note values in mm. 1 and 3. Then sing the same diatonic line starting on scale degree $\hat{6}$, scale degree $\hat{7}$, and scale degree $\hat{1}$. (Stick with an unraised scale degree $\hat{6}$ throughout, but you may raise the leading tone anytime it isn't just before or just after scale degree $\hat{6}$.)

3. Refer to Example 20.1, the Musette in D major. Chant the rhythm of mm. 13–16 (repeatedly) while conducting in two. Notice that the rhythm of these four measures is a palindrome. Moreover, the melody of these measures produces viable counterpoint when played against itself in reverse. At a slow tempo, try singing the melody at the same time as playing its exact retrograde, "G#–A–C#–D–(low)E–D#–(high)E" on the piano. Then sing the backward version while playing the forward version. Sing the forward and backward versions together with a classmate.

CHORALE WORKSHOP: CHROMATIC THIRD RELATIONS

For each of the major-key progressions below, sing just the bass line, and then sing each chord as an arpeggio (up from its bass note and back down) or play it on an instrument. Then, working at a piano, try singing the soprano lines while playing the bass line, and singing the bass while playing the soprano lines. Finally, practice every progression with every soprano line on the piano, in a variety of simple major keys.

Harmony (bass line in left hand)	Possible soprano scale degrees (right hand)
I V⁷ ♭VI iv | V	$\hat{5}$ $\hat{4}$ ↓$\hat{3}$ $\hat{4}$ | $\hat{2}$ $\hat{3}$ $\hat{2}$ $\hat{1}$ $\hat{1}$ | $\hat{7}$
I v⁶ ♭VI ii°⁷ | V$^{8-7}_{6-5}_{4-3}$ I	$\hat{5}$ $\hat{5}$ ↓$\hat{6}$ ↓$\hat{6}$ | $\hat{5}$ $\hat{4}$ $\hat{3}$ $\hat{1}$ $\hat{2}$ ↓$\hat{3}$ $\hat{4}$ | ↑$\hat{3}$ $\hat{2}$ $\hat{1}$ (or ↓$\hat{3}$ $\hat{2}$ $\hat{1}$)
I V⁷ ♭VI ♭III | ii°$^6_5$ V I	$\hat{5}$ $\hat{4}$ ↓$\hat{3}$ ↓$\hat{3}$ | $\hat{2}$ $\hat{2}$ $\hat{1}$ $\hat{1}$ $\hat{7}$ $\hat{1}$ ↓$\hat{7}$ | ↓$\hat{6}$ $\hat{5}$ $\hat{5}$
I $\frac{V^6_5}{♭III}$ ♭III iv | V	$\hat{5}$ $\hat{4}$ ↓$\hat{3}$ $\hat{1}$ | $\hat{7}$ $\hat{1}$ ↓$\hat{7}$ ↓$\hat{7}$ ↓$\hat{6}$ | $\hat{5}$
I $\frac{V^6_3}{♭III}$ ♭III ♭VI | ii°⁶ V I	$\hat{5}$ ↓$\hat{6}$ $\hat{5}$ ↓$\hat{3}$ | $\hat{4}$ $\hat{2}$ ↑$\hat{3}$ $\hat{3}$ $\hat{4}$ ↓$\hat{3}$ ↓$\hat{3}$ | $\hat{2}$ $\hat{2}$ $\hat{1}$ $\hat{1}$ ↓$\hat{7}$ ↓$\hat{7}$ ↓$\hat{6}$ | ↓$\hat{6}$ $\hat{5}$ $\hat{5}$

IMPROVISATION: GAMES AND EXERCISES

1. Try all four Chorale Workshop exercises listed under "Improvisation" in Chapter 15 for the progressions given in this chapter.

2. Sing the melody in the first four measures of Example 20.5. Then, beginning with the upbeat(s) to m. 5, invent a new four-measure melody. Use only staccato quarter notes (or you may imitate the dotted rhythm on the upbeat to m. 5) and aim toward a perfect authentic cadence in m. 8 instead of a half cadence. Sing your melody through, and compare it to your classmates' efforts.

IMPROVISATION: FOCUS ON RHYTHM AND METER

1. The final three measures of John Cage's "Story" are shown in the excerpt below. They draw together all of the rhythmic configurations we have explored thus far. In preparation for your performances at the end of the next chapter, practice singing each line individually, being sure to subdivide appropriately. Remember, your tempo goal is at least 65 beats per minute.

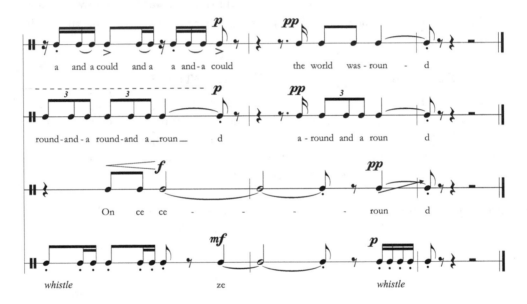

2. Now, working in a group of four and listening to your metronome, try singing the entire exercise four times through, switching parts each time. Decide in advance how you will rotate parts (either shifting down, as in a regular "round," or up). As the point approaches at which every member of the group has sung every part, the group leader should ratchet up the metronome 5 to 10 beats per minute, and then all should start singing again. See how fast you can do this exercise while still maintaining crispness of rhythm and correct articulation and inflection, and following the clearly marked dynamics.

SUGGESTED SMARTMUSIC ASSESSMENTS

Complete SmartMusic assessments 20.1 (top voice), 20.2 (all voices), 20.3 (all voices), 20.4 (both voices, 20.5 (all voices), 20.6 (all voices), and 20.7 (all voices).

SHORT-TERM MUSICAL MEMORY

Fill in the key signature and clef as indicated by your instructor, and write in the initial note(s) on the basis of the given pitch and rhythm information. Note that the key and clef *may not be the same* as in the original example. Your instructor (or practice partner) will play a short progression to establish the key and then count off several beats to establish the tempo. Because of the brevity of each extract, you should have an overall impression of the rhythm, contour, and scale degrees after just one or two hearings. Notate the entire fragment.

1. Example 20.1, m. 13 to downbeat of m. 15, upper voice. Starts on beat 1 (eighth note, high scale degree $\hat{5}$).

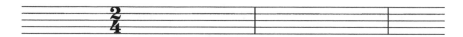

Clef and key
signature

2. Example 20.3, through end of m. 2, upper voice. Starts on eighth-note upbeat (low scale degree $\hat{5}$).

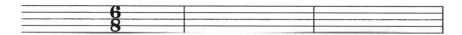

Clef and key
signature

3. Example 20.4, Gavotte II, beat 3 of m. 14 to end, upper voice. Starts with eighth note (scale degree $\hat{3}$).

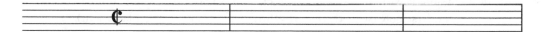

Clef and key
signature

4. Example 20.5, m. 52 to downbeat of m. 55, bottom voice. Starts on beat 1 (quarter note, high scale degree $\hat{1}$).

Clef and key
signature

5. Example 20.1, m. 17 to beat 2 of m. 18, both voices (end dictation on the beat). Both start on beat 1 (sixteenth note and scale degree $\hat{5}$ in top voice, eighth note three octaves lower in bottom voice).

Clef and key
    signature

6. Example 20.5, up to downbeat of m. 3, outer voices. Top voice starts on beat 3 (dotted eighth note, high scale degree $\hat{5}$), bottom voice starts on the first downbeat (quarter note a major tenth lower than top voice entrance).

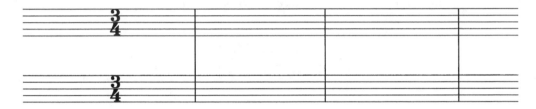

Clef and key
    signature

DICTATION OF LONGER EXAMPLES

Your instructor or a classmate will choose one of the examples listed below and inform you of the key, clef, meter, first note (scale degree, rhythmic value, and metric placement) of one or more parts, and total number of measures. Use a separate piece of staff paper to write down the indicated information. You will hear a short progression to establish the key of the example, and then hear the example several times with breaks between hearings.

Nonmodulating:

1. Example 20.2, mm. 1–8, outer voices.
2. Example 20.5, beat 3 of m. 65 to downbeat of m. 71, outer voices.

Modulating:

3a. Example 20.4, Gavotte I, up to downbeat of m. 8, both voices (or just top voice).
3b. Example 20.4, Gavotte I, beat 3 of m. 8 to beat 3 of m. 14, top voice.
 4. Example 20.6, through end of m. 10, outer voices. Omit grace notes for dictation purposes.
 5. Example 20.7, mm. 9–17, middle and lower voices (line with text and bass line).

CONTEXTUAL LISTENING 20.1

Robert Schumann (1810–1856), "Dein Angesicht" ("Your Face"), op. 127 no. 2

Dein Angesicht	Your Face
Dein Angesicht, so lieb und schön,	Your face, so sweet and lovely,
Das hab' ich jüngst im traume geseh'n	I have just seen it in a dream.
Es ist so mild und engelgleich,	It is so mild and angelic,
Und doch so bleich, so schmerzenbleich.	And yet so pale, so filled with pain.
Und nur die Lippen, die sind roth;	And only the lips, they are red;
Bald aber küßt sie bleich der Tod,	But death will soon kiss them pale,
Erlöschen wird das Himmelslicht,	Out will go the heavenly light,
Das aus den frommen Augen bricht.	Which beams from the pious eyes.

1. The first two phrases are very similar—indeed, the vocal part differs by only one note. What are the singer's first and last scale degrees of the first phrase? What type of cadence is heard?

2. To what key does the second phrase modulate? (Answer with a Roman numeral conceived in comparison to the principal key of the song.) What kind of cadence is heard?

3. The third phrase ("Und nur die Lippen . . .") stays briefly in the new key. What three melodic scale degrees (in the new key) are repeated at the beginning of this phrase?

4. A chromatic descent in the pianist's left hand then takes us to yet another key. What is the vocal melody doing above this bass descent ("Bald aber küßt . . .")?

5. We then hear two presentations of the original melodic material in different keys ("Erlöschen wird . . ." and then back to "Dein Angesicht"). How does the first of these two function in the context of the overall form?

6. Does the opening of the song return in its original form or are there some changes? If you hear some changes, describe them.

CONTEXTUAL LISTENING 20.2

Ludwig van Beethoven (1770–1827), Septet in E♭ major, op. 20, mvt. 3

Dedicated to the Empress Maria Theresa of Austria, Beethoven's Septet is a very popular piece written for clarinet, horn, bassoon, violin, viola, cello, and bass.

This movement is a Minuet and Trio; both sections are in binary form. (You will hear the Minuet, and then the Trio, followed by the Minuet again.)

These questions refer to the Minuet:

1. Does the first reprise remain in the home key or modulate to a new key? If it modulates, what key does it go to? What kind of cadence concludes the first reprise?

2. What prior thematic material (if any) is used in the second part of the second reprise? How has it been changed?

Now for some questions about the Trio:

3. Does the first reprise remain in the home key or modulate to a new key? If it modulates, what key does it go to? What kind of cadence concludes the first reprise?

4. What prior thematic material (if any) is used in the second part of the second reprise? How has it been changed?

Concerning the movement as a whole:

5. On the basis of your answers to these questions, identify the type of binary form for each part. How would you describe the effect of their pairing (either in terms of the difference in binary form or along other lines)?

Name: _____ Date: _____ Instructor: _____

CONTEXTUAL LISTENING 20.3

In addition to this piece for cello and piano, Mendelssohn wrote eight volumes of pieces for solo piano entitled "songs without words." After listening to this piece, compare it to other songs (with text) that you have already seen in earlier assignments, and consider why is it called a song.

1. Is the A section tonally closed?

2. How would you describe the form of the A section?

3. What textural changes highlight the arrival of the B section?

4. Where does the B section first modulate? (Express the new key as a Roman numeral within the key in which the B section began.)

5. Is the B section tonally closed?

6. Is there a retransition back to the A section? If so, describe.

7. Does the A section undergo any changes on its return? If so, describe.

8. Is there a coda? If so, describe.

EXPANDING THE REPERTOIRE 20.4

Aaron Copland, "The World Feels Dusty," from *Twelve Poems by Emily Dickinson* (1951)

A wistful melancholy and an ambiguous tonality characterize this well-known song. Copland's halting rhythm reflects the poet's trademark uses of dashes and other punctuation for expressive purposes.

1. The meter is $\frac{3}{4}$ and the piano begins on the downbeat. What repeating rhythm is heard in the piano part?

2. The vocal part begins on the upbeat to m. 3 with a low D quarter note; the key signature has two sharps. Notate the singer's first four measures; include the words ("The world feels dusty, when we stop to die") below the appropriate pitches.

3. Notice the stepwise ascent on the words "dusty," "stop," and "die." Listen for the continuation of this ascent through two more upward steps; what words are heard on the next two melodic peaks?

4. In what ways does the music change after the words "Honors taste dry"?

5. As the song continues, the vocal part features rests in two places. Compare what happens in the vocal part right before each rest and at the very end of the song.

6. The second rest in the vocal part coincides with a "Tempo I" marking. Which of the two parts seems more closely related to the music at the very opening?

Chapter 21

The Neapolitan Triad and the Common–Tone Diminished Seventh

This chapter introduces two frequently encountered chromatic chords. The Neapolitan is a major triad with a lowered scale degree $\hat{2}$ as its root; it can substitute for a diatonic ii triad in major or minor keys. It most typically appears in first inversion, with scale degree $\hat{4}$ in the bass. The lowered scale degree $\hat{2}$ then sounds in some upper voice and proceeds downward, either directly to the leading tone (if a V chord is what follows) or through scale degree $\hat{1}$ and then to the leading tone (if the dominant harmony is preceded by a cadential six-four or a secondary diminished seventh).

The common-tone diminished seventh is frequently used as a colorful harmonic embellishment of a major or minor triad or a dominant seventh chord. In such cases the root of the upcoming chord is one of the four notes in the common-tone diminished seventh (the common tone). Try harmonizing just the beginning of "Happy Birthday" with a common-tone diminished seventh chord.

In addition to the examples in this chapter, the common-tone diminished seventh is also featured in Examples 22.10 and 24.2.

THE NEAPOLITAN

Example 21.1.   Franz Schubert (1797–1828), "Der Müller und der Bach" (opening), from *Die schöne Müllerin*, op. 25, D. 795 (1824)

Au - gen sich zu und schluch - zen und sin - gen die See - le zur Ruh.

* *Translation*: Where a true heart perishes from love,
    There the lilies wilt in every bed;
    Then the full moon must go into the clouds,
    So that its tears will not be seen;
    Then the angels close their eyes
    And sob and sing his soul to rest.

Note the importance of the words supported by the Neapolitan: "lilies" (symbolic of death), "tears," and the "singing" of angels.

Where does the Neapolitan progress directly to the dominant? Where does it get to the dominant through a secondary diminished seventh?

Example 21.2.   Schubert, "Arpeggione" Sonata, D. 821 (1824), mvt. 1

* Taking note of any and all cadences, can you identify the number of phrases that are contained within this excerpt? Note how fleeting the Neapolitan is in m. 7, but how prominent it is in mm. 9–11, tonicized repeatedly with secondary V $\frac{4}{2}$ chords. (Where does Schubert anticipate this bass motion of E♭ to D in a disguised way?)

Example 21.3.   Wolfgang Amadeus Mozart (1756–1791), Piano Concerto K. 488, mvt. 2

* What factors give this melody its emotional character? Provide Roman numerals throughout. How does the trajectory of Mozart's melody serve to emphasize the Neapolitan? Observe also that the root of the Neapolitan triad, G♮, is the last of twelve chromatically distinct tones (pitch classes) to be heard.

Example 21.4.   Ludwig van Beethoven (1770–1827), Bagatelle op. 119, no. 9

* What phrase structure is heard over the first eight measures? What type of binary form is this?

THE COMMON-TONE DIMINISHED SEVENTH

Example 21.5.   Schubert, String Quintet in C Major, D. 956, op. posth. 163 (1828), mvt. 1

* Tremolos have been added in mm. 3 and 13 to better capture the fullness of the quintet's harmonic texture. What two triads are embellished by common-tone diminished sevenths in this excerpt? Notice all the suspensions and other linear dissonances in mm. 8–9 and 18–19: what effects do they have?

Example 21.6.   Robert Schumann (1810–1856), "Ich grolle nicht," op. 48, no. 7 (1840)

* *Translation*: I do not complain, even if my heart may break,
        Ever-lost love, I do not complain.
    What mixture harmony is used in m. 3, to express heartbreak? What kind of chord is supported by the one chromatic bass note in this whole passage?
    Refer to Contextual Listening 21.2 for the complete text and a translation, as well as listening questions.

Example 21.7.   Johannes Brahms (1833–1897), Symphony no. 4, op. 98 (1885), mvt. 4
        (flute solo)

* This chromatic melody is very hard to sing accurately, but it becomes much simpler if you leave out the first of every pair of eighth notes on a given beat. Practice it that way (E–E–G–E–E–G–F♯ . . .) and then restore the decorative notes. Also feel free to change octaves whenever you like.

Where do you hear common-tone diminished seventh chords?

Example 21.8.   Scott Joplin (c. 1867–1917), "Cleopha" (1902)

Example 21.9.   Giuseppe Verdi (1813–1901), "In solitaria stanza" from *6 Romanze* (1838), no. 3

* *Translation:* In a solitary room she languishes in dreadful pain, no words on her lips, no breath in
      her breast.

      Just as in a deserted flower-bed bereft of dew, under the summer heat the soft narcissus
      droops.

      I, by sorrow oppressed, run along the distant paths and the sound of my cries would
      move the stones:

      "Merciful gods, save that heavenly beauty; you might never be able to create another
      Irene."

Note how the common-tone diminished seventh chord in m. 4 is followed by a mixture chord
(comprising the same four scale degrees) before moving back to tonic on the downbeat of m. 5. What
other mixture chords are heard in the first nine measures? Find another common-tone diminished seventh chord toward the very end of the song.

Example 21.10. John Cage (1912–1992), "Story" from *Living Room Music* (text by Gertrude Stein)

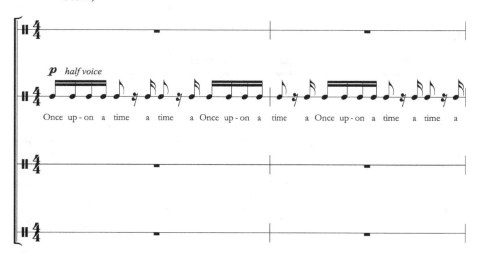

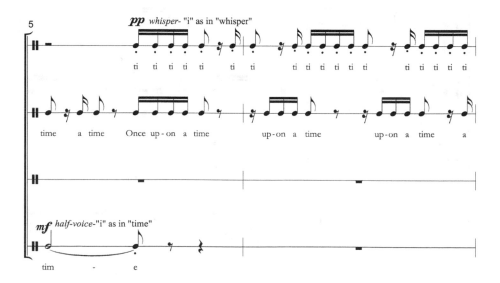

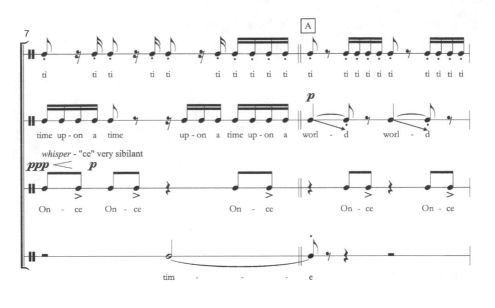

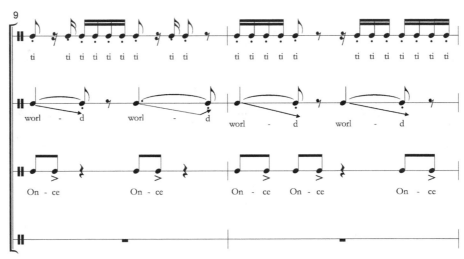

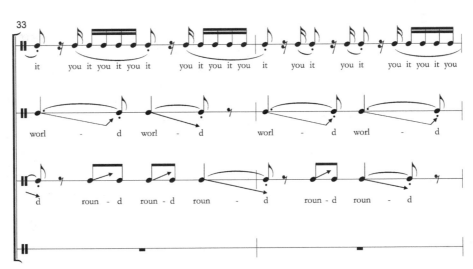

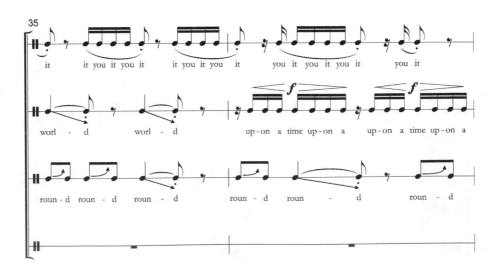

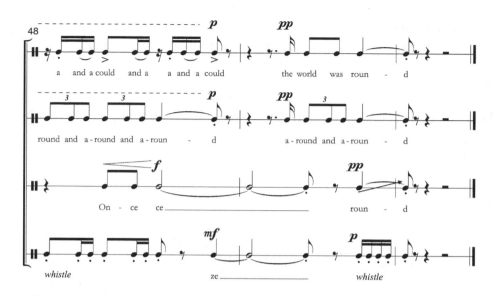

* What form does Cage's piece most resemble? Note how he starts by introducing a single set of thematic materials, then moves to contrasting materials, and finally attempts to assimilate the two.

DRILLS

1. Review the two-step drill, the two-skip drill, and the sliding $\frac{6}{3}$ drill. Here is a new twist on the sliding $\frac{6}{3}$ drill: in a minor key, arpeggiate a tonic triad (high in your vocal range), and then sing the interval qualities ("î–ĵ–ŝ, î–minor–major"). Then, without raising either scale degree 6̂ or 7̂, do the same for first-inversion triads based on scale degrees 7̂, 6̂, and 5̂ ("7̂–2̂–5̂, 7̂–major–perfect, 6̂–î–4̂, . . ."). When you get to scale degree 4̂, sing a Neapolitan triad ("4̂–6̂–low") and the interval qualities. Then do the same for V $\frac{4}{2}$, i⁶, vii°⁶, and i.

2. In a major key, arpeggiate the progression ♭II⁶–$\frac{\text{vii}^{°7}}{\text{V}}$–V–I⁶, up from each bass note in close position and back down, using appropriate scale-degree numbers or solfège syllables. Then reinterpret your concluding I⁶ chord as ♭II⁶ in a new key (one semitone lower than before) and arpeggiate the progression again. Continue this pattern for at least five repetitions. With a partner, try singing a two-voice pattern based on this pattern; one of you should sing the bass line and the other should start on the lowered scale degree 2̂ and continue through scale degrees î, 7̂, and î, before starting again on the same pitches as the new Neapolitan triad. Try switching parts each time. Try singing one line while playing the other, and then try switching parts each time by yourself, singing and playing. Given a random pitch played on the piano or sung by a partner, sing either a minor sixth above or a minor sixth below, and then go through the same contrapuntal paradigm (just once).

CHORALE WORKSHOP: THE NEAPOLITAN

All the following progressions can be realized in major and minor keys. For each progression, sing just the bass line, and then sing each chord as an arpeggio or play it on an instrument. Next, working at a piano, try singing the soprano lines while playing the bass line and singing the bass while playing the soprano lines. Finally, practice every progression with every soprano line on the piano, in a variety of simple keys.

The common-tone diminished seventh chord will be studied in the Chorale Workshop in Chapter 22.

Harmony (bass line in left hand)	Possible soprano lines (right hand)
I | ♭II⁶ V⁷ I or i | ♭II⁶ V⁷ i	$\hat{3}$ | $\hat{4}$ $\hat{4}$ $\hat{3}$ $\hat{1}$ | $\downarrow\hat{2}$ $\hat{7}$ $\hat{1}$
I | ♭II⁶ V$\frac{4}{2}$ I⁶ or i | ♭II⁶ V$\frac{4}{2}$ i⁶	$\hat{3}$ | $\hat{4}$ $\hat{2}$ $\hat{1}$ $\hat{1}$ | $\downarrow\hat{2}$ $\hat{7}$ $\hat{1}$
I | ♭II⁶ $\frac{\text{vii}^{o7}}{\text{V}}$ V⁴⁻³ | I or i | ♭II⁶ $\frac{\text{vii}^{o7}}{\text{V}}$ V⁴⁻³ | i	$\hat{3}$ | $\hat{4}$ $\downarrow\hat{3}$ $\hat{2}$ $\hat{2}$ | $\hat{1}$ (in minor: $\hat{3}$ | $\hat{4}$ $\hat{3}$ $\hat{2}$ $\hat{2}$ | $\hat{1}$) $\hat{1}$ | $\downarrow\hat{2}$ $\hat{1}$ $\hat{1}$ $\hat{7}$ | $\hat{1}$

Try other V-to-I options such as V$\frac{6-5}{4-3}$ I, V$\frac{8-7}{4-3}$ I, and V$\frac{8-7}{6-5}$ I. (Slightly different melodies are available in each case.)

For each of the following progressions, make sure also to try all of the alternative "exits" from the Neapolitan listed above (through V$\frac{4}{2}$ to I⁶ and through $\frac{\text{vii}^{o7}}{\text{V}}$ to V).

I I⁶ ♭II⁶ V⁷ | I or i i⁶ ♭II⁶ V⁷ | i	$\hat{5}$ $\hat{5}$ $\hat{4}$ $\hat{4}$ | $\hat{3}$ $\hat{1}$ $\hat{1}$ $\downarrow\hat{2}$ $\hat{7}$ | $\hat{1}$
I $\frac{\text{V}\frac{6}{5}}{\text{IV}}$ ♭II⁶ V⁷ | I or i $\frac{\text{V}\frac{6}{5}}{\text{IV}}$ ♭II⁶ V⁷ | i	$\hat{5}$ $\hat{5}$ $\hat{4}$ $\hat{4}$ | $\hat{3}$ $\hat{1}$ $\hat{1}$ $\downarrow\hat{2}$ $\hat{7}$ | $\hat{1}$
I ♭VI ♭II⁶ V⁷ | I or i VI ♭II⁶ V⁷ | i	$\hat{5}$ $\downarrow\hat{6}$ $\downarrow\hat{6}$ $\hat{5}$ | $\hat{5}$ (in minor: $\hat{5}$ $\hat{6}$ $\hat{6}$ $\hat{5}$ | $\hat{5}$) $\hat{1}$ $\hat{1}$ $\downarrow\hat{2}$ $\hat{7}$ | $\hat{1}$
I iv⁶ ♭II⁶ V⁷ | I or i iv⁶ ♭II⁶ V⁷ | i	$\hat{5}$ $\downarrow\hat{6}$ $\downarrow\hat{6}$ $\hat{5}$ | $\hat{5}$ (in minor: $\hat{5}$ $\hat{6}$ $\hat{6}$ $\hat{5}$ | $\hat{5}$) $\hat{1}$ $\hat{1}$ $\downarrow\hat{2}$ $\hat{7}$ | $\hat{1}$
I $\frac{\text{V}\frac{4}{2}}{\text{IV}}$ iv⁶ P$\frac{6}{4}$ | ♭II⁶ V⁷ I or i $\frac{\text{V}\frac{4}{2}}{\text{IV}}$ iv⁶ P$\frac{6}{4}$ | ♭II⁶ V⁷ i	$\hat{3}$ $\hat{3}$ $\hat{4}$ $\hat{5}$ | $\downarrow\hat{6}$ $\hat{5}$ $\hat{5}$ (in minor: $\hat{3}$ $\uparrow\hat{3}$ $\hat{4}$ $\hat{5}$ | $\hat{6}$ $\hat{5}$ $\hat{5}$) $\hat{1}$ $\hat{1}$ $\hat{1}$ $\hat{1}$ | $\downarrow\hat{2}$ $\hat{7}$ $\hat{1}$

Use a minor passing $\frac{6}{4}$, even in major.

I V⁷ ♭VI $\frac{\text{V}\frac{4}{2}}{♭\text{II}}$ | ♭II⁶ V⁷ I or i V⁷ VI $\frac{\text{V}\frac{4}{2}}{♭\text{II}}$ | ♭II⁶ V⁷ i	$\hat{5}$ $\hat{4}$ $\downarrow\hat{3}$ $\downarrow\hat{3}$ | $\hat{4}$ $\hat{4}$ $\uparrow\hat{3}$ (in minor: $\hat{5}$ $\hat{4}$ $\hat{3}$ $\hat{3}$ | $\hat{4}$ $\hat{4}$ $\hat{3}$) $\hat{1}$ $\hat{7}$ $\hat{1}$ $\hat{1}$ | $\downarrow\hat{2}$ $\hat{7}$ $\hat{1}$

IMPROVISATION

1. Try all four Chorale Workshop exercises listed under "Improvisation" in Chapter 15 for the progressions given in this chapter.

2. Sing through the Schubert excerpt in Example 21.2 again. Sing the first four measures; then improvise a new continuation that incorporates the Neapolitan but comes to a perfect authentic cadence after only four bars. Feel free to borrow from Schubert's own materials. Now, improvise an alternative to Schubert's first four measures, so that a half cadence is reached in measure 4. Then improvise a new consequent phrase in parallel to what you just invented, again incorporating the Neapolitan.

3. The Mozart excerpt in Example 21.3 uses the typical rhythmic feel of the "siciliano," a rustic dance that found its way into much of the music of the Classical era. Improvise your own short siciliano, borrowing your rhythms from Mozart's piano concerto. Start with a typical antecedent-consequent design, and then try to use Mozart's own harmonic progression as a basis. Compare your improvised siciliano with Mozart's.

SUGGESTED SMARTMUSIC ASSESSMENTS

Complete SmartMusic assessments 21.1 (top two parts), 21.2 (all parts), 21.3 (all parts), 21.4 (both parts), 21.5 (top and bottom parts, 21.6 (all parts), 21.7 (top three parts), 21.8 (all parts), and 21.9 (top part).

SHORT-TERM MUSICAL MEMORY

Fill in the key signature and clef as indicated by your instructor, and write in the initial note(s) on the basis of the given pitch and rhythm information. Note that the key and clef *may not be the same* as in the original example. Your instructor (or practice partner) will play a short progression to establish the key and then count off several beats to establish the tempo. Because of the brevity of each extract, you should have an overall impression of the rhythm, contour, and scale degrees after just one or two hearings. Notate the entire fragment.

1. Example 21.2, beat 3 of m. 4 to beat 2 of m. 6, upper voice. Starts with three eighth-note upbeats (the first of which is scale degree $\hat{5}$).

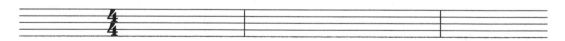

Clef and key
signature

2. Example 21.5, m. 3 to beat 2 of m. 6, upper voice. Starts on beat 1 (whole note tied to quarter note, scale degree $\hat{1}$).

Clef and key
signature

3. Example 21.7, nine notes starting on last eighth note in m. 5, upper voice (starts on scale degree $\hat{6}$).

Clef and key
signature

4. Example 21.4, mm. 2–4, both voices. Both start on beat 1 (eighth note and high scale degree $\hat{5}$ in top voice, quarter note a perfect twelfth lower in bottom voice).

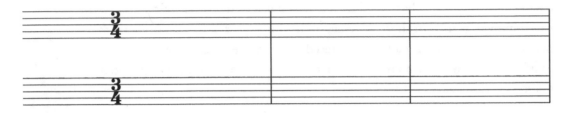

Clef and key
signature

5. Example 21.6, m. 9 to end, outer voices. Both start on beat 1 (whole note and low scale degree $\hat{5}$ in bottom voice; half note tied to dotted quarter note in top voice, a perfect twelfth higher).

Clef and key
signature

6. Example 21.8, m. 2 to downbeat of m. 4, outer voices. Both start with quarter notes on beat 1, both on scale degree $\hat{1}$ an octave apart.

Clef and key
signature

DICTATION OF LONGER EXAMPLES

Your instructor or a classmate will choose one of the examples listed below and inform you of the key, clef, meter, first note (scale degree, rhythmic value, and metric placement) of one or more parts, and total number of measures. Use a separate piece of staff paper to write down the indicated information. You will hear a short progression to establish the key of the example, and then hear the example several times with breaks between hearings.

Nonmodulating:

1. Example 21.1, m. 3 to downbeat of m. 10, upper voice (or outer voices).
2. Example 21.3, mm. 1–4, outer voices.

Modulating:

3. Example 21.5, m. 13 to end, bottom voice. Starts on beat 1 with whole note tied to quarter note and scale degree î (in temporary key).
4. Example 21.9, mm. 10–17, upper voice with just the bass pitches on beats 1 and 3 (each sustained across two beats).

CONTEXTUAL LISTENING 21.1

Joseph Haydn (1732–1809), Theme from *Variations in F minor*, Hob. XVII:6

Although many late eighteenth-century variation sets borrowed a preexisting melody for the theme, composers also quite often composed their own themes. Listen for the special harmonic arrival near the end of Haydn's theme that suggested its inclusion in this chapter.

1. Does the first reprise remain in the home key or modulate to a new key? If it modulates, what key does it go to? What kind of cadence concludes the first reprise?

2. What prior thematic material (if any) is used in the second part of the second reprise?

3. Provide your best guess as to what harmony it is that Haydn articulates (and then arpeggiates) so prominently, very close to the end of the second reprise. Speculate as to why Haydn gives this harmony such special treatment. For extra credit, listen to how this harmony is treated in the following variations, and describe the two most interesting instances.

4. On the basis of your answers to questions 1 and 2, identify the type of binary form.

CONTEXTUAL LISTENING 21.2

Robert Schumann (1810–1856), "Ich grolle nicht," op. 48, no. 7

This famous song belongs to Schumann's best-known cycle *Dichterliebe*, written in 1840 (his so-called *Liederjahr* or "year of song"). Read through the translation of the text. What are some ways in which Schumann represents the text through his music?

Ich grolle nicht	I do not complain
Ich grolle nicht, und wenn das Herz auch bricht,	I do not complain, even if my heart may break,
Ewig verlor'nes Lieb! Ich grolle nicht.	Ever-lost love, I do not complain.
Wie du auch strahlst in Diamantenpracht,	Though you shine in diamond splendor,
Es fällt kein Strahl in deines Herzens Nacht.	No beam falls into the night of your heart.
Das weiß ich längst.	I knew it long ago.
Ich grolle nicht, und wenn das Herz auch bricht,	I do not complain, even if my heart may break,
Ich sah dich ja im Traume,	I truly saw you in my dreams,
Und sah die Nacht in deines Herzens Raume,	And saw the night in the room of your heart
Und sah die Schlang', die dir am Herzen frißt,	And saw the snake that is eating your heart,
Ich sah, mein Lieb, wie sehr du elend bist.	I saw, my love, how very miserable you are.

1. The first section ends with a repetition of *Ich grolle nicht* and a chromatic ascent in the pianist's left hand. Is this section tonally closed?

2. What kinds of intervallic and/or rhythmic differences are heard as the following section begins (*Wie du auch strahlst . . .*)? What is happening harmonically here?

3. Just before the return of the opening material, the singer sings *"Das weiß ich längst"* (I knew it long ago) with a long held tone. How does this part of the song function in the context of the overall form?

4. Does the opening of the song return in its original form, or are there some changes? If you hear some changes, describe them.

CONTEXTUAL LISTENING 21.3

Brahms, Piano Quintet in F Minor, op. 34, mvt. 3

This work originated as a string quintet; Brahms later transcribed it as a sonata for two pianos. The third movement, featured here, ends with a prominent melodic gesture. How is this gesture transformed at the beginning of the fourth movement?

The contextual listening on "Satin Doll" (Expanding the Repertoire 21.5, below) will provide a special perspective on one of the questions in this assignment.

1. What is the instrumentation of a piano quintet?

2. What is the first scale degree performed by the viola in this excerpt?

3. Transcribe the missing notes of the piano part. A single-line staff is provided to help you identify the rhythm, the texture (number of notes), and the voicing. Then, provide Roman numerals in the key of C minor.

4. The entire excerpt fluctuates between two sonorities. Write letter-name *chord symbols* (not Roman numerals) for these sonorities under the score above.

5. How is the D♭⁷ sonority related (in terms of function and structure) to both the Neapolitan chord used in common practice and to the tritone substitution chord used in "Satin Doll" and countless other jazz and popular styles?

Name: _____ Date: _____ Instructor: _____

EXPANDING THE REPERTOIRE 21.4

Roberto Murolo, "Marechiaro"

Roberto Murolo, "Lo Guarracino"

Renato Carsone, "Maruzzella"

Because of the frequent use of a major chord built on the ♭2̂ scale degree by the Neapolitan school of Italian opera (Alessandro Scarlatti, Domenico Cimarosa, et al.), this sonority has been referred to as the Neapolitan triad. Both the chord and the ornamental use of ♭2̂ remain favorites of contemporary and popular musicians of the Napoli region.

1. Identify the key of each song:

   a. "Marechiaro": _____

   b. "Lo Guarracino": _____

   c. "Maruzzella": _____

2. Which song includes a typical incidence of the Neapolitan chord, and which provides the best example of the use of scale degree ♭2̂ as a melodic coloring device?

	Neapolitan Chord	Scale Degree ♭2
"Marechiaro"		
"Lo Guarracino"		
"Maruzzella"		

3. Transcribe the melodic introductions (played on a guitar) of "Maruzzella" and "Marechiaro." Make sure to include the time signature and key signature for each transcription.

4. Both "Lo Guarracino" and "Marechiaro" feature a brief tonicization of a diatonic harmony. Which harmony is tonicized?

   a. Dominant   b. Mediant   c. Subdominant   d. Submediant

EXPANDING THE REPERTOIRE 21.5

Duke Ellington and Billy Strayhorn, "Satin Doll"

This jazz standard has been recorded by countless artists, becoming a well-established instrumental piece before Johnny Mercer wrote its clever lyrics. It is included here because of its use of a sonority that shares three of its notes with the Neapolitan yet functions quite differently in the context of jazz and popular music. This sonority is understood as a *tritone substitution* (TS) chord built on $\flat\hat{2}$.

1. What is the form of the song?

   a. A B A B   b. A A B A   c. A B B A   d. A B A A

2. After a four-measure introduction, the A section begins with a harmonic sequence based on a two-chord progression often used as a "turnaround" (a passage at the end of a section that leads to the following section). Transcribe the melody of this sequence, and provide Roman numerals according to the suggested key areas:

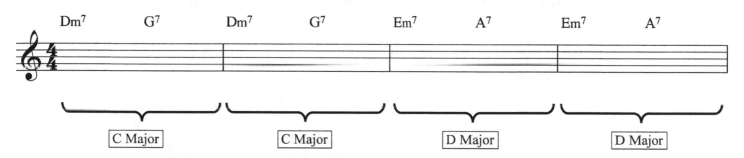

3. Then the next four measures slow down the harmonic rhythm and provide a cadence to tonic. Transcribe the melody of this segment:

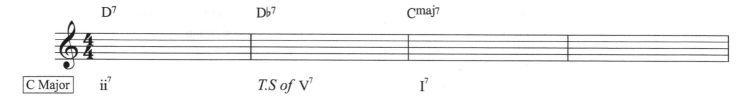

4. Write the notes of both a D♭ chord (i.e. the Neapolitan in C major) and the notes of a D♭7 chord. How many notes do they have in common?

5. Observe that by adding a fourth pitch the sonority changes considerably. In fact, it becomes a substitution of V^7 because it shares the most sensitive pitches with it. Which pitches are they? (Write the notes of V^7 and of the TS of V^7 in C major below.)

6. Clearly, this sonority is a good substitute for V^7. Why do you think it received the label *tritone* substitution?

7. Write the TS of the following chords, observing their common tones:

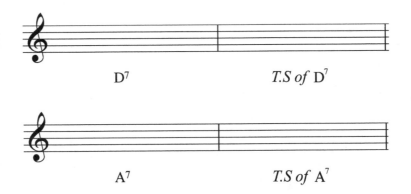

8. On the basis of the harmonic syntax of "Satin Doll," how would you say a Neapolitan chord and a TS of V^7 chord differ in terms of their resolution?

9. On the basis of the melody, speculate why a TS of V^7 is used more often in this style than a straightforward V^7.

Unit IV Advanced Chromaticism and Larger Forms

Chapter 22

Introduction to Augmented-Sixth Chords

Augmented-sixth chords provide an especially intense way to approach a dominant chord. The intensity derives from the fact that both notes forming the interval of the augmented sixth are only a semitone away from scale degree $\hat{5}$. The augmented sixth is formed by the bass voice with scale degree $\hat{6}$ in minor, or lowered scale degree $\hat{6}$ in major, and an upper voice with a raised scale degree $\hat{4}$. The bass voice will move down a semitone to scale degree $\hat{5}$, the root of the dominant; the raised scale degree $\hat{4}$ in the upper voice usually also moves to scale degree $\hat{5}$.

We have already encountered this interval's characteristic behavior in Examples 10.12, 13.1, 14.1, 14.7, 17.3, 18.2, and 20.5. Study the progression in Example 20.5 from beat 3 of m. 3 into beat 1 of m. 4. The upbeat to m. 4 is an *Italian sixth*, one of three types of augmented-sixth chords. It features scale degree $\hat{6}$ (in minor, or lowered scale degree $\hat{6}$ in major) in the bass, a raised scale degree $\hat{4}$ in the middle voice, and scale degree $\hat{1}$ in the top voice. When an Italian chord is used in a texture of more than three voices, scale degree $\hat{1}$ will be doubled and may move by step toward the leading tone and toward scale degree $\hat{2}$.

We will also discover the *French sixth*, which has all three of these scale degrees along with scale degree $\hat{2}$ in another upper voice, and the *German sixth*, which again has all three of these scale degrees but also a perfect fifth above the bass (scale degree $\hat{3}$ in minor, or a lowered scale degree $\hat{3}$ in major). Since the German sixth has a perfect fifth above the bass, composers take care (usually!) to avoid parallel fifths into its resolution, by either inserting a cadential six-four or simply moving the voice with (lowered) scale degree $\hat{3}$ to some note in the dominant chord other than scale degree $\hat{2}$.

The first two examples in this chapter again feature the "lament bass" in various forms. Refer to Examples 14.1, 19.4, 19.5, and 19.6 for prior instances of this pattern. It is quite common to approach an augmented-sixth chord via downward stepwise motion in the bass voice.

Example 22.1.   Barbara Strozzi (1619–1677), *Diporti di Euterpe*, op. 7 no. 4, "Lagrime mie, a che vi trattenete"

* *Translation*: My tears, why do you hold back?

How do this slightly decorated lament bass and highly florid melody relate to the text? Note the similarity between the two cadences, both of which are decorated by anticipations in the melody. Which one of them involves the interval of an augmented sixth?

Example 22.2. Wolfgang Amadeus Mozart (1756–1791), String Quartet in D minor, K. 421/417b (1783), Minuet

* What type of binary form is this? Provide Roman numerals for the first reprise. You can count the first three measures as a tonic expansion. (In the full string-quartet texture, both D and G♯ are heard on beats 1 and 3 of m. 7.) What type of sequence is heard in mm. 22–27? Comment on the harmonies in m. 28.

Example 22.3.   Ludwig van Beethoven (1770–1827), Piano Sonata op. 109 (1820), Andante

* Note the use of the German sixth chord in m. 8 (in the full piano texture, the G♮ sounds on beat 2 as well, before moving to B on beat 3). What kind of binary form is this? Identify all four cadences.

Example 22.4.   Franz Schubert (1797–1828), "Die Liebe hat gelogen," op. 23, no. 1, D. 751 (1822)

* *Translation*: Love has lied, and care weighs heavily,
        Betrayed, ah! betrayed by all around me!

    Provide Roman numerals for the first two measures, which feature different chromatic pre-dominants. Notice the use of lowered scale degree $\hat{2}$ midway through m. 1, and diatonic scale degree $\hat{2}$ on beat 2 of m. 2; both tones are critical to their harmonies.

    Schubert changes to C major in m. 5. Analyze the remaining three measures in C major before attempting to perform this challenging excerpt. Note Schubert's use of an A-major triad in m. 5, the expected function of which as a secondary dominant is denied. (See Examples 24.2, 24.3, and 24.4 for further examples of this kind of denied dominant function.)

Example 22.5.   Fanny Hensel (1805–1847), "Abendlich schon rauscht der Wald," op. 3 no. 5

* *Translation*: Evening breezes rustle already in the wood; from the deepest sources;
Above the lord will soon; ignite the stars.
How silent in the chasms! Just evening breezes in the wood.
Everything goes to its rest. Wood and world vanish;
shuddering, the wanderer listens, yearning straight for home.
Here in the quiet retreat of the forest, Heart, at last too go to rest.

Be sure you can identify the types, location, and functions of the augmented sixth chords here.
How do they relate to Eichendorff's deeply Romantic text?

Example 22.6.   Pyotr Ilyich Tchaikovsky (1840–1893), "Dance of the Sugar Plum Fairy,"
from *The Nutcracker*, op. 71 (1891–92)

* What phrase structure is heard from m. 5 to the end of this excerpt? What type of augmented-sixth chord is heard in m. 12? What type of sequence is heard in mm. 17–19?

Example 22.7.   Mozart, Serenade no. 1, K. 439b, mvt. 1

* Which type of augmented-sixth chord is heard at the end of m. 15? What are the Roman numerals for mm. 16–18? Identify the two half-note triads in mm. 8 and 11, and compare the effects of each triad's resolution into the following downbeat.

Example 22.8. Mozart, "Lacrimosa," from *Requiem*, K. 626 (1791)

25

e - is, do - na e - is re - - - qui -

28

em! A - - - men.

Translation: That sorrowful day, on which will arise from the burning coals
Man accused to be judged: therefore, O God, do Thou spare him.
Faithful Lord Jesus, grant them rest. Amen.
Provide Roman numerals for mm. 5–8. Also identify the augmented-sixth chord heard in m. 16.

Example 22.9.   Clara Schumann (1819–1896), "Er ist gekommen in Sturm und Regen," op. 12 no. 2

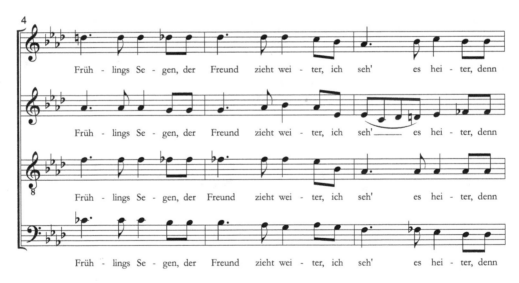

* *Translation:* For he remains mine, on any road.

       Now has come the blessing of spring.

       My love travels afar, I watch cheerfully,

       For he remains mine, on any road.

    Be sure to identify the location and function of any chromatic chords. To what chords do they resolve, and in which keys?

Example 22.10. Richard Strauss (1864–1949), "Di rigori armato il seno," from *Der Rosenka-valier*, op. 59 (1909–10), Act I

* *Translation*: With determination I armed my heart and I rebelled against love
But in a flash I was conquered on seeing two lovely eyes.

In just the first sixteen measures, find an augmented triad, an augmented-sixth chord (what type?), and a common-tone diminished seventh.

DRILLS

1. Review the two-skip drill, the sliding $^6_3$ drill in major, and the minor-mode variant with the Neapolitan. Here is a drill for diminished sevenths: in a fairly high range, arpeggiate a vii^{o7} chord upward using scale-degree numbers. Then arpeggiate a minor tonic triad downward ($\hat{5}$–$\hat{3}$–$\hat{1}$) with the $\hat{5}$ just a semitone below the highest note of your diminished-seventh chord. Then sing the same diminished-seventh chord on a neutral syllable such as "la" or "loo," and this time resolve it into a major triad ($\hat{5}$–$\hat{3}$–$\hat{1}$") whose $\hat{5}$ is a *whole tone* below the highest note of the diminished-seventh chord. Continue with the vii^{o7} of this new tonic, resolving to a *minor* triad, and repeating the steps above. Complete at least five entire repetitions.

2. Refer to Example 22.2. Starting in a fairly low register (perhaps from a low D in your range) and using scale-degree numbers, sing the very beginning of the top part, up to the downbeat of m. 2. Then sing the same notes again as follows: "$\hat{1}$–$\hat{5}$–$\hat{3}$, $\hat{1}$–perfect *fourth*–minor *sixth*" (with "fourth" and "sixth" falling on the new notes). Move this figure up one step ("$\hat{2}$–$\hat{6}$–$\hat{4}$, $\hat{2}$–augmented *fourth*–major *sixth*"), then up another step and so on. Do not raise the leading tone when singing "$\hat{3}$–$\hat{7}$–$\hat{5}$," but do raise it when singing "$\hat{5}$–$\hat{2}$–$\hat{7}$," after which you should just sing a final "$\hat{1}$."

3. The second reprise of Example 22.2 features a familiar kind of sequence through mm. 22–27. With a partner, perform just the top two parts, which proceed chromatically downward in parallel tritones. One of you can begin with the two Ds on the upbeat to m. 22. This may be hard to keep in tune and on pitch, but continue the pattern as long as you can. Try playing just a single bass note on every downbeat (see the score) on the piano or another instrument while you are singing, or get someone else to do so. The chords should be clearer to your ear that way. Finally, at the piano, try playing sustained parallel tritones (just held tones, no dotted-rhythm values) in your right hand while also playing the same pattern of descending fifths in your left hand.

CHORALE WORKSHOP: COMMON-TONE DIMINISHED SEVENTH CHORDS

For each of the following progressions, sing just the bass line, and then sing each chord as an arpeggio (up from its bass note and back down) or play it on an instrument. Then, working at a piano, try singing the soprano lines while playing the bass line, and singing the bass while playing the soprano lines. Finally, practice every progression with every soprano line on the piano, in a variety of simple keys. The modality of each progression is specified.

Our notation for common-tone diminished seventh chords does not indicate their inversion, since it would be hard to decide which note is "really" the root. For this reason, the bass line has also been specified for each progression below. The normal situation is for the voice with the common tone to stay on the same note (becoming the chordal root of the resolution), and for most or all notes of the other chord tones to move by step.

The standard uses of augmented sixths will be studied in the Chorale Workshop at the end of Chapter 23.

Major keys:
Harmony
(bass line in left hand)

Possible soprano scale degrees
(right hand)

$\text{I} \quad \text{CT}^{o7} \quad \text{I}$
(bass: $\hat{1} \quad \hat{1} \quad \hat{1}$)

$\hat{5} \;\; \hat{6} \;\; \hat{5}$
$\hat{5} \;\; {\uparrow}\hat{4} \;\; \hat{5}$
$\hat{3} \;\; {\uparrow}\hat{2} \;\; \hat{3}$

$\text{I}^6 \quad \text{CT}^{o7} \quad \text{I}^6$
(bass: $\hat{3} \quad {\uparrow}\hat{2} \quad \hat{3}$)

$\hat{5} \;\; \hat{6} \;\; \hat{5}$
$\hat{5} \;\; {\uparrow}\hat{4} \;\; \hat{5}$
$\hat{1} \;\; \hat{1} \;\; \hat{1}$

$\text{I} \quad \text{V}^4_3 \quad \text{CT}^{o7} \mid \text{I}^6$
(bass: $\hat{1} \quad \hat{2} \quad {\uparrow}\hat{2} \mid \hat{3}$)

$\hat{3} \;\; \hat{4} \;\; {\uparrow}\hat{4} \mid \hat{5}$
$\hat{1} \;\; \hat{7} \;\; \hat{6} \mid \hat{5}$

Amaze your friends: if the above progression were played in reverse order, it would no longer contain a common-tone diminished-seventh chord! The Roman numerals would be $\text{I}^6 - \dfrac{\text{vii}^{o4}_2}{\text{V}} - \text{V}^4_3 - \text{I}$.

$\text{I} \quad \text{CT}^{o7} \quad \text{V}^4_3 \quad \text{CT}^{o7} \mid \text{I}^6$
(bass: $\hat{1} \quad {\uparrow}\hat{1} \quad \hat{2} \quad {\uparrow}\hat{2} \mid \hat{3}$)

$\hat{5} \;\; \hat{5} \;\; \hat{5} \;\; \hat{6} \mid \hat{5}$
$\hat{3} \;\; \hat{3} \;\; \hat{4} \;\; {\uparrow}\hat{4} \mid \hat{5}$

$\text{I} \quad \text{V}^4_3 \quad \text{I}^6 \mid \text{CT}^{o7} \quad \text{IV} \quad \text{V}^4_2 \mid \text{I}^6$
(bass: $\hat{1} \quad \hat{2} \quad \hat{3} \mid \hat{4} \quad \hat{4} \quad \hat{4} \mid \hat{3}$)

$\hat{3} \;\; \hat{4} \;\; \hat{5} \mid {\uparrow}\hat{5} \;\; \hat{6} \;\; \hat{7} \mid \hat{1}$
$\hat{1} \;\; \hat{7} \;\; \hat{1} \mid \hat{7} \;\; \hat{6} \;\; \hat{7} \mid \hat{1}$

$\text{I}^6 \quad \text{CT}^{o7} \quad \text{I}^6 \mid \text{IV} \quad \text{CT}^{o7} \quad \text{IV} \mid \text{V}$
(bass: $\hat{3} \quad {\uparrow}\hat{2} \quad \hat{3} \mid \hat{4} \quad \hat{4} \quad \hat{4} \mid \hat{5}$)

$\hat{5} \;\; \hat{6} \;\; \hat{5} \mid \hat{6} \;\; \hat{7} \;\; \hat{6} \mid \hat{5}$
$\hat{1} \;\; \hat{1} \;\; \hat{1} \mid \hat{1} \;\; \hat{7} \;\; \hat{1} \mid \hat{7}$

$\text{I} \quad \text{V}^6 \quad \dfrac{\text{V}^4_2}{\text{IV}} \mid \text{IV}^6 \quad \text{CT}^{o7} \quad \text{IV}^6 \mid \text{V}^7 \quad \text{CT}^{o7} \quad \text{V}^7 \mid \text{I}$
(bass: $\hat{1} \quad \hat{7} \quad {\downarrow}\hat{7} \mid \hat{6} \quad {\downarrow}\hat{6} \quad \hat{6} \mid \hat{5} \quad \hat{5} \quad \hat{5} \mid \hat{1}$)

$\hat{3} \;\; \hat{2} \;\; \hat{1} \mid \hat{1} \;\; \hat{7} \;\; \hat{1} \mid \hat{7} \;\; {\uparrow}\hat{6} \;\; \hat{7} \mid \hat{1}$
$\hat{1} \;\; \hat{2} \;\; \hat{3} \mid \hat{4} \;\; \hat{4} \;\; \hat{4} \mid \hat{4} \;\; \hat{3} \;\; \hat{4} \mid \hat{3}$

Minor keys:
Harmony
(bass line in left hand)

Possible soprano scale degrees
(right hand)

$\text{i} \quad \text{vii}^{o6} \quad \text{i}^6 \mid \text{CT}^{o7} \quad \text{VI} \quad \text{ii}^{o6} \mid \text{V}^6_4 - {}^5_3 \mid \text{i}$
(bass: $\hat{1} \quad \hat{2} \quad \hat{3} \mid \hat{6} \quad \hat{6} \quad \hat{4} \mid \hat{5} - \hat{5} \mid \hat{1}$)

$\hat{5} \;\; \hat{4} \;\; \hat{3} \mid \hat{2} \;\; \hat{3} \;\; \hat{4} \mid \hat{3} - \hat{2} \mid \hat{3}$
$\hat{3} \;\; \hat{2} \;\; \hat{1} \mid \hat{7} \;\; \hat{1} \;\; \hat{2} \mid \hat{1} - \hat{7} \mid \hat{1}$
(both leading tones raised)

The long dashes in the progression above indicate the missing second beat in triple meter.

IMPROVISATION: PUTTING IT ALL TOGETHER

1. Try all four Chorale Workshop exercises listed under "Improvisation" in Chapter 15 for the progressions given in this chapter.
2. Referring to Example 22.3, improvise a different melody in answer to the first four measures. Approach a perfect authentic cadence in E major. Try creating a

new bass line as well, and performing the entire eight measures in two-voice texture with a classmate or with an instrument.

3. Employing the distinctly florid rhythms from Strozzi's lament in Example 22.1, improvise a completely new melody over the lamento bass. Start by staying completely diatonic, and then add chromatic dissonance.

SUGGESTED SMARTMUSIC ASSESSMENTS

Complete SmartMusic assessments 22.1 (top part) and 22.2 through 22.10 (all parts).

SHORT-TERM MUSICAL MEMORY

Fill in the key signature and clef as indicated by your instructor, and write in the initial note(s) on the basis of the given pitch and rhythm information. Note that the key and clef *may not be the same* as in the original example. Your instructor (or practice partner) will play a short progression to establish the key and then count off several beats to establish the tempo. Because of the brevity of each extract, you should have an overall impression of the rhythm, contour, and scale degrees after just one or two hearings. Notate the entire fragment.

1. Example 22.5, m. 35 to end, top voice. Starts on beat 1 (dotted quarter note, scale degree $\hat{3}$).

Clef and key
signature

2. Example 22.7: two possibilities! Either (a) m. 8 to downbeat of m. 11, top voice; or (b) m. 13 to downbeat of m. 16, bottom voice. Both possibilities start with an eighth note on beat 1 (scale degree $\hat{1}$) followed by an eighth rest.

Clef and key
signature

3. Example 22.8, mm. 9–10, upper voice. Starts on beat 1 (dotted quarter note tied to eighth note, low scale degree $\hat{5}$).

Clef and key
signature

4. Example 22.8, m. 18 to downbeat of m. 19, top voice. Starts on beat 1 (dotted quarter note tied to eighth note, high scale degree $\hat{1}$).

Clef and key
signature

5. Example 22.3, up to downbeat of m. 3, outer voices. Both start with quarter notes on beat 1 (scale degree $\hat{3}$ in top voice, and a major tenth lower in bottom voice).

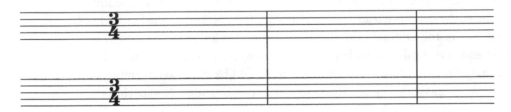

* Clef and key signature

6. Example 22.4, up to beat 3 of m. 2, alto and bass voices. Both start with quarter notes on beat 1, both with scale degree $\hat{1}$ an octave apart.

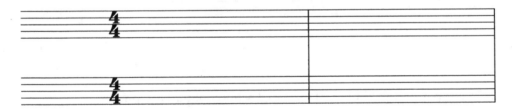

Clef and key
signature

7. Example 22.9, beat 4 of m. 5 to downbeat of m. 7, outer voices. Both start with eighth notes on beat 4 (scale degree $\hat{3}$ in top voice, scale degree $\hat{1}$ a major tenth below in bottom voice).

Clef and key
signature

8. Example 22.10, mm. 11–12, outer voices. Both start on beat 1 (eighth note and low scale degree $\hat{5}$ in top voice, half note a minor sixth or thirteenth lower in bottom voice).

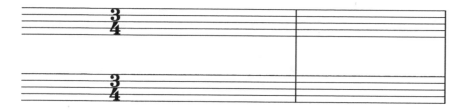

Clef and key
signature

DICTATION OF LONGER EXAMPLES

Your instructor or a classmate will choose one of the examples listed below and inform you of the key, clef, meter, first note (scale degree, rhythmic value, and metric placement) of one or more parts, and total number of measures. Use a separate piece of staff paper to write down the indicated information. You will hear a short progression to establish the key of the example, and then hear the example several times with breaks between hearings.

Nonmodulating:

1. Example 22.4, last eighth note of m. 2 to end (or only up to beat 3 of m. 6), outer voices.
2. Example 22.6, m. 5 to beat 2 of m. 12, outer voices (or only upper voice).
3. Example 22.7, up to downbeat of m. 8, middle and bottom voices.
4. Example 22.8, mm. 3–8, outer voices.

Modulating:

5. Example 22.5, mm. 1–8, outer voices.

Name: _____ Date: _____ Instructor: _____

CONTEXTUAL LISTENING 22.1

Mozart, Serenade no. 10 "Gran Partita," K. 361, mvt. 6 (Romance)

This serenade is written for twelve wind instruments and a double bass. Do you think this may have been the precursor to the modern concert band?

1. The first thirty seconds of music are repeated. Do these measures modulate? If so, to what key?

2. Another repeated subsection begins immediately after that. What harmonic function is emphasized over the first half of this new subsection? What music is heard beginning at the midpoint of this subsection?

3. How would you describe the form of the first large section of this movement?

4. Describe the metric and textural changes that set the B section apart.

5. Provide a Roman numeral that identifies the key in which the B section begins, with respect to the principal key of the movement.

6. How would you describe the form of the B section of this movement? (Consider the entire span that features the quickly moving bassoon line.)

7. What section of the movement begins after the bassoon's quickly moving passage concludes?

8. Does the A section undergo any changes on its return? If so, describe.

9. Is there a coda? If so, describe.

CONTEXTUAL LISTENING 22.2

Beethoven, Piano Sonata op. 14, no. 1, mvt. 2 (Allegretto)

This is one of the most often performed of Beethoven's thirty-two sonatas for piano; its lightness of character neatly disguises its technical challenges.

1. How would you describe the phrase structure of the first twenty seconds of this movement?

2. Identify the key to which the music moves in the immediately following phrases, with respect to the principal key of the movement.

3. A half cadence is heard in the home key, after which the opening music then returns. Describe any changes that you hear.

4. Soon we are hearing only one note in the bass over and over. What part of the A section is this?

5. Is the A section tonally closed?

6. How would you describe the form of the A section?

7. Provide a Roman numeral that identifies the key in which the B section begins (with respect to the principal key of the movement).

8. The B section begins with a repeated subsection. What kind of modulation occurs within this repeated unit?

9. Listening for any returning themes within the B section, how would you describe its form? (Reasonable listeners might disagree about this one.)

10. Is the B section tonally closed? (Disregard the brief retransition back to A.)

11. Does the A section undergo any changes on its return? If so, describe.

12. What is heard in the last thirty seconds of the movement? What part of the form is this?

CONTEXTUAL LISTENING 22.3

Robert Schumann (1810–1856), "Widmung," op. 25, no. 1

"Widmung" is the opening song from Schumann's song cycle *Myrthen*, one of five songs in the cycle written on text by Friedrich Rückert. Schumann composed this cycle as a wedding present to his bride, Clara Wieck (who later composed your Example 22.9).

Widmung	Dedication
Du meine Seele, du mein Herz,	You my soul, you my heart,
Du meine Wonn', o du mein Schmerz,	you my delight, o you my pain,
Du meine Welt, in der ich lebe,	you my world, in which I live,
Mein Himmel du, darein ich schwebe,	My heaven, through which I soar,
O du mein Grab, in das hinab	o you my grave, into which
Ich ewig meinen Kummer gab.	I ever bury my sorrows.
Du bist die Ruh, du bist der Frieden,	You are rest, you are peace,
Du bist vom Himmel mir beschieden.	you are from heaven given to me.
Daß du mich liebst, macht mich mir wert,	That you love me makes me feel worthy,
Dein Blick hat mich vor mir verklärt,	your gaze has transfigured me in my own eyes,
Du hebst mich liebend über mich,	you lift me lovingly above myself,
Mein guter Geist, mein beßres Ich!	my good spirit, my better self!

1. Is the A section tonally closed?

2. Is the A section a single unit, or is it itself in binary or ternary form?

3. What rhythmic change highlights the arrival of the B section?

4. What kind of modulation is heard as the B section begins? Provide a Roman numeral that identifies the key in which the B section begins, with respect to the principal key of the song.

5. Is the B section tonally closed?

6. Is the B section a single unit, or is it itself in binary or ternary form?

7. Does the A section undergo any changes upon its return? If so, describe.

Name: _____   Date: _____   Instructor: _____

EXPANDING THE REPERTOIRE 22.4

Irving Berlin (1888–1989), "There's No Business Like Show Business" (1946)

Written for the musical *Annie Get Your Gun,* this song addresses the glamor and excitement of show business. It has been recorded by numerous artists from Judy Garland to Frank Sinatra and was later featured in the film *All That Jazz.*

1. Before you embark on the transcription and analysis of "There's No Business Like Show Business," notate these sonorities in the key of C:

    a. Tritone substitution of $\frac{V^7}{V}$:

    b. A♭$^{7(♭5)}$:

    c. French augmented sixth chord:

    d. Describe the similarities and differences of these chords:

2. On the staff below:

    a. Transcribe the last twenty-four measures of the melody.

    b. Analyze the chord progression with Roman numerals in the key of C major, according to the chord symbols provided. Your decision as to how to analyze the B♭$^{7(♭5)}$ and the A♭$^{7(♭5)}$ chords might be informed by question 1 of this assignment.

c. Speculate about the use of "$^{(\flat5)}$" in several chords. Why do $B\flat^{7(\flat5)}$ and $A\flat^{7(\flat5)}$ suit the melody better than $B\flat^7$ and $A\flat^7$?

Roman Numerals

Chapter 23

Rondo Form

This chapter introduces some aspects of rondo form. Rondo form involves the alternation of a recurring "refrain" (A) with various "episodes" (B, C, . . .) and includes such structures as ABACA, ABACABA, ABACADA, and so on. The A section returns in the tonic key but may be abbreviated, embellished, or otherwise modified in its reappearances. The contrasting sections are usually of an audibly different musical character, and they are often in a key other than tonic (or are in the parallel mode). Alternatively, as is also common in ternary form, a contrasting section may not achieve tonal closure in any key. In certain rondos, some or all of these sections will themselves be in binary form. A transition may connect an A section to an ensuing contrasting section, and a retransition may be used to approach the returning A section. A coda may be heard following the final presentation of the A section.

The pieces presented here for study and performance all conform to the model of a five-part rondo, involving the alternation of a recurring A section with contrasting B and C sections (ABACA). Some of the contextual listening exercises at the end of the chapter will also deal with five-part rondos, but some will prove to be larger rondo forms, which may extend to seven parts or even more. A common option during the Classical era was a sonata rondo in ABACABA format, where the B section is at first in a nontonic key (often the dominant) and then returns in the tonic key, and the C section is markedly developmental in character.

The first two examples are drawn from opera. Each example features an orchestral introduction and conclusion, which can be considered as separate from the rondo form itself.

Example 23.1.   George Frideric Handel (1685–1759), "Verdi prati," from *Alcina*, HWV 34
(1735)

Ver - di pra - ti,   sel - ve   a - me - ne,

pra - ti,   sel - ve   a - me - ne,   per - de -

re - te   la bel - tà.   E   can - giato   il

va - go og - get - to   all or - ror   del pri - mo a -

spet - to   tut toin voi ri - tor - ne -

rà.   tutto   in   voi   ri - tor - ne -

rà.   Ver - di___ pra - ti, sel - ve a -

me - ne,   per - de - re - te   la bel -

tà,   per - de - re - te   la bel - tà.

* *Translation*: Green meadows, pleasant woods, you will lose your beauty.

  Pretty flowers, running rivers, your charm, your beauty, will soon be changed.

  Green meadows, pleasant woods, you will lose your beauty.

  And, everything of beauty changed, you will return to the horror of your initial aspect.

  Green meadows, pleasant woods, you will lose your beauty.

Identify the closely related keys that are visited in the contrasting sections. Which of the contrasting sections is followed by a retransition back to the A-section material? How does the text at this point reinforce the idea of a retransition?

Example 23.2.   Christoph Willibald Gluck (1714–1787), "J'ai perdu mon Eurydice," from *Orphée et Eurydice* (1762–1774), Act III

bit - ter— plight,————————— my— bit - ter— plight.

* Only one of the two contrasting sections in this aria features tonal closure in a nontonic key. Which section? Which key?

Examine and compare the two cadences heard in mm. 40–41 and 47–48 (both involve a raised scale degree $\hat{4}$ followed by scale degree $\hat{5}$ in the melody). What are the harmonies in each case?

Example 23.3.   Ludwig van Beethoven (1770–1827), Sonata op. 13 ("Pathétique"), mvt. 2

* Each contrasting section begins in a different minor key and then moves toward an authentic cadence in a (nontonic) major key. Which keys are these? Which of the two contrasting sections seems to be followed by a more clearly defined retransition?

Example 23.4.   Joseph Haydn (1732–1809), Sonata in D major, Hob. XVI:37 (1780), mvt. 3

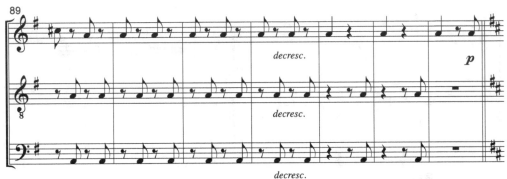

* In this rondo, the A, B, and C sections are all in binary form, and all are tonally closed. What keys are they in, and what types of binary form are heard? Where do you find a retransition? How is the final A section changed from its earlier appearances?

Example 23.5. Wolfgang Amadeus Mozart (1756–1791), "Coronation" Mass K. 317, Agnus Dei

* Which of the two contrasting sections is tonally closed in a nontonic key? Which key? Where do you hear an augmented-sixth chord extending over two full measures?

DRILLS

1. Review the two-skip drill, the sliding $^6_3$ drills from Chapters 20 through 22, and the diminished seventh drill from Chapter 22.

2. Composers often move between distantly related keys by reinterpreting the German sixth as a dominant seventh chord, to which it is enharmonically equivalent. Using scale-degree numbers and starting in the middle of your range, arpeggiate a dominant seventh chord up from the bass note in close position ($\hat{5}$–$\hat{7}$–$\hat{2}$–$\hat{4}$), and then sing a zigzag cadential line, "$\hat{3}$–$\hat{1}$–$\hat{2}$–$\hat{7}$–$\hat{1}$" (or "E–I–E–I–O" if you prefer). Now sing the notes of the same dominant seventh again, but using the scale-degree numbers of a German sixth chord in major ("low–$\hat{1}$–low–raise"). Move up by just one semitone and sing "$\hat{5}$–$\hat{3}$–$\hat{4}$–$\hat{2}$–$\hat{1}$" in a new key, one semitone lower than you began. Start again from your new key.

CHORALE WORKSHOP: AUGMENTED-SIXTH CHORDS

All of the following progressions can be realized in major and minor keys. For each progression, sing just the bass line, and then sing each chord as an arpeggio (up from its bass note and back down) or play it on an instrument. Then, working at a piano, try singing the soprano lines while playing the bass line, and singing the bass while playing the soprano lines. Finally, practice every progression with every soprano line on the piano, in a variety of simple keys.

Harmony (bass line in left hand)   **Possible soprano scale degrees (right hand)**

I | It^{+6} V I $\hat{5}$ | $\uparrow\hat{4}$ $\hat{5}$ $\hat{3}$
or $\hat{1}$ | $\hat{1}$ $\hat{7}$ $\hat{1}$
i | It^{+6} V i

I | Fr^{+6} V I $\hat{5}$ | $\uparrow\hat{4}$ $\hat{5}$ $\hat{3}$
or $\hat{3}$ | $\hat{2}$ $\hat{2}$ $\hat{1}$
i | Fr^{+6} V i $\hat{1}$ | $\hat{1}$ $\hat{7}$ $\hat{1}$

I Ger^{+6} V$^{8-7}_{6-5\ 4-3}$ | I $\hat{5}$ $\uparrow\hat{4}$ $\hat{5}$ $\downarrow\hat{4}$ | $\hat{3}$
or $\hat{3}$ $\uparrow\hat{2}$ $\hat{3}$ $\downarrow\hat{2}$ | $\hat{1}$ (in minor: $\hat{3}$ $\hat{3}$ $\hat{3}$ $\hat{2}$ | $\hat{1}$)
i Ger^{+6} V$^{8-7}_{6-5\ 4-3}$ | i $\hat{1}$ $\hat{1}$ $\hat{1}$ $\hat{7}$ | $\hat{1}$

A cadential six-four is used in the above progression in order to avoid parallel fifths with the bass.

I $\frac{V^4_2}{IV}$ IV^6 It^{+6} | V$^{8-7}_{6-5\ 4-3}$ I $\hat{3}$ $\hat{3}$ $\hat{4}$ $\uparrow\hat{4}$ | $\hat{5}$ $\hat{4}$ $\hat{3}$
or   (in minor: $\hat{3}$ $\uparrow\hat{3}$ $\hat{4}$ $\uparrow\hat{4}$ | $\hat{5}$ $\downarrow\hat{4}$ $\hat{3}$)
i $\frac{V^4_2}{iv}$ iv^6 It^{+6} | V$^{8-7}_{6-5\ 4-3}$ i $\hat{1}$ $\hat{1}$ $\hat{1}$ $\hat{1}$ | $\hat{1}$ $\hat{7}$ $\hat{1}$

Try using Fr^{+6} or Ger^{+6} instead of It^{+6}. Also try using iv^6 in major keys, and using IV^6 in minor keys (appropriate in this case because the bass line continues down through the lowered scale degree $\hat{6}$).

I V^7 ♭VI It^{+6} | V$^{8-7}_{6-5\ 4-3}$ I $\hat{3}$ $\hat{2}$ $\hat{1}$ $\hat{1}$ | $\hat{1}$ $\hat{7}$ $\hat{1}$
or
i V^7 VI It^{+6} | V$^{8-7}_{6-5\ 4-3}$ i

I V^7 ♭VI Fr^{+6} | V$^{8-7}_{6-5\ 4-3}$ I $\hat{5}$ $\hat{4}$ $\downarrow\hat{3}$ $\hat{2}$ | $\uparrow\hat{3}$ $\hat{2}$ $\hat{1}$
or   (in minor: $\hat{5}$ $\hat{4}$ $\hat{3}$ $\hat{2}$ | $\hat{3}$ $\hat{2}$ $\hat{1}$)
i V^7 VI Fr^{+6} | V$^{8-7}_{6-5\ 4-3}$ i $\hat{3}$ $\hat{2}$ $\hat{1}$ $\hat{1}$ | $\hat{1}$ $\hat{7}$ $\hat{1}$

I V^7 ♭VI Ger^{+6} | V$^{8-7}_{6-5\ 4-3}$ I $\hat{5}$ $\hat{4}$ $\downarrow\hat{3}$ $\downarrow\hat{3}$ | $\uparrow\hat{3}$ $\hat{2}$ $\hat{1}$
or   (in minor: $\hat{5}$ $\hat{4}$ $\hat{3}$ $\hat{3}$ | $\hat{3}$ $\hat{2}$ $\hat{1}$)
i V^7 VI Ger^{+6} | V$^{8-7}_{6-5\ 4-3}$ i $\hat{3}$ $\hat{2}$ $\hat{1}$ $\hat{1}$ | $\hat{1}$ $\hat{7}$ $\hat{1}$

Two progressions featuring all three augmented sixths in succession (a long dash indicates the second beat in triple meter):

Harmony (bass line in left hand)   **Possible soprano scale degrees (right hand)**

$I - V^4_2/IV \mid It^{+6} \; Fr^{+6} \; Ger^{+6} \mid V^{8-7}_{6-5}_{4-3} \mid I$

or

$i - V^4_2/iv \mid It^{+6} \; Fr^{+6} \; Ger^{+6} \mid V^{8-7}_{6-5}_{4-3} \mid i$

$\hat{5} - \hat{5} \mid \uparrow\hat{4} \; \uparrow\hat{4} \; \uparrow\hat{4} \mid \hat{5} - \downarrow\hat{4} \mid \hat{3}$

$\hat{1} - \hat{1} \mid \hat{1} \; \hat{2} \; \downarrow\hat{3} \mid \uparrow\hat{3} - \hat{2} \mid \hat{1}$

(in minor: $\hat{1} - \hat{1} \mid \hat{1} \; \hat{2} \; \hat{3} \mid \hat{3} - \hat{2} \mid \hat{1}$)

$I \; V^4_2/IV \; IV^6 \mid Ger^{+6} \; Fr^{+6} \; It^{+6} \mid V^{8-7}_{6-5}_{4-3} \mid I$

or

$i \; V^4_2/IV \; iv^6 \mid Ger^{+6} \; Fr^{+6} \; It^{+6} \mid V^{8-7}_{6-5}_{4-3} \mid i$

$\hat{3} \; \hat{3} \; \hat{4} \mid \uparrow\hat{4} \; \uparrow\hat{4} \; \uparrow\hat{4} \mid \hat{5} - \downarrow\hat{4} \mid \hat{3}$

(in minor: $\hat{3} \; \uparrow\hat{3} \; \hat{4} \mid \uparrow\hat{4} \; \uparrow\hat{4} \; \uparrow\hat{4} \mid \hat{5} - \downarrow\hat{4} \mid \hat{3}$)

$\hat{5} \; \hat{5} \; \hat{4} \mid \downarrow\hat{3} \; \hat{2} \; \hat{1} \mid \hat{1} - \hat{7} \mid \hat{1}$

(in minor: $\hat{5} \; \hat{5} \; \hat{4} \mid \hat{3} \; \hat{2} \; \hat{1} \mid \hat{1} - \hat{7} \mid \hat{1}$)

Also try using iv^6 in major keys and IV^6 in minor keys (as discussed above).

IMPROVISATION: PUTTING IT ALL TOGETHER

1. Try all four Chorale Workshop exercises listed under "Improvisation" in Chapter 15 for the progressions given in this chapter.

2. Referring to Example 23.2, sing through the melody of the refrain (mm. 7–16, with the upbeat to m. 7). Then, using the same or similar rhythm, improvise an accompanying melody that is in agreement with the harmonies of the phrase. You may "shadow" the given melody in thirds or sixths as much as you think appropriate.

3. Referring to Example 23.3, sing through the melody of mm. 1–8 (stopping right on beat 3 of m. 8). Then, using the same or similar rhythm, improvise an accompanying melody that is in agreement with the harmonies. Feel free, again, to "shadow" the supplied melody in thirds or sixths to some extent. Perform your accompanying melody along with the two given outer voices.

4. See the "extended techniques" improvisation exercise at the end of Expanding the Repertoire 23.3 below.

SUGGESTED SMARTMUSIC ASSESSMENTS

Complete SmartMusic assessments 23.1 (all parts), 23.2 (outer parts), 23.3 (top part, only A section), 23.4 (all parts), and 23.5 (all parts).

SHORT-TERM MUSICAL MEMORY

Fill in the key signature and clef as indicated by your instructor, and write in the initial note(s) on the basis of the given pitch and rhythm information. Note that the key and clef *may not be the same* as in the original example. Your instructor (or practice partner) will play a short progression to establish the key and then count off several beats to establish the tempo. Because of the brevity of each extract, you should have an overall impression of the rhythm, contour, and scale degrees after just one or two hearings. Notate the entire fragment.

1. Example 23.1, mm. 49–52, upper voice. Starts on beat 2 (half note, high scale degree 1̂).

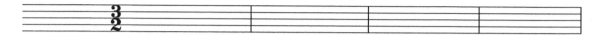

Clef and key
signature

2. Example 23.3, beat 4 of m. 25 through m. 27, upper voice (starts with dotted sixteenth note, low scale degree 5̂).

Clef and key
signature

3. Example 23.4, last eighth note of m. 60 to beat 2 of m. 62, upper voice (starts with eighth note, low scale degree 5̂).

Clef and key
signature

4. Example 23.5, m. 38 beat 3 through m. 41, upper voice (starts with dotted eighth note, low scale degree 1̂).

Clef and key
signature

5. Example 23.1, mm. 10–12, outer voices. Both start on beat 1 (dotted half note and scale degree 5̂ in top voice, half note a minor tenth lower in bottom voice).

Clef and key
signature

6. Example 23.2, m. 4 beat 4 to downbeat of m. 6, outer voices (or just upper voice). Both start on beat 4 (quarter note and scale degree $\hat{3}$ in bottom voice; top voice enters a minor tenth higher with the first of two several eighth notes).

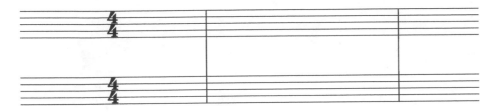

Clef and key
signature

DICTATION OF LONGER EXAMPLES

Your instructor or a classmate will choose one of the examples listed below and inform you of the key, clef, meter, first note (scale degree, rhythmic value, and metric placement) of one or more parts, and total number of measures. Use a separate piece of staff paper to write down the indicated information. You will hear a short progression to establish the key of the example, and then hear the example several times with breaks between hearings.

Nonmodulating:

1. Example 23.2, beat 4 of m. 6 to beat 2 of m. 14, outer voices.
2. Example 23.3, up to beat 2 of m. 8, outer voices (disregard triplets at end of m. 8).

Modulating:

3. Example 23.1, mm. 21–26. All three voices to be played; notate outer voices and Roman numerals (taking modulation into account).
4. Example 23.4, up to downbeat of m. 8, outer voices.
5. Example 23.5, m. 9 to beat 2 of m. 20

CONTEXTUAL LISTENING 23.1

Beethoven, String Quartet op. 74 "Harp," mvt. 2 (Adagio ma non troppo)

The "Harp" Quartet is so named because of the characteristic pizzicato sections in the first movement. The second movement achieves a very different hymnlike texture.

1. The first phrase of the refrain begins after two tonic chords (in the key of A♭ major) with the melody in the first violin. What cadences conclude each of the first two phrases? (Depending on how you state your answer, you may need to specify the key or keys in which a phrase concludes.)

2. Toward the end of the refrain, the cello plays a lengthy tonic pedal and then which three scale degrees?

3. The first episode begins right after that with a change to the parallel minor key, A♭ minor. What are the first six scale degrees in the violin melody here?

4. The music modulates fairly soon to a major key—confirming this move with a perfect authentic cadence. Identify this key with a Roman numeral in relation to the home key of A♭ major. (Hint: it's the relative major of A♭ minor.)

5. A sparser texture then seems to anticipate the upcoming return of the refrain. What is the term for this subsection?

6. What rhythmic element is introduced on the return of the refrain?

7. a. After a transition consisting of only three chords, the second episode begins. Is this the same theme as featured in the previous episode or a new theme?

   b. In relation to the home key of the movement, what key is the second episode in?

   c. When the cello takes over the melody, which instrument takes over the bass line?

8. How is the refrain varied at its next appearance?

9. Is there a coda? If so, what musical material is heard?

10. Indicate the form of the movement (with capital letters—A, B, etc.—for each section).

CONTEXTUAL LISTENING 23.2

Mozart, Clarinet Concerto in A major K. 622, mvt. 3 (Rondo: Allegro)

This work is among the most-performed clarinet concertos. Mozart was particularly fond of the clarinet and famously rewrote his Symphony no. 40, adding in two clarinet parts.

1. What kind of phrase structure begins the piece? (Heard over the first twelve seconds, and then repeated.)

2. We hear the opening theme coming back after about thirty seconds, after some slightly different melodic material. Was that long enough to hear it as a separate intervening episode already, or was that entirely within the refrain?

3. a. The arrival of authentic cadences accelerates toward three conclusive tonic chords. Then a new theme arrives (scale degrees $\hat{3}-\hat{4}-\hat{3}-\hat{4}-\hat{5}$), though still in the home key of A major. What section is this?

   b. This theme repeats down an octave and modulates to what key?

4. What section begins with octaves in the horns? Which scale degree are they playing, with respect to the home key?

5. Which previously heard theme returns after that? Has anything been changed, added, or omitted since it was heard earlier?

6. a. Yet another new theme is introduced. What key have we moved to by this point?

   b. Provide scale-degree numbers for the first seven notes of this melody.

7. Mozart soon modulates to the subdominant key, D major, as a new (quite leapy) theme is heard. Which theme then returns, in the tonic key?

8. A rapidly modulating passage based on this theme begins after a half cadence. What is the function of the music heard about a minute later, with the entrance of the horns?

9. The refrain returns again, complete. What section begins after that, with urgent upward arpeggios sounding in the solo part?

10. Indicate the form of the movement (with capital letters—A, B, etc.—for each section).

EXPANDING THE REPERTOIRE 23.3

Henry Cowell (1897–1965), "The Banshee" (1925)

Henry Cowell's solo piano pieces introduce numerous extended techniques (i.e., playing instruments in nontraditional ways). His term *string piano* refers to the manipulation of the strings inside the instrument, rather than performing with the conventional hammer-key action.

1. This piece involves two techniques: (a) a sort of pizzicato (plucking the strings with the nail), and (b) a longitudinal scraping and sweeping of the strings. How does the juxtaposition of these two techniques create a distinct formal design?

2. In the timeline below, make note of the "sections" as defined by the various sonic environments (the length corresponds to that of the video online).

0:00   3:30
├──┤

3. What term best describes the form of this piece?

4. How do parameters other than texture contribute to shape the piece? (Think of register, dynamic level, tempo, etc.)

5. Compose a piece that illustrates the same formal structure as the one present in "The Banshee." Use extended techniques on your own instrument to delineate the various sections, but use other parameters to create a climax. Notate the various elements in the timeline below:

0:00
├──┤

Chapter 24

Further Uses of Augmented-Sixth Chords

This chapter illustrates the use of augmented-sixth chords in several larger forms and also introduces some more advanced uses of this type of sonority.

Example 24.1.   Franz Schubert (1797–1828), Sonatina for Violin and Piano, op. posth. 137 no. 2 (D. 385), mvt. 3

* Locate an augmented-sixth chord in each of the two reprises of the Menuetto. What type of binary form is the Menuetto? The Trio is the same type of binary form, but how does it contrast with the Menuetto?

Example 24.2.   Schubert, Moment Musical in A♭ major, op. 94 no. 6, D. 780 (1824), Allegretto

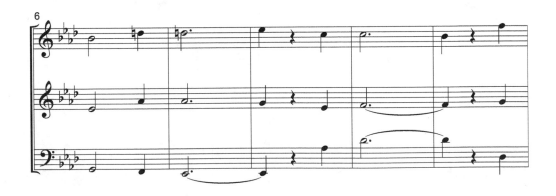

* What type of binary form is this? What phrase structures are heard over the first eight measures, and over the first sixteen measures? When you sing the melody of the first reprise, how does it feel to *descend* from E♮ to E♭? This coincides with the denial of the C-major triad's expected dominant function. (See Examples 24.3 and 24.4 for further examples of this kind of denied dominant function.)

What harmony is heard at the beginning of the second reprise, and again eight measures later? What key is attained at m. 29, where the key signature changes for the first time? How does this relate to the home key of A♭ major? Hint: consider its enharmonic equivalent. What type of chromatic chord is used in mm. 34 and 37? Note how smoothly Schubert reattains the home key with the use of an augmented-sixth chord in m. 41.

How does the later tonicization of A major (leading into m. 68) function in the home key of A♭ major? Hint: notice the direct resolution of an A-major triad in first inversion (in mm. 68 and 73) to the dominant of A♭ major (in mm. 69 and 74).

Example 24.3.   Wolfgang Amadeus Mozart (1756–91), "Voi, che sapete," from *Le nozze di Figaro*, K. 492 (1786), Act II, scene 3

per. Non tro-vo pa - ce not-te, nè di, ma pur mi pia - ce lan - guir co - sì.

Voi, che sa - pe - te che co-sa è a-mor, don - ne ve - de - te,

s'io l'ho nel cor, don - ne, ve - de - te,___ s'io l'ho nel cor.

don - ne, ve - de - te,___ s'io l'ho nel - cor.

Translation: You, ladies, who know what love is, look to see if I have it in my heart!

  I'll tell you what I'm going through. It's new to me; I can't understand it.

  I feel an affection full of desire that now is pleasure, now is agony.

  I freeze, and then feel my soul burning, and in another moment go back to freezing.

  I look for something beautiful outside of myself, I don't know who has it, I don't know

    what it is.

  I sigh and groan without wanting to, I quiver and tremble without knowing it,

  I find no peace night or day, and yet I like suffering this way!

  You, ladies, who·know what love is, look to see if I have it in my heart!

The modulatory goal of A♭ major (attained in m. 29) is perhaps an unusual goal in an aria by Mozart whose home key is B♭ major. But in comparison to the dominant key, F major—which is heard just before this—A♭ major represents the more common "mixture" goal of ♭III. (Plan your performance of these modulations accordingly.) Note that the dominant harmony (V in the key of F) heard in m. 28 is denied its expected resolution, as we abruptly enter the key of A♭ major.

What is the form of this aria? Hint: consider the brief but tonally stable eight measures in A♭ major (mm. 29–36) as the second main section of the piece. What part of the form directly precedes this section? What is the formal function of the music that is heard between these central measures and the return of the opening theme (in the home key) in m. 54?

The next example introduces the German diminished-third chord. This is simply a German sixth with the raised scale degree $\hat{4}$ in the bass instead of in an upper voice. Just like its more common sibling, it also resolves to a dominant harmony via stepwise motion from the raised scale degree $\hat{4}$ to scale degree $\hat{5}$ in the bass, and from scale degree $\hat{6}$ (lowered scale degree $\hat{6}$ in major) to scale degree $\hat{5}$ in an upper voice. This interval is usually a diminished tenth rather than an actual diminished third, but the harmony is called a German diminished-third chord anyway.

For other examples of German diminished-third chords, see Example 17.4 (at the end of the first reprise, in the second measure of the second ending) and Example 22.8 (at the end of m. 11).

Example 24.4. Frédéric Chopin (1810–1849), Prelude in E minor, op. 28, no. 4 (1839)

* Chopin denies quite a few dominant-seventh chords their expected resolution through this short prelude, including the (respelled) V $\frac{4}{3}$ chord heard on the third beat of m. 2, and the downbeats of mm. 4
and 7. The chord in m. 23 is spelled as a dominant seventh chord; judging from its resolution, however,
how should it be spelled?

What phrase structure is heard over the course of this piece? (Several other of Chopin's Preludes
have the same overall structure.)

The next few examples feature augmented-sixth chords that resolve unusually. As
with the standard types of augmented-sixth chords, however, the two notes spanning the
interval of an augmented sixth will lie just a semitone away from an upcoming chord
tone, and one or both of them will resolve to that tone.

Example 24.5. Edvard Grieg (1843–1907), "Death of Ase," from *Peer Gynt Suite no. 1,* op. 46 (1875)

* Examine the augmented-sixth chord in m. 5 and its resolution into m. 6. (In Grieg's full texture, the last chord in m. 5 also has a B, resulting in a complete French sixth.) Compare its effect to the use of the V triad in m. 1. Note that when the opening material returns up a perfect fifth (in m. 9) the corresponding chord on beat 3 of m. 13 is spelled as a dominant seventh. Nonetheless, it is still functioning as an augmented-sixth chord, in the same way as in m. 5.

How do the augmented-sixth chords in mm. 25 and 29 compare to the one in m. 5, in terms of how they resolve?

Example 24.6.   Grieg, "Med en Primula veris" ("With a Primrose"), from *Five Songs*, op. 26, no. 4 (1876)

* *Translation*: You lovely, gentle child of spring, take the spring's first flower.

And don't throw it away because you know the rose of summer will follow.

Summer certainly is radiant and beautiful and the autumn of life is rich,

But spring is the loveliest with the play and pleasure of love.

And you and I, my slender maid, are in the glow of spring!

So take my flower, but in return give the sweetness of your young heart.

Note the use of the raised scale degree $\hat{2}$ in the very first measure, transforming a diatonic V⁶ triad into an augmented triad and clearly forecasting a densely chromatic style. Through mm. 9–16, Grieg's bass line goes through the pattern of falling minor thirds to get from scale degree $\hat{5}$ down to the lowered scale degree $\hat{2}$ (A♭, in m. 16). Given that this A♭ chord resolves back to G major, how "should" Grieg have spelled it?

Example 24.7.   Johannes Brahms (1833–1897), "Im Herbst," from *Fünf Gesänge*, op. 104 (1888)

Translation: Solemn is the Autumn. And when the leaves fall, the heart also sinks to troubled woe.

       Still is the meadow, and towards the south journey the singers in silence, as if to the

          grave.

       Pale is the day, and colorless fog enshrouds both sun and hearts.

       Early comes the night: for all Powers celebrate and deeply withdrawn rests the being.

       Soft becomes the man. He sees the sun sink; he foresees the end of life and of the year.

       Moist becomes the eye, yet in the tear-sparkle gushes the heart's most blessed outpouring.

       (Klaus Groth)

    Like Example 19.3, this song is in modified strophic form and alternates between major and minor modes. It begins in C minor and ends in C major, although the key is a little vague at the very beginning. The upbeat to m. 2 contains all four notes of a standard German sixth (A♭, C, E♭ and F♯) and resolves toward a cadential six-four as expected, but it has a C in the bass instead of an A♭. How are these same four notes reused in mm. 5, 10, and 20? How do the augmented sixths in mm. 24–26 function? Find two notes in the altered dominant chord on the upbeat to m. 31 that span an augmented sixth, and examine their resolution. Where do this same chord and this same resolution recur a little later?

Example 24.8. Pyotr Ilyich Tchaikovsky (1840–1893), "Waltz of the Flowers" (two excerpts) from *The Nutcracker*, op. 71 (1891–92)

(a) Beginning

* What phrase structure is heard over the course of this excerpt? What (different) structure is heard over each sixteen-measure phrase?

Note Tchaikovsky's use of a secondary augmented-sixth chord (built on the lowered scale degree $\hat{7}$ in the bass) in m. 10 and a standard augmented-sixth chord (with the lowered scale degree $\hat{6}$ in the bass) in m. 15. How does the augmented-sixth chord in m. 24 help to accomplish the modulation to F♯ minor?

(b) Ending

* Temporarily ignoring the upper neighbor notes in the triplet figures, provide Roman numerals for the long hemiola passage. Begin on a V^6 triad in m. 11 of this excerpt, but feel free to label any passing $^6_4$ chords as P $^6_4$ and passing diminished-seventh chords as P^{o7}. Then perform your analysis as arpeggiated triads ascending and descending in close position above each bass note in turn.

DRILLS

1. Review the minor-mode parallel $^6_3$ drill with the Neapolitan, the diminished-seventh drill, and the V^7 reinterpretation drill from Chapter 23.

2. Here is a V$^4_2$ reinterpretation drill, focusing on the German diminished-third chord. Using scale-degree numbers in a major key and starting in the middle of your range, arpeggiate this progression from the bottom of each chord to the top and back down: V–V$^4_2$–I^6. Then sing the same notes that you sang for the V$^4_2$ chord, but sing the scale-degree numbers for a German diminished-third chord ("raise, low, $\hat{1}$, low"), and move into the dominant triad to which it should resolve (with the root just a semitone above the raised scale degree $\hat{4}$ in the German chord).

CHORALE WORKSHOP: GERMAN DIMINISHED-THIRD CHORDS AND SECONDARY AUGMENTED SIXTHS

All of the following progressions can be realized in major and minor keys, except where specified. For each progression, sing just the bass line, and then sing each chord as an arpeggio (up from its bass note and back down) or play it on an instrument. Then, working at a piano, try singing the soprano lines while playing the bass line, and singing the bass while playing the soprano lines. Finally, practice every progression with every soprano line on the piano, in a variety of simple keys.

Since the chord after a secondary augmented sixth will not (necessarily) sound like tonic, it would be confusing to use the "fractional" notation that we use for secondary dominants and secondary diminished sevenths. We will enclose the secondary augmented sixth symbol within square brackets and will provide an arrow pointing to its resolution. In these cases the bass line will be specified.

German diminished-third chord:

Harmony (bass line in left hand)	Possible soprano scale degrees (right hand)
I Ger^{o3} V or i Ger^{o3} V	$\hat{5}$ $\downarrow\hat{6}$ $\hat{5}$ (in minor: $\hat{5}$ $\hat{6}$ $\hat{5}$) $\hat{1}$ $\hat{1}$ $\hat{7}$
I | IV Ger^{o3} V or i | iv Ger^{o3} V	$\hat{5}$ | $\hat{6}$ $\downarrow\hat{6}$ $\hat{5}$ (in minor: $\hat{5}$ | $\hat{6}$ $\hat{6}$ $\hat{5}$) $\hat{1}$ | $\hat{1}$ $\hat{1}$ $\hat{7}$
I $\frac{\text{V}^4_2}{\text{IV}}$ $\flat$VI Ger^{o3} | V or i $\frac{\text{V}^4_2}{\text{iv}}$ VI Ger^{o3} | V	$\hat{5}$ $\hat{5}$ $\downarrow\hat{6}$ $\downarrow\hat{6}$ | $\hat{5}$ (in minor: $\hat{5}$ $\hat{5}$ $\hat{6}$ $\hat{6}$ | $\hat{5}$) $\hat{1}$ $\hat{1}$ $\hat{1}$ $\hat{1}$ | $\hat{7}$
I $\flat$II^6 Ger^{o3} V^7 | I or i $\flat$II^6 Ger^{o3} V^7 | i	$\hat{3}$ $\hat{4}$ $\downarrow\hat{3}$ $\hat{2}$ | $\uparrow\hat{3}$ (in minor: $\hat{3}$ $\hat{4}$ $\hat{3}$ $\hat{2}$ | $\hat{3}$) $\hat{1}$ $\downarrow\hat{2}$ $\hat{1}$ $\hat{7}$ | $\hat{1}$

Secondary augmented sixths:

In major keys:

$$\text{I}^6 \mid \text{ii}^7 \; [\text{Fr}^{+6}] \rightarrow \text{I} \qquad\qquad \hat{5} \mid \hat{4} \; \hat{4} \; \hat{3}$$
$$(\text{bass:} \quad \hat{3} \mid \hat{2} \quad \downarrow\hat{2} \qquad \hat{1}) \qquad\qquad \hat{1} \mid \hat{1} \; \hat{7} \; \hat{1}$$

In minor keys:

$$\text{i} \; \text{V}^6 \; \text{i} \; [\text{It}^{+6}] \rightarrow \mid \text{VII} \; \text{Fr}^{+6} \; \text{V} \qquad\qquad \hat{5} \; \hat{5} \; \hat{5} \; \hat{3} \mid \hat{4} \; \uparrow\hat{4} \; \hat{5}$$
$$(\text{bass:} \quad \hat{1} \; \hat{7} \; \hat{1} \quad \hat{7} \qquad \mid \downarrow\hat{7} \quad \downarrow\hat{6} \quad \hat{5}) \qquad \hat{3} \; \hat{2} \; \hat{3} \; \hat{3} \mid \hat{2} \; \hat{2} \; \hat{2}$$

In major keys:

$$\text{I} \; [\text{Ger}^{\circ 3}] \rightarrow \frac{\text{V}}{\text{V}} \; \text{V}^7 \mid \text{I} \qquad\qquad \hat{5} \; \hat{5} \; \uparrow\hat{4} \; \downarrow\hat{4} \mid \hat{3}$$
$$(\text{bass:} \quad \hat{1} \quad \uparrow\hat{1} \qquad \hat{2} \quad \hat{5} \mid \hat{1}) \qquad\qquad \hat{3} \downarrow\hat{3} \; \hat{2} \; \hat{2} \mid \hat{1}$$

In major keys:

$$\text{I} \mid \text{V}^6_5 \; [\text{Ger}^{+6}] \rightarrow \text{P}^6_4 \leftarrow [\text{Ger}^{\circ 3}] \mid \text{V}^7 \qquad \hat{5} \mid \hat{5} \; \uparrow\hat{5} \; \hat{6} \; \uparrow\hat{6} \mid \hat{7}$$
$$(\text{bass:} \quad \hat{1} \mid \hat{7} \quad \downarrow\hat{7} \qquad \hat{6} \qquad \downarrow\hat{6} \mid \hat{5}) \qquad \hat{3} \mid \hat{4} \; \hat{4} \; \hat{4} \; \hat{4} \mid \hat{4}$$
$$\hat{1} \mid \hat{2} \; \hat{2} \; \hat{2} \; \hat{2} \mid \hat{2}$$

This is a lament-bass progression that was popular among nineteenth-century composers. It is the basis for a more extended pattern called the "omnibus" progression. Note that the secondary Ger$^{\circ 3}$ applies to the passing six-four rather than to the following downbeat. It has the same four notes as the secondary Ger^{+6} just before. Note also the voice exchange occurring between the bass and an upper voice (connecting the two dominant-seventh chords on the downbeats).

IMPROVISATION: PUTTING IT ALL TOGETHER

1. Try all four Chorale Workshop exercises listed under "Improvisation" in Chapter 15 for the progressions given in this chapter.

2. Taking a cue from Example 24.4, improvise a series of close-position harmonies with just one hand on the piano. Begin with i^6 and V$\frac{4}{3}$ in a minor key, and then from that point on just move one chord tone down by one semitone at a time. Make sure the chords that result are always some kind of seventh chord or augmented-sixth chord. Optional: make a flowchart showing which chord types could turn into other chord types in this way.

3. Refer to the Grieg song given in Example 24.6. Sing the melody of mm. 1–4. Then improvise an answering phrase (in the same style) that does not modulate but instead approaches a perfect authentic cadence in the home key. Now pick two closely related keys and one distantly related key as modulatory goals for three more alternative answer phrases. See which works best, and compare notes with classmates.

4. Listen to a recording of Antonio Carlos Jobim's (1927–1994) song, "The Girl from Ipanema." See if you can notate the bass line and melody of the chorus. Now, have your classmates sing the bass and improvise a new melody, using the same distinct syncopated rhythms as found in the original melody. Try writing down your new melody; then add new text, preserving the original's pattern of strong and weak syllables.

SUGGESTED SMARTMUSIC ASSESSMENTS

Complete SmartMusic assessments 24.1 Menuetto (all parts), 24.1 Trio (all parts), 24.2 through 24.7 (all parts), and 24.8a and 24.8b (all parts).

SHORT-TERM MUSICAL MEMORY

Fill in the key signature and clef as indicated by your instructor, and write in the initial note(s) on the basis of the given pitch and rhythm information. Note that the key and clef *may not be the same* as in the original example. Your instructor (or practice partner) will play a short progression to establish the key and then count off several beats to establish the tempo. Because of the brevity of each extract, you should have an overall impression of the rhythm, contour, and scale degrees after just one or two hearings. Notate the entire fragment.

1. Example 24.1, up to beat 2 of m. 3, upper voice. Starts on beat 3 (quarter note, low scale degree $\hat{5}$).

Clef and key
  signature

2. Example 24.3, mm. 29–32, top voice. Starts with quarter note on beat 1, scale degree $\hat{3}$).

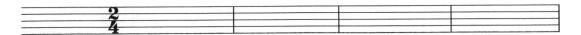

Clef and key
  signature

3. Example 24.6, beat 6 of m. 20 to beat 4 of m. 22, upper voice (starts with eighth note, scale degree $\hat{3}$).

Clef and key
  signature

4. Example 24.7, mm. 40–42, upper voice (starts with dotted half note on beat 1, high scale degree î).

Clef and key
signature

5. Example 24.2, m. 33 up to downbeat of m. 36, top and middle voices. Both start on beat 1 (half note and scale degree î in top voice, dotted half note a minor sixth lower in middle voice).

Clef and key
signature

6. Example 24.5, mm. 3–4, outer voices. Both start with quarter notes on beat 1 (scale degree 3̂ in top voice, scale degree î over two octaves lower in bottom part).

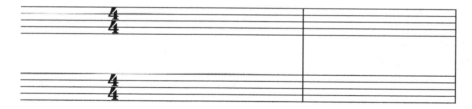

Clef and key
signature

7. Example 24.7, m. 20 to downbeat of m. 22, alto and bass voices. Both start with dotted half note on beat 1 (high scale degree î in bass voice, and a minor third higher in alto voice).

Clef and key
signature

8. Example 24.8(a), up to downbeat of m. 3, soprano and tenor voices. Notate both voices on the same staff. Both start with quarter notes on beat 1 (low scale degree $\hat{5}$ in soprano voice, and a minor third lower in tenor voice).

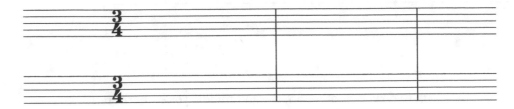

Clef and key
signature

DICTATION OF LONGER EXAMPLES

Your instructor or a classmate will choose one of the examples listed below and inform you of the key, clef, meter, first note (scale degree, rhythmic value, and metric placement) of one or more parts, and total number of measures. Use a separate piece of staff paper to write down the indicated information. You will hear a short progression to establish the key of the example, and then hear the example several times with breaks between hearings.

Nonmodulating:

1. Example 24.2, up to downbeat of m. 16, outer voices.
2. Example 24.3, mm. 1–12, top voice along with just the downbeats of the bottom voice (sustained throughout each measure).
3. Example 24.4, up to downbeat of m. 10, outer voices.

Modulating:

4. Example 24.1, Trio section up to downbeat of m. 38, outer voices.
5. Example 24.5, mm. 25–32, outer voices. (Treat first bass note as scale degree $\hat{4}$.) It's possible that more than two keys may be heard.
6. Example 24.6, up to middle of m. 9, outer voices. Top voice starts with eighth-note upbeat (low scale degree $\hat{5}$), bottom voice starts on first downbeat (quarter note a perfect twelfth below top voice entrance).

CONTEXTUAL LISTENING 24.1

Ludwig van Beethoven (1770–1827), Piano Sonata in C minor ("Pathétique"), op. 13, mvt. 3 (Rondo: Allegro)

Like that of Tchaikovsky's sixth symphony, this sonata's subtitle pertains to its emotional *pathos*. Compare the form of this final movement to that of its slow movement, given as Example 23.3.

1. A contrasting period is heard at the outset (in the home key of C minor): an antecedent phrase reaches a half cadence and a consequent phrase reaches a perfect authentic cadence. What material is then immediately repeated and extended?

2. After a quite loud cadence, we hear a couple of secondary V $^4_2$ chords and arpeggiated melodies. What part of the form is this?

3. A new theme is introduced, featuring an Alberti bass and a repeated syncopation in the melody. What key have we arrived in, and what scale degree is being repeated in the melody?

4. After the next cadence and a short rest, we hear a new, calmer-sounding, hymn-like texture (with a repeated scale degree $\hat{2}$ in the melody). What part of the form is this?

5. Some quick triplet figures bring us back to a dramatic dominant seventh chord. What theme is heard immediately after that, and in what key?

6. Describe the character of the following section, which features a highly disjunct melody in steady rhythm. Which major key is attained here?

7. Soon after, a pedal tone is heard in the bass. What harmonic function is high-lighted and extensively arpeggiated? What part of the form is this?

8. The refrain is then heard again. How is it changed?

9. We then have our Alberti bass texture returning, but not in the key it was in before. What key is it in now?

10. How is the hymnlike material changed from its earlier presentation?

11. After the refrain, what part of the form begins with the triplets? (Notice the partial reference to the refrain, but transposed dramatically to the submediant, halfway through this final section.)

CONTEXTUAL LISTENING 24.2

Brahms, Piano Quartet in G minor, op. 25, mvt. 4 (Rondo alla zingarese: Presto)

Scored for violin, viola, cello, and piano, this piece was completed in 1861 and memorably orchestrated by Schoenberg in 1937. This movement's "alla zingarese" marking refers to its Hungarian characteristics. Brahms later composed a set of twenty-one "Hungarian Dances" for which he achieved great renown.

1. a. Notate the first six scale degrees of the opening tune (heard in the home key of G minor).

    b. After this opening motive is heard twice, the melody then descends twice from the same scale degree. What scale degree is this?

2. The opening tune then returns, presenting a kind of a–b–a ministructure (the first of many) within this first section. How is this opening section linked to the following quicker-moving material?

3. a. After the miniature a–b–a is complete, what musical factors help us hear a new section beginning? (This suggests that the a–b–a noted previously constitutes a single larger section in the overall scheme of the movement.)

    b. The piece began in G minor; what key is heard in this new section?

    c. What are the first eight scale degrees in the very quick melody here?

    d. Listening for exactly where the repeats are in this section, what form would you say is heard? Does this section seem to be tonally closed?

4. The refrain is then heard again. What is somewhat different about how it ends, compared to before?

5. a. Describe the character of the following section. What key is it in?

   b. What are the first seven scale degrees in the melody?

   c. Again listening for repeats, what is the form of this section? Is it tonally closed?

6. a. A new theme is heard, featuring triplets. What key is heard here?

   b. What form is heard in this section? Is it tonally closed?

7. Several previously heard themes are then reprised in close succession. Identify which themes these are, in order of their appearance.

8. After a freer-sounding cadenza section, things start to accelerate again. Which two themes are then referenced?

9. Which theme is the last to be heard?

10. Outline the form of this movement using capital letters (A, B, etc.).

EXPANDING THE REPERTOIRE 24.3

The Ronettes, "Be My Baby" (1963)

This song placed number twenty-two on *Rolling Stone*'s list of the five hundred greatest songs of all time. The initial drumbeat and the repeated eighth-note chord accompaniment pattern took on iconic significance and influenced countless other popular songs, such as Billy Joel's "Say Goodbye to Hollywood," Meat Loaf's "You Took the Words Right Out of My Mouth," and many others.

1. Using a piano or other instrument, identify the chords of the verse for "Be My Baby" and analyze the progression with Roman numerals in E major:

E		F#m	B
I		ii	V

The night we met I knew I needed you so

and if I had the chance I'd never let you go.

So won't you say you love me,

I'll make you so proud of me.

We'll make 'em turn their heads every place we go.

So won't you, please, BE MY BE MY BABY

2. All chains of secondary dominant-seventh chords feature two chromatically descending lines at the distance of a tritone; these lines are formed by an alternation of the third and seventh of the secondary dominant chords. In the staff below, notate the descending lines, specifying the chord and the chord member. (The first chord is provided).

G#⁷

Chapter 25

Sonata Form

This chapter introduces sonata form. In the context of your familiarity with binary form, a movement in sonata form may strike you as a combination of rounded continuous binary and balanced continuous binary.

The first section (the *exposition*) typically presents thematic material in two keys, often a major key and its dominant, or a minor key and its relative major. A *transition* takes you from one key to the other, and *closing* material serves to confirm the second key at the end of the section. You may sometimes find a *codetta*, or a kind of coda within the exposition.

The second large section is often described in two parts, the *development* and the *recapitulation*. The development revisits some thematic elements from the exposition in new keys or contexts (often featuring thematic fragmentation, sequences, or multiple modulations) and usually concludes with a *retransition* emphasizing the dominant of the returning home key. The recapitulation presents all the thematic material from the exposition in the home key—thus resolving the tonal "conflict" of the exposition.

The exposition may be preceded by an *introduction* of some sort, often at a slower tempo; the recapitulation is often followed by a *coda*, separate from and subsequent to the closing material.

We begin this survey with a Clementi sonatina, in which the development is quite minimal in length. Following two fairly archetypal Classical-era sonata forms by Mozart and Beethoven, we will then study two (so-called) "three-key expositions" by Schubert and Brahms, disregarding the remainder of these movements for reasons of space. The complete first movement of Franck's Violin Sonata rounds off this chapter.

Example 25.1.   Muzio Clementi (1752–1832), Sonatina in C major op. 36 no. 1 (1797), mvt. 1

* Where does the modulation occur in the exposition? The very short eight-measure development is still focused on the note that was the goal of the modulation, but it no longer sounds like a local tonic; how and why is this true? How is the recapitulation different from the exposition?

Example 25.2.   Wolfgang Amadeus Mozart (1756–1791), Serenade in G major, K. 525
                "Eine kleine Nachtmusik" (1787), mvt. 1

130

134

* In the exposition, where do you think the transition, the secondary tonal/thematic area, and the closing section begin? (The closing section is fairly long.)

Note, in mm. 70–75, a six-measure emphasis on the dominant of the returning home key. What part of the form is this, and how does Mozart *approach* this dominant?

What does Mozart change in the recapitulation in order not to modulate, as the exposition did? What is heard at the very end of the movement?

Example 25.3. Ludwig van Beethoven (1770–1827), Piano Sonata op. 14, no. 1, mvt. 1

* Although it doesn't sound transitional at first, where in the exposition does the transition begin? Where does the secondary tonal/thematic area begin, and what new key is reached? If the closing material is heard to begin with the bravura gestures in m. 46 (or possibly earlier), then do you find a codetta a little later on?

After passing through A minor and C major in the development, Beethoven then reapproaches the home key—colored, as in Example 25.2, with modal mixture. Where do you notice a dominant pedal beginning, and signaling the retransition? Where does the recapitulation begin, and how is it different from the exposition?

722 SONATA FORM

Example 25.4.   Franz Schubert (1797–1828), Sonata in B♭ major, D. 960, mvt. 1 (exposition only)

Analytical questions:

1. What phrase structure do you notice over the first eighteen measures?
2. a. What type of harmony does the ensuing fourteen-measure tonicization of G♭ major lead into (in mm. 34–35)?
   b. Since it then appears that we haven't yet modulated away from the home key after all, is there a single Roman numeral to use for those fourteen measures?
3. What type of harmony is used in mm. 45–46, and how does Schubert use it to modulate into F♯ minor? How does F♯ minor relate to any previously tonicized keys?
4. a. What key is attained in m. 79, and how is it prepared?
   b. If this section sounds most like closing-style music, where should we locate the secondary theme?
5. Describe the very interesting sequence that is heard in mm. 102–106.

Example 25.5.   Johannes Brahms (1833–1897), Clarinet Sonata op. 120 no. 1 (1894), mvt. 1 (exposition only)

* This "three-key exposition" features three distinct themes as well, in mm. 4, 38, and 53. What are the three keys in question? (It may be difficult to tell without performing the excerpt or listening to a recording.) Do you hear a transition leading into the theme at m. 38? What part of the form is heard over the last twelve measures of the exposition?

Example 25.6.   César Franck (1822–1890), Violin Sonata in A major (1886)

* Note the unusual augmented-sixth usage right after we first hear the tonic of the home key, A major, in m. 8. If the second tonal/thematic area arrives in m. 31, where would you say the transition begins in the long seamless stretch before that? Perhaps the primary tonal/thematic area simply "becomes transitional" in a gradual way.

The soloist takes a long break from the downbeat of m. 31 to the downbeat of m. 47, reentering with the theme from m. 4 in C♯ minor, which can be heard as the beginning of the development. (The accompanimental texture also thickens at this point.) The primary theme returns in the home key shortly thereafter; identify exactly where, and describe how the exposition is altered in the development. What does the ten-measure coda remind you of?

DRILLS

1. Review the diminished seventh drill from Chapter 23, the V^7 reinterpretation drill from Chapter 23, and the $V \frac{4}{2}$ reinterpretation drill from Chapter 24.

2. Refer to Example 25.5, specifically the rhythm of the clarinet part (the upper part) from beat 3 of m. 60 to the downbeat of m. 67. Disregard the pitches, and perform this rhythm at a slow (though not glacial) tempo by chanting the number of each beat; stutter appropriately for any rhythmic articulations that are encountered prior to the next on-beat note. Your performance will begin like this: "three-ee WHUH—un two—oo-oo-oo . . ." etc. (You may as well continue the vowel of "two" through the first beat of m. 62, since that was the number of the previous on-beat note.) Pay special attention to the quintuplets! Do not perform them as either 2+3 or 3+2, but exactly in between, so that the subdivisions of the quintuplets are utterly even.

3. In Example 25.6, as mentioned previously, the development begins in m. 47 with the return of the opening theme, transposed to C♯ minor. Try singing a long C♯

beginning in m. 47, and then stepping down chromatically along with the melody as its focal pitches steadily descend (C♮, B, B♭, A, etc.) toward the F♮ in m. 60.

CHORALE WORKSHOP: LONGER PROGRESSIONS

For each the following progressions, sing just the bass line, and then sing each chord as an arpeggio (up from its bass note and back down) or play it on an instrument. Then, working at a piano, try singing the soprano lines while playing the bass line, and singing the bass while playing the soprano lines. Finally, practice every progression with every soprano line on the piano, in a variety of simple keys. The modality of each progression is specified.

The use of quotation marks around a cadential six-four indicates the evasion of its cadential tendency. Bass lines are specified in certain instances for clarity. Where $V-\frac{4}{2}$ is specified, the bass line is intended to be performed as two eighth notes within one beat of a $\frac{4}{4}$ meter.

Harmony (bass line in left hand)

Possible soprano scale degrees (right hand)

In major:

$$I \ CT^{o7} \ I \ \frac{V^7}{IV} \ | \ iv \ Ger^{o3} \ V^{8-7}_{\substack{6-5\\4-3}} \ | \ I$$

$\hat{5} \ \hat{6} \ \hat{5} \ \downarrow\hat{7} \ | \ \downarrow\hat{6} \ \downarrow\hat{6} \ \hat{5} \ \hat{4} \ | \ \hat{3}$
$\hat{5} \ \uparrow\hat{4} \ \hat{5} \ \hat{5} \ | \ \hat{4} \ \hat{4} \ \hat{3} \ \hat{2} \ | \ \hat{1}$

In major:

$$I \ vii^{o6} \ CT^{o7} \ I^6 \ | \ IV^6 \ P^6_4 \ \frac{V^6_5}{V} \ V \ | \ I$$
(bass: $\hat{1} \quad \hat{2} \quad \uparrow\hat{2} \quad \hat{3}$)

$\hat{8} \ \hat{7} \ \hat{6} \ \hat{5} \ | \ \hat{4} \ \hat{5} \ \hat{6} \ \hat{5} \ | \ \hat{3}$
$\hat{3} \ \hat{4} \ \uparrow\hat{4} \ \hat{5} \ | \ \downarrow\hat{4} \ \hat{3} \ \hat{2} \ \hat{2} \ | \ \hat{1}$
$\hat{3} \ \hat{2} \ \hat{1} \ \hat{7} \ | \ \hat{1} \ \hat{1} \ \hat{1} \ \hat{7} \ | \ \hat{1}$

In major:

$$I \ \frac{V^4_2}{IV} \ iv^6 \ V-\frac{4}{2} \ | \ I^6 \ ii^7 \ "V^6_4-" \ \frac{vii^{o7}}{vi} \ | \ vi$$
(bass: $\hat{5} \qquad \uparrow\hat{5}$)

$\hat{5} \ \hat{5} \ \hat{4} \ \hat{2} \ | \ \hat{1} \ \hat{1} \ \hat{1} \ \hat{7} \ | \ \hat{1}$
$\hat{3} \ \hat{3} \ \hat{4} \ \hat{5} \ | \ \hat{5} \ \hat{4} \ \hat{3} \ \hat{2} \ | \ \hat{1}$

In minor (similar to above):

$$i \ \frac{V^4_2}{iv} \ iv^6 \ V-\frac{4}{2} \ | \ i^6 \ \flat II^6 \ "V^6_4-" \ \frac{V^6_5}{VI} \ | \ VI$$
(bass: $\hat{5} \qquad \hat{5}$)

$\hat{3} \ \hat{3} \ \hat{4} \ \hat{5} \ | \ \hat{5} \ \hat{4} \ \hat{3} \ \hat{2} \ | \ \hat{1}$
$\hat{5} \ \hat{5} \ \hat{4} \ \hat{2} \ | \ \hat{1} \ \hat{1} \ \hat{1} \ \hat{7} \ | \ \hat{1}$

The first of these progressions is also viable in minor if you use a "common-tone augmented sixth" instead of a common-tone diminished seventh. This is just the same as a common-tone diminished seventh except for one note: a common-tone augmented sixth resolving to a tonic triad in a minor key would contain a minor-mode scale degree $\hat{6}$ (instead of the raised scale degree $\hat{6}$ in a common-tone diminished seventh). For that reason, it usually sounds more appropriate in minor keys.

IMPROVISATION: PUTTING IT ALL TOGETHER

1. Try all four Chorale Workshop exercises listed under "Improvisation" in Chapter 15 for the progressions given in this chapter.

2. Refer to the melody over the first seven measures of Example 25.4. Begin singing this melody on scale-degree numbers and in a comfortable range. After the second downbeat, continue with the given rhythm, but with a different pitch for every given melodic element. Finish with scale degrees $\hat{2}$ and $\hat{1}$ (instead of $\hat{3}$ and $\hat{2}$) in m. 7. If you are truly inventing a new melody in real time without pre-planning what you are going to sing, it is actually quite difficult to avoid every single one of the given pitches!

3. Refer to Example 25.5, specifically the clarinet's melody (the upper part) in mm. 5–12, which ends with a half cadence. Singing on scale degree numbers, improvise a second eight-measure phrase that begins the same (at least three notes the same, and perhaps as many as eight notes) but ends on scale degree $\hat{1}$, as if supported by a perfect authentic cadence. Write down your answering phrase, or some version of what you improvised, and perform for a classmate (or do so in teams). Take one another's answering phrases in dictation.

4. Refer to Example 25.6, mm. 1–12. Have your friends sing the lower parts while you improvise a new melody, employing Franck's distinctive rhythmic motive and its variations. Once you have used his exact rhythms, try varying them further.

SUGGESTED SMARTMUSIC ASSESSMENTS

Complete SmartMusic assessments 25.1 (both parts), 25.2 (all parts), 25.4 (top part, up to downbeat of m. 27), 25.5 (top part, through m. 61), and 25.6 (outer parts, all).

SHORT-TERM MUSICAL MEMORY

Fill in the key signature and clef as indicated by your instructor, and write in the initial note(s) on the basis of the given pitch and rhythm information. Note that the key and clef *may not be the same* as in the original example. Your instructor (or practice partner) will play a short progression to establish the key and then count off several beats to establish the tempo. Because of the brevity of each extract, you should have an overall impression of the rhythm, contour, and scale degrees after just one or two hearings. Notate the entire fragment.

1. Example 25.1, beat 4 of m. 17 to beat 3 of m. 19, upper voice (starts with quarter note, scale degree $\hat{1}$).

Clef and key
signature

2. Example 25.2, beat 2 of m. 72 to downbeat of m. 74, upper voice (starts with last five eighth notes of the measure, first of which is a low scale degree $\hat{5}$).

Clef and key
signature

3. Example 25.3, m. 17 to downbeat of m. 19, upper voice (starts with quarter note on beat 1, scale degree $\hat{7}$).

Clef and key
signature

4. Example 25.3, m. 134 to downbeat of m. 136, upper voice (starts with dotted quarter note on beat 1, scale degree $\hat{5}$, with a turn figure).

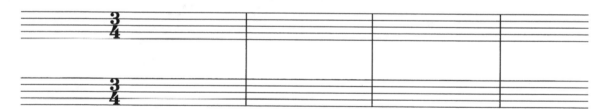

Clef and key
signature

5. Example 25.5: two possibilities! Either (a) m. 1 to downbeat of m. 4, top voice; or (b) m. 13 to downbeat of m. 16, top voice. Both possibilities start with a quarter note on beat 1 (m. 1 starts with scale degree $\hat{5}$; m. 13 starts with a raised scale degree $\hat{7}$).

Clef and key
signature

6. Example 25.4, up to beat 3 of m. 2, top and middle voices. Both start on beat 4 (quarter note and scale degree 1̂ in top voice, first of several eighth notes a minor sixth lower in middle voice).

Clef and key
signature

7. Example 25.5, m. 38 to downbeat of m. 41, both voices. Bottom voice starts on beat 1 (half note, scale degree 3̂); top voice has a quarter rest on first downbeat, and then half note on beat 2 in bottom voice (a minor tenth above bottom voice).

Clef and key
signature

8. Example 25.6, m. 110 to downbeat of m. 112, outer voices. Both start on beat 1 (dotted quarter note tied to quarter note in top voice, scale degree 5̂; dotted half note a minor tenth lower in bottom voice).

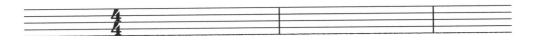

Clef and key
signature

DICTATION OF LONGER EXAMPLES

Your instructor or a classmate will choose one of the examples listed below and inform you of the key, clef, meter, first note (scale degree, rhythmic value, and metric placement) of one or more parts, and total number of measures. Use a separate piece of staff paper to write down the indicated information. You will hear a short progression to establish the key of the example, and then hear the example several times with breaks between hearings.

Nonmodulating:

1. Example 25.2, m. 101 to downbeat of m. 108, outer voices.
2. Example 25.3, beat 3 of m. 30 to beat 2 of m. 38, middle and bottom part.
3. Example 25.5, mm. 5–12, outer voices.

Modulating:

4. Example 25.1, mm. 1–8, both voices.
5. Example 25.6, m. 5 to downbeat of m. 13, outer voices.

CONTEXTUAL LISTENING 25.1

Beethoven, Symphony no. 5 in C minor, op. 67, mvt. 1

One of his best-known works, Beethoven's fifth symphony features an unprecedented intensity and seriousness of purpose. Beethoven unified the entire symphony with a particular rhythmic motive, heard at the opening of the piece.

1. a. Notate the scale degrees of the opening eight notes.

   b. Identify the type of the first cadence.

2. A modulation occurs at the end of the next phrase. A long crescendo over a tonic pedal is followed by a move to V, which leads into a very loud chord with brass and timpani. Identify what type of chord this is. (Hint: listen to the arpeggio in the violins.) What new key is achieved immediately after this? Provide Roman numerals (in the new key) for the loud pivotal chord and its resolution.

3. Shortly before the repeat, the opening rhythmic motive returns. What section of the exposition coincides with this motivic recall?

4. What key is tonicized at the beginning of the development?

5. What striking new element does Beethoven introduce shortly after the recapitulation begins? Why do you think he does this?

6. The same chord from question 2 comes back at the parallel place in the recapitulation, but it now leads to a different chord and key than before. What key now follows? Provide Roman numerals (in the new key) for this chord and its new resolution.

7. After the three repetitions of the opening rhythmic motive (with which the exposition concluded) at the end of the recapitulation, there is still a good minute and a half to go in the movement. What term would appropriately identify the music that follows? What important tonal change (a key change of sorts) occurs as this ending section begins?

CONTEXTUAL LISTENING 25.2

Mozart, Clarinet Quintet in A major, K. 581, mvt. 1

Like Mozart's clarinet concerto, this is one of the first definitive works for the instrument. It is scored for clarinet and string quartet and projects the clarinet part into very much of a soloistic role.

1. a. Notate the scale degrees of the first ten notes in the first violin part.

    b. Notate the harmonic progression (three chords) implied by the clarinet's opening arpeggios.

2. a. The opening phrase repeats (slightly modified), and the clarinet's arpeggio is echoed in the upper strings. What part of the form begins immediately thereafter, with the turn figure in the clarinet?

    b. The cello takes over the clarinet's melody, presenting it in a new key (the "second tonal/thematic area," or STA, of the movement). What key is this?

3. After a prominent arrival on V^7 in the new key, the violin presents a new theme (launching itself repeatedly with three upbeats. Then the clarinet takes us on quite a disorienting tonal journey—moving first to a minor key and then cadencing in a new, distantly related major key. What is the relationship between this new major key and the STA, and how does the music get back to the STA?

4. a. Describe the closing theme.

b. What theme is briefly referenced at the very end of the exposition?

5. What key is visited as the development begins? What theme is revisited, and what instrumental exchange has occurred?

6. After a relatively brief (and heavily arpeggiated) development, the recapitulation begins with the same instrumental switch as in the development and a few other changes. This time around, what key is the cello melody in?

7. Would you say the closing section is expanded, or would you say there is a coda? Why?

CONTEXTUAL LISTENING 25.3

Felix Mendelssohn (1809–1847), Overture to *A Midsummer Night's Dream*, op. 21

Many years after composing this overture, Mendelssohn wrote a number of additional pieces of "incidental music" for Shakespeare's play. The popular "Wedding March" from this suite is excerpted in Example 15.6.

1. a. We begin with an E-major chord. Provide Roman numerals for the unusual opening progression (which you will hear recurring throughout the piece).

   b. Just as strangely, what surprising "change" immediately follows the four-chord introduction?

2. Describe the thematic material heard when the full orchestra enters again, quite loudly.

3. Where do you hear the transition beginning? Describe what is happening in the music.

4. The secondary key area features a repeated descending chromatic melody. What key is this?

5. Quite a brass-heavy section follows (still in the secondary key area). What section of the form is this?

6. What material is recalled when the dynamics suddenly drop back down? What part of the form is this?

7. You will soon hear the recapitulation begin (in the same key as the piece began). Just before the recapitulation, we hear an extended cadence in a different key; what is it?

8. What thematic material is missing from the recapitulation before the second theme returns? What key is the second theme now heard in?

9. A coda presents the first theme once again, and follows with a slow version of which theme?

10. Not including its initial presentation, how many times did you hear the opening chord progression come back?

EXPANDING THE REPERTOIRE 25.4

Sergei Prokofiev (1891–1953), Symphony no. 1 "Classical," mvt. 1

Sergei Prokofiev modeled this symphony after those of Haydn, not only in terms of formal structure but also in its surprising and refreshing content.

1. In what key does the first theme begin? A sudden, abrupt modulation makes possible the sequencing of the first theme; does it sequence up or down?

2. How would you describe the character of the first theme? Which instrumental section of the orchestra performs the first theme?

3. At what time (give a precise timing) do you hear a dominant harmony that segues into the second theme?

4. What is the key of the second theme? Is it sequenced?

5. How would you describe the character of the second theme?

6. Do you hear a closing theme? What is its key?

7. Does the development start in major or minor? With the first theme or the second theme?

8. How is the second theme altered in terms of dynamic level and character during the development?

9. There is a clear *stretto* involving the second theme; give a precise timing of when this occurs. Can you identify the instrumental sections involved in the *stretto*?

10. What is the key of the first theme in the recapitulation? Similar to the exposition, the first theme contains a sudden, abrupt modulation; to what key?

11. What is the key of the second theme in the recapitulation?

12. Do you hear a closing theme at the end of the recapitulation?

13. The symphony begins and ends with an arpeggiated gesture typical of the pre-classical period. What is the name of such gesture?

    a. Mannheim Rocket   b. Plagal cadence   c. Basso continuo

14. On the basis of your answers, describe how this symphony follows the model of "Classical" sonata form. Now, identify several ways in which it deviates from the sonata model.

Chapter 26

Advanced Melodic and Harmonic Chromaticism

This chapter introduces a more extreme degree of melodic and harmonic chromaticism in music from Vivaldi to Coltrane. We will also encounter the phenomenon of equal division of the octave, which usually involves the tonicization of a series of triads whose roots are either all major thirds apart or all minor thirds apart. At a larger level, the overall modulatory schemes of entire movements by late-nineteenth-century composers will sometimes proceed along this same kind of cycle: up or down by a uniform distance, either a major or minor third, so that the initial tonic eventually returns.

Example 26.1.   Antonio Vivaldi (1678–1741), Concerto op. 8, no. 2, "L'estate" (Summer)

* This chromatic passage begins in D minor and ends in G minor, tonicizing numerous keys along the way. For purposes of scale-degree numbers or solfège, you might want to shift into C minor in m. 4 or 5, then into E minor in m. 8, then into B♭ major in m. 16 or 17, and so on. The longer melody notes give you an opportunity to change numbers or syllables.

After arriving in G minor (by m. 27), we have a lot of A♭s above a C pedal; what harmony is suggested?

Example 26.2. Johann Sebastian Bach (1685–1750), tenor recitative from Cantata no. 78 ("Jesu, der du meine Seele")

* *Translation*: Ah! I am a child of sin, Ah! I stray far and wide.

Sin's leprosy, which is found in me, will not leave me in this mortal life.

My will strives only after evil. My spirit indeed says: Ah! Who will set me free?

But to overcome flesh and blood and to carry out what is good is beyond all my strength.

Even though I would not hide my failings, I cannot count how often I fail.

Therefore I now take the sorrow and pain of sin and the burden of my cares

that would otherwise be unbearable for me and with sighs hand them over to you, Jesus.

Do not count my misdeeds which have angered you, Lord! (Francis Browne)

This recitative directly precedes the aria given in Example 16.8. Identify the cadence types and local keys heard in mm. 8, 12, 15, 20 (not exactly a cadence, but an unambiguous tonicization), and 24. Although you may need to consider the first eight measures more closely, the quick pace of cadences after that will help to keep your performance oriented toward the correct key.

Example 26.3.   Wolfgang Amadeus Mozart (1756–1791), *Don Giovanni*, K. 527 (1787), Act I, scene 13.

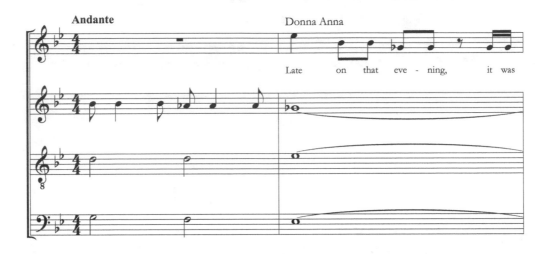

* This excerpt begins and ends in the key of G (minor at first, and then major at the end) but tonicizes two distantly related keys along the way. What do you notice about the local tonics of E♭ and B♮, in relation to surrounding G tonic pitches?

Example 26.4.   Johannes Brahms (1833–1897), Symphony no. 4, op. 98 (1885), mvt. 1, beginning.

* What do you notice about Brahms' ordering of all seven scale degrees in mm. 1–4, and then in mm. 5–8 as well? What kind of sequence is heard in mm. 5–8? Locate an augmented-sixth chord.

Example 26.5.   Brahms, "Immer leiser wird mein Schlummer," from *Fünf Lieder* op. 105, no. 2 (1886, pub. 1888)

wacht   und öff - net dir,

ich er - wach'   und wei - ne bit - ter - lich,   wei -

- ne bit - ter - lich.

Ja, ich wer - de ster - ben müs - sen,

Translation: Ever more peaceful grows my slumber,
    Only like a veil my sorrow lies trembling upon me.
    Often in dreams I hear you calling outside my door,
    No one wakes and lets you in, and I awake and weep bitterly.

    Yes, I will have to die;
    Another will you kiss, when I am pale and cold.
    Before the May breezes blow, before the thrush sings in the woods:
    Will you see me once more? Come, oh come soon!

This song is in modified strophic form. Both strophes begin (and soon cadence) in C♯ minor and then modulate to E major. Perhaps the most harmonically surprising passage is mm. 14–19 (*niemand wacht und öffnet dir*), where the underlying sequence moves from E major through IV–I in D major and then IV–I in C major. Considering the bass note C as persisting throughout m. 19, what harmony does the C-major triad turn into, in order to get back to the dominant of E major in mm. 20–21? Hint: notice the A♯ at the end of m. 19.

Examine the parallel place in the second strophe: Brahms reapproaches the home key (now spelled as D♭) through an ascending cycle of minor thirds.

Example 26.6.   Richard Wagner (1813–1883), Prelude to *Tristan und Isolde* (1857–1859)

* The first three measures of this Prelude present what is surely the most famous half cadence in history. Note the two chromatic melodies proceeding in opposite directions (down from F and up from G♯). In the full orchestral texture the iconic harmony in m. 2—the "Tristan" chord—has a B in an inner voice, as well the three notes given here. The iconic chord on the downbeat is equivalent to a half-diminished seventh chord, but it becomes a French sixth on the last eighth-note beat of m. 2 and resolves into a dominant seventh chord in m. 3. Two similar half cadences follow, resolving onto dominant seventh chords on G and B (which themselves do not resolve). Note the deceptive cadence into m. 17, which leads into a recurring theme (the "Glance") in the keys of C major and then E major. The two chromatic melodies from mm. 1–3 return at the climax (mm. 81–85), at first reinterpreted in E♭ major but then slipping back to the original A-minor key.

Example 26.7.   Pyotr Ilyich Tchaikovsky (1840–1893), "Waltz," from *The Sleeping Beauty*,
op. 66 (1889)

* This familiar piece features a number of interesting chromatic usages, such as the passing dominant-seventh sonority in m. 11, the augmented sixth in m. 22, and the recurring two-part gesture first heard in mm. 33–35. This gesture's quarter-note alternation anticipates the rhythmic character of the eighteen-measure hemiola that begins in m. 93. (Compare it to the extended hemiola in Example 24.8b, which Tchaikovsky wrote just a couple of years later.)

DRILLS

1. Review the diminished seventh drill from Chapter 23, the V^7 reinterpretation drill from Chapter 23, and the V_2^4 reinterpretation drill from Chapter 24.

2. Practice the following arpeggiation exercises, in which triads alternate with secondary dominants or diminished sevenths so as to equally divide the octave into three major thirds or four minor thirds. Start with a triad. Arpeggiate up from each bass note in close position, and back down. You may use major or minor triads, or both, for exercises a. through d.

    a. Triads descending by major thirds; every other chord is the V_3^4 of the upcoming triad.

    b. Triads descending by minor thirds; every other chord is the V_3^4 of the upcoming triad.

    c. Triads ascending by minor thirds; every other chord is the vii^{o7} of the upcoming triad.

    d. Triads ascending by minor thirds; every other chord is the V^7 of the upcoming triad.

    e. Major triads descending by major thirds; every other chord is the V^7 of the *previous* triad.

    f. Major triads descending by minor thirds; every other chord is the V^7 of the *previous* triad.

3. Notice how ascending and descending chromatic lines overlap at the very beginning of Example 26.6. Practice chanting just the rhythm of the first three measures in a duet with a partner; one of you can chant "He's Ri . . . chard Wag . . . ner . . ." in the rhythm of the middle part, and the other can come in at the appropriate moment with "Ri . . . chard Wagner . . ." in the rhythm of the top part. Try this in a larger group: once someone starts with the middle-line rhythm, the next person will come in with the top-line rhythm and then start the next duet performance with the middle-line rhythm. Then, one person should sing the middle line, beginning on any randomly chosen note (with or without text), and an answering singer should sing the top line beginning on the correct pitch in relation to the pitch of the middle line. Once you have correctly sung the top line in coordination with someone else on the middle line, you get to choose your own starting pitch for the next duet performance!

CHORALE WORKSHOP: LONGER PROGRESSIONS

For each the following progressions, sing just the bass line, and then sing each chord as an arpeggio (up from its bass note and back down) or play it on an instrument. Next, working at a piano, try singing the soprano lines while playing the bass line, and singing the bass while playing the soprano lines. Finally, practice every progression with every soprano line on the piano, in a variety of simple keys. The modality of each progression is specified.

The use of quotation marks around a cadential six-four indicates the evasion of its cadential tendency. Bass lines are specified in certain instances for clarity.

Harmony (bass line in left hand)	Possible soprano scale degrees (right hand)
In major: I CT^{o7} I $\frac{\text{V}_2^4}{\text{IV}}$ | IV^6 It^{+6} V V$_2^4$ | I^6 ♭II^6 $\frac{\text{vii}^{o7}}{\text{V}}$ V | I	$\hat{5}$ $\uparrow\hat{4}$ $\hat{5}$ $\hat{5}$ | $\hat{1}$ $\hat{1}$ $\hat{7}$ $\hat{7}$ | $\hat{1}$ $\downarrow\hat{2}$ $\hat{1}$ $\hat{7}$ | $\hat{1}$ $\hat{3}$ $\uparrow\hat{2}$ $\hat{3}$ $\hat{3}$ | $\hat{4}$ $\uparrow\hat{4}$ $\hat{5}$ $\hat{5}$ | $\hat{5}$ $\hat{4}$ $\downarrow\hat{3}$ $\hat{2}$ | $\hat{1}$
In minor: i $\frac{\text{vii}^{o4}_3}{\text{V}}$ V^6 $\frac{\text{V}_3^4}{\text{VI}}$ | VI Ger^{o3} "V$_4^6$—" V$_2^4$ | i^6 iv ii$^{\o7}$ V | i (bass: $\hat{5}$ $\hat{4}$)	$\hat{5}$ $\uparrow\hat{4}$ $\hat{5}$ $\hat{5}$ | $\hat{6}$ $\hat{6}$ $\hat{5}$ $\hat{5}$ | $\hat{5}$ $\hat{1}$ $\hat{1}$ $\hat{7}$ | $\hat{1}$ $\hat{3}$ $\hat{3}$ $\hat{2}$ $\downarrow\hat{2}$ | $\hat{1}$ $\hat{3}$ $\hat{3}$ $\hat{2}$ | $\hat{1}$ $\hat{1}$ $\hat{4}$ $\hat{2}$ | $\hat{3}$
In major: I IV CT^{o7} I^6 | ii^6 $\frac{\text{V}^7}{\text{V}}$ V $\frac{\text{V}^7}{\text{vi}}$ | vi Fr^{+6} V$_{4-3}^{6-5}$ | I (bass: $\hat{1}$ $\hat{2}$ $\uparrow\hat{2}$ $\hat{3}$)	$\hat{1}$ $\hat{7}$ $\hat{6}$ $\hat{5}$ | $\hat{6}$ $\hat{1}$ $\hat{7}$ $\hat{2}$ | $\hat{1}$ $\hat{2}$ $\hat{3}$ $\hat{2}$ | $\hat{1}$ $\hat{3}$ $\hat{4}$ $\uparrow\hat{4}$ $\hat{5}$ | $\hat{6}$ $\hat{6}$ $\hat{5}$ $\hat{4}$ | $\hat{3}$ $\hat{2}$ $\hat{1}$ $\hat{7}$ | $\hat{1}$

IMPROVISATION: PUTTING IT ALL TOGETHER

1. Try all four Chorale Workshop exercises listed under "Improvisation" in Chapter 15 for the progressions given in this chapter.

2. Play the simple bass line from Example 26.1 several times. Then improvise a new chromatic melody consisting of straight eighth notes (or the occasional quarter-eighth pairing). Some of the chromatic bass notes could be treated as leading tones (denied their upward resolution); some could be treated as chordal sevenths. Write down your improvisation.

3. Refer to the first eight measures of Example 26.4. Disregarding the given inner voice, invent a new inner voice (or a descant part) that repeats a particular rhythmic figure every measure, and that complements the melody and bass line. Suggested rhythms: alternating dotted quarter notes with eighth notes, or a quarter rest on the downbeat followed by four eighth notes and a quarter note, or the rhythmic figure from mm. 9–12 in the melody.

SUGGESTED SMARTMUSIC ASSESSMENTS

Complete SmartMusic assessments 26.1 (both parts), 26.2 (all parts), 26.3 (all parts), 26.4 (all parts), 26.5 (all parts), 26.6 (all parts), and 26.7 (all parts).

SHORT-TERM MUSICAL MEMORY (DRAWN FROM CHAPTERS 26 AND 27)

Fill in the key signature and clef as indicated by your instructor, and write in the initial note(s) on the basis of the given pitch and rhythm information. Note that the key and clef *may not be the same* as in the original example. Your instructor (or practice partner) will play a short progression to establish the key and then count off several beats to establish the tempo. Because of the brevity of each extract, you should have an overall impression of the rhythm, contour, and scale degrees after just one or two hearings. Notate the entire fragment.

1. Example 26.3, m. 2 to beat 3 ("mid-night"), vocal line. Starts on beat 1 (quarter note, high scale degree î).

Clef and key
signature

2. Example 26.4, up to downbeat of m. 4, upper voice. Starts on beat 4 (quarter note, high scale degree ŝ).

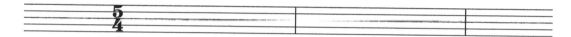

Clef and key
signature

3. Example 27.1, mm. 1–2, top voice. Treat as if consistently in quintuple meter (last note will be written as third downbeat). Starts on beat 1 (quarter note, low scale degree ô).

Clef and kcy
signature

4. Example 27.6, mm. 1–3, top voice. Starts on beat 1 (two sixteenth notes, scale degrees ŝ–î).

Clef and key
signature

5. Example 26.1, up to downbeat of m. 3, both voices. Both start on beat 1 (dotted quarter note in bottom voice, first of several sixteenth notes in top voice), both on scale degree î two octaves apart.

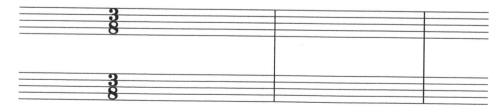

Clef and key
signature

6. Example 26.5, up to beat 3 of m. 2, top and middle voices. Both start with dotted quarter notes on beat 3 (scale degree $\hat{5}$ in top voice, a major third lower in bottom voice).

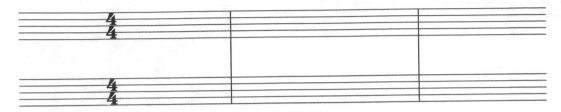

Clef and key
signature

7. Example 26.6, up to downbeat of m. 3, middle and lower voices. Middle voice begins with eighth-note upbeat (low scale degree $\hat{1}$), lower voice rests until entrance on downbeat of m. 2 (dotted half note, scale degree $\hat{6}$ a major third below middle voice entrance).

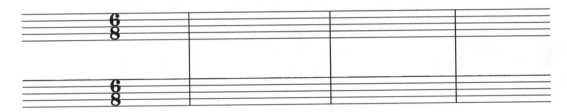

Clef and key
signature

8. Example 26.7, m. 33 to downbeat of m. 36, outer voices. Top voice starts on beat 1 (quarter note, scale degree $\hat{5}$), bottom voice rests for two beats and then enters a minor tenth lower on beat 3 (quarter note tied to the downbeat).

Clef and key
signature

DICTATION OF LONGER EXAMPLES (DRAWN FROM CHAPTERS 26 AND 27)

Your instructor or a classmate will choose one of the examples listed below and inform you of the key, clef, meter, first note (scale degree, rhythmic value, and metric placement) of one or more parts, and total number of measures. Use a separate piece of staff paper to write down the indicated information. You will hear a short progression to establish the key of the example, and then hear the example several times with breaks between hearings.

Nonmodulating:

1. Example 26.2, beat 3 of m. 15 to beat 3 of m. 20, outer voices.
2. Example 26.7, mm. 1–17, outer voices.
3. Example 27.1, m. 8 to beat 3 of m. 11, outer voices. Treat as if consistently in $\frac{6}{4}$ time.
4. Example 27.7, up to downbeat of m. 11 (or just up to the downbeat of m. 7), middle and bottom voices.

Modulating:

5. Example 26.6, middle of m. 17 to just before the middle of m. 22, outer voices.

CONTEXTUAL LISTENING 26.1

Felix Mendelssohn (1809–1847), Violin Concerto in E minor (1844), mvt. 1

One of Mendelssohn's final large-scale works, this violin concerto is a standard in the violinist's repertoire. The location of the cadenza in the first movement is very unusual, but somehow it sounds perfectly appropriate.

1. How many thematic or motivic ideas do you hear before the orchestra comes in with a second presentation of the soloist's opening melody? Describe each distinct idea.

2. After a prominent authentic cadence in the home key, a staccato texture in the bassoons (about ninety seconds in) marks the beginning of what new section?

3. The soloist then moves to a triplet texture over (for a while) a pedal tone in the bass. What is the importance of this bass note, with respect to upcoming material?

4. The second theme—in a slower tempo, and featuring a "2–3–4–1" rhythm—is first played in the winds and then in the solo part. What new key has been reached?

5. Within this new key area, the soloist then picks up the tempo with a brief recall of which theme?

6. All the fast triplet passagework coming up sounds like closing material and remains in the same key, but we never get another strong authentic cadence in the second tonal area, and there is no repeat marked. Where or when do you think the exposition ends and the development begins? (It may be best to think about this after listening all the way through.)

7. Following the very dramatic orchestral chords, alternating with fragments of the opening motive, which themes do you hear returning?

8. a. Quite unusually, the cadenza in this movement does not occur toward the end of the recapitulation, but rather before the recapitulation even begins. What harmony is heard in the orchestra just before the cadenza? What section of the form is this?

   b. Provide the Roman numerals for just the first four chords that the soloist arpeggiates in the cadenza.

   Bonus: for an added challenge, give Roman numerals for the whole cadenza on a separate sheet of paper.

9. Are any of the thematic or motivic ideas that you identified in question 1 missing from the recapitulation, before the second theme? If so, which one(s)?

10. Would you consider the accelerating final section to be part of the recapitulation, or separate from it? Why?

CONTEXTUAL LISTENING 26.2

Brahms' second violin sonata may be the most lyrical of the three he wrote. Compare the characters of the themes you hear to the themes in his Clarinet Sonata, op. 120 no. 1 (the exposition of which is given in Example 25.5).

When listening to this movement, note that the exposition does not repeat. The development begins (after a measure of silence) with a recall of the opening theme.

1. a. Write out the scale degree numbers for the first eight notes in the violin part.

   b. What type of harmony is heard just before the violin reprises the piano's opening melody?

2. What part of the form begins with the violinist's presentation of the opening melody?

3. After an obvious formal boundary, the piano takes over the spotlight again with a new melody, featuring a rhythmic motive of a dotted quarter note and three eighth notes. What new key has been attained?

4. A new rhythmic motive, consisting of two quarter notes and a triplet, is soon heard. What part of the form is this?

5. a. The development first deploys the opening theme through an extended modulatory passage. What theme then dominates the rest of the development?

b. A long pedal tone in the bass eventually cadences to a relatively stable minor key within the development; what key is this? (There is no dominant preparation for the return of the home key; the mystery minor key changes to major near the end of the development and then abruptly moves back to the home key for the recapitulation.)

6. Which themes are reprised in the extended coda, and in what order?

CONTEXTUAL LISTENING 26.3

Tchaikovsky's ability to write memorable melodies is exemplified in his many ballets, serenades, and symphonies. Do you hear a connection to the opening of Beethoven's Fifth Symphony in the opening motif that Tchaikovsky uses?

1. Which two scale degrees are repeated over and over at the end of the introduction? (These are the first two notes of the upcoming principal theme.)

2. Following the first authentic cadence, the low strings initiate an upward gesture. How do you think the composer came up with this melody? (Hint: compare to the principal theme.)

3. After a very loud recall of the principal theme in the home key, the composer suddenly introduces a new key for the "subordinate theme"—heard at first in the clarinet's low range, and then in the higher winds. (The composer moves to a new major key at first, since it is closely related to the home key . . . but then the clarinet changes this new key to minor.) What is the tonic of this new major-then-minor key?

4. An "accompanying theme" then emerges in the cellos (featuring some falling thirds) against the subordinate theme. Describe the musical effect of the simultaneous presentation of these two themes.

5. a. Against the "accompanying theme" in the upper strings, which instruments bring back the first reminders of the principal theme?

   b. Which instruments have the "accompanying theme" next, and which have the principal theme?

6. A prominent "third" theme (involving a descending $\hat{5}$–$\hat{3}$–$\hat{1}$ melody) is then presented. What key has been achieved? (It is quite distantly related to the opening key. If you aren't sure about a Roman numeral, you might suggest more than one possibility.)

7. Which theme is brought back in the brass (a couple of times) at the end of the exposition? What formal function does this serve?

8. What thematic material do you hear in the development?

9. Just before the recapitulation, the introductory fanfare is recalled three times in the brass, and the low strings then descend to a rumbling pedal. Which two scale degrees are heard quickly alternating in the low strings?

10. What key is the principal theme now heard in (and after that, the "subordinate" and "accompanying" themes)? (Hint: this is not the home key.)

11. The recapitulation modulates to F major, the parallel major of the home key. Thematically speaking, what is missing from the recapitulation?

12. What theme announces the beginning of the coda? What theme is heard (greatly elongated) at the end of the coda?

EXPANDING THE REPERTOIRE 26.4

Cole Porter (1891–1964), "What Is This Thing Called Love?" from *Wake Up and Dream* (1929)

Cole Porter is one of the most celebrated American jazz musicians. He claimed that the alternations of major and minor key centers in this song were inspired by Moroccan folk music. The inclusion of alternating major and minor here, however, is made possible by the similarities between the German-sixth chord and the tritone substitution of V^7/V.

Although these two chords are equivalent in terms structure, they differ in their voice-leading conventions and to some extent in their function: while the German-sixth chord appears most commonly as a dominant preparation, the tritone substitution of V^7/V is (as its name implies) a dominant substitute.

1. What is the form of the song?

   a. A B B A   b. A A B A   c. A B A B   d. A A B B

2. The piece navigates various key centers using the ii–V–I progression that is so common in jazz idioms. Transcribe the entire melody, and give Roman numerals according to the key centers provided:

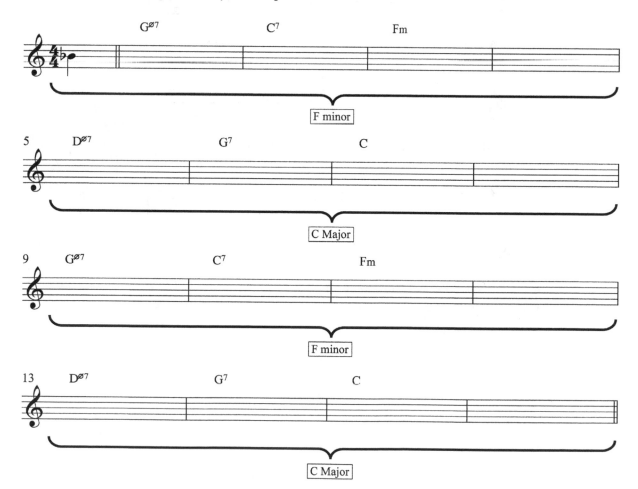

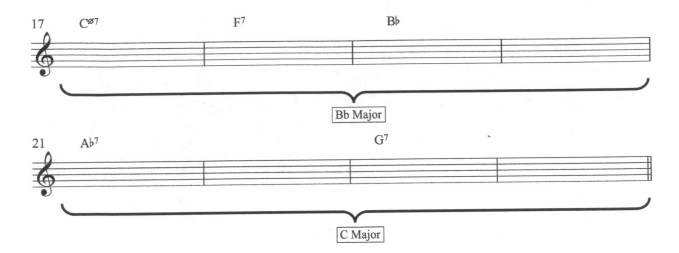

17   C⌀7   F7   B♭

Bb Major

21   A♭7   G7

C Major

3. As you recall from the contextual listening on "Satin Doll" (Expanding the Repertoire 21.5) a tritone substitution may replace any dominant sonority. Below, write and compare the requested pair of chords:

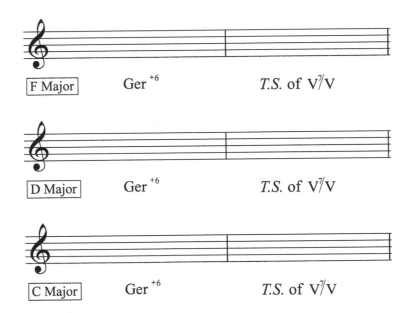

F Major   Ger +6   *T.S.* of V⁷/V

D Major   Ger +6   *T.S.* of V⁷/V

C Major   Ger +6   *T.S.* of V⁷/V

4. On the basis of your answers above, supply a harmonic analysis of mm. 21–22 of "What Is This Thing Called Love?"

EXPANDING THE REPERTOIRE 26.5

Duke Ellington and Irving Mills, "Sophisticated Lady" (1932)

As with many Duke Ellington songs, this jazz standard was originally an instrumental piece. The beauty of its melody is matched by its difficulty. In listening to "There's No Business Like Show Business" and "Be My Baby" earlier in this book, you observed how a chain of secondary dominants could be transformed to include tritone substitutions. Keep this notion in mind while listening to and analyzing "Sophisticated Lady."

1. What is the form of the song?

   a. A B B A   b. A A B A   c. A B A B   d. A A B B

2. In the score below:

   a. Transcribe the missing melody. Note that most of the notes correspond to the root or fifth of the chords, which is highly unusual.

   b. Give the Roman numerals, keeping in mind the presence of tritone substitutions in place of secondary dominants.

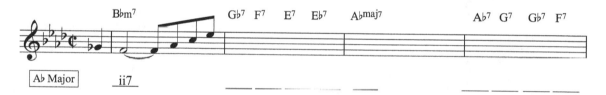

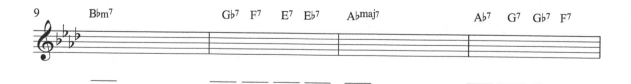

795

3. Optional assignment: although the melody for the A section (which you have just transcribed) generally outlines the root or fifth of the chord changes and is largely based on stepwise motion, the melody for the B section is quite a bit more complex. Transcribe the melody of the B section below:

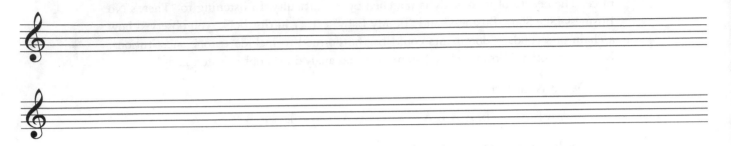

EXPANDING THE REPERTOIRE 26.6

John Coltrane, "Giant Steps" (1960)

Saxophonist John Coltrane recorded this song and released it on his 1960 album of the same name. Its harmonic progression, which experiments with equal divisions of the octave, stimulated harmonic thinking in jazz. Many other composers and musicians (particularly Freddie Hubbard) subsequently adopted the progression for their own pieces.

1. Keeping in mind that the octave spans twelve semitones (half-steps), how many equal divisions can you think of, other than semitones themselves?

2. Transcribe the missing melody notes and the missing chord symbols.

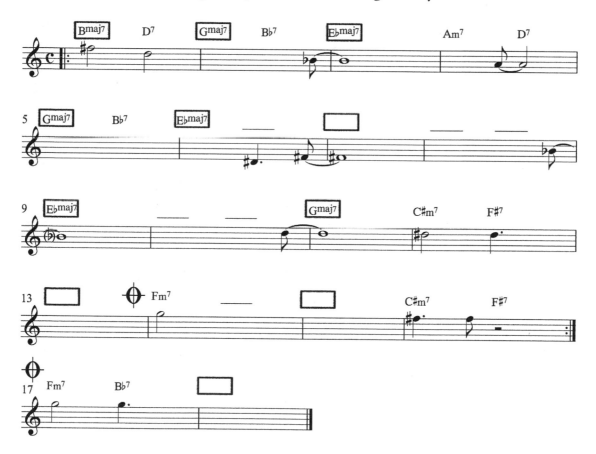

3. The song's title reflects the giant leaps between consecutive established tonal areas (depicted within boxes in the score above). How does Coltrane divide the octave?

4. How does the song establish the various tonal centers?

5. Listen to the head (opening section) of the song. Does the piano's "comp" (the background groove furnished by the rhythm section) follow the melody's syncopated rhythm?

Chapter 27

Later Tonal Styles

This chapter presents a selection of highly chromatic excerpts and complete works by Russian, French, and American composers. It includes no improvisatory exercises or drills, since all of these excerpts depart in certain ways from tonal practices that we have studied to this point. You or your teacher may think up some drills or other kinds of focused practice strategies, possibly incorporating improvisation, which could help to solidify the skills that these pieces demand.

Example 27.1.   Modest Mussorgsky (1839–1881), "Promenade," from *Pictures at an Exhibition* (1874)

* What type of scale is represented by the opening melody (mm. 1–4)?

Example 27.2.   Gabriel Fauré (1845–1924), *Pavane*, op. 50 (1887)

Translation: It's Lindor! It's Tircis! And all our conquerors!

> It's Myrtil! It's Lydé! The queens of our hearts!
>
> How provocative they are, how proud are they always!
>
> How they dare to reign over our destinies and our days!

Fauré's music is tonally ambiguous; sometimes it seems to be floating between two or three keys, though F# minor clearly predominates here. Compare this piece to the next example, which is another Pavane, written by Fauré's student (for fourteen years) Maurice Ravel.

Example 27.3.   Maurice Ravel (1875–1937), *Pavane for a Dead Princess* (1899)

* The inclusion of ninth chords in the cadential gestures in mm. 11, 18, and 25–27 (and elsewhere) characterizes Ravel's extended tonal style, even in this early work of his.

Example 27.4.   Ravel, "Forlane," from *Le tombeau de Couperin* (1914–1917)

* This lengthy and challenging piece can be tackled in sections, according to the alternation of refrain and *couplet* that Ravel borrowed from Couperin's model.

Example 27.5. Sergei Prokofiev (1891–1953), *Peter and the Wolf* (1936), theme

* The close similarity of the first four measures to the next four allows Prokofiev to nearly replicate the modulation up a minor third from G major to B♭ major, in order to arrive on D major (this time a major third higher) and thus return to G.

Example 27.6.   Aaron Copland (1900–1990), *Fanfare for the Common Man* (1942)

* This familiar piece may not fall in and around the written downbeats in quite the way a listener would expect. Do mm. 4–6, for instance, suggest a meter other than the notated $\frac{4}{4}$?

    Although Copland remains within the diatonic B♭-major scale for most of the work, the accidentals multiply toward the end, and his final chord is quite distant from where he started.

Example 27.7. George Gershwin (1898–1937), Prelude no. 2, from *Three Preludes for Piano* (1926)

* This central section of Gershwin's Prelude can be compared to a standard twelve-bar blues pattern in F♯ major. The first four measures embellish an underlying I chord, followed by two measures each of IV and I, one measure each of V⁷/V and V⁷, and then (essentially) four measures of I. Note the particular emphasis on chromatic tones in the melody, such as the E♮s in m. 8 and the A♮s in m. 9.

Example 27.8. Gershwin, "It Ain't Necessarily So," from *Porgy and Bess* (1935)

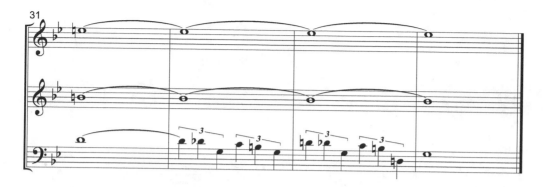

* What scale would be heard if the flats in the opening eight-measure melody were converted to naturals? These "blue notes" serve as chromatic passing tones in mm. 1–8, but they add a very different modal color to the subsequent scalar passages.

Example 27.9.   Paul Desmond (1924–1977), "Take Five," from *Time Out* (1959)

* Notwithstanding the difference in notation, it is customary to perform all "eighth, eighth" or "dotted-eighth, sixteenth" pairs equivalently ("swung," that is). As in Example 27.8, the repeated melodic gesture in mm. 4–8 initially circulates among scale degrees $\hat{1}$, $\hat{3}$, $\hat{4}$, $\hat{5}$, and $\hat{7}$ in a natural minor scale (what scale type is it?) with chromatic passing tones playing an important role. Then, as in Example 27.8, the melodic scope soon expands into a fully diatonic context.

SUGGESTED SMARTMUSIC ASSESSMENTS

Complete SmartMusic assessments 27.1 (all parts), 27.2 (top part), 27.3 (all parts), 27.5 (all parts), 27.6 (all parts), 27.7 (all parts), 27.8 (top two parts), and 27.9 (top part).

Name: _____   Date: _____   Instructor: _____

CONTEXTUAL LISTENING 27.1

Wolfgang Amadeus Mozart (1756–1791), Piano Sonata in F Major, K. 332, mvt. 1 (Allegro)

In his book *Classic Music: Expression, Form, and Style*, Leonard Ratner introduces the concept of "topics," a term designating the succession of recognizable musical types embedded within a single movement or piece. Topics can be exported to a nonnative context; for example, a waltz can be the genre or title of a piece, but it can also be a *style* that is evoked in a nonwaltz composition. The first movement of Mozart's Sonata K. 332 features a rapid succession of topics (and is sometimes referred to as the "Topics Sonata").

1. From the "universe of topics" listed here, identify the ones you find most fitting. If more than one topic fits a particular segment, list all of them. Then, describe the musical characteristics that suggest those topics. The timings below correspond to the exposition section of this movement as found in the online version.

- Alberti bass
- Amoroso
- Aria
- Brilliant style
- Buffa style
- Cadenza
- Chaconne bass
- Chorale
- Concerto style
- Fanfare
- Fantasia style

- French overture
- Fugato
- Galant style
- Gavotte
- High style
- Horn call
- Learned style
- Mannheim Rocket
- March
- Military figures
- Minuet

- Ombra style
- Pastorale
- Popular style
- Recitative
- Sigh motif
- Singing style
- Strict style
- Sturm und Drang
- Trommelbass
- Turkish music
- Waltz

Segment	Topic(s)	Description
0:00–0:16		
0:16–0:29		
0:29–0:51		
0:51–1:11		
1:11–1:28		
1:28–1:37		
1:37–1:45		
1:45–1:57		

2. Identify the main key areas of this sonata-form exposition. Observe how the various topics correlate with the key areas. Comment on what seems typical or atypical about that correlation.

CONTEXTUAL LISTENING 27.2

Ludwig van Beethoven (1770–1827), Piano Sonata in C Minor, op. 13
("Pathétique"), mvt. 1

As defined by Ratner, "topics" are musical signs. In order to perceive these signs, a certain degree of "competency" with eighteenth- (and nineteenth-) century musical styles is needed.

1. From the "universe of topics" listed here, identify the ones you find most fitting within the *Grave* section of the first movement. In this case you will have to provide the segments (with timings), as well as the topics and a description of the musical qualities that suggest those topics.

- Alberti bass
- Amoroso
- Aria
- Brilliant style
- Buffa style
- Cadenza
- Chaconne bass
- Chorale
- Concerto style
- Fanfare
- Fantasia style
- French overture
- Fugato
- Galant style
- Gavotte
- High style
- Horn call
- Learned style
- Mannheim Rocket
- March
- Military figures
- Minuet
- Ombra style
- Pastorale
- Popular style
- Recitative
- Sigh motif
- Singing style
- Strict style
- Sturm und Drang
- Trommelbass
- Turkish music
- Waltz

Segment	Topic(s)	Description

2. How does topical contrast add to the expressive nature (and overall drama) of this section?

3. How ambiguous (or clearly defined) are the topics here, in comparison to Mozart's Sonata in F major (Contextual Listening 27.1)? Speculate about artistic trends in the Classic versus Romantic periods that might have influenced composers to choose clearly defined (or less clearly defined) topics.

EXPANDING THE REPERTOIRE 27.3

John Coltrane, "Central Park West" (1960)

This song, like "Giant Steps," experiments with equal divisions of the octave. It uncovers a sensuous and surprising beauty within a more reflective mood.

1. Transcribe the missing melody notes and chord symbols.

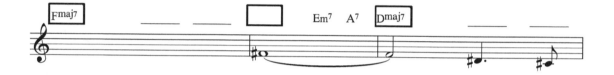

2. The tonic areas in the squares above divide the octave into equal parts. What is the intervallic distance between tonics? Are tonics ordered according to a particular interval?

3. What typical chord progression helps establish the various tonal centers?

4. Our culturally established competency with musical discourse prepares us to expect modulations (or tonicizations) of relative keys when traveling the distance of a minor third. Speculate as to how the tonal design in this piece acts against these tonal expectations.

EXPANDING THE REPERTOIRE 27.4

Main Titles/Episode Intro to "Them, Robot," from *The Simpsons*

The main title theme for the series (and movies) was composed by Danny Elfman; under-scoring for each episode, however, has been composed by Alf Clausen. The intro to this episode is in A B A′ form, featuring the main title theme in sections A and A′, while mu-sically diverging in the B section. The B section accompanies the scenes introducing the subject of the TV episode and establishes both the time and place in which the episode takes place. In "Them, Robot" (and in *The Simpsons* in general), the notion of the "passage of time" is depicted with a particular scale, as you will find out in this assignment.

1. Transcribe the main theme. On which "mode" is this theme based? (Hint: it con-tains raised $\hat{4}$.) Does it come back during the introduction? Is it altered in any way?

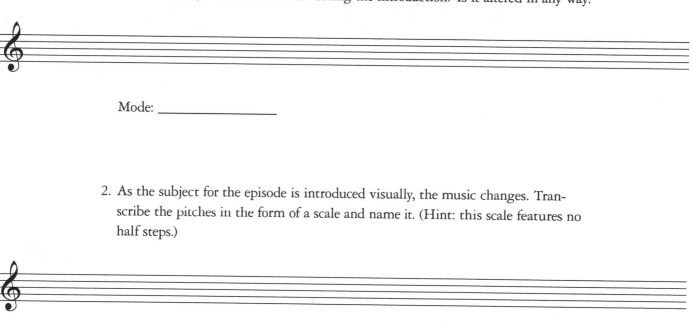

         Mode: _____

2. As the subject for the episode is introduced visually, the music changes. Tran-scribe the pitches in the form of a scale and name it. (Hint: this scale features no half steps.)

         Scale: _____

3. Although any pitch could serve as the gravitational focal point for the scale out-lined here, this excerpt seems to establish C♯ as the most important pitch. How does the composer (and sound designer) achieve this? (Hint: listen closely to the piano bass pattern, and to the "ching" sound of the counter.)

4. *Optional assignment*: speculate about the form of the introduction and how the music helps shape that design. Watch other episodes of *The Simpsons*, and analyze the introduction in a similar manner.

Index

CPSIA information can be obtained
at www.ICGtesting.com
Printed in the USA
BVHW011507161022
649418BV00002B/2